Red at Heart

Red at Heart

HOW CHINESE COMMUNISTS FELL IN LOVE WITH THE RUSSIAN REVOLUTION

Elizabeth McGuire

OXFORD
UNIVERSITY PRESS

OXFORD
UNIVERSITY PRESS

Oxford University Press is a department of the University of Oxford. It furthers the University's objective of excellence in research, scholarship, and education by publishing worldwide. Oxford is a registered trade mark of Oxford University Press in the UK and certain other countries.

Published in the United States of America by Oxford University Press
198 Madison Avenue, New York, NY 10016, United States of America.

Library of Congress Cataloging-in-Publication Data
Names: McGuire, Elizabeth, author.
Title: Red at heart : how Chinese communists fell in love with the Russian Revolution / Elizabeth McGuire.
Description: New York, NY : Oxford University Press, 2017. |
Includes bibliographical references and index. |
Identifiers: LCCN 2017008881 (print) | LCCN 2017012238 (ebook) |
ISBN 9780190640569 (Updf) | ISBN 9780190640576 (Epub) |
ISBN 9780190640552 (hardcover : acid-free paper)
Subjects: LCSH: China—Relations—Soviet Union. |
Soviet Union—Relations—China. | Chinese—Soviet Union—History. |
Revolutionaries—China—History—20th century. |
Revolutionaries—China—Biography. | Communists—China—History—20th century. |
Soviet Union—History—Revolution, 1917–1921—Influence. |
China—Foreign relations—1912–1949. | China—Foreign relations—1949–1976.
Classification: LCC DS740.5.S65 (ebook) | LCC DS740.5.S65 M38 2017 (print) |
DDC 303.48/2510470904—dc23
LC record available at https://lccn.loc.gov/2017008881

1 3 5 7 9 8 6 4 2

Printed by Sheridan Books, Inc., United States of America

For my parents
Thomas Roger McGuire and Patricia Mae Ainsworth

CONTENTS

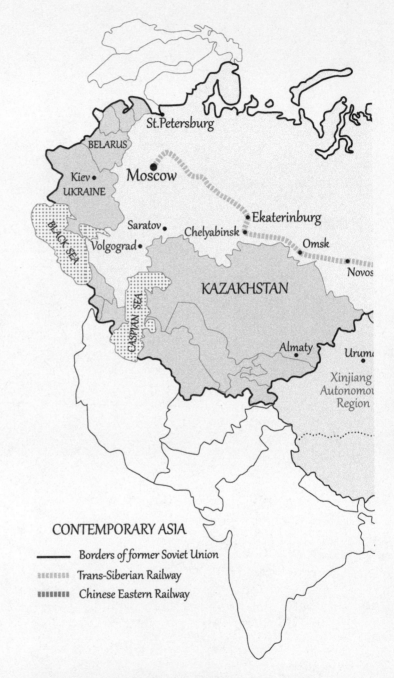

St.Petersburg

BELARUS

Kiev •
UKRAINE

Moscow

BLACK SEA

Saratov •

Volgograd •

CASPIAN SEA

Ekaterinburg

Chelyabinsk •

Omsk

Novos

KAZAKHSTAN

Almaty •

Urum

Xinjiang
Autonomo
Region

CONTEMPORARY ASIA

—————— Borders of former Soviet Union

∎∎∎∎∎∎∎∎ Trans-Siberian Railway

∎∎∎∎∎∎∎∎ Chinese Eastern Railway

Map of Contemporary Russia and China.

Map by Oksana Limankina.

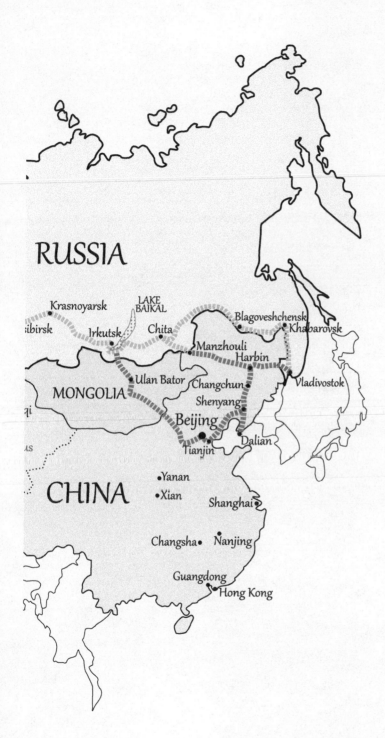

Prologue

At Vova's

IT IS A hot summer afternoon in July of 2004, too hot to be wandering the long, quiet streets lined with huge apartment blocks in the Fuxingmen district of Beijing. Where is number 14? Something isn't right. The map shows two streets very close to each other with long names that differ by only one character, and this is the wrong one. That is why there is no number 14.

It's an hour after the meeting time but finally here is number 14. In a little guard's office next to the gate, a middle-aged man glances up. Before he can even hear the question, he gestures to enter and points to the back right corner of the courtyard. He's used to this, it seems. Across the courtyard, through the entryway, up a little flight of steps, and through an open door.

A flurry of polite greetings in Chinese for the wife, and then a flood of affectionate Russian scolding from Vova. How could you be so late? Did something happen to you? Did you get lost? How come you didn't call? Sit down, sit down. What do you want to know? Here, let me show you some pictures. Now let me show you my video from our last reunion in Ivanovo.

An hour passes, then two—it's time for dinner and the table is set. There is sautéed eggplant and a fish, poached whole, Chinese style. But there is also a Russian salad, potatoes sautéed with onions and mushrooms, and beef cutlets. Russian cutlets, with some haunting of Chinese flavor, just enough to make them not quite Russian, not enough to make them actually Chinese. There are chopsticks on the table but Vova and his wife quickly offer forks. There are glasses, for juice, with napkins in them. And there are shot glasses, rimmed in gold leaf. The meal is served. It is a perfect meal, Sino-Soviet style.

After dinner Vova says, look I have a garden, it is a Russian garden. What does he mean? He is explaining himself, pointing out the plants. A neighbor peeks out the first-floor window from the building across. Vova greets her and starts talking to her. But he's forgotten, for a moment, where he is. It's been fifty years since he returned to China from Russia, but three hours and a few shots later, and he's back. He speaks to her in Russian. She shakes her head and draws back from the window.

Does he realize his mistake? It's hard to say, he moves on. There are too many stories to tell.

Introduction

Serious Romance

BEGINNING IN THE 1920s, thousands of Chinese revolutionaries set out for Soviet Russia, just at that moment of youth when a journey can define a lifetime. Once there, they studied Russian language and experienced Soviet communism. Many also fell in love, got married, or had children. In this they were similar to people from all over the world, East and West alike, who were enchanted by the Russian Revolution and lured to Moscow by it.

But there was a difference: the Chinese went home, fought a war, and then, in the 1950s, carried out a revolution that became the Soviet Union's most geopolitically significant legacy. They also sent their children to study in Moscow and passed on their youthful affinities to millions of Chinese, who read Russia's novels, watched its movies, and learned its songs. Russian culture was woven into the memories of an entire generation that came of age in the 1950s—an attachment that has outlasted not just the Chinese Cultural Revolution and the collapse of the Soviet Union but also the subsequent erosion of socialist values and practices.

This multi-generational personal experience has given China's relationship with Russia an emotional complexity and cultural depth that were lacking before the advent of twentieth-century communism—and have survived its demise.

This book uses the metaphor of a life-long romance to tell a new story about the relationship between Russia and China. It offers an alternative to the metaphors of brotherhood or friendship more commonly used to describe international socialism. Rather than focusing on the "Sino-Soviet split" of the 1960s, it asks, "How did these two countries get together in the first

3

place?" To answer this question, it looks at the lives of those who experienced Sino-Soviet affairs most intimately: Chinese revolutionaries whose emotional worlds were profoundly affected by their journeys to Russia and connections to its people and culture.

Sino-Soviet relations has traditionally focused on leaders, ideology, geopolitics, and political parties. During the Cold War, scholars debated the extent and mechanisms of Moscow's influence, asking whether Chinese communism was indigenous or imposed and how deep later conflicts really ran.[1] When Russian archives opened after 1991, it became possible to calculate how much money had passed from the Soviet Union to the Chinese Communist Party in its early years and to read transcripts of angry conversations between Mao and Khrushchev later on.[2] Newly available information from archives all over the Eastern Bloc enabled well-documented and highly nuanced studies, including research on Sino-Soviet competition in the Third World and the end of the Cold War.[3] Yet Sino-Soviet relations remained relatively untouched by cultural and social analyses that were transforming the broader history of communism.

After the Soviet archives opened and the sensation of "secret histories" had subsided, it became clear that one of the most closely held assumptions about communist societies—of an inherently oppositional unofficial culture—was not fully validated by the new evidence. Behind the cynicism of Soviet jokes and the indignation of dissidents lay not a citizenry seething with discontent but instead ordinary people working the system to economically benefit themselves and their families, patriots whose commemorations of war turned out to be genuine, and letters and diaries of citizens who poured their hearts out in earnest attempts to understand and fit into communist society. As full-fledged nostalgia for the Soviet era appeared in Russia in the 1990s, landmark studies emphasized symbiosis in the relationship between state and society under socialism.[4]

Gradually, new approaches emerged as well to international socialism, which could also be seen as an individual experience, a personal belief, and a way of life. New studies of relationships between Russians and other nationalities inside the Soviet Union made the surprising discovery that even as non-Russian nationalities were required to become Soviet, the Soviet Union promoted non-Russian ethnic nationalism.[5] And analyses of interactions between Soviet people and foreigners they encountered—as visitors to Soviet lands, as fellow fighters in the Spanish Civil War, as enemies in the

Second World War, and as objects of Soviet tourist curiosity after the war—asked how these cross-cultural exchanges affected people's feelings about global communism and about themselves.[6]

While the material and emotional lives of Europeans, Americans, and other foreigners inside the Soviet Union have been examined, few works have looked at the Chinese—even though some ended up as leaders of the only other great power communist country in the world.[7] More strikingly, numerous books describe Chinese experiences in Europe, Japan, and the United States—though none of these countries was as central as Soviet Russia in shaping China's twentieth-century transformation.[8] It is almost as if the thousands of Chinese who traveled to Moscow over the course of decades are considered containers for ideology first, pawns of geopolitics second, and flesh and blood individuals as an afterthought. In fact, long before some became national leaders of China and Taiwan, they had been transnational leaders of one of the twentieth century's most fascinating—and romantic—cross-cultural encounters.

"Romance" has many meanings and functions in this book, but none would be possible had the theme not emerged so clearly from historical sources. Not only are Chinese accounts tinged and sometimes even saturated with romance, but Moscow archives full of Party documents also contain collections of letters and reports that show how wracked by love and overcome with desire the Chinese in the red capital were. In the 1920s and 1930s, no matter how hard the authorities tried, they could not keep the Chinese from carrying on illicit affairs, getting pregnant and aborting at an alarming rate, and pursuing their rivals in love using every means at their disposal—including denunciation during times of political purge. They also could not stop them from heated arguments about the relevance of Goethe's romantic novel *The Sorrows of Young Werther* or the applicability of Alexandra Kollontai's free-spirited theory of sex to their own lives in Russia. And even if the Soviet press machine could ensure that China's first journalist in revolutionary Moscow filed his reports in line with *Pravda*'s expectations, they could do nothing about the fact that the moment he got home, he sat down and wrote the *History of the Heart in the Red Capital*—one of the most influential pieces of "red propaganda" ever written.[9]

No history that attempts to explain the great attraction of the Russian Revolution for the first generation of Chinese radicals can ignore, or take for granted, this overt mingling of the intimate and the ideological. Far from a peripheral concern or a colorful footnote, love, sex, desire, and romance were a central and historically meaningful element of Sino-Soviet history. Emotion and geopolitics were intertwined in the biographies of Chinese communists who traveled to Russia and did much to structure the relationship to come.

Early accounts of Russian romances resonated in China because they dovetailed with major social and cultural changes there. The 1920s was a period of experimental ideas about family, love, sex—and literature—in both places. In China, radical young people began to refuse arranged marriages while some Soviet youth rejected marriage entirely. Chinese readers devoured translated works by nineteenth-century European novelists including Turgenev and Tolstoy. Russians were reading the homoerotic poetry of Esenin and satirical sketches of love under communism by Zoshchenko. A young Chinese person who boarded the Trans-Siberian Railroad, then, was traveling between two cultures equally obsessed with revolutionizing love and literature, but in different ways.[10] Very quickly, Moscow became a place where young Chinese imagined and did things they might never dare in their hometowns or even in Shanghai. Was it really just the chance to read Marxist-Leninist tracts that got them on that train?

Once they were aboard, they became agents of a much larger historical interaction, forging human ties between two revolutions. Traditionally, when social scientists have tried to understand how separate revolutions are related, they crafted definitions and typologies of revolution, or (taking their cue from Marx) generated causal explanations that could apply to multiple cases, or compared particular aspects of revolutions, or identified an underlying process by which revolution evolves as it moves through time and space. They have also shown how ideas generated by one revolution inspired others, or how one revolution might "expand" and force or foment revolutions elsewhere.[11]

This last approach most heavily influenced historians of the Sino-Soviet relationship. When considering the role that human beings played as individuals—as opposed to members of political parties and economic classes or leaders of nations—they have tended to focus on the "advisors" and "experts" who went to China as part of a larger Soviet initiative to influence China's development. Indeed for many Chinese, Soviet people appeared as teachers—a relationship that this book tracks as a sub-theme from the 1920s through the 1960s.[12] And yet these political operatives, military officers, or engineers were most often mid-ranking male professionals for whom time in China was a brief episode in their lives, not a unifying theme. They did not learn Chinese or take Chinese wives, and many would not necessarily have chosen the assignment. By contrast, younger Chinese went eagerly to Soviet Russia as ordinary radicals but returned as high-ranking revolutionaries; some became poets and presidents.

This difference between Soviet people who went to China and Chinese people who went to the Soviet Union reflected a deep truth: this was an asymmetrical love affair. Since Peter the Great's first "Westernization" campaigns, the development of Russian elite culture has been unambiguously European. Russia's great revolutionary romance was French; as Tolstoy suggested in *War and Peace*, the very idea of a Russian Revolution first emerged through Russia's encounter with Napoleon's France, which inspired the Decembrist revolt of 1825. Russian revolutionaries imagined themselves as Danton or Robespierre, and if they could have gotten on a time travel train, they would have gone back to experience Paris of the 1790s just as surely as the Chinese made their way to 1920s Moscow. After 1917, the Bolsheviks remained obsessed with the idea of a Russian Bonaparte, a conservative who would roll back their radical social agenda just as Napoleon had done to the Jacobins. Meanwhile, they focused on encouraging (and eventually forcing) European revolutions; Germany was the dream but Hungary would suffice. In the 1930s, even as Stalin's regime redefined socialist internationalism in increasingly restrictive ways, the Spanish Civil War ignited what was arguably the Soviet Union's most passionate romance, one that carried over into postwar feelings for Cuba.[13]

After World War II, early Soviet concepts of socialist internationalism enjoyed a renaissance, one that ultimately excluded China altogether. New communist states in Eastern Europe and decolonization in Africa and Latin America gave the Russian Revolution the kind of global sweep that first-generation Bolsheviks had only imagined. Trade, aid, tourism, and cultural exchange opened up new worlds to the citizenry of global socialism, whose members traveled along complex itineraries that could bypass the Soviet Union entirely. China participated in this exchange for a time, and historians have been eager to include Chinese in the story of postwar internationalism. Yet in the 1960s, the Chinese withdrew from this exchange and, from the perspective of the Soviet Union, came to embody all that was repressive and dangerous about communism. China was once again relegated to the shadowy periphery of the Russian imagination, even as Maoism reached the zenith of it global influence.[14]

Traditionally, when Russian leaders thought about "the East," they primarily meant territories to the southeast and even southwest of European Russia—Central Asia, the Caucasus, the Near East—or perhaps India, the Middle East, occasionally Japan.[15] Even during the Enlightenment, when Europe was fascinated with China and Russia with Europe, Catherine the Great wrote to Voltaire: "Sir, you have lavished so much praise on China . . . yet my own dealings with this state would go a long way toward destroying any notions about their *savoir-vivre*."[16] For Catherine and her successors, China was primarily a trading partner and a sometimes "quarrelsome" border state.[17] After 1917, though China occasionally captivated Soviet political and cultural elites—once in the late 1920s and again in the late 1960s—for the most part it was a peripheral concern for the Russian elite. On the one hand, Russians could never quite let go of their identities as lovers of the West long enough to be somebody else's West. On the other hand, insofar as Russia enjoyed being the center of a new universe defined by its own revolution, this entailed creating a new world of which China was just one part.[18] China, of course, objected to being peripheral in that world.

Today, as growing numbers of Chinese immigrate to Russia, those who study them anxiously discover an often stereotyped "other" not inclined to assimilate, lamenting that "Russia and China are distancing themselves from each other and are becoming strangers emotionally and ideologically."[19] "Eurasianists" who emphasize Russia's cultural ties with "the East," however defined, are marginal voices in a country that has always measured itself against a European standard.[20]

And yet, stepping back, the Russian and Chinese revolutions were clearly deeply interrelated. If revolution is defined as a process that begins with attempts to destroy an old order, peaks with a revolutionary movement in power that is transforming society, and ends when living memories of the transformation fade, then the Russian and Chinese revolutions were contemporaries. China toppled the Qing Dynasty and established a republic in 1911, six years before Russia overthrew the Romanovs. In both cases, periods of complex military struggle and political uncertainty followed. In the late 1920s, as the Bolsheviks were preparing a Five-Year Plan to fundamentally reshape Soviet society, China's Nationalists also pursued state-sponsored social transformation. In the 1930s, Stalin's show trials obliterated his opposition and Chiang Kai-shek ruthlessly suppressed Chinese communists—who also purged their own ranks.

World War II ultimately worked in favor of China's Red Army, helping to enable radical social change, as World War I had done in Russia. It also vindicated the Soviet experiment, particularly in the eyes of Chinese communists. In the early 1950s, the People's Republic of China embarked on an industrialization campaign in line with the Soviet Union's own postwar technocratic agenda. And yet, the first-generation Chinese communists who still held power in the 1950s stayed true to the radical agenda they had first imagined and seen in Soviet Russia. China's Great Leap Forward and Cultural Revolution were reminiscent of the Soviet 1930s, a legacy that Russia's second-generation leaders were already questioning. On the other hand, by the 1970s China was liberalizing its rural economy in a way that Russia would not really accomplish for decades. In 1989, with the fall of the Berlin Wall and the Tiananmen Square massacre, Russia and China appeared headed in opposite directions. Yet China's booming economy and increasingly globalized culture and Russia's uncertain political reforms blur the distinctions from a twenty-first-century perspective. In retrospect, Russia and China seem to have tag-teamed their way through a century-long transformation that profoundly affected all of Eurasia.

The Chinese who traveled to live and study in Moscow in a steady stream over the course of decades were a key human interface between the two revolutions, and their stories illustrate the emotional investment backing ideological, economic, and political change. They embodied an attraction strong enough to be felt by young people in their provincial hometowns, strong enough to pull them across Siberia to a place that before their own revolution had begun had held no interest at all. If they eventually helped to lead a revolution that resembled Russia's in remarkable ways, it was not only because class struggle intensified in China due to international imperialism, as Lenin had predicted it would, or because Bolsheviks arrived in China to ensure that it did. It was also because in their youths they had been captivated by the potential of the Russian Revolution to help them to become new people, and to create a new China.

What this book calls the Sino-Soviet romance began in the 1920s when young Chinese revolutionaries first conflated Russia with romance and revolution.

Some deliberately wove romance into the stories they told about Russia or literally inscribed it into their own biographies through their love affairs. They used romance as a metaphor—that is, an evocative way of connecting two things whose relationship is hard to establish by overt, systematic comparison—not only rhetorically but also in practice. Would-be Chinese revolutionaries who wanted to find a connection with Soviet Russia could overcome language barriers, learn history, and master ideology. In the meantime, they could certainly flee arranged marriages at home, board the train for Moscow, and once there, strike up a relationship where few words were necessary. If that proved impossible, they could write stories about Russian romances and quote Pushkin to Chinese love interests.

Metaphors have always been important to understanding political, cross-cultural, and international dynamics. Many of the most fundamental concepts of international relations such as "balance" of power or "hard versus soft" power are metaphors, and states are often de facto described as individuals.[21] Kings have always been "fathers" of their people—in Confucian China as in absolutist Europe—and killing them was considered an act of "patricide" to create a more egalitarian polity of "brothers."[22] Alliances have long been called "marriages," fascinations with foreign cultures "romances," and brutal military rampages "rapes." Actual human interactions—marriages between ruling houses, love affairs in the midst of cross-cultural encounters, and rapes in the context of military invasions—also took place.

Chinese revolutionaries who used romance as a way of imagining and enacting connections to Soviet Russia were not doing something particularly new, but their choice created a peculiar and often overlooked emotional subtext for the Sino-Soviet alliance. Setback felt like heartbreak and disagreement like betrayal—both of which complicated real-life Sino-Soviet love affairs and families. All along, romance clashed with the dominant metaphors of brotherhood or friendship that prescribed how they were supposed to feel about the Soviet Union. The Bolsheviks had leaned heavily on the metaphor of communist "brotherhood" throughout the Civil War and the 1920s, while Stalin promoted a "friendship of peoples" both within the multi-ethnic Soviet empire and abroad in the 1930s. After World War II, these metaphors permeated descriptions of social and cultural exchange across the Eastern Bloc.[23]

When the Chinese Communist Party finally took power in 1949, it vigorously promoted both brotherhood and friendship to communicate its vision of the relationship between the People's Republic and the Soviet Union to a younger generation of Chinese. Leaders in China and Taiwan kept information about their own emotional histories out of the public eye. Romance had caused no end of trouble, and even metaphorically it was fragile and complicated in comparison to brotherhood and friendship. A second look at the 1950s, however, shows that despite the onslaught of propaganda using these male metaphors, romance and family themes involving women cropped up repeatedly, remained in the imaginations of some Chinese throughout the Cultural Revolution, and re-emerged in the 1980s. In the 1990s, an entire generation of Chinese Russophiles who had come of age in the 1950s and 1960s resumed study of their beloved language and literature, producing an enormous second wave of scholarhip and memoir about Sino-Russian cultural relations. Today, young Chinese scholars of Russian literature are attempting to bring what one specialist has called a "more serious and rational" attitude to a subject so long entangled in romance, both personal and political.[24]

Meanwhile, historians have appropriated the mishmash of metaphors without an attempt to untangle them, incongruously referring to Russia and China in the 1950s as brothers but using the terms "split" or "divorce" to describe the 1960s, without thinking about the union that had preceded it in romantic terms.[25] In reality, once the Sino-Soviet romance began in the 1920s, it continued to inform cross-cultural juxtapositions for decades to come. Again and again, in the late '20s, mid-'30s, late '40s, mid-'50s, early '60s, and mid-'80s, Chinese traveled to Moscow to witness and participate in an ongoing transformation that felt ever more related to their own. Each individual processed this experience differently, and once the metaphor was in circulation, Sino-Soviet romance could be creatively interpreted and mobilized to project new visions of the relationship. Precisely because it was a fickle human metaphor, the Sino-Soviet romance did not necessarily translate to unequivocal affection for Russia or "pro-Soviet" positions in ideological or geopolitical disputes. Whereas "friends" and "brothers" are supposed to be steadfast and moderate in their affections, "lovers" can be passionate and mercurial, oblivious or obsessed. "Romance" thus gave people a way of interpreting radical swings in Sino-Soviet relations intuitively and emotionally.

Nobody could lay claim to this kind of knowledge better than people who had traveled to Russia. Over time, their journeys created a recognizable emotional topography for the Sino-Soviet relationship as a whole.

Mirroring the life cycles of first-generation Chinese revolutionaries, the feelings associated with Russia as the Sino-Soviet relationship ran its course corresponded with those common to many lifelong romances. The excitement of anticipation, first encounters, and unquenchable yearning led to affairs and love children—but also gave way to heartbreak, disillusion, and distance. The exigencies of middle age brought official marriage and legitimate offspring. But the tensions of balancing real-world responsibilities with increasingly complicated family lives led to emotional rupture and divorce. None of this prevented a second or even a third generation from wonder and curiosity about the love affairs that had led to their own creation. Nor did it spell a bitter end to the Sino-Soviet romance. As time passed, memories of hostility faded, replaced by a sincere nostalgia that lingers even today.

The pages that follow draw upon some of the conventions of romance as a literary genre to capture an element of emotional truth in Sino-Soviet relations while presenting a work of archival and cultural history. On one level, the Sino-Soviet romance is a story of unrequited love, or an asymmetrical love story. But it also carries overtones of romance in the medieval sense: a tale of a heroic quest to an exotic place, told without irony. The protagonists of this story were all familiar with China's great medieval romances— *Journey to the West, Water Margin, Dream of the Red Chamber*—and some drew explicit parallels between their own lives and these fabled tales. Because this is the emotional history of a lived metaphor, the characters explain their feelings and tell their stories while archival sources, memoirs, interviews, and works of history describe their environments and contextualize their claims whenever possible. Emotions are taken as expressed, physical appearances as described, and musings as recalled. No details are imagined or conversations invented.

Structured around the romance metaphor, this book unfolds in a series of chapter cycles: First Encounters, School Crushes, Love Affairs, Families, and Last Kisses.[26] While a small cast of major characters carries the story forward, numerous others make appearances as well.

One peculiar aspect of the history of Chinese in the Soviet Union is that it includes a great many major Chinese political figures, such as Liu Shaoqi, Deng Xiaoping, and Jiang Zemin. They are not necessarily the protagonists of the Sino-Soviet romance because, with the exception of Liu, they did not engage with or illuminate the metaphor in obvious ways, nor did they leave particularly interesting autobiographical statements of their time in Russia. And yet because this book may help to indirectly shed light on their experiences, the story does occasionally pinpoint the presence of leading figures. Similarly, while China did not occupy a large space in Russia's imagination, those moments where the Chinese revolution did capture Russian attention are noted. Although this book is not a history of Russian culture in China, literature consistently sparked and fed the curiosity that fueled the journeys.

First Encounters describes the initial journeys to Russia of two of the story's most important protagonists. The first is Qu Qiubai, author of *History of the Heart in the Red Capital,* a key figure in cross-cultural literary politics and briefly a general secretary of the Chinese Communist Party. The second is Emi Siao, a childhood friend of Mao Zedong, an early leader of China's Friendship Association, and the premier poet of the Sino-Soviet relationship. Their stories locate the origins of the Sino-Soviet romance in the broader fascination with foreign literature and education that accompanied China's revolution in the first decades of the twentieth century.

School Crushes follows Qu, Emi, and others into Soviet and Chinese revolutionary schools. In truth, there is a fine line between studying a thing and loving that thing, and Soviet archives contain vivid evidence of all the ways in which Chinese students conflated romance and revolution while in Moscow—and how hard it was for Soviet schoolmasters to conceptualize an appropriate revolutionary pedagogy for them. This cycle introduces a third major character, the son of Jiang Jieshi (Chiang Kai-shek), Jiang Jingguo, who would spend a tumultuous decade in the Soviet Union and ultimately become the president of Taiwan. It also describes the quest of Chen Bilan, a protégé of Qu Qiubai, to become the first Chinese woman to study in Moscow. School Crushes ends with the heartbreak of China's 1927 revolutionary debacle as it played out among Chinese students in Moscow.

Love Affairs focuses more narrowly on a series of high-profile, individual Sino-Soviet romances that occurred in the 1930s, when the two revolutions were relatively estranged—circumstances that ironically allowed some Chinese-Soviet personal ties to deepen. Jiang's quiet marriage to a Belorussian worker contrasts with Emi's high-profile marriages, first to a Russian and then to a German Jewess in the Soviet Union. Liza Kishkina is introduced—a Russian woman born to an aristocratic family, who marries the famous Chinese labor agitator and one-time Communist Party leader

Li Lisan. The Soviet sojourn of He Zizhen, the second wife of Mao Zedong, offers a Maoist twist on the Sino-Soviet affair. The sudden appearance of dozens of Chinese love children in Soviet orphanages shows how literally the choices of one generation can shape the next. A boy named Yura Huang Jian contributes the perspective of a black sheep on the upbringing of these love children as part of a peculiar Russian international socialist family.

Families opens in the 1950s, as Liu Shaoqi and other members of the first generation of Chinese students in the Soviet Union confronted the children they left behind there, juggling geopolitics by day and skirmishes with their Russian-educated children by night. These chapters follow Emi, Liza, Yura, and others as they take on leadership roles in the massive cultural exchange of the 1950s, contrasting overt brotherhood metaphors with their private lives as well as with the romantic subtext of many of the most popular Soviet movies, novels, and songs. They also introduce Wang Meng, a writer and Russophile who came of age in the 1950s and eventually became China's minister of culture in the late 1980s. He did not get to participate in the second great wave of Chinese students sent to study in the Soviet Union in these years, described here as a sanitized reprise of the 1920s experience. Yet Wang's attraction to Russian literature and music was profound, and his later travelogues describe his lifelong emotional engagement with Soviet history and culture.

Last Kisses takes a close look at tensions in Sino-Soviet families beginning in the 1950s, even before the Sino-Soviet split. From the perspective of people whose lives had been shaped by a decades-long relationship between the Russian and Chinese revolutions, the enthusiastic "friendship" of the early 1950s and the melodramatic "split" of the early 1960s seem more like a single period of volatility in which the emotional valence of the relationship swung from one extreme to the other. These chapters show the cross-cultural and trans-revolutionary dilemmas Sino-Soviet parents and children faced throughout the period, following Liza, Yura, and others into and out of the Cultural Revolution. The continued story of Wang Meng highlights a renaissance in the Sino-Soviet romance and a return to beginnings. When finally given the chance, he travels to Moscow with great anticipation, chronicling his quest to find the "real" Russia—that is, the Russia that history has placed in his own heart.

Now that the Sino-Soviet romance has ended, Russia and China are left to grapple with its legacy. When the twentieth century began, the two were distant imperial rivals, but communism brought their people and cultures together in unexpected ways. The individual love affairs described in this book mirrored a larger process by which Russia and China became deeply, and irrevocably, related.

Part I
FIRST ENCOUNTERS, CIRCA 1921

I

Emi's Adventures

Changsha-Paris-Moscow

IT's THE WINTER of 1922, and just over the border from Latvia, a young Chinese man is stepping down from a Moscow-bound train carrying a little sign, handwritten in Russian, that says, "I want to eat." He can't speak Russian, but his French is good; a fellow passenger, a Belgian, has written the sign for him. He has a round face and a warm smile, European clothes, and glossy black hair, which he tends to leave a bit long. He's twenty-six and he calls himself Emil Siao. Siao is a Latinized spelling of his family name; Emil is after Emile Zola. At some point the "l" is dropped and his foreign friends just call him Emi. He finds a cafeteria where they give him "soup" and "bread." The soup is water with a few pieces of fish in it, and the bread is so hard he thinks they must have needed an axe to cut it, plus it's got straw in it.[1]

Would you believe it if I told you that Emi's disembarkment from the train constituted a world-historical event? Since the beginning of World War I, politically aware Chinese students had been streaming to Western Europe, along with hundreds of thousands of Chinese laborers. Because the overthrow of the Qing Dynasty in 1911 did not lead to comprehensive social reform, many intellectuals looked to the United States and Europe as models of successful revolution. France was a particularly popular destination for "work-study" youth, who earned a living in factories like other immigrants but also attended night school and banded together in small groups to read and think. Poor working conditions caused some left-leaning students to become interested in Marxism and to abandon the liberal ideals of the French Revolution. They became curious about Soviet Russia, with its anti-imperialist rhetoric and emphasis on social justice.

Emi was the first such student to leave France for Russia.[2] His own life marked the moment when the westward-bound river of radical Chinese intellectuals changed course, streaming "backward" from Paris to Moscow.

From the Village to Changsha

That Emi would arrive in Moscow in 1922 was completely inconceivable in 1911, when he left his hometown in Hunan at the age of fourteen.

Emi was born into a minor gentry family in a small village. His father was among the educated men who failed the examinations to enter state service. A few failed candidates—perhaps frustrated by their exclusion from the existing political system—ended up leading major rebellions. But more often these aspiring scholar-bureaucrats became teachers in small villages or large families. No one in Chinese society had more affectionate humor heaped upon them than these provincial instructors.[3]

Emi might have ended up like his father, except that the exams had been abolished in 1905 in an effort to modernize the school system, and Emi's father had decided to use this historic change to transform his personal identity. In 1904 at the age of thirty-four, he went back to school to study new subjects like physics and math. He went on to teach science in a nearby middle school and brought his sons to be educated there too.[4]

When Emi and his brother graduated in 1911, his father sent them to the capital of Hunan Province, Changsha, to attend one of the brand-new teaching colleges that were being promoted throughout China by gentry reformers. Tuition was waived in exchange for the boys' agreement to teach for several years in provincial elementary schools after graduation.[5]

Emi's journey to Moscow, then, began with an exhausting thirty-mile walk to catch a boat up the Xiangjiang River to Changsha. The riverboat, which was owned by a foreign shipping company and so was called a "foreign" boat, remained etched in Emi's memory to the end of his life: the ten rows of ten seats apiece in the upper cabin with its low canvas roof, and the pickles and sausage that he and his brother ate while eyeing the more expensive hot dishes sold on the boat.[6]

In Changsha, the brothers experienced the quintessentially modern shift of perspective on first arriving in a city far larger than one's own: the buildings seemed impossibly high and the streets so wide compared to those at home. The pedagogical school, called Hunan First Normal, was on the edge of Changsha, in the only modern building in the city. It was set against the hills, with five hundred stone steps that led to the railroad tracks; a little beyond that lay the banks of the Xiangjiang River.[7]

Perhaps because Mao Zedong was a student there, memories of Hunan First Normal have been preserved. Taking walks along the river was a favorite pastime for the students; on the river was an island with so many orange trees that when the trees were filled with fruit, it looked from a distance like a "golden-red cloud floating on the water." At least this was how the students described it in the poems they composed together as they walked, each boy taking his turn at extemporizing a verse.[8]

If it sounds like a dream world, it was, and not only of the students' making. Dreams for the future are the foundation of so many schools; in late imperial and early republican China, school building was a craze. The institutions that resulted were reflections of utopian visions, in which math from the West and poetry from the East would lead China to a preeminent position in the modern world.

Hunan First Normal's curriculum included an ambitious array of subjects from Confucian classics to chemistry. Competition in the school was sharp; the best essays were hung up for all to read, and there was a clear pecking order among the students. No model student, Emi's best subjects were language and music and he lived in fear of exams. Afraid of losing his free tuition, he calculated the grade average he needed across all his subjects to avoid being kicked out. Meanwhile, his older brother excelled and his prize-winning essays were publicly posted on a regular basis.[9]

Living in the shadow of one's older brother is a common curse; the historically peculiar aspect of Emi's situation was that his brother, Yu, happened to become the best friend of Mao Zedong. The two of them seem to have left Emi behind in their river walks and heated discussions of educational reform and the fate of China.[10]

1911 as Revolutionary Childhood

In 1911, when the Siao boys arrived in Changsha, their own "revolutionary path" was still far off. The 1911 revolution was the political achievement of an older cohort of men acting in their prime years. After overthrowing the Qing dynasty and replacing it with a republic, revolutionary elites set about defining a Chinese nation, opening the way for an entire century of change.[11]

But for Emi and his generation, the 1911 revolution was distant gunshots on a cloudy day, a student rally and a march through the dusk, hundreds of lanterns flickering against the darkening sky. Mao would later tell a story about being late for the 1911 revolution because it was raining and he couldn't find a pair of galoshes to wear. In fact all three boys were, in a way, late to the revolution—as was the entire generation of students arriving in the new provincial normal schools in the early 1910s, after an earlier wave of student radicalism had subsided. [12]

As teenagers in the aftermath of 1911, Emi and his classmates had new latitude to set their own courses of study. Emi focused on Sherlock Holmes, beloved Chinese novels like *Hongloumeng* (Dream of the Red Chamber), folklore collections, and serial novels published in Shanghai newspapers. Yu and Mao, on the other hand, were staying up late, watching the city lights of Changsha and talking about how to save China. Yu recalls that in one all-night session in 1914 he and Mao decided to start an informal student association devoted to national reform through the moral improvement of its members.[13]

After graduating in 1916, Emi found a job in a village clan school that was attempting to modernize. All the students and all the school officials were named Huang. Though he tried to introduce some ideas for reform that he had picked up at Hunan First Normal, teaching there was exhausting, low-status work, so Emi jumped at the chance to get out. In the spring of 1917, he found a job traveling around to start Boy Scout troops and then settled back in Changsha as a troop leader. While Emi was busy with the Boy Scouts, Yu and Mao were turning their little group into a formal organization: the New People's Study Society. Yu was the first president; Emi joined as a member.[14]

The New People's Study Society was one of many such groups coalescing all over China in support of the Beijing-based New Culture Movement. This movement arose after the 1911 revolution, when a series of military coups undermined the authority of China's national government and left de facto political power in the hands of provincial warlords. Disappointed, middle-aged intellectuals decided that the 1911 revolution had failed because it was purely political. How could China become a modern nation, they reasoned, if it was still in the grip of Confucian values? Between 1915 and 1917, prominent reformers took over Beijing University and began to publish a magazine, *New Youth*, encouraging Chinese students everywhere to question tradition.[15] Many of the intellectuals who led the New Culture Movement had studied abroad and wholeheartedly endorsed foreign exchange as a means of national renewal.

The idea wasn't new, but it wasn't very old either. In the 1870s, government reformers had tried sending small batches of students to the United States or Europe for middle school, college, or naval training. But the idea of studying abroad didn't really catch on until after the Sino-Japanese war of 1895. In 1898, a Qing official wrote a memo explaining that key Japanese reformers had studied abroad and attributed the success of the so-called Meiji Restoration to these foreign exchange students. He advised Chinese young people to study in Japan.[16]

This suggestion represented a sea change in Chinese mentality. Japan was traditionally a vassal state that had been sending students to study in China for over a thousand years. Now it was seen as an inexpensive, linguistically, and culturally amenable shortcut to Europe. In the first decade of the twentieth century, Chinese students began going in earnest to Japan, where they could read all manner of Western political philosophy in Japanese translation and openly join anti-Qing organizations. Russian anarchism was particularly popular among Japanese radicals, whose translations in turn influenced Chinese revolutionaries and inspired some isolated incidents of terror. By 1911, 10,000 Chinese had received some sort of Japanese education.[17]

After 1911, increasing numbers of Chinese began going to the United States to study. The new Ministry of Education had a relatively small budget for study abroad, and much of the initiative for sending students passed into the hands of local officials. The United States was the most expensive option, and while in any given year there were several thousand Chinese students there, they were likely to be from wealthy families. Less successful families had to look elsewhere.[18]

Russia was the least expensive European alternative, but study there was nearly impossible to arrange. The imperial Russian foreign ministry considered requests by Chinese to study in higher institutes of education on a case-by-case basis. Most applications around the turn of the century were for study of technical subjects, including military ones, a few of which the Russian government refused on grounds of national security. One of the eight Chinese students who remained in Petrograd in 1917 recalled that even before the war, there were fewer than thirty Chinese students in the capital.[19]

On the other hand, thousands of Chinese laborers streamed into Western Europe to work in factories during World War I, so reformers came up with a new strategy: students could go to Europe and work their way through school as laborers. Formal organizations like the Work-Study Association and the

Sino-French Educational Association endeavored to make a European education both affordable and accessible.

Hunan to Beijing

Just after the official founding of the Hunan New People's Study Society in the spring of 1918, Mao, Yu, and Emi received some Work-Study propaganda materials. In June, they called a meeting and decided to send one of their members to Beijing to investigate. By August, Emi, Yu, Mao, and about twenty other students left Changsha by train for Beijing.[20]

Life in Beijing was tough but exciting. Mao got a job in the Beijing University library, but Emi and the rest of the students studied French at the Work-Study Association preparatory school. Emi shared a room with eleven of the others, who all slept together on the same big *kang*, the traditional northern Chinese heated bed. They had no idea how to cook with the wheat that formed the basis of the northern Chinese poor man's diet. But they hadn't come to Beijing to live the good life; they had loftier things to think about as they studied French and contemplated freedom, equality, and fraternity.[21]

It wasn't only the language classes or French revolutionary ideals that made life in the capital so compelling. Emi and his friends had arrived on the eve of the May Fourth movement, the moment when the Chinese paradox of patriotic iconoclasm burned just hot enough to internally combust. In the final days of World War I, Japan had demanded that Germany hand over its Chinese territories, a grab that China hoped the Great Powers would deny at Versailles. In late April 1919, the Chinese public discovered that Japan was indeed to take Germany's place, and hostility against both the Chinese and European governments exploded.[22]

Like students all over Beijing, Emi and his friends at the French prep school organized to participate in the great May Fourth march of 3,000 students toward the gates of the Forbidden City, the demonstration that would politicize what is now known as Tiananmen Square. The demonstration was peaceful until the students arrived at the foreign legations, where they scuffled with police; one student died and others were arrested. The incident galvanized public opinion and touched off a series of nationwide strikes, which ultimately succeeded. On June 28, the Chinese government refused to sign the peace treaty with Germany.[23]

In late June, Emi traveled back to Hunan where he joined up with Mao, who had returned to Hunan before May Fourth and started a radical journal.

Emi wrote hot-headed articles and sold the early issues on the street with Mao. They organized meetings and marches and made arrangements for Hunanese to travel to Shanghai and Beijing to participate in student activities there. This kind of circulation between big cities and provincial towns spread and intensified May Fourth activities.[24]

It also underscored the importance of travel for exposure to new ideas. While some young people continued their struggle against Confucianism by arguing with their families and aspiring to new lifestyles in China, in the aftermath of the May Fourth movement other students like Emi and Yu redoubled their efforts to get to France. Yu managed to get a job as a secretary in the Sino-French Educational Association and became a trusted assistant to its leader, a famous, wealthy anarchist. In early 1919, Yu left with his new employer for France.[25]

Emi and the others weren't as lucky. Faced with students' overwhelming enthusiasm for the work-study program, the Work-Study Association raised the price of the trip to 550 yuan, a large sum for a poor family. The Hunan work-study group gave Emi the nearly impossible job of gathering funds and organizing the students' departure from Shanghai. At some point he even schemed for students to open restaurants and laundries to raise money for the trip. Finally, though, it was a visit to a powerful friend of Yu's patron that yielded the funds needed for the Hunan group's departure.[26]

And so it was that two years after the Bolsheviks took power in Moscow, the most radical students in China were headed to France, partially bankrolled by a wealthy aristocrat. For many Chinese, the journey to Russian communism started out with an exploratory trip to European liberal democracy.

Shanghai to Paris

On May 9, 1920, Emi and 126 other work-study students left Shanghai for Paris on a fourth-class ship—a huge, converted cargo boat. The plank beds had bedding made of coarse blue material, filled with straw. It was dark inside the boat, the food was meager and terrible, and everyone was seasick.

The students did what they had already learned to do in response to adverse circumstances: they organized. Each province elected two representatives to a "going to France on the boat self-governing organization," which had life sections, news sections, French sections, and music sections, and which assigned people meal and cleanup duty. Each student was given a number, which was written on a little white strip of cloth and attached to his or her clothing. Emi was in charge of news, music, and gymnastics.[27]

Not all of the students who boarded this and other ships were as politically active as the Hunan contingent. For some students, the boat ride itself, with its exposure to other young people with radical ideas, was a life-altering experience. One student who had not participated in the May Fourth movement called the journey "my personal May Fourth."[28]

The boat sailed from Shanghai to Hong Kong, then to Singapore, on to Djibouti, through the Red Sea and the Suez Canal, and across the Mediterranean before arriving in Marseilles on June 14, thirty-eight days later. On their first night in the long-dreamed-of country, they roamed around visiting parks and museums, and only ate dinner at 9 PM—their first French meal, arranged by the Work-Study Association, in a huge restaurant. They saved money by staying a couple of nights in train cars before their departure for Paris.[29]

In Paris, all the students from Emi's boat were divided up and sent to two-month French-language crash courses that the French government had set up in various schools. Emi was sent to Fontainebleau, where his French teacher remarked on his quick progress in French and invited Emi to his house. Emi became a regular at the teacher's home, an early experience that distinguished him from other Chinese students.[30]

Once, one of the French teacher's children walked up and pressed his finger on Emi's nose, a teasing gesture Emi took to mean that his Chinese nose was too flat. And so Emi crooked his own index finger over the bridge of his nose, to suggest that French noses were too prominent, sending the children into gales of laughter. Another time, when some of the Chinese studying in Fontainebleau got upset over portrayals of Chinese as backward in a local drama production, Emi organized an evening of student theater to acquaint the French with Chinese culture. The show sold out, an early indicator of Emi's talent for cross-cultural performance and mediation.[31]

After two months in Fontainebleau, Emi moved to Montargis, about seventy miles south of Paris, where some fellow Hunanese were already living. They organized a meeting of the New People's Study Society there in July of 1920. Besides debating their own political organization, the group also split up the French newspapers; Emi was in charge of Le Monde. At this point, some members of the group, including Emi, had begun to read Marxist-Leninist tracts in earnest. In December of 1920, the group sent Emi to Le

Havre to investigate the conditions of Chinese workers there, and he filed a damning report for a Shanghai newspaper.[32]

The material conditions of the work-study group were none too easy either. Over half of the students were unemployed, and in 1921, two hundred students had nowhere to live except tents that had been set up for them on the lawn of the main Chinese cultural center in Paris.[33] Material hardship set many students thinking about whether France was really a revolutionary destination. One student recalled his attempts to find the revolution in France:

> But what about the France that we saw around us? Solemnly pacing Catholic priests in black robes came to the school each day to preach to the students; the students viewed the principal and the housemaster as mice view cats; they had not the slightest notion of how to run a movement and never talked about resistance, revolution, socialism, atheism, anarchism, and the rest; the books and magazines they read never broached such subjects. Could it be that France had not yet had its May Fourth? . . . Luckily, a recently arrived issue of *New Youth* carried a translation by Zhang Songnian of a "Manifesto of Independence of Spirit" signed by Romain Rolland, H. Barbusse, Bertrand Russell, and a host of others I had never heard of. [34]

Only through Chinese periodicals could this student get in touch with contemporary revolutionary currents in France.

Different students responded differently to these conditions. Not all were hell-bent on revolution. Some turned to a life of crime; others took a pull-ourselves-up-by-the-bootstraps approach; some joined church-sponsored organizations; and many probably just suffered through it. Emi's friends in Montargis took the most radical tack. The Marxist-Leninist theorist of the group convinced them that working in factories would make them objects of capitalist exploitation; the obvious solution was to petition the Chinese government for financial support. They organized supporters and in February 1921 they went to Paris to the Chinese consulate to protest their poor living conditions. There they clashed with the French police.[35]

In the following months student protests were so frequent that the Chinese government began offering free passage home for some students and forcibly deporting others.[36] Like the earlier experience in Japan, the French

study-abroad movement had been politicized. It also ended with the departure of many students and ultimately helped move Chinese politics to the left.

Cross-Cultural Mediator

Some students, including Emi, managed to stay in Europe. With no source
of income and no prospects, Emi and a friend decided in late 1921 to go to
Berlin where they heard the living was cheaper. Emi managed on a little bit of
money from a brother-in-law; he and his friend slept in a cheap hotel and ate
in a small Chinese restaurant. If there was a moment when Emi might have
disappeared from history, it was probably this one.

But he didn't. In the spring of 1922, Zhou Enlai—who had been in Europe
on a scholarship and therefore had more time for political organization—
came to visit and told him about a new, more radical organization forming
in Paris. Emi returned there just in time for the June 1922 organizational
meeting of the European Communist Youth Corps, an early branch of the
Chinese Communist Party, in the Bois de Boulogne. He got a job at a factory
that produced insulation and befriended a middle-aged Frenchwoman amid
the mostly-female workforce.[37]

At the same time, he was placed in charge of the Youth Corps's relations with the outside world, because by then it was clear that he possessed
superior linguistic skills. Emi was the liaison with the newly formed French
Communist Party, which he and four others joined through their new friend,
Ho Chi Minh. Mostly, they just attended humdrum local meetings where
members squabbled over personnel issues, but Emi also got to hobnob a bit
with well-known French radicals. He and his friends would rent out cafés on
Sundays and invite French theorists to come and speak to the Chinese. He
also wrote an article about the situation of Chinese worker-students for a
French journal; he signed it Emi Siao.[38]

The public debut of this new, Zola-inspired name marked Emi's debut as
an independent player in the hazy world of international radicals. For the
first time, he had an identity separate not just from his brother but also from
the rest of the students in the group. He was the one who could best communicate with outsiders, his warm, open face and smooth language bridging
the cultural gap that separated even the most ideologically compatible comrades. Neither exactly Chinese nor exactly European, his name was easy for
everyone to say and remember.

Emi Siao, also called Xiao San. Courtesy of the Siao Family.

One day when Emi was at the French Communist Party headquarters, the French head of colonial affairs mentioned that a new university had opened in Moscow for students from "eastern" countries and asked if he would be interested in going. Of course, Emi said—thinking that at the very least he could get back to China through Siberia. He told the man he had heard of it from one of its students while in Berlin and had already tried to go but hadn't had any luck getting a visa. The Frenchman took out his card, scribbled a few words in Russian on the back of it, and told him to try again.[39]

So Emi returned to Berlin in the winter of 1922. When he produced the Frenchman's card at the consulate, he was given a passport and entry visa to the USSR within half an hour. Emi thanked the official who helped him in German, and then—having spent some time learning a few words of Russian the previous week—Russian. "Can you speak Russian?" the official asked. Emi produced the one sentence he had memorized in Russian: "I can't speak Russian, but I can speak German and French."[40]

So almost by chance, Emi would become the first of many students from Paris who, disillusioned with France, would leave for Moscow. At this point the Communist International, the Soviet organization dedicated to promoting world revolution (also known as the Comintern), was not directly involved in the European branch of the nascent Chinese Party; it took a random encounter at French Party headquarters to produce the visa for Emi.[41]

Yet it wasn't random chance that Emi was selected first. In the course of his travels halfway around the world and through France and Germany, it seems he thrived in the gap between cultures and on the border between languages. His experiences suggested that one could only enter the no-man's land by leaving one's compatriots behind and that, with just a touch of charisma, one might transform one's own cultural difference into a public identity. It was hardly an accident, then, that he was the first of all Chinese radicals in Europe to set off for Russia—that it was *his* life that contained the moment when the Chinese left Paris for Moscow.

Berlin to Moscow

Alone, Emi took a train from Berlin up to the German coast. From there he crossed the Baltic Sea on a Latvia-bound ship and then caught the train that brought him to the small stop just inside the Russian border, where he sought out his dinner. At this point, only a few hours separated him from Moscow.[42]

When his train finally arrived in the capital, there was no Educational Association to greet him. Instead, he found a Red Army soldier willing to help him get to the Comintern office downtown. There, the women at the front desk helped him find someone he'd known back home. This friend brought him right away to the Lux Hotel on Tverskaia where the Comintern delegates lived. They went to a big room, where they found a whole group of Chinese, including some leading lights of the brand-new Chinese Communist Party that just had been founded back in Shanghai under the Comintern's watchful eye.

After the round of introductions was over, Emi realized that he recognized several of the people in the room. Among them was a man he'd never met but whom he identified instantly, from his refined conversational tone. Years later, Emi would recall meeting the famous journalist Qu Qiubai: "One look at him," he would write, "and you knew, this was a big intellectual."[43]

2

Qu's Quest

Tolstoy and the Trans-Siberian Journey

IF EMI RECOGNIZED Qu, it was probably because anybody from China who cared about Russia knew Qu Qiubai, who had been sending the very first Chinese eyewitness sketches of revolutionary Russia back to a Beijing newspaper since early 1921. The young Chinese who devoured the articles could piece together what Qu might be like from his writing alone: "erudite, sensitive, a brilliant conversationalist, with a good sense of humor, a pale-faced scholar."[1]

A pale-faced scholar Qu certainly was, the smooth white flatness of his perfectly oval face hardly interrupted by his sparse eyebrows, his too-small eyes, his too-flat nose. At the moment Emi met him, Qu—who would later serve as general secretary of the Chinese Communist Party—was in the midst of a profound physical and emotional transformation. A year in the rough and tumble of Moscow was bringing the man out of the boy.[2]

Reluctant Russian Student

Qu was born in 1899 in the coastal province of Jiangsu to a mother who taught him Tang poetry and encouraged his studies from an early age. His father was a sometime landscape painter who dabbled in occult Daoism, smoked opium, frittered away the gentry family's dwindling fortunes, and finally left his wife with their six children to live in disgrace in the clan temple. It fell to Qu, the eldest child, to make the furtive trips to a pawnshop to sell the family's calligraphy, their paintings, and even their furniture.[3]

Qu entered middle school in Changzhou, Jiangsu, in 1909. He was an excellent, apolitical student who helped start a poetry club and dreamed of spiritual transcendence. A year before his graduation, his family's inability to pay his tuition led him to quit his studies and become the principal of a primary school in a tiny village. Meanwhile, his mother had become the family scapegoat for his father's failures. In early 1915, she killed herself by drinking the red tips of phosphorous matches dissolved in tiger-bone wine.[4]

Later in life, Qu recalled that in the aftermath of his mother's death, he made a series of decisions with no clear direction.

> After my mother committed suicide and my family scattered, I went alone to Beijing, just hoping to test into Beijing University's Chinese literature department and spend my life as a teacher. I had no great ambition to "rule the world," unfortunately I was just the reading type, a bookish art lover who wasn't so focused on making a conventional career and getting on in the world. After I got to Beijing, I lived with a cousin from home. I was hoping he could help me with the tuition for Beijing University, but he really couldn't, so he told me to go and take the ordinary civil service exam, but I didn't pass that either, so I chose to enter the Ministry of Foreign Affairs' tuition free Russian Language Institute. That's how I started to study Russian in the summer of 1917. I had no idea Russia was having a revolution, and I didn't know anything about the value of Russian literature either, I was just looking for a way to make a living.[5]

Qu's indifference to the language, literature, and revolution that would so profoundly shape his life is not surprising. Accurate news of the revolution was slow to reach China, and until the Bolsheviks won the Civil War in 1921, Russia seemed to many Chinese like just another fragmented country ruled by warlords. Little was known of Russian literature and not much was to be gained from learning Russian.

Like study abroad, foreign language had only become stylish in China at the turn of the century, and Russian was neither as easy as Japanese nor as popular and lucrative as English. Merchants in the borderlands became proficient in pidgin Russian for trading purposes, with a school in Zhangjiakou offering lessons in this Sinicized form of the language. But the literati in Beijing showed little interest, because the career possibilities for Russian speakers were still marginal. In the early 1900s, there were only ten schools in all of China that taught Russian, and most of them had Chinese, not Russian, teachers.[6]

The Beijing Russian Language Institute where Qu matriculated was the best in China, and graduates were guaranteed jobs somewhere in Manchuria or the Russian Far East. In 1896, after China's defeat at the hands of the Japanese, Russia and China agreed to the joint construction of the Chinese Eastern Railroad across northeastern China to link the Russian cities of Chita and Vladivostok. So few Chinese were fluent in Russian, and vice versa, that written agreements between officials were garbled, so the railroad's Chinese general inspector decided to create a Russian language school at the Foreign Ministry.[7] The fact that students paid no tuition and received a stipend shows the low valuation placed upon the Russian language among educated Chinese.

On the Russian side, the Institute involved some of its most qualified and charismatic China specialists, intent on creating positive impressions of Russia among the Chinese. Co-founder Dmitrii Pozdneev was the editor of a world-class book on North Manchuria, a high-ranking official in Russia's Ministry of Finance, and one of only a few dozen people in the entire Russian empire with an education in the Chinese language.[8]

In 1900, just after the Russian Language Institute had opened its doors, the anti-imperialist Boxer Rebellion swept through Beijing and put a violent halt to its operations. The rebels, angry at territorial concessions to Russia, set fire to the school buildings and killed one of its Russian teachers; the school's Chinese co-founder had his legs cut off with a wood saw before being killed, apparently on orders from Empress Dowager Cixi herself, for his assistance to foreigners.[9] A year later, after the Boxer Rebellion had been put down, the school reopened.

The teachers faced a daunting task: not only were there no textbooks nor even a readily available Chinese-Russian dictionary; there were also no direct translations of Russian literature into Chinese. There were a few renderings of Russian fables and short stories, but these were secondhand translations via Japanese and could not give students even a sense of the language they were trying to learn. Gradually the school's instructors compiled a textbook for the students full of Russian proverbs and short excerpts of literature as well as an early stage Russian-Chinese dictionary.[10]

The very first direct translation of a major Russian classic, *The Captain's Daughter*, Pushkin's story of love during a time of rebellion, was published in

China in 1903. Although not Pushkin's most celebrated work, it was a fitting introduction to Russian literature for a Chinese audience. The novel was set in the late eighteenth century during the Pugachev Rebellion, a great peasant uprising against Catherine the Great, led by the most infamous "false tsar" in all of Russian history. The hero is a loyal subject who is accused of treason and sentenced to death, then pardoned by the empress herself.[11] Considering that in 1898 China's empress had turned a blind eye to the Boxer Rebellion—less than forty years after China had finally defeated the Taiping rebels, who were led by one of the greatest pretenders to the throne in Chinese history—*The Captain's Daughter* was topical for Chinese readers.

The Captain's Daughter's characters and plot twists would have been immediately familiar to readers of popular Chinese novels as well. At the beginning of the story, the hero gives his coat to a stranger—who turns out to be Pugachev himself. Later, the hero is captured by Pugachev's forces, but Pugachev recognizes and frees him. The hero falls in love with the daughter of a military captain and defends her honor against the crude advances of a traitor. Magnanimous rebel leaders, providential kindness to strangers, scandalous seductions, and the fine line between treason and loyalty were also key features of Chinese classic tales like *Shui hu zhuan*, a historical novel about outlaws who band together and eventually offer their services to a vulnerable emperor. The 1903 translation of *The Captain's Daughter* was a watershed in linking up themes of Russian and Chinese cultures.[12]

The Captain's Daughter joined a group of low-brow Chinese stories about Russia that were popular in the early twentieth century: tales about so-called Russian nihilists. In the 1870s, young Russian intellectuals traveled to villages to educate peasants and incite them to rebellion, and then, when the peasants were unresponsive, turned to terrorism, carrying out numerous attacks that culminated in the assassination of Tsar Alexander II in 1881. News of these deeds reached China, and as frustration with the Qing dynasty grew, so too did fascination with Russian nihilism. "Nihilists, nihilists! I love you, I worship you," read the introduction to a 1904 book about them; "Your undertakings are brilliant and glorious. You never fail to startle heaven and earth with your ability to kill those emperors (the damned bastards) to rescue the multitudes of your suffering brothers and sisters. The comrades of your party are diverse indeed—beautiful women in disguise, young boys, and the most unusual stalwart men—but all are Bodhisattva redeemers."[13] Bodhisattvas were gender-neutral popular figures in Buddhist lore, beings who delayed their own final redemption to help others on the path to illumination.

Chinese were particularly fascinated with female nihilists like Sofia Perovskaia, who was sentenced to death for her role in the assassination of Alexander II but lived a second life as Su Feiya in a number of Chinese stories about her. A popular Chinese book called *Heroines of Eastern Europe* gushed, "There have probably never been so many beautiful patriotic heroines as in Russia." Attractive and intelligent, these Russian women used their charms in the name of revolution, luring wealthy officials into marriage to secure funds for their movement.[14]

After the overthrow of the Qing in 1911, Chinese infatuation with Russian nihilists died down. While a dozen or so translations of Russian classics appeared in the decade after *The Captain's Daughter*, it was ultimately the New Culture Movement that shifted Russian literature to Chinese high culture and made the Russian language into something exciting for a young man with literary pretensions like Qu.

Spring Torrents

When reformers began the New Culture Movement in 1915, one of their primary goals was to overhaul the Chinese language. China had never experienced a vernacular revolution in literature, so most poetry and prose was written in classical language very different from spoken Chinese of any dialect. For centuries, China's educational system had been geared toward increasing literacy in classical Chinese. Even after 1911, when a Chinese revolutionary penned a critique of the government, he could write most naturally in classical idiom; anything else felt experimental. Language seemed to constrain political and social change.[15]

As they searched for ways to explain their thoughts, some writers became preoccupied with translating foreign literature. Many in the New Culture Movement had studied abroad and, for them, exposure to new ideas went hand in hand with experience of new languages and lifestyles. When they looked at China's existing stock of literature translated from foreign languages, they were appalled. The leading translator was a man called Lin Shu, who could not read a word of foreign language but worked with a team of sixteen assistants who could. They would sit with a book and talk it through with him, as he simultaneously retranslated it into absolutely fluent and decidedly old-fashioned classical Chinese, at a rate of 1,500-2,000 characters an hour. He produced 180 book-length translations this way— 105 of which were British, 33 French, 20 American, and 7 Russian. Some of the texts that resulted, such as his rendition of *La Dame aux Camelias*, were literary achievements in their own right and became instant classics in China. However, they were exactly what the New Culture Movement opposed: translation that obscured linguistic and cultural difference in order to fit foreign texts into Chinese paradigms, rather than highlighting difference to destabilize tradition.[16]

In 1915, a key leader of the New Culture Movement, Chen Duxiu, started a magazine called *New Youth*—and its inaugural issue featured a translation of a very different kind of love story, Ivan Turgenev's *Spring Torrents*, followed by a translation of the more celebrated *First Love*. In political terms, Turgenev was one of nineteenth-century Russia's tamer writers, and if a Chinese revolutionary were to choose a Turgenev novel for an iconoclastic journal, *Fathers and Sons*, which portrayed the conflict between nihilists and their reformer fathers, would be the natural choice. So it's curious that Chen selected *Spring Torrents* for the first issue of *New Youth*.[17]

In *Spring Torrents*, a young Russian nobleman goes to Germany, where he falls in love with the beautiful and innocent daughter of the owner of a candy shop and woos her away from her German fiancé. But then, a passionate, freethinking, married Russian noblewoman distracts, seduces, and enchants him. He abandons the innocent young German girl and lives most of his life under the spell of his countrywoman. As an older man, he discovers that his German love has moved to the United States, and the story ends as he makes plans to move there himself.[18]

On one level, *Spring Torrents* was about a romantic young man journeying to enlightened Europe—as many young Chinese imagined themselves doing and as Chen had done himself—only to be lured hopelessly back to the debauched ways of his native land. Yet the story's anti-heroine was a serious addition to existing and growing lore about a new kind of woman: the passionate, independent, strong-willed Russian noblewoman, so unlike both her Chinese counterparts, who were secluded and weakened by Confucian social mores, and Western European women, who were constrained by bourgeois morals. Similarly, the heroine of *First Love* is a young, impoverished yet confident and playful noblewoman who has many young suitors but chooses a passionate affair with a married man over respectable offers of marriage.

The fact that these stories end tragically does nothing to diminish the charisma of their Russian heroines.

Right before *Spring Torrents* in the first issue of *New Youth*, Chen placed a short article about male-female relations, with the English original by Max O'Rell right next to direct translations into Chinese of little sayings:

> Women were not born to command, but they have enough inborn power to govern man who commands, and, as a rule, the best and happiest marriages are those where the woman has most authority. . . . It is a great misfortune not to be loved by the one you love, but it is still a greater one to be loved by the one you have ceased to love.[19]

Then he included a brief biography of Turgenev, which noted correctly that the author had lived much of his life in France, been arrested briefly in Russia, and was all too familiar with the kinds of "conflicts" discussed in the story. In 1915 at thirty-seven, Chen was nearly old enough to be the father of young radicals like Mao, Emi, or Qu, who lined up to get new issues of *New Youth*. He knew firsthand that nothing was more upsetting to many younger Chinese intellectuals than their arranged marriages to uneducated women. Chen carried on a lifelong love affair with his wife's sister and was also a legendary womanizer, yet like so many radical men his age, he could not bring himself to leave his arranged marriage. He became convinced that no political change would bring meaningful freedom to people like himself unless the Confucian moral system that structured more fundamental things—like language and emotion—was destroyed. As a "father" urging "sons" to sustained rebellion against tradition, Chen knew that, in the Chinese context, *Spring Torrents* was actually the more incendiary text.

While China's system of arranged marriage proved impervious to all kinds of torrents, classical Chinese fell surprisingly quickly to a new vernacular. The increasing flow of translations from Western languages brought not only a flood of foreign loan words but also a steady stream of foreign grammatical constructions and conventions of self-expression, changing the rules for all writers of Chinese.[20]

Just two years after its first publication, *New Youth* published a short story called "Diary of a Madman"—not a translation of the famous Russian novella by Nikolai Gogol but rather one of twentieth-century China's most innovative pieces of writing. The author, Lu Xun, had been translating

European literature from English or Japanese versions for years.[21] Whereas Gogol's madman is a lowly bureaucrat who gradually becomes convinced he is the king of Spain, Lu's is a minor gentry scholar whose intense study of the Confucian classics reveals to him that the words "eat people" are written between the lines. He becomes convinced that everyone in his village intends to eat him. Lu used classical Chinese to write an introduction to the story, in which a friend explained that the writer of the diary has since been cured of his insanity. The diary itself, however, was written in a powerful vernacular.

Lu Xun's "Diary of a Madman" is a concise, elegant, prophetic demonstration of China's ability to appropriate Russian frameworks and leverage them to instigate revolutionary shifts in Chinese practices. While Lu read widely across European fiction, when he sat down to write a story designed to change Chinese literature, he chose a Russian prototype.

Lu Xun loved Gogol and Chen Duxiu loved Turgenev, but no Russian writer was more broadly influential in early twentieth-century China than Tolstoy. No matter what genre or theme Tolstoy chose, he most consistently conveyed a vision of life that resonated with Chinese readers, and, for many of them, his moral politics were a way into his art.[22]

Before 1911, Tolstoy was one of several Russian anarchists (including Bakunin and Kropotkin) whose writing deeply influenced Chinese revolutionaries via Japanese translations. In their opposition to state and social hierarchy, anarchists had something in common with China's oldest philosophy, Daoism. Russian anarchists, including Tolstoy, were aware of this connection. Daoism did not oppose the state per se, but it did insist that all human beings, including rulers, should act only in accordance with a deeper natural order, which opposed violence or the imposition of artificial hierarchy and social convention. The main Daoist text, *Daodejing*, is terse and enigmatic—and especially open to appropriation and translation. Tolstoy spent five months with a visiting Japanese scholar as a guest in his home to produce a Russian translation of the work from classical Chinese. He read into it his own rejection of the injustices of Russian tsardom and the violence of warfare, as well as his distaste for St. Petersburg social conventions and preference for the nature-based rhythm of rural life.[23]

By 1917, of the dozen or so major canonical works of Russian literature available in Chinese translation, five were by Tolstoy: *Sevastopol Stories, Resurrection, Living Corpse, Childhood, Boyhood and Youth*, and, debuting in 1917, just as Qu arrived at the Russian Language Institute, an abridged

Anna Karenina.[24] *Anna Karenina* added yet another beautiful woman to a growing Chinese pantheon of Russian heroines willing to break the rules for love. Anna also fit perfectly into the New Culture Movement's radical social agenda, bent on destroying a family system widely seen as cruel to women and men alike.

At the same time, Tolstoy's deep, paradoxical affection for noble ways mirrored the nostalgia so many young Chinese felt for the heritage they had lost.[25] Reading Tolstoy was a way for Chinese to pay loving tribute to the aristocratic culture and the literary values they were so determined to transform and would eventually destroy, and to retain the idea of literary aesthetics as political and social power.

"History's Mistake"

In 1917, the Beijing Russian Language Institute was run by a White Russian émigré who also served as an advisor to the Chinese Foreign Ministry. Harbin, Shanghai, and to a lesser extent Beijing were common destinations for White Russians from the Soviet Far East who had opposed and fled the Bolshevik revolution. The school gave Qu Qiubai and his classmates snippets of nineteenth century Russian literature in the original. This, it seems, got Qu's attention. Later in life, attempting to explain the beauty of the Russian language, Qu used the Chinese term *i-chu*, which is "the aesthetic expression of an idea," like "'color on mountains, taste in water, bloom in flowers, posture in women.'"[26]

Qu spent his early years at the institute studying long hours, reading Buddhist texts, growing increasingly irritated with life in the capital, writing for a little magazine published with friends, and ruminating on the pointlessness of his life. As soon as his Russian was good enough to read fiction, he lost interest in the political ferment around him.

In 1918 I started to read a lot of new magazines, and my thinking seemed to make a certain amount of progress, a new person was starting to take shape. But, in accordance with my personality, what was happening was not so much the formation of a revolutionary ideology, as an intellectualization of world-weariness. So at first when I and [my friends] organized the "New Society" magazine, I was closer to a Tolstoyan anarchist, and what's more, in a fundamental sense, I was not a "political animal." After just a short time of political activity, pretty soon I was able to read works of Russian literature looking words up in a dictionary, so most of my attention went to literature and art.[27]

The first translation Qu published, in 1919, was the preface to one of Tolstoy's didactic fables of Christian life, *Work While Ye Have the Light*. It's not hard to see what attracted Qu to the preface, a little story about a family debating whether or not its members should opt out of conventional life to work for the spiritual improvement of themselves and the world. In Qu's translation, Tolstoy's young man exclaims:

> Why do we have to live this kind of a life? Even though we don't approve of it, why do we go and do it? Why can't we find the power to change our lives? We ourselves know that our luxury, our property, most importantly our arrogance, our lack of respect, our separation from life, it's all a harmful trap. In order to gain fame and fortune, we set aside all the joy of life. We live in the city, cooped up all day . . . all the way until we die. . . . I don't want to live like this anymore.[28]

The passage reflected Qu's own frustrations, studying eleven hours a day for the purpose of getting a boring official job.

Yet history intervened and gave Qu a way out. Later in life, as Qu sat in prison trying to figure out how he had gotten there, he identified the May Fourth movement as the beginning of it all. "That," he wrote, "is when 'history's mistake' began." By this Qu meant that this was the moment when he first became involved in politics.

> It was like this: the May Fourth movement had just started, and I was one of the Russian Language Institute's general representatives to it, and because none of my classmates was willing to do it, I had to be the school's "political leader," and I had to organize the student body to go and participate in the political movement.[29]

Qu's claim that he became the default leader just because nobody else wanted to do it sounds a bit hollow. Given his own complaints of restlessness and isolation, the chance to join like-minded souls in dramatic action may have had some allure.

And dramatic it was: Qu marched with fellow students and participated in clashes with the police. Back at home, he began to cough up blood, the harbinger of a lifelong struggle with tuberculosis. In Qu's representations of himself, politics would always be a disease, infecting his scholarly pursuits. He was arrested briefly in June 1919.

Perhaps riled, perhaps chastened by his experiences with street protest, Qu decided to become a writer. Like so many other new writers at that time, he started by translating—first Tolstoy's "Chitchat," and then his "Prayer," and "What People Live By," the afterword of "Kreutzer Sonata" and reviews of it, and the article, "On People's Education." Qu also translated short pieces of Gogol and parts of a minor French novel.[30]

By late 1919 he was participating in the new Marxist Research Society at Beijing University, his Russian language skills giving him entrée into this nascent radical elite.

> Not long after that Li Dazhao, Zhang Songnian and those guys orga-nized their Marxist Study Group (or was it maybe "Russian Study Group"?) and because I'd read a few paragraphs of a Russian language version of Bebel's "Woman and Society," I got curious about socialism, especially in its most idealistic forms, and interested in researching it, so I joined. This was at the end of 1919 or the beginning of 1920.[31]

The confusion Qu claims as to whether Li's group was a "Marxist" or "Russian" study group highlights the vague relationship between Marxism, Russia, and revolution on the part of participants. Though Li Dazaho, along with Chen Duxiu, would soon help to found a Chinese Communist Party, very little was actually known about Soviet Russia even in this radical group, partly because so few Chinese writers had actually been there.

China's First Moscow Correspondent

Qu was thinking about doing his own translation of Tolstoy's *Resurrection*, when he was given an opportunity he couldn't refuse. The politically moder-ate *Beijing Morning Post* (*Chen Bao*) was launching a special section devoted to coverage of the Russian Revolution and offered him 2,000 yuan a year to go to Moscow as one of three Russia correspondents for the newspaper.[32] Qu's salary in the primary school had been a fraction of this; now, in Beijing, despite the free tuition and stipend at the Russian language institute, he was still dependent on his cousin for financial assistance. Beyond the money, it was hard for Qu to reject an opportunity to use the language skills he'd been developing and to see for himself the country that was the subject of increasing excitement among young intellectuals.[33]

Here Qu's path diverged from that of so many other Chinese Russophiles at the time, the vast majority of whom never had the desire or the chance or the nerve to go to Russia. A common career for intellectuals who fell in love with Russia was to become translators of Russian literature—sometimes also becoming writers in their own right—honing their reading and writing skills to levels that Qu would never reach. Yet no armchair traveler or other journalist did as much to shape Chinese perceptions of Soviet Russia as Qu.

For him, a lucrative job as the first Chinese journalist in red Moscow was a perfect way to end hours holed up in pointless study, worries about a stultifying career as a railroad official, and financial woes. His choice made less sense to his friends and family, some of whom had heard of the harsh material conditions to the North and implored him not to go. In their remonstrance, Qu found his story: he was going to the Soviet Union, he said, precisely because it was the Land of Hunger. He was referencing an essay by an eighteenth-century Chinese scholar about the nobility of seeking death through starvation. It read:

> The Land of Hunger is located at the extremity of the Cosmos and is separated from China by immeasurable distances. . . . The first stages of the journey are unendurably hard; but if fortitude should urge the traveler on, the destination may be reached within less than ten days. The entrance will take him into an open bright country, which looks as if it were a new universe. . . . Nevertheless, unless they are unshakable in their determination to accept death for the sake of truth they will turn back even when they have almost arrived.

"I shall find in the Soviet Union," said Qu, "my Land of Hunger."[34]

Pesky Peripheries

On October 16, 1920, Qu left Beijing and began a hundred-day journey through a succession of borderlands to Moscow, traveling in train cars with diplomats who embodied a transitional moment in Sino-Russian relations. The traditional pattern—of borderland trade and confrontation between two old regimes with mutually incomprehensible cultures seeking material gain and geopolitical advantage—was in crisis as the old regimes crumbled and the new ones fumbled.[35]

Qu embodied a new idea: bringing the central values and traditions of the two cultures face to face to somehow merge in the center. But to realize this ambition, Qu first had to reach the center, which could only be done by crossing the border on the very train lines that were the subject of so much sordid haggling, with the very people who engaged in it.

The first borderland to cross was Manchuria, whose railroads reflected the realities of imperialism in northern China. On October 18, Qu left Tianjin on a Chinese train headed north, running at first along the scenic coast of the Yellow Sea, then turning inland toward the heart of Manchuria. In Fengtian he changed trains, boarding the Japanese-controlled Southern Manchurian line. Qu's middle school history books had said that Manchuria was Chinese territory, but here there were Japanese everywhere, including all the train personnel. Where were the Chinese coolies, he wondered? On October 20 he reached Changchun, where he left the station to take a look around this wintry land; it seemed that "the world had already changed color."[36]

Here in Changchun, Qu had his first taste of Russia.

A lot of Russian-style carriages were parked outside the station, and the grooms were Russian too, with badly worn, greasy fur hats on their heads; when the wind blew it fiddled with the silky fur on their hats, constantly whisking their long eyebrows about, giving them all the more that Russian look of miserable anxiety.[37]

He then switched to the Chinese Eastern Rail line, where the service people were mostly Russian and the police Japanese. The station was filthy and disorderly, "not even as tidy as a station in a small town in Jiangsu," Qu's home province. Things didn't improve on the train: third class was "sixes and sevens," teeming with Russians carrying large bags on their backs, their mouths full of cigarettes and spit, women dragging their children along behind them.[38]

But "Russia" really began in Harbin, where the train station was Russified, "pure and simple." Qu and his travel companions got a horse carriage and headed toward an inn that had been recommended to them by a Chinese they had met on the train. The inn was "wretched beyond belief," full of small traveling traders who had the "absolutely foul" smell of northerners. It was expensive too, but Qu's traveling companions couldn't find something more livable. They resigned themselves to the filth of it. " 'We' pitiful, laughable, 'civilized' Chinese people," reflected Qu, "the minute we really entered Chinese life, we felt it was unbearable, and the half-Europeanized Russian civilization also shocked us. 'It turns out 'Western' people are also like this.' "[39]

Soon Qu discovered that his progress to the center was delayed indefinitely in the borderland. Battles between the White general Semenov and the Chita people's army were spreading, a key bridge in the middle of Chita had been blown up, the train lines were obstructed and train travel was halted. Qu bought Russian language papers every day hoping for good news, but in vain. Meanwhile it was getting colder and harder for Qu with his tubercular lungs to breathe. As the ice on the windows of the room at the inn became thicker, he began to feel he was trapped in a crystal palace.[40]

But Qu was supposed to be a reporter, so he had to leave the palace to investigate the dirty imperial miscegenation that was Harbin.[41] To Qu, Harbin was a cultural wasteland, where Japanese economic influence squeezed out both Russians and Chinese. He found only Hubei barbers and Ningbo tailors, who made Western-style clothes for the Russified Chinese merchants of Harbin with Russian wives.

Throughout Harbin, Qu found only three or four Chinese schools and a few newspapers; the book selection was paltry, so Chinese life in Harbin felt static. His former Russian language institute classmates, whom he found working in official posts at all the train stops in Manchuria, were big fish in this small pond, even though their lives compared to students back home who had studied English or French were much more frugal and cold. The lower classes, including lots of coolies who worked for the railroad, lived the "dirty life of the Russian village." Everyone spoke a little pidgin Russian. "The ash colored life of the Chinese once they arrived in Harbin" became even more black."[42]

As for the Russians in Harbin, Qu characterized them as Whites and capitalists who spent their time "running around with the Japanese coming up with fresh tricks." The few sympathetic Russians he met knew nothing of Chinese high culture; when he asked them what they thought about China, they all said, "We haven't arrived in China yet. You thought Harbin

was China?" and then expressed polite interest in "ancient eastern culture."
Yet they seemed no more current on the situation in Moscow than Qu.
Eventually Qu invited the few passable Russians he had gotten to know for
a real Chinese dinner; they were stunned by how good it was. Surrounded
on all sides by Chinese, they had never had a Chinese meal.[43] And so, to Qu,
Harbin appeared as a desolate borderland, where, in the cold, mad imperial-
ist rush for wealth, the streams of two cultures had dwindled to a trickle and
frozen.

Qu took refuge in the creation of propaganda that would transform the
drudgery around him into beautiful words. He began an account of his
travels, *Journey to the Land of Hunger*, in which he wrote about Harbin and
about himself, in a strange language that was hardly classical Chinese and
hardly vernacular. [44] As one scholar has noted, Qu had a "queer ability to
perceive . . . a hyperawareness of, the philosophic implications of words."[45]
Here is Qu on the natural world of Harbin:

> A grey sky, full of snow, reflected in the clouds of dusk, like the peeling
> skins of silkworms in the spring, slowly coming out through the bright,
> severe winter light; the private whisperings of the short trees, the pierc-
> ing, cruel winter wind passing through the forest; an open plane, the
> waning grasses submerged in the white snow, here and there suddenly
> poking up, shaking with the wind, rustling and swishing the threads
> of snow; reflecting high and low clouds and snowdrifts, as if thickly
> speaking words straight from the heart, sighing with complaint over
> the dullness of life.[46]

Chinese was just beginning to include long sentences filled with modi-
fiers, and it shows as Qu's references slip and slide through the sentence.
Impressionistic, stream of consciousness narration of a subjective self was all
the rage in Beijing; it hardly mattered whether it made much sense, as it was
the sensibility that counted.[47]

From the day of his departure for Moscow, Qu became an instant celebrity intellectual. When he left Beijing, his friends mailed the farewell poems
they had written him to *Chen Bao*, which published them, hyping the trip
even before it began. Throughout November and December of 1920, Qu sent
his articles regularly and the newspaper printed them immediately.[48] The
transitional language Qu used to describe his transitional frame of mind in

this transitional place was bound to stir the longings of young readers back home for a new language and, ultimately, a new world.

Trans-Siberian Reveries

As the days passed into weeks and threatened to become months, Qu and his friends, like the travelers in the eighteenth-century Land of Hunger, began to have their doubts and to consider turning back. "This trip," his fellow journalist said later, "is like ploughing with a dog because you have no cow." Finally, in early December they received word that the battle that had halted train travel was over. Qu and his friends ran around buying large quantities of food to continue their journey to the Land of Hunger, food that would last them through their first months in Moscow. Finally, on December 10, fifty-five days after their arrival, they departed Harbin.[49]

Once the long train ride was under way, Qu passed the time in a half-asleep half-awake mode of reverie. "The train lines fly by," he wrote "you hear the Northern wind, trembling the hard walls of the icehouse that was the snowy sky, the red terror and the eastern sun countries' god of wealth, capitalism, have begun a final battle, lifting the skies and moving the earth."[50] Or, later,

> Inside the rail car, the cold air has seeped in, between thick quilts, lying on the railcar seats, listening with my eyes shut to the surging of the engine, the howling voice of the snowy wind, as if a thousand troops and ten thousand horses were suddenly galloping close, revealing a cosmically vital, magnificent valor. A limitless imagination, a limitless shocking sway arises in the heart, a child of ancient Eastern culture enters Western Europe's new and old cultures.[51]

Qu might like to have remained undisturbed with his dreams of the red capital, but he was drawn into unwanted conversation with his traveling companions instead. Qu, representing China's new youth, hurtled toward Moscow in a compartment with three Chinese from the Moscow consulate, representing China's old guard, "two consciousnesses coming into contact."[52]

One issue preoccupying the Chinese diplomatic community at that point was the fate of the hundreds of thousands of Chinese laborers in the Russian Far East. They had first begun to arrive en masse in the late nineteenth century, when Russia found itself short of workers to develop the region and the Chinese found they could earn twice or triple their usual salaries by emigrating. By 1910, there were upwards of 200,000 Chinese in the Russian Far East. Their already poor working and living conditions plummeted as Russia descended into civil war, and their plight attracted elite attention. According to the gossip of Qu's travel companions, the old Chinese diplomatic corps had been corrupt and ineffective, embezzling funds the Chinese government sent to aid emigrant workers. In 1917, when other countries' envoys were busy arranging for their citizens' safe passage home, the Chinese envoy "ran for his life," arranging a chartered car and trying to sneak out of town unnoticed, leaving a couple of students to handle the affairs of the miserable masses.[53]

The three Chinese traveling with Qu were sent to replace the diplomats who had fled, and so they were open about the weaknesses of their predecessors, but Qu also found fault with them. The new general consul quickly betrayed his own venality by demanding extra payments from Qu and his friends, supposedly for their travel fees to Moscow. Occasionally at stops along the way, local Chinese business leaders would board the train to discuss their run-ins with the "red nose Bolshevik fools." But when three Chinese got on board to ask the consul to speak to the three hundred Chinese workers at a small stop near Irkutsk, he refused.[54]

All of this was damning enough, but to Qu the worst thing about the new envoy was that he knew nothing of Russian culture and couldn't speak a single phrase of Russian, despite having lived in Petersburg for seven years.[55] Even the very center of Sino-Russian relations, it seemed, was characterized by the marginality of the periphery; it was as if the cultural indifference of Harbin extended to China's most elite representatives in the heart of Russia.

On December 13, Qu's party arrived in Manzhouli, the town on the border between Manchuria and the Soviet republic of Chita. Four days later, they received permission from the government in Chita to proceed; theirs was the first train to leave Manzhouli after the Whites' retreat. The train inched toward Chita over temporary tracks laid on the ice in segments to replace those destroyed in the civil war.[56]

They stayed two weeks in Chita, where they were warned so urgently against continuing to Moscow that they felt once again like the sojourners to the Land of Hunger who wanted to "turn back even when they have almost arrived." Instead, the group left Chita on January 4. Qu became the first Chinese radical to describe the beauty of Lake Baikal and relate the taste of Russian black bread. "Its bitterness and sourness, smelling of rotting grass mixed with mud, was something that no Chinese has ever tasted or can imagine."[57]

Finally, on January 25, 1921, at 11 PM, the train pulled into Moscow's Iaroslavskii Vokzal. Delegates from the Commissariat of Foreign Affairs brought him to an old hotel, Kniazhii Dvor (Prince's Court), where Commissariat employees now lived.[58]

History of the Heart

Qu's life as a foreign journalist in Moscow was smoothed by an introduction from the Eastern Division of the Commissariat of Foreign Affairs to the editor of *Pravda*. The editor explained to Qu how to get interviews and provided him with a translator, V. S. Kolokolov, who became Qu's friend and a source of information about Russian life.[59]

In Moscow, Qu began a new set of reports, some of which he sent to *Chen Bao* and others which he published after his return to China in a book he called *Chi Du Xin Shi*, or *History of the Heart in the Red Capital*. Qu's reports are verbal polaroids done hastily for immediate consumption. They capture not just the focal point but all the arbitrary background, and they make no attempt to disguise the author's utterly subjective vantage point. The opening lines of *History of the Heart* announce Qu's approach to his experience: Life, he says, passes

> like polished images on the heart's bright, clear mirror, flashing and wasting away, bizarre and motley. . . . Life's meaning seems objectively even, you only see the continuous images of the movie, but in reality they are individual, independent images.[60]

Qu's reportage of the red capital gives impression after impression, bizarre and motley, allowing readers to create their own narratives and to insert themselves in Qu's place. It is a peculiar and at times exquisite piece of propaganda, perhaps one of the most paradoxical and effective pieces of "red" propaganda ever written. Despite its dated language, it is still read by young Chinese interested in Russia.

Qu made the rounds of all the "sights" that the new Soviet government deemed worthy of showing, attended all the "events" that it thought relevant, and duly reported on them. Appropriately enough for a young Chinese radical on a journey from Tolstoyan anarchism to Soviet socialism, the first big event he attended in mid-February 1921 was the funeral of Kropotkin, the Russian anarchist beloved by Chinese radicals since the turn of the century. One can only imagine the vicarious thrill readers back home would feel as they heard how Qu was shoved this way and that in the crowd of banner-wielding anarchists, Socialist Revolutionaries, Mensheviks, and artists' study groups.[61] Amid that throng, Qu symbolized a moment in Chinese radical development when each young person found himself shoved this way and that among a crowd of new ideas.

In the coming months, Qu filed reports on Moscow under the draconian policies of War Communism, the Kronstadt rebellion, Russia's attempt to revive international trade and relations, the big Comintern meetings of the summer of 1921, his brief encounter with Lenin (a staple of early Chinese accounts), the famine of 1921–1922, and the New Economic Policy designed to jumpstart the Soviet economy after the Civil War.

Qu Befriends the Tolstoys

Woven through the barrage of images of a new socialist world is a subplot leading from the last days of the old regime. Himself the child of a disgraced gentry family, Qu wrote with particular empathy about the fallen Russian aristocracy and its culture. In the Tretyakov Gallery a few days after his arrival, Qu finds "the gold among the old culture's grit." "Wandering far away, you can enjoy yourself so much that you forget to go home." Later Qu points out the traditional hatred of the Russian "aristocratic and intellectual classes" for capitalism, praising the "repentant aristocracy" and contending that there were a good number of former aristocrats in the ranks of the Communist Party. One of Qu's more poignant passages describes aristocratic youths reduced to selling their jewelry, their antiques, even their rugs by the side of the road.[62]

But these are just hints of a coherent subplot that emerges toward the end of *History of the Heart*.

One evening, Qu attended a meeting of the Proletcult, a Soviet group dedicated to the creation of a new proletarian culture. Tolstoy's granddaughter Sofia came to speak, and invited Qu to visit Tolstoy's Moscow apartment, which had been turned into an exhibition. She gave Qu a tour, explaining the paintings on the walls (including one drawing by Tolstoy himself) and sprinkling in personal reminiscences of her grandfather.

This visit reduced Qu to poetry; his next entry is a translation of Lermontov and after that, a Chinese poem he wrote for Sofia. "The luminous moon falls into the sea; its fragmentary reflection shakes from afar; physiology is very much like this; great waves of desire without boundaries."[63] Whether or not Qu gave Sofia the poem is unclear, but it was nevertheless a gift to his readers, who could thereby imagine themselves writing in their very own language of love to Tolstoy's granddaughter.

At Easter, Qu attended the famous midnight mass at Church of Christ the Savior, officiated by the Russian Orthodox Patriarch who had just been released from prison. He describes the experience in reverent terms:

> Deep night. Even though it's the "May weather" of the Russian poets, a late chill still sneaks through the coats of passersby. The dense streets of downtown Moscow are still for a moment, then faintly saturated all around with the rich ringing of the churches' holy bells, precipitously breaking the deep silence of God's night. Silhouettes of people in groups of threes and fives gradually appear at street corners, each instant more numerous than the last. Church bells ring, the longer the more, the later the mightier. The sky echoes with the rhythmic and solemn sound of hymns. By one or two in the morning, a large crowd, dark and silent, gathers before the steps of the church, the candles in the hands of believers bits and pieces of dazzling illumination, the ritual entrance into the church of rows of priests beneath the icons painted high above, the old beggars, tattered, weary and weak, holding out their joined hands, waiting for Christian mercy—the midnight mass for Easter had begun. We crowded into a sea of people at the Cathedral of Christ the Savior, there must have been twenty or thirty thousand at least, it was impossible to see the entire ceremony clearly. Eventually we squeezed our way out, by the time we got home it was past four and we were exhausted. Yet Moscow was still trembling and vibrating with the chiming of bells from over 1,500 churches, disturbing the sleep of "heretics."[64]

Qu also wrote about Easter practices, including the custom that girls exchange presents and kisses with their boyfriends at Easter. This Easter is especially festive, he says, because Lenin's New Economic Policy has brought back to the markets ingredients for traditional feasts.

On May 1, Qu goes to visit an unidentified "female acquaintance," passing various state-sponsored secular celebrations in and around Red Square along the way. His descriptions of these events pale in comparison to his lavish language of mass religious faith the night before. As he described himself arriving at the young woman's house, he relates a conversation between them. She naively but sincerely asks whether Chinese have Easter, and Qu gives a brief soliloquy on Chinese spiritual beliefs. Qu confesses that he doesn't kiss the girl because of "Eastern shyness."[65]

Qu's romance with the Tolstoys faced an ominous threat—from the Soviet government itself. Qu relates that one night when he went to Sofia's apartment, several Russian girls sat with him in the small kitchen, "talking about feelings with the child of the East." There Sofia told him she had been visited by a "very important Bolshevik," she claimed, none other than "the secretary of the central executive committee."

Whoever this Bolshevik might have been, he exclaimed: "The Chinese reporter has also come here!" Then he asked, pointedly, whether Sofia's mother's wages were sufficient and offered a veiled threat in the form of a story about his own experiences with the imperial police. Qu conveyed the incident without comment; it is a moment when his two great romances—Russian revolution and Russian literature—conflict in a way that even he cannot, or chooses not to, resolve.[66]

Tolstoy Time Warp

Given Qu's subsequent political development and the various uses the Chinese Communist Party found for his writing, it's a bit odd to find among his short, impressionistic sketches of Soviet life a seven-part narrative of a visit to Tolstoy's country estate. What seems disproportionate or incongruous in retrospect was a brilliant rhetorical move on Qu's part. He managed to touch the space and time in Russia that corresponded to China's contemporary reality, without ignoring the ways in which the Russian past had irretrievably altered the Chinese present. Tolstoy's era was a moment when the Russian aristocracy still set the tempo of social change, before radical leaders emerged from other, poorer classes—who would eventually turn the aristocracy's houses into museums.

China, too, had a gentry-based intelligentsia that traditionally defined political culture. Yet when Chinese youth disaffected with the results of

China's 1911 revolution went looking for a more thorough solution, they could turn to communism. While Russian communism took decades to develop, Chinese like Qu could latch onto it quickly and directly. Moreover, increasing transnational travel and communication meant that Chinese like Qu could personally and physically transcend differences separating Russia and China.

It was still a big jump to make, especially for gentry children like Qu, ambivalent about the loss of their families' social and political status. As a thinker, Qu implicitly addressed questions that no one had yet articulated. His comprehension of the chronological complexity of two simultaneous and intertwined revolutions was more sophisticated than that of subsequent Soviet and Chinese Marxists, who were forever trying to figure out which moment in Chinese history most corresponded with Russia's 1905. By his own presence at the Tolstoy museum, Qu relayed a message: we Chinese intellectuals, right here and now, can both reach back to our moment in Russia's past and reach across to a new moment in Russia's present, and thereby reimagine China's future.

Given the complexity of the relationship between contemporary Russian and Chinese political developments, it was no wonder that Qu described his trip to Tolstoy's country home in such detail.

Qu traveled to Iasnaia Poliana along with twenty schoolchildren and their two teachers, a couple of Tolstoy's relatives, and a "Soviet young lady" who was taking advantage of the chance to hitch a ride back to her home village. Qu had already encountered several "Soviet young ladies," the young, beautiful, impoverished women who, he explained, became secretaries in the new government bureaucracies with the understanding that they would become mistresses to their bosses. Qu gave the reader to understand that he personally had nothing to do with them, but he clearly implied how many beautiful, hungry, and willing young ladies lived in the city.[67]

After a night at an old house near the train station, Qu and the children set out for Tolstoy's. The walk was an occasion for one of Qu's rhapsodic descriptions of the natural world, where "shadows of trees bow and peep on the brook, water and clouds ripple in reflection," the grass is like "nature's wool rug," the "weak fall clouds occasionally cover the sun," so that it seems to greet people, "stroking their shoulders and then passing." As Qu's urban gloom washed away, he passed through the final canopy of flowers leading to Tolstoy's house in a state of exaltation.[68]

Never have a piano, a reading table, and some family photos been so moving as these relics of Tolstoy were to Qu that day. The keeper of the museum, Tolstoy's grandson Alexander, assured Qu that nothing had been touched since Tolstoy's death. There were two library rooms, and Alexander explained that Tolstoy had wanted to consolidate them to a single library, but had never done it. Among the family photos on the wall was an empty frame; Alexander explained that it was a picture of Tolstoy's uncle that was taken down because of his excessive drinking and gambling. On the bookshelf, Chinese characters caught Qu's eye: it was an English-Chinese version of the *Daodejing*. Here in this far-away land he found all of his fathers.[69] After the tour, they went outside to the tree where Tolstoy used to sit and talk with peasants; the schoolchildren were nearby, covering Tolstoy's grave with fallen leaves.

That night Qu had dinner with Tolstoy's relatives. As a nephew read from the collected works of the nineteenth-century writer Ivan Goncharov, Qu inquired about his schooling. It turned out that the boy didn't even go to school—Soviet schools were inadequate, according to the Tolstoys. One of the women asked Qu whether Chinese gamble, and she referred to her own past gambling losses in Paris. She took out a box of family photos and began showing them to Qu; they came across a picture of her son "killed by evil Bolsheviks."[70]

Qu took the night train back to Moscow with the schoolchildren and a small party of Tolstoy's relatives. To Qu, he, the schoolchildren, and the Tolstoy family represented three different cultures, his ideal travel companions: the fallen nobility who, he says, "are doing their very best to become ordinary Russians but whose aristocratic manners come through whether they like it or not"; the laughing, teasing schoolchildren; and the "child of the East" would all reach Moscow together.[71] In a lyrical mood, Qu drifted off to sleep.

3

New Youth, New Russians

As Qu INCHED his way toward Moscow, the first serious representative of the Communist International was finding his footing in China. The Bolsheviks had seized power in Moscow in 1917, firmly convinced that communist revolutions in Europe would quickly follow. Instead, they were forced to give up Ukraine and the Baltics and found themselves mired in civil war, which dragged on in the Far East. Vladivostok remained in the hands of Whites backed by Japanese troops until late 1922. Yet the Bolsheviks remained certain that Russia's was a revolution without borders, and the radicalism of China's May Fourth movement caught their attention.

The interplay between Qu's reporting from Moscow, the overtures of Soviet representatives, and the actions of thousands of young Chinese intellectuals in 1920–1921 begins to convey the complex process by which Chinese and Russian communism came to be so deeply intertwined. For many first-generation Chinese communists, 1920–1921 was their first meaningful exposure to Soviet Russia, and it created a set of tropes that proved remarkably durable.

"Old Hairy People"

The process by which "Russia" shifted from repellant to attractive among some young Chinese wasn't exactly logical or linear. One early communist recalled that prior to 1921,

> for the average Chinese intellectual versed in international affairs, Tsarist Russia was filled with corruption, darkness, despotism, and backwardness. It had eaten into the Northern borders of China and aggressed against the Northeast (Manchuria). The Russians were

looked upon as curious Arctic creatures, covered with long hair, dressed in heavy furs, and given to drinking and arrogance. They were called "Old Hairy People (Lao Mao-tzu)."[1]

While the publication of Russian literary classics acquainted Chinese readers with a handful of sympathetic Russians who were certainly not "Old Hairy People," interest in these new fictional heroes did not cancel out animosity toward their historic counterparts.

The complexity of "Russia" for radical Chinese intellectuals is perfectly captured by the career of Chen Duxiu. Born in 1879, the same year as Trotsky, in 1902 he went to study in Japan for five years. There he became an active revolutionary, forming a "Youth Society" inspired by Mazzini's Young Italy. One of his earliest political crusades was against Russian incursions into Manchuria. Chen formed a volunteer army and offered its services to the Qing to fight the Russians, then later organized anti-Russia student demonstrations in his home province. At the same time he also wrote a novella, *Hei Tianguo*, or *Black Paradise*, a love story about a Russian revolutionary in Siberian exile.[2] For Chen, "Russia" encompassed both the geopolitically threatening empire against which he crusaded and the romantically inspiring revolution about which he dreamed.

Yet for Chen and many others, "revolution" was not an exclusively Russian phenomenon. In early 1917 in the context of the New Culture Movement, Chen wrote glowingly:

> What is the foundation stone of contemporary Europe which lies so brilliantly before us? It is the gift of revolutions. The term revolution in Europe means a change from the old to the new, which differs absolutely from what we call the change of dynasties. Since the Renaissance in Europe, there have been revolutions in the fields of politics, religion, ethics, morality, literature, and the arts, and because of these revolutions there have been rejuvenation and progress. The history of modern Europe is the history of revolution.[3]

Chen believed that one of the reasons Europe was able to dominate China was that it possessed a powerful transformative faith—Christianity. It's remarkable that even after he began cooperating with the Bolsheviks, for whom communism and Christianity were mutually exclusive, Chen still considered Christianity a viable alternative for China.

"Russia" was not exclusively equated with "socialism," either. And "socialism," let alone "communism" or "Marxism," was hardly the first choice among ideologies for many leftist intellectuals. In the aftermath of the May Fourth movement, some young people were undergoing an inchoate process of radicalization, joining study groups and debating the very idea of ideology. Anarchism was far more popular than socialism, which was known via Japanese translations of a wide variety of European socialist tracts. In fact, China already had a small socialist party that was founded in 1911. Its leader only visited Russia later in the 1920s and was critical of what he saw.[4] Similarly, many Chinese learned about socialism via Bertrand Russell, who made a widely publicized visit to China in 1919 right after he left the Soviet Union. Russell was pro-socialist but anti-Soviet; his visit to China received broad press coverage, and his works were translated into Chinese and widely read.

Even when *New Youth* magazine devoted an entire issue to Marxism on May 19, 1919, there was only one article that whole-heartedly endorsed it, written by Li Dazhao. Li had written the first article in a Chinese newspaper to celebrate the Russian Revolution, which he heralded not so much as a Marxist revolution as the harbinger of a great, worldwide transformation that would usher in a new era, when backward countries like Russia and China would leap ahead of the West.[5] Young people brought copies of the May 19 *New Youth* from cities to hometowns and passed them among relatives and friends. Yet even the most eager readers understood little about how Marxism was related to events in Russia.

In short, people who thought they could organize young Chinese radicals into a Leninist party and mobilize them to agitate for a Soviet-style revolution in 1920 would have been wrong.

This didn't stop some in the Russia-dominated Communist International from dreaming and scheming, however. Excited by the radicalism of the May Fourth movement yet aware of the enmity most Chinese had for Russian imperialism, in 1919 the Bolsheviks issued the Karakhan Manifesto, renouncing the unequal treaties the tsarist government had concluded with China. Ostensibly this meant giving the valuable Chinese Eastern Railway to China, forgoing extraterritoriality for Russian citizens in China (most were Whites anyway), and abandoning Russian territorial concessions—all of which had been sore points with patriotic Chinese for years. The Bolsheviks later reneged on Karakhan. And yet, for Chinese revolutionaries in 1920, the Manifesto was a key event, since it seemed to fulfill all the broken promises of Wilsonian diplomacy that had sparked the May Fourth movement in the first place.[6] It also projected a new vision of Russia and defined a gold standard for Russo-Chinese relations, against which many Chinese would measure Russian actions for decades to come.

Just as news of the manifesto was spreading—not coincidentally—the first serious Comintern representative of Soviet Russia, Grigorii Voitinskii, arrived in Beijing. Only twenty-seven when he came to China, Voitinskii had already lived three lives. The son of an office clerk, at age twenty he'd gone to the United States and then Canada, where he had been a worker-student. He returned to Vladivostok in 1918 and joined the Russian Communist Party. He worked in the city's underground against the Whites, who captured and imprisoned him on Sakhalin Island. Freed in January 1920, he immediately contacted the Comintern and, only four months after his release from Sakhalin, arrived in Beijing.[7] So recently liberated, Voitinskii well might have brought a special enthusiasm to his work.

Voitinskii met directly with Chen Duxiu, but he also held a series of open discussions that were attended by people curious about the Soviet Union. Soon all but the most radical young students stopped attending the talks, and he began to identify his most natural ideological allies.[8] Yet Voitinskii, like Chen Duxiu, was anything but a simple conduit for revolutionary theory. To certain Chinese, Voitinskii seemed the very embodiment of a new sort of Russian. The future communist who described Russians as "Old Hairy People" remembered that Voitinskii was the person who changed his perceptions. "I talked a good many times with Voitinsky," he recalled.

> We touched on a wide variety of subjects, such as basic Communist beliefs, principles of organization, the founding of the Comintern, what happened in the Russian Revolution, and the Chinese revolution. We were principally interested in exchanging views and did not attempt to arrive at any conclusions. . . . Filled with youthful enthusiasm, he [Voitinskii] very easily fell in with people that held the new attitudes of the generation of the May Fourth Movement. And he drew no distinction between Chinese and foreigners, between the yellow

and white races. . . . His behavior showed him to be truly a new kind of Russian emerging from the Revolution.[9]

With Voitinskii's help, Chen Duxiu organized a Marxist Research Society in his own house in the French Concession in Shanghai, where he had moved after being released from prison for his May Fourth activities. Chen had considerable influence in radical circles and could count on the support of a number of young students for any move he endeavored to make—regardless of the exact idea behind it. He and Voitinskii created a Socialist Youth League and a bureau to translate articles from the Soviet press into Chinese and place them in Chinese journals. After the Bolsheviks captured Irkutsk from White forces in January of 1920, they were able to establish a telegraph connection with China and thereby transmit news and propaganda directly. With the help of a separate office in Beijing, the bureau was able to place pieces in over thirty different newspapers. Voitinskii also got hold of a printing press, which he used to duplicate materials he received from Vladivostok. Eventually he opened offices in Tianjin, Wuhan, Hankou, and Jinan.[10]

A Chinese Bolshevik

Voitinskii was assisted by a capable right-hand man named Yang Mingzhai, who in 1920 was the closest thing to a Chinese Bolshevik. Like so many other young, poor Chinese born into large peasant families in China's northeastern provinces at the turn of the century, Yang Mingzhai migrated to Vladivostok in search of work in 1902. This was such a common move that there was a local saying to the effect that "When the going gets rough, Northeasterners go to Vladivostok." After working in a small factory for several years, Yang moved farther west into Siberia to work as a miner.

Yang studied while he was working and became preoccupied with the poor conditions of Chinese migrant workers in Russia, not least his own. As World War I got under way, Yang worked for the tsarist ministry of foreign affairs; his Chinese biographer claims that he also secretly assisted the Bolsheviks, representing Chinese Red Army volunteers, and that he joined the party before the revolution. He was not alone; some sources claim that as many as 30,000–40,000 Chinese fought in the Red Army and one Chinese even served in Lenin's personal forces.[11]

What was important about Yang was that he was a "conscious" Chinese/worker/Bolshevik, in direct contradiction to popular images in civil-war era Russia of Chinese Red Army soldiers as, along with the Latvians, unthinking Bolshevik henchmen. Later, in 1925, Mikhail Bulgakov would publish a short story called "A Chinese Tale," featuring a coolie whose Russian vocabulary was largely limited to single words and the phrase "your mother," who had a preternatural ability with a machine gun and killed unthinkingly for the Red Army in exchange for bread and opium.[12]

Yang, on the other hand, spoke good Russian and understood Marxism. An ideal right-hand man for Voitinskii, he was one of the only people who could effectively serve as a linguistic, cultural, and ideological mediator between the Russian and Chinese revolutions. One person who encountered him at this time called him "a half-Russian Chinese, or more exactly, a Chinese doubling as a Russian." What made Yang seem so Russian? He was "disorganized and vehement," "brutally honest," "brusque with a heart of gold," generous, and dedicated to the language of Tolstoy and Pushkin.[13]

Yang's singularity underscored the need to expand the human revolutionary interface. To this end, in the fall of 1920, with a cash infusion of $20,000 in the form of liquidated diamonds from the Siberian Bureau of the Bolshevik Party, Voitinskii and Chen Duxiu opened a new school and made Yang Mingzhai its head teacher.[14] The Shanghai Foreign Languages School, as it came to be known, was the first place in China where young leftists could come to study Russian, not to obtain a government job or even to become a translator of literature, but to learn about the Russian Revolution.

To Moscow via Shanghai

The Shanghai Foreign Languages School operated for less than a year, but in that time it managed to recruit and send the first group of Chinese students to study in the Soviet Union. This group included a number of young men who would influence the development of Chinese communism in the 1920s, as well as an even more rarefied handful who would shape Sino-Soviet relations under the People's Republic of China (PRC), from President Liu Shaoqi, to the dean of Russian Studies at Beijing University, Cao Jinghua.

Xiao Jingguang, who later served as the PRC's deputy secretary of defense, sat down in 1981 to write an account of his journey. Xiao was a middle school student in Changsha during the May Fourth movement, and he remembered that the first time he heard about the Russian Revolution was in school, where one day,

> the teacher suddenly said in a very serious manner: "Right now in the world there's a new type of thinking, Russian extremism. These people say what's yours is mine. Do you approve?" We listened, confused. He said again: "Raise your hand if you approve!" No one raised their hand. Then he said "Raise your hand if you don't approve." And a few scattered people raised their hands.[15]

In the summer of 1920, after a year of feverish May Fourth activity, Xiao was eager to go to France, but he was only seventeen and had missed the departure of Emi's group. One day his roommate, Ren Bishi, came running home shouting, "There's a way! There's a way!" Ren had heard from a friend about the Russian Research Society that Mao had formed in Changsha with the assistance of a former teacher, which was organizing a small group of students to go to Russia. Xiao and Ren had not yet graduated from middle school, but no sooner had they expressed an interest in going than they found themselves along with four others from Changsha at 6 Yuyang Street in Shanghai, enrolled in the Shanghai Foreign Language Institute.[16]

Even more mature members of the group recall equally haphazard paths to Shanghai, suggesting that ideology was an excuse for adventure. For example, Peng Shuzhi was as eager as anyone could be to learn about the ideology of revolution. Peng had been born to a large family of gentry farmers in a small rural village in southwest Hunan and had defied his father—who expected him to settle down in an arranged marriage and manage the family farm—to attend secondary school in Changsha. Like Emi and Qu, upon graduating, Peng became a secondary school teacher. [17]

At home on holiday in 1919 he met some other young Pengs who had been studying at Hunan First Normal along with Mao and other rabble-rousers. Peng's cousin passed on to him the infamous May 19, 1919, issue of *New Youth* magazine devoted to Marxism. Peng began devouring radical journals, started a feverish diary about ideas to save China, left his job in the school, and pronounced himself an anarchist. He also made the acquaintance of an older man with Shanghai connections who had already sent four of his students to Chen's group; plans were afoot to send the four students to Moscow to study. Obsessed with ideas he did not yet fully understand, twenty-five-year-old

Peng decided that he too would go to Moscow. Scarcely a year after hearing of the Russian Revolution for the first time, a few short months after having decided that he was, in fact, an anarchist—if not a socialist (whatever that was)—Peng was off to Shanghai.[18]

The Shanghai Foreign Languages School began instruction in the fall of 1920. The students focused on Russian in the morning and in the afternoon some participated in the activities of Chen's Socialist Youth League and Chinese-Russian Correspondence Society, also headquartered in the school. At Voitinskii's behest, the first complete Chinese translation of the Communist Manifesto was produced for the students to read. Xiao Jingguang remembers that while he understood each word, the meaning escaped him. He also remembers helping out with the physical labor of Bolshevik propaganda—engraving steel plates, stamping leaflets, and bringing them to factories. At 6 Yuyang, students did not necessarily have to participate in overt politics or even care about ideology to be counted among China's most radical community. Simply studying the Russian language in this way in this place was a political statement. "Foreign language," one Chinese historian of the school has commented, "is a weapon in the struggle for life."[19]

Precisely at this moment—when China's first group of students began to learn Russian because they were interested in the Russian Revolution—Qu Qiubai's reports began running in *Chen Bao*. Peng Shuzhi remembered the intensity with which he and the others read Qu's articles. Later, Peng realized, much of the concrete "information" these writings contained about the Soviet Union were artful rearrangements of *Pravda* pieces. But it was Qu's selective, innovative, subjective translations that made his reports feel so relevant. At 6 Yuyang, at least some of the students, including Cao Jinghua, had been classmates with Qu at the Beijing Russian Language Institute, a personal connection that further amplified the effect of Qu's writing. Whereas studying Russian or Marx in translation might provoke exciting confusion about an inaccessible revolution, reading Qu's ongoing travelogue made that revolution seem much more immediate and personal.

One student, a committed anarchist, claimed the higher-ups had held them back from leaving for Moscow. According to him, at first the students were told that they only needed 30 yuan to make the trip to Russia and that five hundred students could go, but then the fee rose to 100 yuan and the quota dropped to fifty students.[20]

In early spring 1921, about two dozen students departed for Moscow in groups of two or three so as not to attract attention. In Shanghai, they boarded a Russian merchant vessel headed to Japanese-controlled Vladivostok. The approach to Vladivostok was hair-raising because they had been told that Japanese officials would check their belongings carefully. The students had letters of introduction from Voitinskii that were supposed to smooth their way in the Soviet Union. Nevertheless, Peng Shuzhi remembered that he and his friend got so nervous about the Japanese police finding the letter that just as Vladivostok came into view they ripped up the letter and threw it into the ocean, a split-second decision they came to regret when they were later detained by Red Army soldiers convinced they were Japanese spies. Others remember throwing away their Russian language textbooks in similar moments of panic.[21]

Xiao Jingguang recalled that several were in fact detained in Vladivostok by the local representative of the Chinese warlord Zhang Zuolin, who believed the students were emissaries of Sun Yatsen. Liu Shaoqi was among them; he convinced Zhang's officials he was a tailor and they let him go. Ren Bishi was held as a possible plague carrier. However difficult Vladivostok was, the alternative river route was no easier. Some students crossed over to Khabarovsk on the Songhua/Sungari river, whose banks were policed on one side by Chinese and the other by Soviets, and whose waters were patrolled by both as well. In short, none of this first cohort of students arrived in Soviet territory without experiencing some moment when they believed all was lost.[22]

Most of the students proceeded directly from Khabarovsk to Moscow, but two—Peng Shuzhi and Ren Zuomin—were held back. Hearing that a group of literate Chinese were in town, local Bolsheviks ordered them to choose two people to stay behind and help them to establish a newspaper for the new Union of Chinese Workers. Nobody wanted to do it, but Peng and Ren got stuck with the job.[23]

For several months Peng and Ren lived in Khabarovsk's Chinese ghetto, eating Chinese food, speaking Chinese, and producing the Chinese newspaper. They got news about China and Japan from journals smuggled through at Blagoveshchensk along with various pipes and teas required for Khabarovsk's Chinese community. When they needed to translate items from the Russian press, the one Chinese in the Union who could actually read Russian would orally translate articles that Peng and Ren would polish into proper Chinese, attaching explanations of new words like soviets and syndicates.[24]

Finally, a letter arrived to rescue Peng from the Khabarovsk: the chief political commissar of the Army of the Republic of the Far East had heard that there were some young Chinese students in Khabarovsk, and he requested their help for a mission much more glamorous than the newspaper. The Republic of the Far East had recruited a large group of Chinese bandits to help the Red Army against the Japanese. But these bandits—Red Beards the Soviets called them—were quite unruly.[25]

So Peng got to spend his days talking to a real live bandit king, whom he remembered as "so courageous, so violent, so generous." The idea was to persuade the rank and file that if only they first fought the Japanese for the Soviets (and in the process came to appreciate the virtues of Bolshevism), later they would be able to go back and fight the Japanese for China and get rid of the warlord Zhang Zuolin. Peng embraced this work enthusiastically, motivated by visions of personally convincing not just these particular bandits but indeed the Chinese masses as a whole to rise up and fight their oppressors.[26] Drawing parallels between the Red Beards and the bandits of *The Water Margin*, Peng Shuzhi wrote himself into China's most beloved tale of rebellion, underscoring how important the element of adventure was even to him, one of the older and more pedantic students to go to Moscow in 1921.

Five months after their comrades, Peng and his friend finally got word that they could proceed to the capital. After a short stay in Irkutsk, they boarded the Trans-Siberian, Moscow-bound. For all of Qu's fancy descriptions, Peng more profoundly absorbed the beauty of Siberia. Passing through it at summer's end, Peng remembered how, after sunset, the waters of Lake Baikal became an "immense, shimmering carpet of stars," which seemed to him the most beautiful thing he had ever seen. In September of 1921, after days riding entranced and starving through the forests of central Russia, the last two students from the Shanghai Foreign Languages Institute finally arrived in Moscow.[27]

Part II
SCHOOL CRUSHES, 1920S

4

School Dramas

THE FINAL MOSCOW destination for Emi, Qu, Peng, and thousands of Chinese who would follow in their footsteps could hardly have been more glamorous. The so-called Communist University for the Toilers of the East (hereafter, Communist Eastern University) was one of the most exotic and theatrical of all revolutionary sites. It was also located in one of the most beautiful neighborhoods of Moscow.

After the revolution, the Bolshevik government had appropriated the prestige of Moscow's oldest addresses for its newest institutions. The Toilers of the East were given several splendid, old-regime buildings in and around Strastnaia Square, a ten-minute walk from the Kremlin up Tverskaia Street, sometimes called the Champs-Élysées of Moscow.

Thirty Chinese Guys on Tverskaia Street

Nothing about the building's lovely façade indicated the poverty and chaos within. Conditions were every bit as rudimentary as at 6 Yuyang. The thirty Chinese were given a single large room on the second floor furnished only with beds, just a couple of planks covered with straw mattresses and blankets; a few "tables," pieces of wood held together by studs; and some stools. The one luxury they enjoyed was central heat.[1]

The spartan conditions would have been easier to endure if only the students weren't so hungry. Breakfast was boiling water, perhaps with a little sugar. The bread they were given resembled bread only for a little while; left overnight it turned to powder and could only be eaten with a spoon. They ate two meals a day at the university cafeteria, usually potatoes or soup, sometimes with a tiny piece of meat or dried fish. In fact, they were receiving Red Army rations, some of the best in Moscow at the time. But they were still so hungry that sometimes they could barely make it up and down the four flights of steps to the cafeteria, and they spent a fair amount of their free time lying in bed, smoking whatever tobacco they could find.[2]

When Peng arrived at the university a few months after his friends, Liu Shaoqi related a tale of woe. The terrible material conditions of the university had caused dissension among the Chinese. They had just discovered that the two students who spoke Russian better than the rest had been stealing bread. These two had added fake names to the list of Chinese students that the university administration used to distribute bread rations and hoarded the extras, sneaking off to eat by themselves. When the other students would complain of hunger, they would say: "Come now, was it to live the high life or to study the theory and practice of revolution that you've come to Soviet Russia?" Peng was appalled by the disorganization and confusion that had overtaken his enthusiastic compatriots in just a few short months.[3]

First Impressions

Years later, when Liu Shaoqi sat down with a group of young Chinese students headed to Russia in the early 1950s, it was the Moscow of 1921 that was on his mind. By all accounts, Liu hadn't been happy in Russia back then. One biographer characterized his mood as "romantic and depressed," quoting a poem Liu allegedly wrote to a friend back home: "Your eyes are heavy with sadness; your thoughts are foolish but sincere. Here at the busiest thoroughfare you are recognized by no one. These sentiments you can only send to a bosom friend far away." Decades later, he took a more matter-of-fact tone when speaking with young people about to depart for Moscow. "There are lots of things worth studying there," he told the young people, "but there are also things you can't bear to see, like women wearing necklaces and rings with precious stones. Not everything in the Soviet Union is good; they also have beggars, thieves, and drunkards."[4] Liu's comments are a reminder that 1921 was one of the most chaotic and contradictory moments of the Russian Revolution.

The Bolshevik Red Army had just declared victory in the Civil War, yet to get to Moscow, the Chinese students crossed territory still held by White Army forces collaborating with the Japanese. The goal of the Revolution was to take power and property from wealthy elites and redistribute it to the have-nots, yet Bolsheviks and Whites alike had implemented such harsh war requisitioning that even the most loyal troops had rebelled, the economy had come to a standstill, and the country was suffering from a terrible famine. Peng remembered a huge photo exhibit in Moscow about the famine that few foreigners bothered to attend but that the Chinese visited as a group.[5] To stimulate the economy, the Bolsheviks had just announced the New Economic Policy, which led to a new class of wealthy private traders.

Because the Chinese were perched at the heart of one of Soviet Russia's most elite and experimental educational institutions, they had an excellent view of one of the new regime's strongest selling points: its determination to teach everyone to read. Liu and his classmates were in Russia as the direct result of their own New Culture Movement, an explicit goal of which was to expand literacy through vernacularization. Eastern University's mission—to teach illiterate poor people from non-Russian groups basic literacy and political organization—was a logical step on the path to the kind of unified and egalitarian society that both the Bolsheviks and their Chinese protégés envisioned.

Academy of Anti-Imperialism

Communist Eastern University had technically opened in April 1921, staffed by recent graduates of another relatively new institution, Sverdlov University. Sverdlov was a Communist Party school that had grown out of Civil War–era crash courses for agitators, just one of a profusion of early revolutionary educational experiments.[6] In the spring of 1921, Deputy Commissar of Nationalities Grigorii Broido came to Sverdlov University and rounded up thirty-five students from the Soviet Union's eastern republics who were about to graduate. Broido informed these surprised young people that they would be starting a new university with him as rector.[7]

The curriculum at Communist Eastern University was supposed to be similar to that of Sverdlov, and the school was originally intended for easterners and emigrants from the Soviet Union's own "backward" republics, not foreign revolutionaries. The foreign sections of Communist Eastern University were tacked on to an institution designed to meet the domestic personnel needs of the new communist bureaucracy.[8]

At first, there were relatively few foreigners at the university—about fifty or sixty in a student body of about eight hundred. But between 1921 and 1925 the foreign group grew constantly, so that by 1924–1925 there were almost three hundred foreigners among over one thousand Soviets. Besides Chinese, the largest groups were Koreans, Turks, Persians, Mongolians, Arabs, and Jews. There were a few Malaysians, Indians, and Japanese.[9]

If the composition of the student body at Communist Eastern University was any indicator, in its early days the Bolsheviks assumed that revolution could spread "east" through southeastern and southwestern Soviet territories to more or less geographically contiguous regions, where their tsarist predecessors had also attempted to establish spheres of influence. By bringing foreign students from the geographic periphery and educating them in a Tverskaia Street school for domestic cadres from the Soviet "east," the Bolshevik government took an expansive, optimistic view of its borders, or at least of the potential borders of socialism.

The foreign students who represented the future socialist world were all individual products of major geopolitical shifts. Their journeys to Moscow were motivated by factors similar to those that catalyzed Chinese journeys. In Iran (Persia), for instance, British and Russian imperial incursions had fueled patriotic radicalism, which crested in opposition to the treatment of Persians by the Versailles Peace Conference. Imperial Russia had been a major competitor for influence in the region, but now the Bolsheviks renounced the old unequal treaties and encouraged the formation of an Iranian Communist Party. The Turkish and Vietnamese revolutionary movements were also closely tied to post-Versailles resentment, and the first Korean Communist Party had its origins in opposition to the Japanese occupation of Korea.[10]

The Chinese in Moscow were just another ragtag group of would-be revolutionaries with no special place in the imagined global revolution. But that wasn't exactly how they saw it, and that wasn't how it played out, not even in the very first years when the global revolution was mostly a figment of Moscow's imagination.

Costumes and Characters

When the Chinese matriculated at Eastern University in the fall of 1921, they were given new clothes and new names and set about learning new lines in a new language.

As the weather got colder that fall the students were in desperate need of warm clothes and so they were given the discarded uniforms of demobilized Red Army fighters, with their hempen overcoats and motley assortment of peaked hats. The Chinese found themselves literally trying to fill the enormous shoes of the victorious Russian revolutionaries. They could shorten the pants, they could take in the coats, but there was nothing to be done about the boots. Only when they wrapped their feet in layers of newspapers could they begin to walk in these boots.[11]

Along with the costumes came names. For some of the Chinese, the name they received in the registrar's office at Eastern University wasn't their first false name. Students from France usually already had noms de guerre. One remembered the process of naming that occurred in France:

> Li Weinong spent several days trying to think up a name, but to no avail; eventually, he decided to call himself Chu Fu (hoe-ax) after studying the emblem on the masthead of our paper *Youth*, even though the emblem showed not a hoe but a sickle and not an ax but a hammer. Wang Zekai called himself Luo Ti (naked); he had often represented political movements in the past and been wrongly accused of various crimes, so he wanted to show that he was above reproach. . . . Zhang Bojian was called Hong Hong (red swan). In those days, names with "red" in them were very popular. . . . Li Weihan called himself Luo Mai, which, according to some people, stood for the first two syllables of the word "romanticism." Wang Ruofei was called Lei Yin (thunderous noise) but I do not know why.[12]

Sometimes Chinese kept their prior assumed names, or even their own names, once in Moscow, but more often than not they were given new names. Just as they donned the clothes of Russia's victorious fighters, they often were called by the names of famous revolutionaries. One particular group of twelve students, for instance, was given the names of the twelve members of the Petrograd Soviet arrested in 1905. There was also an Oktiabr'skii and a Fevralin and a Fevral'skii; a Proletariev, a Boevoi ("fighter"), a Barrikadov, an Avangardov, and a Dinamitov; there was a Lunacharskii and a Molotov and even a Stalin. Ren Bishi was given the name Belinskii after the famous literary critic but everyone mispronounced it so that even in Comintern records Ren shows up as Brinskii.[13]

Pronunciation was, in fact, a major problem for the Chinese. One Chinese student famously characterized the demand that they learn Russian as tantamount to asking "a toothless man to chew iron and steel."[14] It is certainly true that in linguistic terms the gap between Russian and Chinese is wider than the gap, say, between Chinese and Japanese, or Russian and German.

But any given language gap is also partly determined by the availability of bilingual people, teaching materials, and dictionaries, as well as by the desire to communicate. The year 1921 was more or less the beginning of a long history of Sino-Soviet attempts to narrow the gap between Russian and Chinese, part of a broader revolutionary reorientation of the relationship between Russia and the rest of the non-European world.

For the thirty Chinese on Tverskaia, the most obvious problem was the lack of a decent dictionary. As in Beijing, the students were stuck with a Russian-Japanese dictionary. They had a Russian-Chinese dictionary that had been published in Harbin, but it was less useful than the Russian-Japanese one. The best Russian-Chinese dictionaries had been compiled in the late nineteenth century by the Russian ecclesiastical mission in Beijing. But even if these had been available to the students in Moscow, they could hardly have helped them learn how to speak the new Bolshevik jargon.[15] Liu Shaoqi recalled:

> How do you even translate "tovarishch" correctly? Is "partners in planning" good? Or is it better to translate it as "people who lend a hand to take care of matters"? . . . When we first came to Moscow, we saw that on the ruble note there was the slogan, "Workers of the world, unite." It had all different languages. The Chinese characters had been translated by regular Chinese immigrants, there was no good translation for "the working class," so they took this slogan and translated it into the Chinese expression, "Everyone within the four seas is brothers." . . . At the time words like "comrade," "the proletariat," "capitalists," "imperialists," just didn't exist, it was all still being considered.[16]

At first the Chinese spent fruitless hours with their Russian-Japanese dictionaries hunting down the acronyms that were part of the new Soviet Russian taking shape around them but could not be found in any textbook or dictionary.

Even with a good dictionary, the phonetic and grammatical gaps were still huge. As of 1921, there was no universally accepted system for transliterating Chinese sounds into Russian and vice versa. Qu would later create one of the first standardized systems to transliterate Chinese into Russian (and hence Russian into Chinese).[17] For the time being, students had to rely on the imaginations of their teachers to help them cross even this phonetic divide, coaxing from the Chinese sounds they knew the Russian sounds they didn't. Never mind untangling the serious differences in grammatical structure between the two languages. The Chinese found themselves sitting every morning with empty stomachs through two or three hours of largely ineffective Russian language instruction. Once a teacher got fed up and told them they could study their whole lives and still never properly learn Russian.[18] Among the students was Cao Jinghua, who later became a renowned translator and language educator.

The students who were determined to learn did so through self-study, poring over grammar books, memorizing new words by heart, and practicing on other students. This way, some students reported that by the end of a year they could more or less follow lectures in Russian. But the more numerous, less gifted, or less determined students never overcame the language gap.[19] They would be cursed to depend perpetually on translators, deaf-mutes wearing clothes that didn't fit, with names they couldn't pronounce.

Dilemmas of Teaching Revolution

Whether or not would-be revolutionaries should be required to learn Russian was a key question in the pedagogy of international revolution, one of many that would echo through the halls of Soviet international schools for the next seven decades.

If a revolutionary is a devout believer, how to instill and strengthen belief? If a revolutionary is a loyal worker, how to inspire loyalty? If a revolutionary is a person of action, courage, and skill, how to define and impart those skills outside of the environment in which they will be performed? If a revolutionary is a killer, how to transform idealistic young people into fighers ready to shed blood?

Can revolution even be taught at all in a school, or is it a purely practical pursuit that can only be learned hands-on, so that a school dedicated to teaching revolution can really only be a place to study history, religion, and the requisite languages? Is there any reason why the school must be in Moscow? Is Moscow itself a school of revolution? Or is Moscow an insult to the perfect revolution of the future, so that foreign students in Moscow must be shielded from the city itself, or at least from its harshest realities?

Was Russia one link in a long chain of revolutions or was it the hub anchoring the many spokes on the wheel of global revolution? Would each revolution have its own chronology, or would it become entangled in the chronology of the ongoing Russian Revolution?

And what does the Russian language have to do with it? If the Chinese (and everyone else) were required to learn Russian, was it to take orders as functionaries of a new world revolutionary bureaucracy, or was it to translate the textbooks that summarized past experience, or was it to study sacred texts in the original? Or, was it to demonstrate loyalty with no other purpose than to manifest that loyalty through the propagation of the Russian language back home? Was Russian centrality to revolutionary history a fiction, so that the Chinese were learning Russian simply to play a part, to represent world revolution to the Russians themselves?

As might be expected, the answer to these questions was, it depends.

The Translator

The first translator Communist Eastern University hired for its Chinese students was Qu Qiubai. As he remembers it, "I was just a communist sympathizer with only an approximate understanding of it . . . but, in Moscow at that time, besides me, there wasn't a translator to be found."[20] He found himself doing a crash course in Marxism-Leninism, setting his own writing aside to prepare for the lessons he was supposed to translate. Up to this point, Qu had had the luxury of time and space to compose his artful, culture-hopping translations of the Russian Revolution for his growing readership back in China. Suddenly he was face to face with two dozen real people for whom he had to translate in real time, with no room to think. The impression he created was mixed.

Peng Shuzhi admitted that even after they arrived in Moscow, he and his friends relished Qu's written reports, but in person Qu seemed downright inarticulate. "Qu Qiubai gave me a bad impression right from the start," Peng remembered.

> He almost always had a cigarette in his mouth, even when he was talking to you. But what bothered me most about him was his obvious lack of simplicity and straightforwardness. His conversation was difficult to follow, he seemed to think it unnecessary to articulate in a clear fashion the words of the phrases he deigned to utter to his listeners.[21]

Cao Jinghua, Qu's friend and former classmate, retrospectively had a bit more sympathy:

> Qiubai, it was 1922 wasn't it, we were in Moscow, your tuberculosis was really bad, the doctor said your lungs were already worn out, you had two or three years at most. But you wouldn't rest. You'd lecture and sometimes you'd get so tired your face would go pale and lifeless, you could hardly breathe, but you were indefatigable.[22]

Whether it was because he didn't really understand the lessons himself, or because he was better on paper than in person, or simply because he was sick, Qu wasn't a very good translator, and yet, there wasn't anyone better.

Between 1921, when the first group of Chinese arrived, and the end of 1922, by which point most of this cohort of future Chinese Communist Party luminaries had departed, Eastern University hardly taught them at all. Course listings were erratic, lectures garbled in translation, and professors often absent on Comintern business.[23] Under these conditions, students became infected with malaise. Their progress was determined by self-study. One student recalled that they studied Russian and politics together, using Bukharin's *ABC of Communism* as a textbook, which they read aloud and memorized.[24]

Eventually, the curriculum filled out a little bit. In their second year at Eastern University, the students who remained remembered learning history of the workers' movement, history of the October revolution, economics, and natural sciences (which, one student claimed, made everyone want to "throw up"). Some students desperately wanted to learn about historical materialism, but the only teacher to be found was an old woman who "treated us like schoolchildren and gave us only a smattering of general knowledge." The teacher for history of the labor movement was "a Jew called Something-stein who . . . brought new materials and viewpoints to his lectures . . . [but] worked for the Profintern [Red International of Labor Unions] and often arrived late—after a few months, he stopped coming altogether." As time went on, students whose Russian language skills developed most quickly would be designated as translators; it would be their job to stand up in class and simultaneously translate lectures, or to re-teach in Chinese the lectures they had heard in Russian.[25]

In addition to these basic Marxist courses, the school also tried to teach more tailored material that dealt with current developments in the foreign

East. The problem with these specific subjects was that the university's teaching staff wasn't prepared to teach them. Even in 1925, the star teachers were either early Sverdlov University grads or agitprop guys from places like Tiflis and Tashkent who were not familiar with the politics of China. Broido, the rector, was considered Moscow's resident expert on Turkestan, having spent three years there during the Civil War. Once the first batch of students had graduated, the university supplemented its Soviet teaching staff by holding some foreign graduates back as lecturers.[26]

At the Comintern's insistence, the school also added "practical courses," like party building and underground technique. This last was taught only to "qualified workers of brotherly eastern parties," a group to which, of Chinese students, only Peng later admitted to belonging.[27] The students were aware of uncertainty on the part of higher-ups over what they should be studying. One remembered that when he first arrived in Moscow in 1921, there was an idea bandied about, associated with Bukharin, that since there were no real proletarian revolutionary forces in China, the Chinese students at Eastern University should be taught a bourgeois profession in order to become screens for underground work. On the other hand, Lenin, it was said, believed that at least some Chinese should receive more serious training as professional revolutionaries. And so, somehow, Xiao Jingguang and three other students were sent to a Red Army military school to study.

When Chen Duxiu came to Moscow a year later and discovered that the students were receiving military training, he got angry and scolded them. What do you mean, no proletariat in China? What, he wanted to know, were they studying to become—warlords? And so they were pulled from the military school and sent back to Eastern University. But this hardly ended the idea of strictly military training.[28]

If the Chinese were worried about the students becoming warlord turncoats, the Soviets were worried that they would become stupid bureaucrats or useless intellectuals. By 1925, a serious turf war had developed between the school's leadership, who considered that it answered only to the Central Committee of the Russian Communist Party, and Comintern officials, who were constantly trying to meddle in the school's operations. The two groups had different ideas about the training relevant to revolutionaries. To the Comintern's charges that the school's teachings were divorced from the realities of the revolutionary situation in the foreign East as well as from the Comintern's concrete personnel needs, Broido, the rector, answered:

> The Eastern Section [of the Comintern] thinks only about how to get functionaries quickly ... but we are preparing a more finished, polished product, who must differ decisively from what [he] is today, and this is only possible along the lines of education in the spirit of the Russian Communist Party. We have students who protest against the Russian language—this is nationalism. It's impossible to study Leninism without knowledge of the Russian language. It's just as necessary as the study of German was, in its time, for Russian Marxists.[29]

At this point Broido was interrupted by a Comintern representative, who asked him: "And what if we prescribe for the Chinese only one year, then can we do without Russian?" To which he replied:

> If it's one year, then of course. For students the Russian Communist Party and the USSR must become the highest, it must be the basis of all education. .... You do not take into account the enormous meaning that Eastern University students have in each country. For example, the Eastern Section [of the Comintern] could not overthrow any party Central Committee in the East. But if we were given such a task, we could fulfill it through Eastern University students.[30]

This clash of theory and practice, of revolutionary liberal arts and vocational training, of Russian language loyalty and local know-how was long-standing, and hardly resolved in 1925.[31]

Outside the Classroom

If the Chinese students weren't learning much inside the classroom, perhaps they were learning about international revolution from their daily interactions with other students, or about the Russian Revolution from encounters with ordinary Russians.

But the foreign students were generally isolated not only from the Soviet students but also from each other. They stuck to their national groups even within their section, and there were occasional conflicts among national groups.[32] The only time foreign students really mixed was during the summer. All the Soviet students went back to their republics then, but the foreign students couldn't go home and so were sent off to summer resorts outside Moscow.

During the first summer of 1922, about a hundred Eastern University teachers and foreign students ended up in a village in the Moscow suburbs. They decided to implement communism: they formed a commune, whose members were supposed to share food and do communal labor. At school, staff cleaned their floors and made their beds. The students, unused to manual labor, hated the chores and wondered how all those Soviet workers got through their eight-hour days. Once, some students skipped work and so the head of the summer camp withheld all the students' breakfasts. The Chinese were furious and wrote a protest letter; it took an emergency trip from Moscow and a major dressing down to cow them.[33]

Students' encounters with ordinary Russians were hardly brimming with revolutionary solidarity either. One student in the group, an anarchist, conducted his own independent forays into Soviet society, befriending fellow Esperantists dedicated to the spread of a universal language, visiting primary schools, and interviewing workers—an experience that dimmed the enthusiasm with which he had arrived. The interactions of the rest of the Chinese students with ordinary citizens were meager.[34] Later on, hospitality to foreign students became a major Soviet trope, but at this point food was so scarce that a home-cooked meal as an expression of warmth and welcome across cultural barriers wasn't really an option. Nobody remembered going home to a teacher's house for dinner.

Instead, Chinese students found themselves face to face with ordinary Russians in most unrevolutionary and unbrotherly circumstances: at the markets, where they took their sugar and tobacco rations to sell at exorbitant prices that prevailed under Lenin's market-tolerant New Economic Policy. Most claimed they used the money to buy books, but the anarchist said that some of the Chinese students saved their pennies to enjoy "one happy night" with a Russian prostitute. This (increasingly anti-Soviet) anarchist claimed that some of the female students and teachers at Eastern University were reduced to compromising themselves to get by. Besides traders and prostitutes, the students encountered ordinary Russians in the village in summer—where easy girls propositioned them by the river and counterrevolutionary peasants chased them in the forest.[35]

Qu and Emi Try Out Their Parts

What then was left of international revolutionary brotherhood in Moscow in 1921? At this early date, when the international revolution had so little to show for itself and the Russian Revolution had so little to teach or to give, all that either side could do was demonstrate future intentions in symbolic moments of revolutionary drama.

The numerous international meetings and congresses that the students attended to break up the monotony of school life in these early years were high drama. These included the Third (1921) and Fourth (1922) Comintern congresses, and the Second Congress of the Toilers of the East in 1922 (the first had been in Baku in 1920 and had been an inspiration for the founding of the university). Only occasionally was a student appointed as a delegate to these big meetings; it was higher-ups from the party back in China who attended. Instead, the students helped prepare materials, dealt with logistics, and sometimes acted as translators.[36]

By the time of the Second Congress of the Toilers of the East, Qu had a starring role as the main interpreter. The Chinese Communist Party delegate to the congress complained about Qu's Russian, saying his speaking abilities were only mediocre and his written translations were difficult to understand—but also admitted that in all of Moscow there was no one better, among either the Chinese students or the Russian Comintern agents. In this way, Qu's language abilities came to the Comintern's attention. Just after the Congress in early 1922, Qu joined the Chinese Communist Party, sponsored by a childhood friend of his who was attending.[37]

During this period, the Comintern was moving toward its "United Front" stance, whereby foreign communist parties were to cooperate with more moderate socialists and with parties of national liberation. At the time, hardly anyone even attended the talks where the United Front was discussed (except the single Chinese communist delegate, who "ran in there every day and made speeches, bragging about all their accomplishments in China")[38] not least because translation of each talk into English, French, and Russian, none of which most Far Eastern delegates understood well, made these talks excruciatingly boring. And they were already boring; according to a foreign reporter, candidate Politburo member Nikolai Bukharin sat up on stage and composed the following parody:

> People, O People!
> East, O East!
> (I beg pardon) Far East, O Far East!
> Anyway, People, O People!
> I have to apologize to you that you should have today to endure four and
>   twenty addresses of welcome.
> But remember that the sacred of the World Revolution calls for sacrifice.
> Remember, too, that your trials are nothing to ours, who had, during five
>   long years, sword in hand, to read Stekloff's daily editorials in Izvestiia.
> On the Workers' and Peasants' Republic the sun never sets. (That is why
>   we have a famine.)
> The day you arrived in Moscow the snow was falling.
> Pay no heed to that. It was a white plot.
> Und so weiter.[39]

Bukharin had to sit on stage but the delegates fled to the halls and backrooms to gossip. Even when resolutions were translated into Chinese, the delegates still had a sense that they didn't understand the original.[40] Ultimately, the specific content or proceedings of these big gatherings of revolutionaries were less important than that they happened at all.

The delegates were aware that they were showpieces. The Chinese Communist Party delegate to the Congress recalled:

> We delegates were rather like a group of half-deaf, half-dumb students.
> Russian escorts took us here and there. But rather than to say that we were
> taken to look at the various sites, it would be more accurate to say that we
> were taken to the various sites so that the Russians there could look at us.
> For we seemed to be the most fresh and stimulating propaganda objects
> available. . . . This was at a time when the eagerly anticipated Communist
> revolutions in Europe were farther from realization than ever. . . .
> Revolutionary activities in the Far East were like a shot in the arm.[41]

He also remembered that while he and the other Far Eastern delegates were in Irkutsk, the Comintern threw parties for them on Saturday nights, at which each national group was expected to perform. But the Chinese, the largest and most conspicuous group, "were the only ones who could not do anything. We knew nothing about dancing, nor had we ever done any group singing." Finally in desperation a Chinese delegate sang the only song he could think of—a popular, dirty song called "My Little Darling Is Playing Dominoes."[42]

For the Chinese students attending the big meetings, it was the run-up, the off-moments, and the after-party that mattered. Before the Congress of the Toilers of the East, the students spent hours chattering about who the Chinese delegates would be and what the students could do to help ensure that they took the proper view of socialism. They even asked to be allowed to propagandize among the delegates. Once the delegates arrived, the students were horribly disappointed by their weak revolutionary credentials.[43] Still, in off-moments the students had a chance to gossip with the representatives.

So the students heard, for instance, that Lenin had snubbed the big-time Chinese Communist in the delegation to the Congress of the Toilers of the East, instead demanding to speak with real workers. And that class warfare had broken out among the members of the Chinese delegation, with the communists denouncing a woman anarchist for sitting in first class on the train, and the workers telling the Soviets that all the rest of the delegates were intellectuals unqualified to speak for the masses. And that as far as the delegates were concerned the Soviet banquets, which the students viewed as sumptuous, were pitiful. They tried hard to explain to these new initiates that Soviet communism was all about the future, but to no avail.[44]

If students remained behind the scenes at the big Comintern meetings, they were star players at Eastern University. Like the Comintern delegates, they found themselves paraded around Moscow on so-called educational excursions. None other than the famous theater director Vsevolod Meyerhold came to direct the pageant—"Imperialists of Europe and Colonial Politics"—that crowned the ceremonies for the first graduating class of seven hundred students in 1922.[45]

Eastern University also attracted a future notable of the Soviet cinema, Nikolai Ekk, who led the university's drama collective and planned to make a documentary about the school. He envisioned juxtaposing footage of the Strastnoi Monastery with images of minarets, worshippers holding candles with a Chinese student reading a book, maps of the world with the building of the university.[46]

These were discrete moments of drama and fiction; the university itself was a permanent stage, the Soviet site of international revolution par excellence.

Onto this stage walked Emi in the winter of 1922. Qu, perhaps curious about the new arrival from France, was particularly warm to Emi and asked him all sorts of questions about himself. The group demanded a full report about the situation in France from the exhausted arrival. When they heard about the difficulties of the students there, they said, "Tell them to come here to Communist Eastern University," and they badgered Emi about his own plans.

After this initial hazing, Qu took Emi to eat, using his own meal card to feed him, and found him a place to sleep—in a basement storage room of the Comintern building, filled with extra beds and mattresses, with electric lights that blazed all through his first night in Moscow.[47]

The next morning, Emi met with Chen Duxiu, then visiting Moscow. Chen told Emi to study at least for a while at Eastern University before going home. Later in the day some students showed up and brought him over to the university, where he got felt boots and a Red Army coat and hat. In accordance with school policy, he was placed in the French language group.[48]

Emi befriended a student who was making the most of the dramatic opportunities the university offered, a Turk named Nazim Hikmet. This Hikmet was already an aspiring poet who had managed to befriend the premier Russian revolutionary poet Vladimir Mayakovsky. Mayakovsky occasionally came to Eastern University to read his poems and was also said to be one of the Moscow poets who sometimes recited poetry at the statue of Pushkin across from the school.[49]

Once, Mayakovsky took Hikmet along with him to read some poems (Hikmet's were in Turkish) at the Polytechnical Museum. Hikmet was nervous but Mayakovsky reassured him: "Don't be afraid, Turk, they don't understand anyway." Hikmet spent his evenings reading poetry around Moscow and participating in the drama collective at Eastern University. The Turkish group of the collective performed twenty-minute dramas in Turkish before audiences of Moscow workers and suburban peasants, who were given a quick summary of the contents of the performances beforehand.[50] Emi's friendship with Hikmet gave him a a rare vantage point onto a more glamorous, creative side of revolutionary Moscow.

It would be several years before Emi would begin writing his own revolutionary poetry, but at Eastern University he was drawn into the performative side of international revolution. Shortly after his arrival, he and some other students started a project—translating the Internationale from French into Chinese. Emi and the other students also translated various Soviet songs into Chinese, and Emi claims that some of these became very popular with Red Army troops back home. He remembered the moments of singing as highlights of his time in Moscow.[51]

The peak of Emi's creative stardom was his performance in a curious play that the Moscow Chinese performed several times in early 1923. The play was about a recent setback to the revolution in China, a dramatic massacre of striking workers by a warlord named Wu Peifu, played by Peng. At this time, competing warlords ruled vast portions of China, and the Soviet government was always trying to pick the winner. Wu had curried favor with local Chinese unions and had Soviet backing. The Chinese communists, in keeping with Moscow's united front policy, were inching toward an alliance with him. Meanwhile, strike activity in China was up, with a major work-stoppage along the Beijing-Hankou railroad hyping radical enthusiasm to a fever pitch. But in February 1922, Wu turned on his leftist allies and crushed the strike with a brutal massacre.[52]

Emi remembered, "Everyone gave me the responsibility of writing the play," which climaxed when one of the actors cried, "Heads can roll, blood can flow, but the working class cannot be overthrown!" For himself, Emi took the role of a young female worker, donning the clothes of a Soviet woman and capturing the attention of Broido, who jokingly congratulated him on his transformation. The play was a huge success, and it went on the road, including a performance before a group of Old Bolsheviks whom Emi's biographer imagined as all having huge beards just like Karl Marx.[53]

This play dramatized not a moment of revolutionary victory but of loss that was arguably caused by Comintern misapprehensions. But like Soviet classics about the Civil War, the play recast the massacre as righteous martyrdom, giving the Muscovites who saw it a revision of the Chinese revolution and the Chinese who participated a new way of interpreting events. It would be the first of a long series of such representations, some of which were created by Emi as well as by other Moscow-educated Chinese of future generations.[54]

Of all the dramatic moments that Emi and the Chinese experienced during their time in Moscow, perhaps the most significant and theatrical was the funeral ceremony of Lenin in January of 1924. Emi got sick that winter and had been whisked off to a sanatorium outside Moscow, an experience that he remembers fondly. There, a raging fire burned in the fireplace all day and the food was really good. But the best thing was the nursing staff, including one young woman who treated Emi with special care and with whom Emi found an exciting new way to practice Russian. While here, Emi learned of the death of Lenin, which sent all the sick students into hysterics. Emi's nurse gave him two tranquilizers to calm him down. The day after that a woman arrived from the university and taught the ailing students a song to grieve Lenin.[55]

Emi tore himself from his comfortable sickbed and his girlfriend and returned to Moscow. The other students had to wait in the endless line to see Lenin's body, but Emi and Ren Bishi were selected to stand in ceremonial attendance of Lenin's body for five whole minutes[56]—two young harbingers of the Chinese revolution taking a long look at the lifeless embodiment of the Russian one.

Peng's Role: A Proto-Purge

Emi seems to have instinctively understood that he was playing a part in an international revolutionary drama of Soviet creation, and he seems to have embraced the role. But in this he was unique. Other Chinese students made very different dramas of their daily existences. One in particular wanted to direct the show—and that was Peng.

When Peng learned of the bread scandal among the Chinese students on his arrival, he perceived the students as beset by meaningless conflict. He suggested they organize themselves into cells and meet once every three weeks for serious political discussion, and the students agreed. "Finished, the time of pettiness and of quarrels over rice-bread-salt! We would, surely, still clash with one another, but for honorable motives from then on." For Peng, the honorable motives were rooting out the ideologically incorrect, at a moment when nobody was sure what ideology even was.[57]

Far from home, hungry, isolated from those around them, with no clear path of revolutionary action, the Chinese turned on each other. For Peng, it was the ensuing battle against the anarchists in the group that made them into real Marxists. And the anarchists might have said the same, except with "Marxist" given a negative connotation. They perceived the subsequent events as a simple power struggle, in which a group of six or seven students began to try to impose a stricter form of control over the others. These six or seven called a meeting to discuss the matter, where they argued that committee rule was the organizational principle of communism, and that opposing it meant opposing communism. One student ran up to the front of the room and denounced the committee, whereupon one of the six got up and said that the committee represented the dictatorship of the proletariat. Someone asked him, "In our group, who is the proletariat? Who are the capitalists?" at which point he got flustered and angry and simply began to shout, "Dictatorship of the proletariat, dictatorship of the proletariat!"[58]

The meeting adjourned but the six took another tack: they started telling the Russians that there were lots of anarchists inside the group. The anarchists, who heard about this from the Russians, became terrified. The six kept holding meetings, which the opposition found excuses not to attend.[59]

It turns out that the one student who stood up to Peng was Emi. Emi had begun his studies in the French group, but after a time he joined his Chinese compatriots. Emi remembers that the group called Peng "Confucius" because he would stand up in front of them and tirelessly recite meaningless phrases, like "When a person is sick, he needs a doctor. When a society is sick, it needs a revolution"—all in a heavy, incomprehensible Hunan accent that Emi could only understand because he too was Hunanese. Emi's only comment on the workings of the Moscow group is his reference to Peng's teaching style and accent, but the other memoirist from France recalls that Emi openly opposed the dictatorial methods of the Moscow branch of the Chinese Party and was severely criticized for it.[60]

How Emi and Peng clashed and the exact nature of their disagreement are unknown, but each certainly remembered his own behavior in Moscow as if he were playing a role in a drama. And the dramas they envisioned were completely different. Emi's was a play of representation through verbal translation and performance, in which irreconcilable cultural or political differences were temporarily dissolved in unifying moments of camaraderie. Peng's was an unrelenting, culture-blind struggle of ideologically unified comrades for textual truth and moral virtue, and against disorder and duality in thought as in politics. They represented two approaches to Sino-Soviet relations, two approaches to communism, two approaches to life.

China's Role: Rising Star

Emi and Peng were striking their poses in the context of a larger drama: the Moscow-based dress rehearsal of international revolution, in which China itself was emerging as a young star with real potential.

The Chinese Communist Party occupied a unique position among foreign parties in Moscow. Comintern rules prohibited members of the communist party of one country from maintaining a separate organization when they were in another country. This meant that a German communist in France was supposed to be a member of the French party and could not form a German communist branch. But in the early 1920s, there was, in fact, a separate Moscow branch of the Chinese Party.

The first Congress of the Chinese Communist Party had been held in Shanghai in July 1921—several months after the first group of Chinese students left Shanghai for Moscow. At that point, the Chinese Party was hardly a Leninist party with a strong central leadership but rather a loose network of radical cells in cities all over the world—not only Beijing, Wuhan, Guangdong, Changsha, and Jinan, but also Tokyo, Paris, and Moscow. They were connected as much by personal correspondence as by bureaucratic communication. The letters that Paris-based Chinese communists wrote to their Moscow counterparts are from one Chinese comrade to another, with personal descriptions of the failings and strengths of each person leaving Paris for Moscow. There is little attention to a larger party bureaucracy, much less a Comintern one.

Early Chinese communists were ambivalent about joining the Comintern in the first place. Few Chinese in Europe joined the party of their host country and only a few of the Moscow Chinese joined the Russian party. According to the Chinese, their Moscow organization emerged for practical reasons: there were too many Chinese in Moscow for too short a time who spoke no Russian and who needed some sort of management. Until 1925, the Comintern, ever focused on the technical difficulties of international revolution, defended its existence on the grounds of its effectiveness.[61]

In fact, there was a certain organizational and cultural dissonance between the Chinese and Russian Communist parties, which those involved closely with the Chinese Party well understood. Comintern rules assumed homogenous Leninist parties modeled on the current Russian Communist Party and operating as branches of a Moscow-based international revolutionary bureaucracy—the hub model. In reality, the Chinese Communist Party was a loose human network rife with conflict, bereft of stable communications ties, and without clear hierarchies. When Peng, Emi, and Qu were in Moscow, the Chinese Party branch there operated as a somewhat independent organism focused on its own inner development in extremely localized conditions.

And yet, in local Moscow conditions, the Chinese communists were thriving. By 1925, the Chinese outnumbered other foreign groups, a leading position in Soviet international education that China would rarely relinquish until the Sino-Soviet split.[62]

Although some of the students who returned home in 1922 did their best to dispel the illusions of their compatriots innocent of the Soviet experience, they were swimming against a tide that had only gathered force since their own departure from China. Chinese communist leader Chen Duxiu, Russian Research Society activist Mao Zedong, the European branch of the Socialist Youth Corps, and the Comintern were all busy recruiting students for Eastern University, so each student who left seemed to be replaced by three new ones. "Dear Comrade Broido," wrote Chen Duxiu and Mao Zedong via a Russian translator,

> According to Zhang Guotao who just came back from Russia, the Chinese Communist Party can send students to KUTV [Communist University of the Toilers of the East]. But before we send them, we need an explanation of the following questions: 1. How many we can send 2. Who will pay 3. How much money each person needs for the road.[63]

The university was happy to have them, repeatedly projecting an ever-increasing number of Chinese, until finally a new school was founded just for them in 1925.[64]

Costume Change

In 1924, the Chinese delegation to the Fifth Comintern Congress ordered both Emi and Peng to return to China that summer. Apparently their education was complete. Emi made no public record of his return trip, and Peng recalls that the train ride back home was far less eventful than the journey to Moscow had been. But as he approached the Chinese border, Peng realized that he had a problem: his clothes. To safely pass through Manzhouli, he needed to dress as he had not dressed in over three years: exactly as a Chinese. The Moscow act of his life over, it was time for a costume change.[65]

5

Shanghai University and the Comintern Curriculum

IT'S LATE FALL of 1924, cold enough for Qu Qiubai to be wearing a coat as he weaves through the streets of Shanghai's International Settlement to deliver a lecture to a large group of students at a new school for radical youths. He walks into the lecture hall, where an audience has converged in anticipation of imminent spoken wisdom. Hat in hand, Qu makes his way to the front, smiles at the crowd, opens his briefcase, takes out his notes, and starts talking.[1]

When he arrived in Moscow three years earlier, Qu was a pale, slight intellectual just past adolescence. Now, he is a man who has found and perfected his own charisma. His tuberculosis in remission, his thin frame padded by a neat, high-quality Western suit and overcoat, his mind full of literature and politics and women, at times Qu exuded a vitality at odds with his poor health and finicky disposition.[2]

The most obvious change was on his face. Qu routinely wore a pair of round glasses with prominent dark frames, and if these glasses brought the world into focus for him, they also brought his face into focus for the world. A visage that had appeared flat suddenly acquired dimension, with watchful eyes, eyebrows set off by the curvature of the glasses, a nose prominent enough to hold the glasses, and a full mouth that seemed resolute, rather than pursed as before.[3]

Qu at Shanghai University

Qu returned to China from Moscow in January of 1923 and applied to teach at Beijing University (Beida), but China's bastion of high culture rejected

Qu Qiubai. RGASPI, f. 495, op. 225, d. 1014, l. 19.

him.[4] Qu decided that if Beida wouldn't have him, he would create his own Beida.

Shanghai University (Shangda), according to the propaganda Qu wrote for it, was modeled on Beida and was supposed to become a major center of New Culture in the South. Qu's vision of Shangda was motivated by the same belief in a transcendent union of East and West that had saturated his Moscow travelogues. The university was to have three departments: social sciences, literature, and art. In the social sciences, it would reimagine Chinese society according to Marxist-Leninist categories. In literature, Qu assailed the barriers between ancient Chinese and modern Western scholarship, forcing students of Chinese literature to also absorb the history of Western culture, and students of Western languages to continue upper-level study of Chinese. This curriculum put Chinese culture in a global context and framed foreign language as an intellectual pursuit rather than a professional one.[5]

Qu envisioned an institution unlike Moscow's Eastern University, where he had just spent a year and a half teaching and translating. On the surface there were similarities—Eastern University too emphasized social science and foreign language—but the Moscow school rejected the liberal arts in favor of a Leninist curriculum, basic Russian language, and political literacy for communist agitators and teachers.

Qu's Shangda and the real Shangda were two different things, however. The actual school was located in a shabby factory neighborhood and lacked a regular campus. It had been founded on the basis of an existing normal school, when radical students took it over and convinced a prominent member of the Nationalist Party to reorganize it; its President was the Nationalist Party politician Yu Youren. Shangda operated under intense financial pressure, so it had to offer courses in accounting and to teach foreign language for business. Far from being a Beida of the South, its academic reputation was shaky.[6]

Qu lectured partly from his old Moscow notes, offering eager young students from the provinces simple renderings of Marxism-Leninism—cribbed from Bukharin's *Historical Materialism*, Qu's Eastern University textbook—enlivened with illustrations and stories from the Chinese classics and from Western literature. Later he published his lecture notes, which became so popular they went through eleven editions. At the end of his life Qu admitted that he "never touched *Capital*." "My little knowledge of Marxist theory came almost exclusively from some random essays in newspapers and magazines and several pamphlets by Lenin."[7]

In his original plan for Shangda, Qu outlined a comprehensive foreign language program. The Russian language department was to be the most ambitious, because the state of Russian instruction in China, according to Qu, was the most backward of all. The Beijing Russian Language Institute was too focused on producing professionals who could read official documents; Beida's Russian department was immature; and most other Russian language instruction in China was in the Harbin style, geared toward trade. The Comintern-sponsored Shanghai Foreign Languages School had closed its doors after less than a year. In all of China, Qu thought, there might be four or five students qualified to enter a college-level Russian course.[8]

Qu's solution was to establish an experimental Russian department at Shangda, where instruction would be done "Berlitz" style, with eighteen hours of class a week for rapid acquisition of speaking skills. This approach was similar to Eastern University's and diametrically opposed to Chinese methods focused on reading. Grammar, Qu thought, should be taught by a Chinese with deep knowledge of Russian; in the event, two former Communist Eastern University students became Russian teachers at Shangda.[9]

Shangda became legendary for mixing theory and practice. Many of its faculty members were Communists or left-leaning Nationalists, and it quickly became famous as a radical university, the place to go to learn Marxist theory. Students might listen to a course on the history of social movements in the morning, teach a class in a worker's school at night, and, in the run-up to the anti-imperialist labor demonstrations of the May 30th Movement in 1925, spend their days and nights agitating and demonstrating.[10]

When police conducted raids at Shangda after the May 30th demonstrations, they found that students all had pictures of Russian revolutionaries on their dorm walls.[11] Ultimately, the real Shangda was closer in spirit to Communist Eastern University than Qu had intended, and, from a certain Moscow-centric angle, might be seen as a creative translation of Soviet ideals of revolutionary education into a Chinese environment.

Qu Becomes a Politician

In addition to teaching at Shangda, Qu was drawn deeper into the brand-new Chinese Communist Party, which he had joined in Moscow. He leveraged his Russian language skills to advance his political career via the patronage of key Comintern representatives in China.

The First Congress of the Chinese Communist Party had been held in Shanghai on July 23, 1921. Thirteen Chinese attended it, representing groups from six cities plus Japan, and they agreed on almost nothing—except perhaps for their dislike of the Comintern representative at the meeting.[12]

Henk Sneevliet, aka Maring, was by far the most experienced communist Moscow had yet sent to do party work in China. Maring was a forty-year-old Dutchman who had been expelled from the East Indies for his involvement in the labor movement there. In May 1920, he had attended the Second Comintern Congress in Moscow as a representative of the Indonesian Communist Party. There Lenin suggested him for a post in China.[13] Maring arrived in Shanghai weeks before the Communist Party's First Congress.

Qu Qiubai in the mid-1920s.

After a first day of initial remarks and reports at the Congress, Maring got up on the second day and spoke about his own experiences in Java and the importance of an alliance with the Nationalist Party—and then he left. On the third day, heated debates erupted over things that Bolsheviks took for granted, like whether the Chinese Communist Party should agitate illegally among workers or limit itself to intellectual debate, whether the Party should be centralized, and whether members should take official positions in the current Chinese government—never mind whether they should ally with the Chinese Nationalists and join the Comintern, as Maring no doubt assumed they would. Records from this first Congress are murky, but the group decisively voted against an alliance with China's Nationalist Party.[14]

The Nationalist Party (Guomindang, or "National People's Party" in Chinese) had been founded by Sun Yatsen in 1912, and his supporters had played a significant role in the 1911 revolution. By 1921 when Maring arrived on the scene, the Nationalists had managed to take over Guangdong, proclaim a military government, and elect Sun, theoretically, as the president of China. Of course Sun was no such thing—neither the government in Beijing nor even the local warlords supported him. The latter ousted him from Guangdong in the early 1920s. The Nationalists warmed easily to Russian advances; Sun Yatsen was determined to lay his hands on a good army and willing to listen to anyone who offered help in this regard. Sun and his party certainly seemed more viable than the scattered handful of young students interested communism.[15]

After his visit to the First Congress of the Communist Party, Maring departed on a tour of Nationalist strongholds in southern China, which coincided with the largest workers' strike in Chinese history to that time— the Hong Kong seamen's strike of 1922. At this early stage in the development of mass politics in China, the Nationalists, who at least had something of a party infrastructure in place, seemed the more effective party. Maring's travels reinforced his preconceived notions, which fit nicely with Comintern policy.

The Communist International had been trying to promote Marxist revolution across Europe since 1864. Immediately after 1917, the Bolsheviks sincerely believed that their revolution would spread to Germany. Even after German uprisings failed miserably, ultra-leftists in the international party, Trotsky first and foremost, placed their faith in the improbable idea of an immediate global (European) breakthrough to communism. Lenin responded to the dilemma of global non-revolution differently, with a policy called the "United Front," that called upon ultra-radicals to ally with more moderate and hence more popular parties. This policy met with opposition from purists all over the world, from Trotsky to India's M. N. Roy. As for China, few in the Comintern knew much about it, and what exactly the "united front" might mean there was unclear, so China was a key testing ground for the policy.[16]

Many Chinese Communists were initially ambivalent about forming a "united front" with the Nationalists. After all, they had sought to form a new party precisely because they had become disillusioned with existing political forces. They considered the Nationalists "yesterday's people," in the words of one early communist, and the Nationalist Party itself a leftover from the failed 1911 revolution, little better than the warlords with whom it fought.[17]

That Moscow assumed it could dictate revolutionary alliances in the interests of the longevity of the international revolutionary movement as a whole came as a surprise to some Chinese. For many young Chinese communists, revolution was so deeply related to personal freedom—which began with a rejection of the right of patriarchs to decide their marriages and continued through the right of free political activity and association—that any attempt to unite them against their will with another party could only provoke hostile skepticism. Convincing them would take some skill.

Maring was not the man for the job—he didn't like China, and the Chinese didn't like him. Despite the fact that he had a house considered by some Chinese as fit for an ambassador and that he had sent for his Ukrainian mistress, Maring was desperately unhappy in China.[18] As one of the Chinese who liked him least recalled, his attempts to appear sympathetic to Asian people appeared melodramatic and inconsistent:

> One time on the streets of Shanghai, for example, he encountered a foreigner insulting a Chinese coolie. He rushed forward to fight the foreigner. Yet he often dwelt too much upon the backwardness of Asian people, and he joked about the infantile simplicity of Oriental Socialists.[19]

Maring seemed the opposite of the Russian Voitinskii—and he didn't even speak Russian, a fact that did not escape the Chinese.

Qu and Maring

Maring needed a Chinese ally, and he naturally gravitated to Qu. The counsel Qu gave—to spend less time focused on his own objective and more time understanding the preoccupations of his intended partners—was politically astute; even Maring recognized that if only he had the willpower to follow it, he would be much more successful in his maneuverings. Qu, on the other hand, was clearly successful in his efforts to impress Maring; he repeatedly wrote back to Moscow that Qu was by far the most promising of the Chinese comrades.[20]

Qu also turned out to be a Leninist and a key Chinese champion of the United Front policy in the 1920s. He had originally been attracted to the Russian Revolution, like so many other Chinese, as an example of a backward country leaping ahead in historical development, as a transcendence of traditional East-West dichotomies, and as a universal event of enormous spiritual importance. During the Third Congress of the Chinese Communist Party in 1923, which turned out to be showdown about the United Front, Qu made a speech, whose main points Maring jotted down: "Everything is growing," Qu said, after telling his comrades not to be "afraid of the growing of bourgeoisie, at the same time proletariat grows also. We cannot prevent their growth by our separation from them." Qu combined an orthodox Marxist faith in the pure revolutionary nature of the proletariat with a pragmatism that would have made Lenin proud. If the Communists didn't back the Nationalists, Qu argued, the Nationalists would ally with the bourgeoisie and militarists. In the course of the Third Party Congress, Qu became a member of the Central Committee of the Chinese Communist Party.[21]

For his part, Maring got up and brandished a written order he had procured from the Comintern, stating in no uncertain terms that the Communists were to join the Nationalists in a United Front. This time, the Congress voted for it. Maring, however, was removed from his post in China.

Charismatic Borodin

Moscow's replacement of Maring with Mikhail Borodin, along with a large team of military advisors, suggested a new level of interest in the Chinese revolution.[22] Borodin's powers of political persuasion were well known in the world of international communism.

Close to forty when he came to China, Borodin was a Jew, born Grusenberg, in the Pale of Settlement, the western territories where the Russian imperial government required most Jews to live. He had become active in the Jewish Social Democratic Bund in his native Latvia when he was just a teenager. Facing arrest for his activities in the Revolution of 1905, Borodin signed up as a sailor on a British ship and fled to the United States, where he settled in Chicago. On the surface he seemed like a regular immigrant: he married a girl—Fanny (Fraina)—from Latvia, studied for a while at Valparaiso University in Indiana, and opened a school for immigrant children. But in Chicago, Borodin seems to have hosted or met enough high-ranking Russian communists to suggest that he stayed involved in radical politics and still identified himself in those terms. Borodin returned to the Soviet Union in 1918 and became intimate with Lenin, who sent him on various international missions in subsequent years. Borodin cultivated an aura of mystery, playing on his involvement in a failed mission to smuggle jewels to Mexican communists in 1919, for example, to maximum effect. One woman who was quite taken with him said that he was "one of those who, however much they may like one as a woman, they would sacrifice one in a minute if it was necessary for the cause."[23]

When Borodin was called to the Bolshevik Central Committee in mid-1923, he assumed it was to receive the sort of assignment to which he'd been accustomed since his return to Russia—advising communist parties in the West, or perhaps Latin America. He was completely surprised when told he'd be heading to China, as the chief political advisor to Sun Yatsen. He knew this was the mission of a lifetime.[24]

Like Maring, Borodin had never thought much about China before his departure, knew next to nothing about it, and had no romantic notion about it. His best biographer gives a long list of reasons for why he might have been chosen, such as his close association with Lenin and with key Russian diplomats in China, and a long history of revolutionary service, but the most interesting reasons involve his personality. Borodin radiated revolutionary charisma, and his assignments thus far had all involved using this quality to woo foreign revolutionaries.[25]

In China, Borodin summoned all his charm to sway the development of the Chinese revolution decisively. Borodin and Qu became allies, and Qu threw all his weight behind Borodin's efforts. In January 1924, Qu went to Guangdong and stayed with Borodin, angering some communists who huffed that Borodin "treats our party just as if we were the provider of interpreters." Qu was one of a few Chinese Communist Party members elected to the Central Executive Committee of the reorganized Nationalist Party that Borodin was helping Sun to create, and he helped Borodin to draft the Nationalists' new manifesto.[26]

Maring had forced the Nationalists and the Communists into a formal alliance, but it was Borodin who really got them to work together. First he convinced Sun Yatsen to allow Chinese Communists free rein to organize workers and peasants and to appoint them to key political positions in the Nationalist Party. Then he persuaded the Communists to accept those positions and take them seriously. Thus Chinese Communists gained serious political experience—in terms of both high-level realpolitik and regular street logic.

All of this Borodin accomplished through charismatic persuasion combined with the tangible assistance the Kremlin had finally decided to give Chinese revolutionaries.

Red General

In August of 1923, Sun Yatsen sent his trusted lieutenant Chiang Kaishek on a three-month mission to Moscow to seek the military support he so desperately needed. Chiang had studied in a Japanese military academy and was a founding member of the Nationalist Party. [27] Like future communists, he began reading Chen Duxiu's *New Youth* in 1919 and continued doing so when it was edited by Qu and Peng and had already become a Communist Party organ. He struggled through a book about Marxism, where he "found a profound theory which I read with great admiration. I savored it for a long time and could not bear to close the book." He also read the *Communist Manifesto*, a collection of translations of Lenin, a history of the German Social Democratic Party—and histories of the French and Russian revolutions, concluding in 1923 that while the two were quite similar, "the Russians rectified the errors made by the French, which was most valuable." [28]

In Moscow, Chiang pitched a plan for a joint offensive against the warlords in the northeast. He spent most of his time in meetings with Soviet officials who were bent on proving to him that the solution to China's problems was political, not military. Something of the lesson seems to have sunk in, for Chiang left convinced of the efficacy of the one-party dictatorship and the importance of political training for soldiers. The high point of his trip was an impassioned speech he made before four hundred officers of the Red Army. Upon his return to China, so enthusiastically did Chiang advocate the

Nationalist alliance with the Soviet Union that he was nicknamed the "red general."[29]

Like other celebrity Chinese visitors to Moscow, Chiang paid a visit to Communist Eastern University. Hearing of its course on dialectical materialism, he was said to have exclaimed, "Ah! How I would love to take this course, even if it was just as an auditor!" Once, Chiang invited Peng Shuzhi and several of his classmates over to dinner. At the end of that evening in 1923, Peng remembers that as he bade them farewell Chiang cried out, "Long live the world revolution! Long live the Comintern! Long live the Soviets!"[30]

Even so, the Soviets rejected Chiang's joint offensive. In the early 1920s, the Soviet Union had only just brought its own Far Eastern territories to heel, so it probably seemed wiser to seek an alliance with one of the existing military factions—warlords—in Manchuria than to fight all of them at once, as Chiang was asking them to do, with the help of a nonexistent Nationalist army from the South that would somehow have to get to Manchuria first. But the Soviet Union did promise Chiang more military advisors. Thus when Borodin arrived in China he brought with him plans for a new military school in Guangdong, known as Whampoa (Huangpu) Military Academy, of which Chiang became the director.[31]

After Sun Yatsen died in 1924, Borodin seemed to positively run Guangdong, and the Russian presence was palpable, in the form of the hundreds of military advisors.[32] The Nationalists were split between left and right factions that Borodin was endlessly attempting to reconcile. Meanwhile, Qu shuttled back and forth between Guangdong and Shanghai, where China's first big protest movement since May 4, 1919, was gaining steam.

Known as the May 30th Movement, it began when striking Chinese workers at a Japanese factory who had been locked out broke into the factory and destroyed its machinery. The factory's Japanese guards shot at them, killing a worker. More strikes and student demonstrations followed; on May 30, workers and students jammed Nanjing Road, and police gunned down eleven of them. Soon, all of urban China was in an uproar, with a Shanghai general strike that spread quickly to other cities.

In Borodin's Guangdong, cadets from Huangpu Military Academy put on a demonstration of support, in which fifty-two students, soldiers, workers, and even Boy Scouts were killed by the police. A strike launched in Hong Kong lasted sixteen months, was accompanied by a massive boycott of British goods, and was the most serious labor unrest China had ever experienced, a real turning point in the country's development of class consciousness.[33] In Guangdong, the Russian and Chinese revolutions seemed more visibly intertwined than anywhere else in China.

Far from the halls of Huangpu Military Academy and the heated meetings Borodin held in rooms full of Chinese men, however, young Chinese women were imagining a very different kind of Sino-Soviet affair—one that would outlast ephemeral alliances. And Qu Qiubai was encouraging them.

6

A Crush on Russia

Qu's Female Protégés

THERE'S A MAILMAN at the door of a sprawling house in the old Tanhua Woods district of Wuchang, and he has a special delivery letter, registered mail from Hankou, addressed to Chen Bilan. Had he caught a glimpse of her, he'd have seen an energetic young woman, twenty years old, with bobbed hair.[1] Bilan opens the envelope to find a long letter written in proper brush strokes:

> Our two families have intermarried and have been closely interrelated for generations. Furthermore your father and mine are the very best of friends. Before, when I heard that you were studying at the normal school, I was envious; when I heard how well you were doing in your studies I was ashamed of myself. But, recently, I heard that you have been dismissed from the normal school, that you have gotten somewhat of a bad reputation, and that you have cut your hair. . . . I sincerely hope that you let your hair grow long again, because [quoting Confucius] "one's body, hair, and skin are inherited from one's parents and one dares not harm or injure them, this being the ultimate in filial piety." I also hope you can come to study at Hsilita Girls' School in Hankow. If you have any financial difficulties, I will be able to help.[2]

Bilan laughed and her four housemates came and read the letter for themselves. Everyone agreed: now's the time. Bilan sat down and wrote all night long, pouring out her contempt for her fiancée, the "high class mission school" he offered to finance, and the entire system of arranged marriage that had brought them together in the first place. She was proud of her bad reputation, sure of her bright future, and determined to break the marriage contract.[3]

First thing in the morning, she brought the letter to her teacher, who happened to be a leading member of the new Chinese Communist Party's Wuhan branch, and, with his approval, posted it with a feeling of great satisfaction. Eighteen months and a second jilted fiancée later, Chen Bilan was on the train to Moscow.

Chinese Male Feminism

After the May Fourth movement, young people increasingly began refusing their arranged marriages, using politics to change their personal lives and their personal choices to express their politics. Men could more easily refuse arranged marriages than women. In 1923, Chen Bilan really was a rebel, and if she felt it necessary to confer with her male mentors, it was because she knew she'd need their support if her family turned her out. And she had it, because these new-style men needed new-style women.

Like so many other men at revolutionary moments, Chinese men became preoccupied by the "woman question."[4] Chinese men wanted the freedom to love their wives, and they wanted their wives to love them. Ideas of free love were a corollary to the principle of love-based marriage, as were radical notions that marriages should be based on shared political and philosophical beliefs.[5] But broader Chinese society assimilated new ideas of marriage slowly, and with difficulty. A common Chinese saying at the time went, "A college man married to a country girl—hence the tragedy." There was no saying about women with bobbed hair married to men who still quoted the Classic of Filial Piety.[6]

While in theory and practice many Chinese revolutionaries politicized marriage in a serious and high-minded way, the new focus on the element of choice in male-female relations also spiraled into frivolity, melodrama, and pornography in Chinese urban print culture. A bestselling book in Shanghai in the mid-1920s—after Sun Yatsen's *Three People's Principles* and a Chinese translation of the *ABC of Communism*—was called *Sex Lives,* by a Beida philosophy professor who wanted to create a utopian society based on sex. In a more romantic vein, beginning in the 1910s, a new genre of fiction had emerged, called "Mandarin Ducks and Butterflies," which focused on contemporary dilemmas of love and often featured male heroes choosing between traditional and modern women.[7]

In the 1920s, a whole "love and revolution" subgenre developed, fictional stories about the love lives of revolutionaries that explicitly romanticized revolution and revolutionized love. Its most popular author was Jiang Guangci, who had been among the first group of Chinese radicals to travel to the Soviet Union in 1921. Regrettably, Jiang never published a word about his time in Moscow. According to the memories of his fellow students there, he was one of the prime "anarchists" targeted in Peng's campaign at Eastern University. Jiang, apparently, left the university dorm to live with another anarchist in the abandoned Strastnoi Monastery across the street. He immersed himself in avant-garde Russian literary groups and became possessed with fantastic ideas of literary fame, convinced that he was contemporary China's Pushkin. When he returned to China, he began a career as a radical author, on the one hand arguing for the "proletarianization" of Chinese literature, and on the other churning out bestseller after bestseller, combining the themes of love and revolution in utterly formulaic ways.[8] Jiang was also one of the Russian language instructors at Shangda.

In the absence of his own testimony, it is difficult to understand how Jiang's experience in Russia affected him. All we know is that he eventually wrote a florid novel about the adventures of a White Russian noblewoman turned prostitute in Shanghai. Yet even without his private musings, Jiang's biography—a Moscow sojourner, a sometime communist, a Russian student and then teacher, and a romance writer—reflects a Chinese milieu that combined Russia, revolution, and romance like a fizzy cocktail.

Other communists often criticized Jiang—even his friend Qu once said, after he left the room, "That man really has no talent!" Yet Qu as much as Jiang owed his literary success to the romanticism that permeated Chinese radical political culture. At this moment, in 1923 Qu published his *History of the Heart in the Red Capital*, adding his private musings and the long Tolstoy family story to the more basic reports he had written for *Chen Bao*. He collaborated with Jiang to produce a compendium of Russian literature and published several of his own poems, stories, and essays. Qu also applied his literary skill to communist party propaganda.[9]

Russian Literature: A Broader Audience

Qu may have considered himself China's best Russian speaker, but his dismissal of China's other Russian scholars was misplaced, as other Chinese were beginning to surpass him in reading and translation. While Qu was in Moscow, some of his compatriots at home were working their way through the nineteenth-century Russian classics. One of the earliest Chinese to translate Russian literature directly, rather than from a third language, was Qu's classmate at the Russian Language Institute, Geng Jizhi. He began his translation career in 1919, when he published a series of Tolstoy's short stories in magazines; in 1920 he continued to translate Tolstoy but broadened out to include short works by Gogol, Herzen, and Chekhov. In 1922, he translated Turgenev's *Fathers and Sons*.

The direct translations that Geng and others were doing were a new species in the growing population of Chinese translations of Russian literature. Between 1900 and 1916, on average not even one volume of Russian literature was published per year; between 1920 and 1927, the average was ten volumes per year. The Shanghai powerhouse Commercial Press issued multi-volume collections of Russian novels and plays, and popular periodicals regularly offered shorter translations. Russian literature was becoming a commercially viable trend.[10]

China's most popular Russian writers continued to be Tuersetai (Tolstoy), Tugenuofu (Turgenev), and other pre-revolutionary realists. Major canonical works of Russian literature first published between 1917 and 1925 include Turgenev's *On the Eve, Fathers and Sons, Mumu, Virgin Soil,* and his long play, *A Month in Country*; Tolstoy's *Family Happiness, The Power of Darkness*, and *Fruits of Enlightenment*; Dostoevsky's *Brothers Karamazov* and *The Insulted and Humiliated*; and Andreyev's *The Seven Hanged Men*. Notable first translations of shorter works included Chekhov's *Seagull, Cherry Orchard,* and *Three Sisters* as well as a few stories and plays by Gogol, Pushkin, and Ostrovsky.[11]

What appears to be lacking is contemporary literature—an absence all the more notable given that some Chinese Russophiles had met or studied with one or another Soviet writers in Beijing. For example, Aleksei Ivanov, aka Ivin, was a pro-Soviet Russian émigré who had learned Chinese in Paris and taught Russian at Beijing University. Here he hosted the famous journalist Sergei Tretiakov, who spent eighteen months in China and sent reports back to major newspapers such as *Pravda*, and went on to write the well-known play *Roar, China!* Boris Pilniak, world traveler and novelist, also put China on his itinerary in the mid-1920s. Pilniak met Jiang Guangci in Shanghai, as well as the Chinese filmmaker Tian Han. Tian convinced Pilniak to appear in a cameo for a movie he was making called *Go to the People*, inspired by the Russian populist movement of the nineteenth century and featuring a love triangle between two Shanghai students and a waitress.[12] Confronted with a living, breathing Soviet writer in 1920s China, these young Chinese placed him in a movie evocative of 1860s Russia.

The Russia that China was choosing to translate at this moment was not yet a Russia of proletarian revolution but one of young nobles and intellectuals facing major social change, where revolution was a still a question. The nineteenth-century novels that the Chinese were reading modeled history on a human scale, folding major social and political issues into the biographies of charismatic, ambiguous characters. No wonder they were so popular with readers who were still assimilating enormous social and political shifts as individuals, not as members of parties, believers in ideologies, or even, necessarily, modern citizens. The most sensational element of China's social evolution was, of course, the shift in the concept of love.[13]

Pushkin as Aphrodisiac

There are two accounts of how Qu met his first wife, both written by her best friend. One is supposed to be true: it is a memoir that the best friend wrote in the 1950s. The other is supposed to be fiction: it is a novella called *Wei Hu*, written in the immediate aftermath of the marriage. Wei Hu was one of Qu's pen names, so many readers of the novella knew that "Wei Hu" was Qu; years later Qu even signed letters to the author as Wei Hu. The author, Ding Ling, was not overly concerned about the boundaries between truth and fiction.[14]

In real life, a friend of Qu's brought him to see Ding and her friend in the apartment they shared with other free-thinking young women in a rundown neighborhood in Nanjing, just after Qu's return from Moscow. In fiction, Ding imagined that Wei Hu came only reluctantly. He had, she thought, had so many women—traditional Chinese and exotic foreign ones—that he had wearied of them entirely and resolved to channel his passions into politics. He only came to see the girls to humor his friend, who naively offered them up to the cosmopolitan Wei Hu as a novelty: "new" Chinese women.

As such, in real life Ding remembered, she and her friends were used to the clumsy advances of tiresome young men excited by their unconventionality. For them, even communists were yesterday's news, and they knew right away that Qu was a communist.[15]

Yet Qu told them stories of his time in Russia so well that the girls were entranced. In Ding's memory, Qu mentioned Pushkin, Tolstoy, and Gorky, and became all the more voluble when he found that the girls had actually read some Russian literature.[16]

When the conversation turned to romance, the fictional Wei Hu learned that the girls were enamored of Russian women, whom they imagined as an inverse of Chinese women. But Wei Hu flattered his listeners mercilessly. "Russian women have their faults too," he said. "They're strong and healthy, with energy to talk forever. They don't care what you're doing, they'll come in your room without even knocking, squeeze their big thighs into a soft chair, and start smoking. They think they're hilarious, they don't care whether you're listening or not, they'll just keep going on and on in their loud voices."[17]

When Qu met the girls he was in the midst of planning for Shangda, and he used all his powers to convince them to come there. Once they arrived, he proved a most solicitous professor. More often than not, Qu went to see the girls in the evenings after work. He would talk and talk about Greece, Rome, the Renaissance, the Chinese dynasties. And if he didn't care to teach Russian at Shangda, he spared no effort in his private lessons.[18]

> In order to help us to quickly understand the beauty of Pushkin's language, he taught us to read his poems in Russian. His method of teaching was really particular, after studying the phonetics just a little, we'd just directly read the original poem, and in the middle of reading it, discuss the grammar, changing cases, the peculiarities of Russian language use, the beauty of the way Pushkin used words. To read a single poem, we had to read over 200 individual words, memorize a lot of grammar. But these 200 words, this grammar, it seemed that we had entirely eaten them up and spit them out. After reading three or four poems, we thought we had simply mastered the Russian language.[19]

Whatever the results of the language lessons, Qu's efforts paid off in another way: the girls fell hopelessly in love with him, in fact and in fiction. Qu picked not Ding but her friend. When Ding first suspected that Qu was in love, she assumed it had to be with a "dewalisa," a tovarishch—a high-ranking female communist. The day she found out that Qu had fallen for her friend, she blew up at him. "We're not studying Russian anymore! Go away and don't come back!" she yelled at him, and slammed the door in his face. In fact, she remembers, they really didn't study Russian anymore. Her friend, she said, "no longer needed to," and she lost interest.[20]

Ding reconciled herself to the new situation. After Qu married her friend, both girls moved in with him. Qu's apartment was luxurious by student standards. Most impressive to Ding were his shelves and shelves of books, hardcover and foreign, his writing stand with all of its delicate writing tools, his enormous bed with a real spring mattress, and a lamp with a red yarn shade that cast the room in a rosy glow. During the day, Qu would be gone on party and school business, dressed in his meticulous Western suit. At night he would change into an old, comfortable, dark silk gown that Qu told Ding had belonged to his grandfather, a high-ranking Qing official. Qu's new wife was well versed in classical poetry, and the two of them wrote poetry together, Qu engraving little fragments on pieces of stone. They also sang traditional Chinese operas. After several months they moved to a different house, where another communist and his wife lived on the bottom floor.[21]

Eventually, Ding tired of this arrangement and moved out.[22] Her anarchist-thinking-classical-poetry-writing friend died of tuberculosis, perhaps contracted from Qu.[23]

Chen Bilan Becomes Qu's Protégé

Borodin could only combine and direct Chinese revolutionaries; he could not create them. Far more influential in this regard were Chinese mediators like Qu. Qu did literal translation work for Borodin, but he also made the most of his transcultural position in Chinese radical circles, appealing to young people through his writings, his teachings, and his conversation.[24] It seems he had considerable talent as a mentor for young women.

Chen Bilan, who was brought to see Qu by some mutual friends, was a case in point. When Qu met Chen, he sized her up immediately and offered her a new aspiration: to be among the first Chinese women to study in the Soviet Union. So thoroughly did Chen romanticize this idea, and through it her understanding of herself, that it was almost as if she had substituted Russia for a human lover—and in a sense, she actually did.

Chen Bilan had been born in a small Hubei village in 1902 to a large, wealthy landowning clan. Her father was relatively poor but enjoyed high status in his family because he had studied physics and chemistry in Japan, where he picked up progressive tendencies. On the one hand, he insisted in a letter from Japan that Chen's feet not be bound; on the other, he had arranged her marriage, to the son of his best friend there, another forward-thinking Chinese from a neighboring village.[25]

Chen studied in a series of schools of varying quality sponsored by members of her clan, similar to the schools that Emi, Qu, and Peng attended. She eventually earned a diploma from a girls' school, and her father considered her education complete, but she insisted on being allowed to take the entrance exam for the Hubei Teacher's Training College for Women, where tuition was free in return for several years of teaching after graduation. Chen expected to graduate, marry, and become a teacher.[26]

Chen's school wasn't particularly political, but that changed in 1921 when Li Hanjun—one of the earliest members of the Chinese Communist Party—visited her school to talk about "the woman question." Around the same time, a prominent communist came to teach English at the school and a radical Chinese language teacher was hired. They began teaching the "new thinking" and organizing the students in groups. The student body radicalized and clashed predictably with the administration. Chen and her fellow rabble-rousers were expelled; they mobilized and ousted the administration. The communists involved in the school invited her and her four close comrades-in-arms to join first the Socialist Youth Corps and then the Party. Amid this, Chen rebelled against her arranged marriage, sending an article to a local journal attacking the practice in general and thereby throwing down the gauntlet to her own father and fiancé.[27]

Neither Chen's fiancé nor her father was deterred by the article. Her fiancé simply wrote beseeching her to cut her hair and change schools. Her beloved father gently reminded her that she hadn't been home for a year and a half. Her comrades were nervous for her safety as she set off for a visit home; cases were common enough in which families physically imprisoned radical daughters like Chen when they came home for the holidays. But Chen had faith in her family. When she got home, her mother subjected her to a heart-rending account of all the public censure her family had suffered because of Chen's unfilial behavior.[28]

Chen's father reacted quite differently. When Chen produced the letter her fiancé had written to say that cutting one's hair was unfilial, her father, for whom cutting his queue had been a moment of great personal liberation, took Chen's side. He even read the biographies of Marx, Lenin, Rosa Luxembourg, and Karl Liebknecht that Chen had brought home with her. "This communism you believe in is a good thing," he told her. One night, he wrote two matching scrolls of calligraphy on bright red paper, and pasted them outside one of the doors to their house. They read, "Buddha taught the equality of all living things. I hope that all in the world become workers and peasants."[29]

Chen left home and headed to Beijing to try to pass the entrance exams to the National Women's Higher Normal School there. When she failed, the Party proposed that she and her friends move to Shanghai and attend Shangda. When Chen arrived in Shanghai, the comrades there brought her to Qu Qiubai's house. Years later, Chen remembered his comments about her: "She certainly is an exceptional female comrade. I think it would be better to have her attend Shanghai University, and at the same time study Russian, and then, later, send her to the Soviet Union to study for awhile. That way, in future she will be of even more use." Chen was so excited about this idea that she could hardly sleep that night.[30]

But Chen had to flee one more man to live this dream.

In Beijing, Chen had become friendly with Huang, the secretary of the Socialist Youth Corps there, an "elegant, lively intellectual" who gradually made it clear that he had feelings for her. Chen was attracted to Huang but also was determined not to be "duped by my own feelings." She listened carefully to everything Huang said and thought she detected certain faults, certain shortcomings: "a lack of steadiness, vainglory, liking to go around with girls." Moreover, while other comrades were amused by their relationship, Qu, her major mentor by this point, made it clear that he disapproved. When things between Chen and Huang seemed to be transgressing the bounds of friendship, she pulled him up short.[31] Here the matter would have ended had Chen not encountered trouble in her quest to reach the Soviet Union.

To cover her travel expenses, Qu and other senior comrades had taken up a personal collection. They soon raised the $200 she needed, including a $20 contribution from Mao Zedong. In the meantime, Qu had sensed that her spirits were ebbing, so he suggested she move in with him, where he could presumably exert maximum influence over her—and add another adoring young woman to his growing collection.

For Chen, living in the Qu household was a rich but confusing experience. Qu had arranged life to be materially pleasant, socially amusing, and intellectually stimulating. But she was also dismayed because Qu seemed to be carried away in love. He was involved with not one but two politically questionable women, who, she said, "had an abnormally intimate, lesbian relationship," and were both "madly in love with Qu." And Qu,

> being a leader of the Chinese Communist Party, not only did not correct the anarchism in the thinking and behavior of his wife and Ting Ping-chih [Ding Ling], but himself joined them and followed their extreme liberalism and their hedonistic, decadent, indulgent tendencies. During that time, they made no attempt to advance themselves, but spent the whole day diverting themselves with going to the opera, drinking and talking about love. At times, they all buried their heads in bitter weeping. Their emotions were in a very abnormal state. Although Qu's younger brother was in ardent pursuit of Ting Ping-chih and the two were already living together, Ting said in public that she did not love him at all, that it was only a diversion out of loneliness and boredom. In reality, she was in love with Qu Qiubai. In short, their life had fallen completely into decadence, dissoluteness, love triangle, and abnormal amour.[32]

Chen connected Qu's decadent lifestyle with his advocacy of the United Front: ideological and personal promiscuity were all of a piece, in her mind.[33]

Though in retrospect Chen struck a judgmental tone, she also admits that, at the time, she too had great affection for Qu. Like other young women in his circle, she felt singled out by him, had endless admiration for his intellectual abilities—and found any evidence of imperfection on his part disturbing. As for Qu, he continually urged her to apply herself to her studies, even writing a letter to her from Guangdong while he was in the midst of United Front work with the Nationalists, encouraging her to focus on her Russian. In the spring of 1924, Party founder Li Dazhao and others were preparing to attend the fifth congress of the Comintern in Moscow, and it was decided that Chen could go with them. On the eve of her departure, Qu called her in for a special talk, ostensibly warning her of all the dangers, but in the process leading her to affirm her absolute devotion to the journey.[34]

Qu's Anna Karenina

Just after Chen moved out of Qu's house to begin her journey to Moscow, Qu remarried, surprising everyone with the speed of his recovery from the death of the wife whom he had loved so ostentatiously. Chen remembers how one day before she left, the former chairman of the Zhejiang Provincial Parliament (Zhejiang was Qu's birthplace) came to visit Qu.[35] This man was a large landholder, active in the May Fourth movement, and had even visited the Soviet Union. He brought his daughter-in-law, Yang Zhihua. Within months of this visit, Yang had divorced her husband and married Qu.

Yang had first encountered Qu when she attended his lectures as a student at Shangda. Now she had become involved in women's politics and one day was asked to report to Borodin about the Party's work with women in Shanghai. Yang was very nervous and surprised when she arrived to see Qu, who had come to translate for her. "The minute I saw him I felt I had help," she recalled. "I started to calm down. Qiubai used fluent Russian to talk with them, they asked him lots of questions, he translated for me to hear, and also advised me, first you write these questions down and think." Yang noticed that even though Qu called this translation "small" work, he did it "very carefully." This man who had appeared so formidable in class suddenly seemed "modest" and "warm" close up.[36]

Yang, for her part, was "pretty, gentle, soft-hearted, clever, able," well known for being one of the most beautiful of all women comrades. And she was unhappily married, according to the arrangement of her progressive father, to a man who openly loved a Korean woman. When Yang nonetheless had a daughter by this husband, she named the girl Duyi, or lonely. Yang desperately wanted out of her marriage, and divorce was a stigmatizing act even for a radical woman whose husband was eager to be rid of her. Yang's progressive father notified the public of his daughter's change in relationship status by taking out two ads in a Shanghai newspaper. One announced Yang and Qu's marriage, and the other that Qu and Yang's former husband had become friends.[37]

Qu Qiubai and Yang Zhihua. RGASPI, f. 495, op. 225, d. 1014, l. 15.

After their marriage, Yang began to perceive that Qu had a solid imaginary foundation for their relationship. Yang's in-laws had refused to allow
her to bring her daughter to Shanghai with her. Once, she sneaked a visit to
their home and discovered that her daughter had been told she was dead.
When she returned, Qu comforted her by telling her the story of Anna
Karenina, assuring her that, though Anna's situation had turned out badly,
Yang would eventually be happy, because there was going to be a revolution in China. But Qu didn't stop there. He plotted with Yang to kidnap
her daughter. Although the plot failed, the in-laws eventually relented and
Duyi was allowed to move to Shanghai to live with Qu and her mother.[38] Qu
adopted her, and she remembers him as a warm father.

Yang Zhihua, Qu Duyi, and Qu Qiubai.

Shortly after Yang and Qu married, the May 30th protests broke out. Qu stayed home writing propaganda for a new periodical called *Hot Blood Daily*, short-lived but so popular that the printers couldn't get the issues out fast enough. Yang, however, took to the streets, helping major communist labor organizers like Li Lisan by serving as a liaison to female workers. Each day, Yang put on the coarse clothing of a worker, which was, she remembers, Qu's favorite thing. Each night, he waited for her to come home and tell him stories about her encounters with the proletariat.[39]

A Russia Lover

Shortly after Chen Bilan left for Beijing, where a group of prospective students gathered to depart for Moscow, disaster struck. Her boyfriend Huang organized an elaborate farewell banquet in her honor and, along with his friends, insisted that she stay out into the wee hours, while the others departing for the journey went home. That night, the police arrested the other would-be students and carried off Chen's trunks, including her money and travel documents. While she had escaped arrest, jail time might have been less traumatic than what happened next: her grand plans to go to the Soviet

Union completely foiled, Chen was stranded in Beijing and finally succumbed to Huang's charms.[40]

Several months of intense emotional turmoil followed for Chen, whose romantic longings were so abstract that no flesh and blood man could possibly fulfill them.

> Those few months, I felt at the time, were wasted. Love, I felt, was also superfluous, and had happened by chance. And yet, because of the period of friendship we had gone through, it was not entirely by chance: it was the result of the extremely complicated state our lives were in. Although it was my first love, I did not feel any of the intense happiness and delight of young love; my feeling did not even equal the naive, idealistic feeling of love I had when we first knew each other, and exchanged letters. Although he was an elegant, lively, intellectual with a standard build and a debonair manner, yet, because at that time I so much wanted to study, and was so keen on going to the Soviet Union, I did not consider love very important, and for that reason I was not enthusiastic about enjoying the delight and warmth of love. . . . Yet at the same time, I thought of how consoling and considerate he had been when I was in extreme anguish, at a time when I suffered the worst blow I had ever received, and how he was unselfishly making preparations to help me go to the Soviet Union, and I felt extremely moved.[41]

After the police confiscated Chen's things, Huang raised $300 from his family and friends so that she could make her trip and began planning an engagement party, to which he hoped she would invite some of her family.

Chen happily accepted the $300 but declined the engagement party. She moved in with Huang, with the understanding that after her three years of study in the Soviet Union they could have a "normal private life." But Chen was deeply conflicted about even this compromise and devoted herself completely to studying Russian. At first, a Russian from the Soviet embassy came to her house every day to tutor her; then, a Chinese comrade just back from the Soviet Union took his place. "Only in this way was I relieved of my state of inner contradiction."[42]

Finally, Chen had another opportunity to go to Russia. In the fall of 1924, a large group of students were departing for study in Moscow and Germany, among them several of Huang's friends. Huang gathered a merry party to see her off in style; when it came time for her to board her train, they all got on with her for fun and only scampered off when the train began to move. But Huang didn't jump down with all the others; he sat by her side, stretching these last moments all the way to the first suburban stop outside Beijing. Only then did he say goodbye, walking a long way before finding a rickshaw to carry him home.[43]

7

Chiang Kaishek's Son in Red Wonderland

WHILE QU, EMI, and other men who made up China's first communist generation had already returned from their coming-of-age journeys to Russia, a second wave of young people were about to set off with revolutionary aspirations and agendas of their own. It included not only the first Chinese women to go to Moscow to study, but also a second cohort of younger men whose first political engagement was during 1925, not 1919.

Whereas the radicalization of the older men had occurred in an atmosphere of ideologically vague elite ferment, the younger ones were growing up in the midst of mass unrest. Popular protests electrified radical intellectuals with new hopes of class-based uprisings, whose historical possibilities were being articulated in increasingly specific terms, thanks to the labors of Borodin, Qu, and others like them. Qu could have mistaken his trip for a footnote to the great, ancient Chinese *Journey to the West*, and in fact framed it as a modern "Journey to the Land of Hunger" to make it understandable to his readers, but these younger people were in no doubt that their travels to Russia were the prelude to an entirely new story that would have to be written in a new language, with new heroes.

Urban middle schools and normal schools were ripe with prospective pilgrims, but one particular boy's long journey to and within Russia appears to have been as much through history as to a place, with an itinerary composed of major events in the young Sino-Soviet relationship. His own life became a singular expression of that romance, and he cast and recast the story of his journey.

This boy was the fifteen-year-old son of Chiang Kaishek, Jiang Jingguo. Jiang eventually became "Kolia," and even "Kolia-kitaets" to the Russian peasants who befriended him. The process by which Jiang became Kolia was truly fantastic, as was the whole twelve-year Russian episode in the life of the man who would ultimately become Jiang Jingguo, the president of Taiwan.[1]

Son of Chiang Kaishek

In 1925, Jiang was a middle school student in Shanghai. At that point, Chiang Kaishek still very much supported the alliance with the Soviet Union. Jiang was so young when he went to Moscow—at fifteen, he was the youngest student at the university—that he had had little opportunity to make his own decisions.[2]

Jiang had been born in 1910 in Jiangsu province, to his father's first wife, the sort of village girl that so many revolutionaries dreaded. In 1922, Jiang left for Shanghai where he met his stepmother, only five years his senior. She later remembered her first impression of him: "Although young, the boy had closely cropped hair, a square, heavy face that somewhat resembled his [peasant] mother's, a high forehead, large mouth, and prominent buckteeth. He seemed a well-behaved, quiet and docile lad, but far too nervous and ill at ease." She noted that as soon as his father left the room, Jiang relaxed considerably.[3]

In his father's absence, Jiang attended middle school, was swept up in the fervor of the May 30th Movement, and was expelled from school for his participation in it. He then left Shanghai for Beijing, where he attended a foreign language school for the sons and daughters of Nationalist Party officials. He continued to participate in anti-government agitation, for which he was confined by school officials for two weeks. Once he was free, he headed south to Guangzhou to see his father.[4] A few months later, Jiang was on a boat to Vladivostok.

Because Jiang's arrival in the Soviet Union had so much to do with his environment and his family, and because Jiang's independent personal development so clearly began in Moscow, perhaps the best introduction to him comes from a classmate's description of the first time he met Jiang. One night in 1925, shortly after the school opened and students were still getting acquainted, several were preparing to go to sleep, when Chinese Nationalist Party representative Shao Lizi walked into his dorm room and introduced himself. Shao was going to be an honorary student and would eventually send his son there, so he'd come to scout out the school—and also, it seems, to introduce another student. Shao went around the room shaking hands with each student by his bed,

and behind him there was a child, 15 or 16 years old, wearing a
leather jacket and a peaked cap, not tall, just about five foot, but
solid as a rock, coming in from the street all bouncing and lively.
Xu Junhu wanted to ask, who is this kid? That kid actually came
up to Xu on his own, conducting himself normally and properly,
extended his hand, and in a Ningbo accent, said, "I'm Jiang Jingguo,
we're classmates!"[5]

Jiang was apparently eager both to shed his heritage and to trade on it. His
straightforward ease with a group of older strangers, his impression of solid-
ity and energy, and the simple way in which he acknowledged his status ("I'm
Jiang Jingguo") and then swept it aside ("we're classmates!") were traits that
Jiang would display repeatedly. In the Soviet Union, directness, vitality, and
egalitarianism were all markers of good character.

Jiang Jingguo in Moscow. Courtesy of the KMT Party Archives Library, Culture and
Communications Committee, Central Committee of the Kuomintang.

Chinese University

The school that Jiang attended was brand new and very different from the one Emi, Qu, and Peng had attended. The walk from the old Eastern University to the new Sun Yatsen University (also referred to here as Chinese University) took less than an hour: from Strastnaia Square down Tverskaia toward the Kremlin, along the Manezh, and up toward Christ the Savior Church. But the distance between these two educational institutions could only properly be understood in terms of the historical and ideological arc of Russia's international revolution.

Karl Radek, the rector of Chinese University, had been one step ahead of these revolutionary changes. Radek was a Jew from modern-day Ukraine. He participated in the 1905 revolution in Warsaw and then moved to Germany and joined the Social Democratic Party, returning to Russia with Lenin in 1917. By 1918, he was back in Germany, working with great flexibility, wit, and cynicism for the German revolution that was the hope and dream of all Soviet internationalists after 1917. Radek was an early proponent of the United Front, and continually kept awkward coalitions together.[6]

Ultimately, Radek was partially blamed for the defeat of the German revolution and had to act with great circumspection to prevent complete political disgrace. His appointment as rector of Chinese University was an indicator of his status: demoted, but still in the game. It made perfect sense, since in 1925, China was the new Germany, or so diehard Soviet internationalists tried to convince themselves.

Students at Chinese University benefited in every way from Soviet optimism about the Chinese revolution. The university was first organized not under the management of the Ministry of Education like other schools, nor of the Ministry of Nationalities like Eastern University; it was jointly managed by the Central Executive Committees of the Russian Communist Party and the Chinese Nationalist Party.[7] By now, when the Comintern was in full "Bolshevization" mode and actively subjugating foreign communist parties, offering the Nationalists such control was unusual. And no other national revolutionary movement had its own institute of higher education in Moscow.

There was also a Society in Support of Chinese University, with a board chaired by A. Joffe, a high-ranking Soviet diplomat who had been at Brest-Litovsk and who had signed the original Soviet agreement of cooperation with Sun Yatsen. Other board members were Bukharin, Lenin's widow Krupskaia, Radek, and Eastern University rector Broido. Like Eastern University, Chinese University was located in a beautiful Tsarist-era building, but it was extraordinarily well funded.[8]

At first, students at Chinese University were fed five meals a day. They were so stuffed that they actually requested the cancellation of their afternoon tea and night snack. Breakfast alone was eggs, bread and butter, sausages, milk, black tea, and sometimes caviar. They had a constant and steady supply of chicken, duck, fish, and meat, and when they eventually tired of Russian food the school hired a Chinese chef for them, so they could choose Russian or Chinese meals. It took most students some time to figure out that their own standard of living widely diverged from that of the Soviet people around them; they were often scolded, and tensions over lights left on at night in the dorms or crusts of bread thrown away in the cafeteria left student-employee relations tense.[9]

When Chinese University students arrived, they were given "a suit, a coat, a pair of shoes, towels, washcloths, handkerchiefs, shirts, combs, shoe polish, soap, a toothbrush, toothpaste, and all else that one might need in everyday life." Chinese University students could even afford to be fashionable, Russian-style, favoring "high buttoned Lenin jackets or the popular violet Ukrainian style shirts that buttoned up the left side."[10]

Well-fed, well-clothed, the Chinese University students were showered with attention from elite and ordinary Soviet citizens alike. Trotsky came to the opening of the school and announced, "From now on a Russian, be he a comrade or a citizen, who greets a Chinese student with an air of contempt, shrugging his shoulders, is not entitled to be either a Russian Communist or a Soviet citizen." While the Chinese still suffered derisive treatment from some strangers on the street, they were also the beneficiaries of popular goodwill that grew along with mass awareness of the revolutionary situation in southern China. For the hundreds of male students at the school, this translated into a surfeit of female attention. Chinese men at Eastern University had been limited to speculation and furtive exploration regarding Russian women, but Chinese University students commanded attention specifically because they were Chinese.[11]

If these young Chinese students were the recipients of all the best that New Economic Policy–era Moscow had to offer, it might have been partly because by 1925 the Chinese revolution had captured the imaginations of the Soviet leadership at the highest levels. That March, the Politburo of the Russian Communist Party created a "Chinese Commission" to oversee military assistance to the Nationalists, and its chairmen were high-profile generals like Frunze and Voroshilov, as well as secret police vice-chair Unshlikht.[12]

Stalin, Trotsky, and many others had already begun the tortured process of projecting their revolutionary theories, fantasies, and machinations onto China. Stalin conceived a China strategy that involved infiltrating the Nationalist Party with communists, who would transform it into a true revolutionary party—an idea in play at Chinese University and back in China as well. Trotsky, on the other hand, became the darling of the Chinese communist core by prophesying an imminent proletarian revolution and downplaying the importance of nationalism. Stalin and Trotsky both came to speak at Chinese University, as did many other high-ranking celebrity guests, to the delight and fascination of the students.[13]

Jiang's Fairy Tale of Red Moscow

By Jiang's own account, his earliest days in the Soviet Union were full of wonder and curiosity about socialist Moscow, which seemed peopled by workers and soldiers filled with hope for the Chinese revolution. Or else Jiang was full of surprise about the poverty of Siberia and skepticism toward the staged enthusiasm of Soviet people for the Chinese revolution.

Jiang produced two memoirs of his twelve years in the Soviet Union. One, published in English, was called *My Days in Soviet Russia* and is a perfect piece of anti-communist propaganda. The other, *My Life in Soviet Russia*, was published in Chinese, though Jiang may have first written it in Russian and then had it translated.[14] *My Life* lacks the style, ambition, and intimacy of Qu's *History of the Heart*, but it is nevertheless a treasure trove of Sino-Soviet relations. Like Qu's *History, My Life* is supposed to be diary excerpts, peppered with long quotations from other texts, such as essays that Jiang wrote or notes he took during lectures. *My Life* consists of thirteen sample diary entries, one for every year he spent in the Soviet Union (1925–1937). Each entry ostensibly describes a single day, but in fact seems to be a composite designed to convey generic aspects of his experiences and changes in his mindset over time.

What is most striking about Jiang's two accounts of his time in the Soviet Union is the way in which they encapsulate two opposing ideas of "the Soviet experience." In one rendition, Jiang, momentarily swayed by peer pressure to go to the Soviet Union, is miserable there, thinking only of his homeland and his family, but keeping his true feelings secret in the interests of survival. In the other version, Jiang is a communist enthusiast, focused on understanding and fitting into the Soviet system, learning to speak its jargon, examining himself from its perspective, and writing himself into its narrative as he comes to understand it.

In this way a Chinese, the son of Chiang Kaishek no less, captures the paradoxes of Soviet autobiographers—who wrote according to context, necessity, and preference, instinctively grasping the difference between conflicting versions of their own lives, but not quite sure which to use in mapping the surreal psychological terrain of their Soviet existence. There was a crucial difference: for Jiang, physical exit was always at least a possibility. If regular Soviet autobiographers did not have or perceive the option of escape, how sure can we be of our judgments about them? Put another way, how convincing are an autobiographer's attempts to write himself into a society if he feels he has no option to write himself out of it?[15] What is remarkable about Jiang as a Soviet autobiographer is that he wrote both of his accounts after he had left the Soviet Union, adding yet another level of complexity to questions about the relationship between coercion and belief in communist systems.

Jiang's anti-communist account was silent regarding his first impressions of Moscow and Chinese University, but on December 3, 1925, the pro-communist Jiang wakes up early. He goes with the most enthusiastic Chinese students for the morning exercises in the Christ the Savior courtyard that were supposed to begin the model day of a Chinese University student. It is –39 degrees Celsius and there are three feet of snow on the ground, but in Jiang's short time in Moscow, he has already come to feel that without rigorous calisthenics, his "spirit doesn't feel sharp."[16]

Walking along Volkhonka on his way back to campus, Jiang experiences a moment of embarrassment. It's almost eight AM now and there are

more and more pedestrians on the street, gaggles of workers go quickly toward the factories on the banks of the Moscow river, students with book bags head towards MGU [Moscow State University]. You can't see a single idle person on the street. The street at this time seems like a big swirling river. From behind a big group of Red Army soldiers comes, singing solemn military songs, and passes by the school gate. This is the first time I saw Red Army soldiers, their spirit is magnificent.

At the time I was ignorant and I asked a Russian friend, why aren't the Red Army soldiers' uniforms red? And my friend answered, it's red in an ideological sense, because red is the color of communism, the army serves communism so it's called the Red Army. Hearing my friend's explanation I realized how naive I was about the Soviet Union, and I felt ashamed.[17]

Jiang may or may not have been exaggerating his naiveté. Travelers often bring such latent assumptions, and many experience the disorientation Jiang describes, which comes with the realization of the distance between the "imaginary" place they have brought and the "real" place they encounter.

Jiang returns to his dorm where he's "on duty," checking that all eleven of his roommates have made their beds properly. He washes, with cold running water in a sink, instead of a washbasin, a minor difference in daily life that Jiang notes "lots of students" weren't accustomed to "at first."[18] He goes to breakfast where he finds that "no portion is better or worse than any other, they are all strictly regulated," and appreciates the "décor" of the cafeteria— the fresh flowers and portraits of Lenin and Sun Yatsen. And then he has the first of several conversations with people whom he initially takes for "ignorant persons" before learning that they belong to that most exalted of Soviet categories: workers.

While the other students use their free hour after breakfast to read, Jiang becomes acquainted with the boy who stokes the heater in their classroom— Ivanov. Ivanov had been a metalworker making 65 rubles a month. Now as a student at Moscow State University he lives on a stipend of 20 rubles but enjoys a free education. Jiang feels a pang of guilt when he learns that this boy had only black bread and potatoes for breakfast. But Ivanov says he has nothing to be ashamed of: "You are China's revolutionary youth, our only hope for you is that you can liberate the Chinese people quickly." Jiang subsequently becomes friends with Ivanov and practices his Russian with him.[19]

Jiang has three classes on December 3, 1925: social science, economics, and Russian. He gives an oral report in social science class, faithfully reproducing almost two pages of his elementary ruminations on the process of labor specialization in prehistoric times.

After class, Jiang goes shopping with his friends. Upon seeing the clear difference between national stores and private traders, he asks an unnamed Russian friend why the proletarian Soviet Union allows traders. The Russian friend gives him a stock explanation of Lenin's more liberal New Economic Policy. Jiang and his friends choose several items to buy in a state store and become impatient about how long it takes the clerk to tally their bill, complaining that such transactions are a lot quicker in China.

It turns out the shop clerk is also a worker, a blacksmith no less, sent by his factory's party branch to study. "Today I count slowly but tomorrow I'll count quickly; today the country is weak, tomorrow it will be strong . . . you have to know our party decides everything, you do what they tell you to do, you don't decide your own individual life."

In the late afternoon, a trip to the museum of the Russian Revolution has been scheduled for the students. When the Chinese board the trolley, a worker offers his seat to Jiang, saying, "You are the guests, we are the hosts." Through the translator accompanying them, Jiang replies, "We are all equal, please don't give up your seat." Meanwhile, a soldier is busy giving his seat to an elderly woman and helping her to buy a ticket. When Jiang gets back to campus, he attends a small group discussion of "The Chinese Revolution and Our Responsibility."

After dinner, Jiang goes to a Chinese University-Moscow State University mixer where there are official welcome speeches and a dance that lasts until midnight. Before going to sleep, Jiang—who despite being the youngest student in the school and having just arrived has apparently already assumed responsibilities as editor of the school's newspaper—writes an article, in Chinese, titled, "Revolution first requires a change of heart." Then he goes to sleep.[20] A perfect day at Chinese University, and, as far as Jiang's published record of his life in the Soviet Union goes, the only day at Chinese University.

Jiang's First Girlfriend

Of all that he omitted from his accounts of life at Chinese University, one of the most sensational facts is that fifteen-year-old Jiang had a politically incorrect first relationship with Feng Funeng, the daughter of the "Christian warlord," Feng Yuxiang. Far from being a colorful footnote to the history of the school and of Sino-Soviet relations, such affairs were a historically meaningful element of life at Chinese University.

Chinese University rector Radek was in the midst of the most romantic affair of his life while he was at Chinese University, and he set the tone for the school. Radek was married but he had a history of infidelity and seemed to be really in love with Larissa Reisner. Reisner was a revolutionary supposedly so lovely as to inspire paeans of praise from the likes of Trotsky and Lenin, and snide comments from Stalin. Radek installed Larissa as a teacher of Russian language and culture at the school. Actually, several of the Russian teachers appear to have been pretty young women, whose "attitude and teaching methods were lovely" as one student remembers, which meant that "progress in Russian was really quick."[21]

This period of Radek's life may have been an idyllic interlude dominated by the unexpected novelty of a Chinese revolution and by Larissa. Radek threw himself into his work at Chinese University, learning quite a bit about China and impressing his students with the breadth of his knowledge and his extemporaneous speaking skills. With Radek, the students felt themselves in the hands of an experienced revolutionary who genuinely cared about China and the Chinese revolution.[22]

Politically, the fact that Radek was close to Trotsky had a significant influence on the students at Chinese University, some of whom became dedicated Trotskyists. Radek also encouraged the students to follow his lead in their personal lives. At first there was no co-ed dorm, so Radek designated a special room, supposedly for husbands and wives. It was clear that the room was there for any couple who might wander into it. One student who later took issue with this "special boudoir" complained that Chinese University students developed "an aversion to decency."[23]

Even back in China, these revolutionaries were busy conflating love and revolution, experimenting with new kinds of relationships just as they experimented with new kinds of politics. Russia, as the revolutionary country par excellence, was heavily romanticized by Chinese before they departed China. Once they arrived, they discovered a culture in the throes of a great debate over the proper place of love and sex under communism, with frequent discussions in Youth League meetings and the Soviet press of practices ranging from celibacy to free love.[24] Stories of the affairs Chinese students were having in Moscow quickly filtered back to China, so that young revolutionaries came to associate Moscow with exciting romance and/or easy sex in concrete terms.[25]

Chinese University was ground zero for Sino-Soviet romance at its most overt. Although there were numerous liaisons between Chinese men and Russian women, in many cases, Chinese students also fell in love or had casual affairs with other Chinese students. Jiang's relationship with Feng Funeng was a case in point. It almost seems that Jiang and Feng were a match made in a Comintern strategy meeting, for at this point every effort was being made to attract Feng's father to the Nationalists. Feng came to Moscow with her father, who spent several months there in 1924 in negotiations with the Comintern and left her to attend Chinese University.

Feng was fourteen when her father dropped her off in Moscow. She was pretty and flirtatious, and in letters she wrote Jiang while they were apart, she mocked him for being "lovelorn," teased him with mentions of other boys who wanted to "fool around" with her, and suggested that he do as his friends do, and find a foreign girlfriend. Feng was much more interested in her romance with Jiang than in politics, and she was always more excited about going out to eat or hearing what movies Jiang had seen than in politics or schoolwork.[26]

And yet, at Chinese University, this was a hard profile to maintain. As Feng remembered it,

> when I first entered the school my main goal really wasn't to gain an understanding of politics, but rather to achieve my personal goals (studying Russian language and other things), regardless of my father's reasons for sending me. But nearly every aspect of life in our school is completely politicized. No matter how you may want to avoid politics, it will slowly seep into your brain.[27]

Feng's experience at Chinese University and her romance with Jiang underscore the tensions inherent in the Soviet concept of the Chinese United Front. The presence at Chinese University of girls like Feng and other young women—apolitical wives and daughters—suggests a pragmatic acceptance of all sorts of taboos. But these girls nevertheless felt increasing pressure to politicize. One such young woman remembers how she arrived in the Soviet Union with her father—and a long braid down her back. Once she started attending the school, the other young women sporting communist bobs "snickered" at her, and suddenly combing all that hair seemed like a bother. With her father's permission, she cut her braid.[28]

These women were there as concessions to the men who were the real Soviet targets—the Comintern didn't necessarily care about converting them to communism—and yet they found themselves overwhelmed by the milieu of the school. They experienced the ambiguities of the United Front in an intensely personal way: was it okay for them to read novels, keep their hair long, and be objects of attraction, or should they cut their hair and read *Pravda*? Was the Soviet Union serious when it conceded that the Chinese revolution had to be national first, or was this rhetoric to disguise an unambiguous international communist agenda? If historians can't decide even after reading thousands of pages of stultifying documents and ideological claptrap, how could a carefree fifteen-year-old girl Feng or an earnest sixteen-year-old Jiang be expected to know in 1926?

The same atmosphere that made long hair a bother also made Jiang attractive to Feng. Jiang was not only the son of a father every bit as illustrious and important as her own but also, as his "December 3, 1925" diary entry suggests, a politically and socially active young man. By all accounts Jiang was an eager student and a serious politician. Jiang had already joined the Communist Youth League (Komsomol) in December of 1925, and his evaluation at that point noted that he worked on the newspaper, was the secretary of the Komsomol's propaganda group, and was a member of the Komsomol's bureau of party cells. He was also active in non-political extracurricular activities, serving on the school club's board and doing maintenance work at the club. Curiously, the other Chinese student noted as a good political worker by Russian authorities at the time was Deng Xiaoping, whose leadership skills exceeded Jiang's.[29]

Jiang offers an apologetic account of his enormous enthusiasm for politics in his anti-communist memoir:

In the Sun Yat-Sen University, antipathy for some students who were members of the Kuomintang [Nationalist Party] was aroused because of their improper activities. People sometimes thought that members of the Communist Party were better behaved and their activities more promising. The Chinese Communist Party had a branch office in Moscow and its organization and methods of training were very well arranged. Its members were close-knit, strictly supervised and always acted under the direction of the centralized leadership. They all lived frugal and disciplined lives. Therefore, for a moment, I became more interested in their activities and in December 1925, a few weeks after arriving in Russia, I joined the so-called Communist Youth Corps.[30]

In his political evaluation, Jiang was described as "holding firm political positions," "disciplined," with "good theoretical knowledge," but being a bit inclined toward opposition and to stubborn insistence on his own views.[31]

Either Jiang was temporarily influenced and distracted by communist politics, or he was actually a rather promising member of the Komsomol.

But to Feng, Jiang had assimilated to this new, politically charged environment, unlike her.

> Comrade Jingguo! Why is it that meeting you has had such a big influence on me? Such a hardworking person as you with such a fun-loving person like me is really no good, huh? Comrade Jingguo, every time I get a letter from you I really like it, do you know why? Because in every letter you write about how I should study hard. If I'm still such a useless person in the future, I'm really not qualified to be your friend and comrade.[32]

In fact, Jiang eventually came under pressure from his Komsomol friends to break off his relationship with Feng, which had apparently gotten serious enough to warrant the term "jie he," meaning unite, or possibly, marry. Feng, realizing her difficulties, tried to join the Komsomol, but it was too late. A friend of Jiang's advised him:

> Marrying Feng is no doubt a mistake. Hoping that one day she'll become a Communist, and that someday in the future you'll regain your former happiness—it's impossible. There are so many good women in the world, you don't need to keep filthy her in your mind. You said you wanted to talk less and read more. This is of course one way to relieve boredom, but if you need sex urgently, I thought you might also find another woman, to help you give up that dirty girl completely.[33]

Feng herself became lovelorn—"Sometimes at night I dream that you and I, plus Li, Zhao, Qu, Wu and a bunch of people are out having fun, eating, then I wake up and it was just a dream"—and eventually apparently depressed.

> My life is boring and I sleep a lot. . . . It's hopeless, I'm as good as dead. . . . I'm sorry so many people criticize you, saying you're a member of the Komsomol and shouldn't associate with me. I know this.[34]

Later, when she was expelled from the school and Jiang was trying to distance himself from her, he explained the relationship in fluent Bolshevik, "She was given an assignment from her father and wanted to politically work me over. At that time I wanted to politically work her over. Of course, nothing came of this." All that political working over must have had its attractions, though, because Jiang's relationship with Feng lasted two years, despite his official renunciations of her.[35]

The "Rafailovshchina"

For some radical Chinese communist students, the atmosphere of political and personal promiscuity at Chinese University was just too much, and they rebelled by starting a puritanical movement that protested the very terms of the Sino-Soviet romance. Their rebellion was later given a half-whimsical, half-ominous name by the Russian authorities who eventually "uncovered" it: the Rafailovshchina.[36]

The Rafailovshchina had its roots in the activities and mentalities of the Moscow branch of the Chinese Communist Party that Peng had originally founded at Eastern University and that was still vibrant in 1925. The branch underwent several changes in leadership after Peng left, but its basic operating principles remained the same. "Rafail" was the Russian pseudonym of a Chinese student from France named Ren Zhuoxuan, who arrived in Moscow to study at Eastern University in 1925, gained prominence in the Chinese party branch, and then transferred to Chinese University. There, he took charge of party work and continued the practice of frequent small group meetings among the students, where they were encouraged to discuss their personal faults and political progress. In fact, after Chinese University opened in 1925, Moscow's Chinese students were divided, with most at Chinese University and some still at Eastern University. Yet they visited each other frequently, shared news, and more or less remained a single, quarrelsome community.[37]

"Rafail"—who unlike most other students in Moscow in the mid-1920s, was from a working-class background—surveyed the situation at Chinese University, where all lectures were conducted in translation and the course of study was two years, and asked an obvious question: why should the students spend so much time learning Russian? Wasn't the important thing to grasp the basics of revolutionary theory and go home as quickly as possible to participate in the Chinese revolution? And why should the students be divided along party lines, with the Chinese Communist Party students spending so much time trying to recruit the Nationalist students, when they were all supposed to be part of one unified, Chinese revolutionary movement? Rafail himself decided to forget about learning Russian and didn't participate in the many cultural activities designed to acquaint young Chinese with the country around them. "Lenin's tomb—I never went," he recalled.[38]

Rafail and like-minded members of the Moscow party branch began to agitate among the students and even produced a long manifesto, some of which read:

> Systematize thought and study—oppose romanticism. Romanticism is a condition that destroys organization.... We should destroy family, local, and national concepts—the proletariat has no family, no local or national limitations.... Destroy unity based on sentiment— sentimental unity is petty bourgeois unity.... We must employ in our work for the Party the same kind of interest we have in love and literature—love and literature are the foundations of romanticism.... We must studiously avoid academic-type study—academic-type study denies that theory is born of practice.... We must at all times prepare ourselves to return to our country to participate in actual revolutionary work.... We absolutely must not maintain the erroneous idea that we should first study Russian before we study ideology.... We must at all times and everywhere mutually correct each other's errors of thought and actions.... We must have the psychology of thoroughly trusting the organization ... there is absolutely no such thing as individual life or individual free will.[39]

In his own account of his repressive campaign, written many years later, after he had gone over to the Nationalists, Rafail admitted that while in Moscow he was in love and downplayed his antipathy to the Russian language. But other students remember an intimidating struggle waged against them, so that they felt they had to hide not just their enthusiasm for love and literature but even their studies of the Russian language from their zealous classmates. At the height of Rafail's movement, students came under attack for reading a book, being friendly with Russians, and simple conversations with female students.[40]

Most students weren't quite sure what to make of the competing theories about the relationship between the Russian and Chinese revolutions. Was

Marxism-Leninism a universally applicable, scientific theory, a set of formulas that could be learned in any language and applied in any culture if historical conditions were right? If so, why not learn them as quickly as possible in translation, get home, and get busy? Or was there something irreducibly Russian about revolution, something revolutionary about Russia, its language and its people? If so, what could be more revolutionary than spending all one's time studying the language and flirting with Marfa, the proletarian cafeteria worker who had a string of Chinese competing for her affections?[41] Not only did students not agree among themselves about the rules that should govern their behavior, but each individual student was often torn between conflicting priorities. Jiang, for example, admired the discipline of the Moscow branch of the Chinese Communist Party, but he still couldn't get enough of Feng.

Another study in contrasts was Chen Bilan. On the surface, it would appear that Chen would naturally fall in line with the Moscow party branch. Chen was the opposite of Feng, a real radical who had cut her own hair back in China and was already a member of the Chinese Communist Party. She had vowed chastity and had thrown over a perfectly good suitor in order to come to the Soviet Union. Chen tried hard to please her new male mentors in Moscow, who read her correspondence with Huang and repeatedly harangued her for it. She wrote to Huang criticizing his bourgeois tendencies, and Huang, ever polite, wrote back expressing his appreciation for her suggestions. But, as she remembers it,

> every letter he wrote to me thereafter . . . was still filled with descriptions expressing his affection; because of this he was criticized severely by all the members of the Moscow Chinese Communist Party branch. . . . They said he was a typical example of a petty bourgeois, a "love above all" romantic, and not a serious revolutionary. In that atmosphere of heavy academic pressure, this serious criticism of him by the whole committee was a great blow to my morale, and destroyed almost half of my feeling for him. After this, conflict between emotion and reason began in me. Each time a letter from him arrived, the criticism of him became more severe. And his enclosing a finely-embroidered handkerchief for me in one of his letters was criticized particularly severely. . . . I told him not to waste so much time writing letters and, especially, not to send any more handkerchiefs, because I did not need them.[42]

But the Moscow branch of the Chinese Communist Party continued to harass Chen about Huang, and Chen nearly broke down under the pressure.

At least one of the members of the Moscow party branch who threatened Chen in the name of communist morality had ulterior motives. He pursued Chen relentlessly and unsuccessfully, which she omitted from her own account. Chen left Moscow after just one year. Back in China, she met and married none other than Peng Shuzhi, who had only just extricated himself from a complicated love triangle with a married communist, Xiang Jingyu. So heated was the rivalry between Peng and Xiang's husband Cai Hesen that the party leadership—including Qu Qiubai and the womanizing Chen Duxiu—got involved. They broke up the Peng-Xiang relationship, leaving Peng so broken-hearted he allegedly wandered around with a bottle of liquor in his pocket, until he met Chen. The party packed Cai and Xiang off to Moscow, where Xiang took up with a Mongolian student and Cai began an affair of his own.[43]

Observers noted that while many of the Chinese women in Moscow really were strong young people with independent minds who made their own personal and political decisions, others were less so. "Moscow, at the time, was a hive of 'flag-switching,' by which I mean that women with lovers back in China were dropping them for men in Moscow," recalled one student. "The men whose lovers were away in Moscow . . . considered themselves threatened. Comrades who came back to China after attending meetings in Moscow often used to tell stories about the Moscow love scene." Some of the legendary "flag-switching" on the part of Chinese women in Moscow may have been a result of intense pressure from the men around them, who outnumbered them and tended to develop bitter rivalries over them.[44]

Feng Funeng, for example, came under pressure from several male classmates even though she was known to be the girlfriend of Jiang Jingguo. She became so irritated with young men who wanted to "fool around" with her and wrote her "nauseating" letters that she complained to Jiang about it. However smitten she was with Jiang, she was nonplussed about the brazen promiscuity of her classmates. "Everyone is pairing up. It's really tiresome. When they're living together they inevitably have children. There's already 12 who have given birth. There are still many who haven't had babies. The female comrades haven't come here to study, they have simply come to have babies."[45]

Although in many ways the romantic confusion of Chinese students mirrored and no doubt were influenced by similar Soviet controversies, it nevertheless captured the attention of Russian higher-ups, who felt a need to intervene. On the whole, the Russians were against the so-called Rafailovshchina, not only because it represented an alternative, all-Chinese authority structure and opposed the study of Russian but also because the Old Bolsheviks who, for the most part, managed the Chinese, felt it to be too puritanical. When Radek first got wind of the Rafailovshchina, he called Rafail into his office for a confrontation, which Ren Zhuoxuan recalled in his memoirs:

> Later the head of the school Radek found out about it and asked me and several others to come and talk. He emphasized studying Russian, reading Russian books, studying theory. When he spoke it was very witty, very amusing. . . . His manner of speaking was very vulgar, and made the female cadres sitting there laugh incessantly.[46]

Rafail was, in fact, impressed by Radek and even translated some of his lectures on the Chinese revolution and published them back in China. But the tendency that came to be called Rafailovshchina was too endemic to be coaxed down by one of Radek's flippant, racy exegeses. At the end of the 1925–1926 school year, Radek called a four-day meeting of the Chinese University student body, which he concluded by condemning the Rafailovshchina and pronouncing the Chinese Moscow Party Branch dissolved. Rafail and other leaders of his campaign were sent back to China. But conflict over the questions highlighted by Rafail's campaign continued unabated. The four-day summer meeting called in 1926 to "end" the "Rafailovshchina" became an annual affair, sometimes lasting as long as ten days.[47]

In early 1927, Lenin's widow was called to speak to the Chinese students on the topic. Krupskaia reportedly explained that communists needn't be puritans but should avoid play and abuse in love. She also advocated Russian literature and the family in her two-hour speech—and remained afterward for a small informal session with female students. Instead of repeatedly aborting, she said, Chinese women should give birth to their babies and leave them in Russian children's homes. Jiang's girlfriend, Feng, wittily concluded that having babies was "also making little revolutionaries."[48]

Even Krupskaia couldn't end the controversy over love, language, and literature. Of the thousands of pages that document the ongoing turmoil of the Chinese student community in Moscow, one of the most passionate was an anonymous article, handwritten in Chinese and posted on the wall at Eastern University in May of 1928. By this point the Chinese student community had been engulfed in serious political struggles. Not only did these fail to eclipse conflicts over more "trivial" issues like love and litera-ture, but they even seemed to intensify them. The Russians in charge noted that the Chinese expressed "heightened interest in squabbles and the sex question" and were suffering from "love fervor," while at least some Chinese complained about the amount of attention their classmates paid to male-female questions.[49]

The anonymous author of the journal article disagreed. He was respond-ing to an article titled 'No more young Werthers' that had referenced the novel by Goethe, popular at that time among young Chinese, to attack stu-dents' romanticism. The author titled his rebuttal, "Study, revolution, lit-erature, and love—After reading 'No more young Werthers.'" He began by pointing out, along Krupskaia's lines, that reading Russian novels wasn't nec-essarily bad for the revolution, especially if they were novels by Gorky, but his marching pace and political tone unraveled as he launched into a raw diatribe about love, sex, and revolution:

Finally, about the question of "Young Werther type" "introspective worry" love. Now people, unless they no longer have their private parts, all have sexual desires and excitement as well as the painful hopes and desires of love. So love is an uncontrollable element in the lives of people, and unhappiness in sex, although we can use all kinds of methods to lessen it, these all end up wilted flowers, unable to bear any fruit! . . . Unfortunately, the average person's ways and process of loving have hardly been entirely revolutionized! . . . Werther's "worry" bore the evil influence of feudalism! If Lotte and Werther didn't harbor illu-sions of monogamy, and her husband didn't have some petty jealous feelings, then why would Werther resort to killing himself! If people's love—especially Communist Party people's love—can nakedly and without an iota of hypocrisy, on the basis of their common understand-ing of the political line, through ties of sincere love, realize their beauti-ful dreams, what's the "worry," and how can it harm our studies?[50]

Apparently, such articles were so common that the editor of the paper (Shen Zemin, Russian name Gudkov) was instructed to stop publishing them, an order he at first disobeyed, and then was criticized for obeying. In one 1928 marathon meeting, a student mocked him: "About love. Gudkov is probably against love altogether. But now he has a wife. And we don't. Gudkov said that we shouldn't talk about love—as if that's a remnant of the raikom [referring to Rafail's group]. If that's the case, then our Russian comrades are also being raikomovtsy—in the streets." Under fire from all sides, at this meeting Gudkov broke down and admitted his mistakes, including "disobeying the decision of the bureau about not continuing the discussions about love."[51]

The student who pointed out the hypocrisy of Gudkov's position had a point. High-ranking Chinese men were often allowed to bring their wives or girlfriends with them, or like Jiang Jingguo, they easily attracted pretty new girlfriends in Moscow. Curiously though, neither fathers nor husbands, present or far-away, prevented many of the women who arrived with certain men from becoming involved in affairs with others. Even the wife of Zhu De (later a top general in the Chinese Red Army) had an affair that she managed to keep secret from her husband while they were in Moscow. Some male students learned Russian and could find Russian girlfriends; some Chinese men apparently considered Russian women superior to Chinese women.[52]

But ordinary Chinese students, especially the workers who were increasingly favored over intellectuals in Chinese University recruitment, couldn't necessarily find girlfriends. Moscow was supposed to be the experience of a lifetime both politically and romantically for a Chinese revolutionary, but they were lonely and confused.

Probably most students experienced moments of disorientation and homesickness in Moscow and asked themselves the same questions that Rafail had: to which revolution and to which party did the Chinese owe their primary allegiance, and how could or should their daily lives reflect their loyalties? Which language should they speak, when, and how much? What should they read, when, and how much? Whom should they love, how, and how much?

Such questions never died away, always mingling and even interfering with subsequent political struggles in Moscow and beyond.

8

Heartbreak

The Demise of Qu

CHINESE UNIVERSITY HAD been in existence for only a year and a half when something happened that took everybody in Moscow by surprise, shattering the ideological foundation for the United Front and the emotional core of the Sino-Soviet romance. The shock not only led to the end of the institutional experiment that was Chinese University, but it also ultimately stressed to the breaking point the ties that had bound the Russian and Chinese revolutions together with increasing intimacy since the early 1920s.

On July 1, 1926, Chiang Kaishek had ordered the mobilization of troops loyal to the Nationalists for the Northern Expedition, a march north from Guangdong to take territory controlled by warlords and unify China. Graduates of the Soviet-backed Huangpu military academy in Guangzhou formed the backbone of his army, and the decorated Red Army general Vasilii Bliukher served as Chiang's main military strategist. Borodin was less enthusiastic, but despite a falling out with Chiang remained to advise as best he could. In 1926, Chiang's troops quickly took major cities including Wuhan, Hangzhou, and Nanjing. At the same time, Chinese communists were fomenting strikes and peasants were turning against their landlords, putting Chiang in the uneasy position of accommodating unrest in areas he had only just conquered.

From Moscow, this looked like success: Nationalists and Communists working together to unify and revolutionize China. As the Moscow papers reported victory after victory for Chiang, the status of the Chinese students at Chinese University soared.

On March 27, 1927, Chiang's forces took Shanghai, with workers and communists staging strikes and insurrections in support of them. One student remembers the fall of Shanghai as the pinnacle of his experience in Moscow:

> In a mood of wild celebration we thronged into the auditorium and held a jubilant meeting. . . . One of my classmates leapt to the podium, shrieked "Comrades," and then, literally, was so stricken with emotion that he could not go on. He just stood there, his mouth frozen in an ecstatic grin. . . . After the meeting was adjourned we pushed through the gate of the university and quickly formed lines for a demonstration, which eventually included thousands of Moscow residents. . . . On our way [home] we were stopped by the crowds. They cheered us and some even seized some of my fellow students, threw them in the air, and caught them as they fell. Many Russian girls innocently threw us kisses and flirted with us coquettishly. After this memorable day our status increased rapidly. When we walked into theaters, Russian girls clustered around us. They seemed to know that these future revolutionary figures would soon return to China to hold high positions. They also paid us frequent visits at the university. Some of the more daring girls simply offered themselves as loving wives and asked to be taken back to China.[1]

Just five years earlier, Chinese students at Eastern University had been rehearsing the Soviet Union's imagined international revolution in the East. Now, students at Chinese University were the stars of Russia's international revolution.

One of the most engaging aspects of the international revolution was the way in which distant events could be experienced collectively and transnationally. Revolution closed geographical distances that were still daunting in terms of actual travel and communication, and encouraged new kinds of "multi-cultural" communities. Chinese University and its students were the tangible manifestations of a dynamic new idea: the Chinese revolution could and should be reflected and even experienced globally, especially in Moscow, where all revolutionary events ought to reverberate especially loudly. The excitement about an immediate, intimate, personally experienced connection to something otherwise so exotic, faraway, and important—that motivated Russian girls to surround Chinese boys in Moscow theaters—was actually an emotionally constitutive element of Russia's international revolution.

The atmosphere was captured and immortalized by Mayakovsky, who wrote several poems about China, including one that some have claimed was based on his actual experience: asked to recite his best poem in an apartment in Yaroslavl in March 1927, he "bawled out/abandoning my poetic tone/louder/ than the trumpets of Jericho/Comrades!/ with the workers/and the troops of Guangdong/they are taking Shanghai!" Arguably, 1927 was the first moment when excitement about the Chinese revolution overtook Russian cultural elites' dominant and long-standing portrayals of Chinese in negative or comical terms. Just a year before, Mayakovsky had published a very different poem, in which he mimicked common Russian attitudes: "What . . . flings them here over 6000 versts? Is the land there bad? Not enough rice or something?" And Bulgakov had staged a play, *Zoika's Apartment*, which featured two Chinese laundry own-ers/drug dealers. Now, *Roar, China!* continued its run at the Meyerhold theater, and *Red Poppy*, a ballet featuring a coolie and an opium-smoking singsong girl who falls in love with a Soviet captain was being danced at the Bolshoi.[2]

In China, however, the actual revolution was in a precarious position. The coalition that Borodin had held together for so long was beginning to crum-ble from within. A right-wing faction in the Nationalist Party that opposed social revolution became increasingly vocal. Chiang was torn between his aspirations as a revolutionary and his goals as a future head of state. An entry from his diary in August 1926 read, "The communists are causing trouble within; they will not stop until our Party is split and the entire army col-lapses. Trouble and problems everywhere. Endless agony."[3] That he would have mixed emotions is hardly shocking, but his reaction to the conflict brewing in China, and in himself, was a surprise.

On April 12, 1927, Chiang's forces attacked the headquarters of labor unions in Shanghai, killing and arresting union members. When work-ers and students demonstrated against his actions the next day, Nationalist troops mowed them down with machine guns. This action touched off a series of raids by Nationalist-allied generals on leftist groups in their territo-ries. Borodin was crushed; Trotsky appeared vindicated; Stalin was furious. Chen Duxiu, the head of the Chinese Communist Party, was sacked by the Comintern, and Qu took his place.[4]

News of Chiang's coup reached Moscow the day it happened. Students at Chinese University converged on the assembly hall tense in anger and dread to compose an angry telegram to Chiang's government. Many of them belonged to the Nationalist Party, not the Communist, and Chiang's actions touched off a bitter struggle on campus. Not until the 1950s would

Chinese students regain the public approval they had enjoyed in Russia in the mid-1920s.

On the other hand, the failure of the United Front caused widespread disillusionment with Russia among radical Chinese. For the first generation of enthusiastic Soviet sojourners like Emi and Qu, it was a personal tragedy on two levels: the friends they lost were killed in the name of an alliance that had (they rationalized) been Moscow's idea; their faith in a Russian Revolution for China was shattered upon first contact with reality, revealing just how youthful, naive, and romantic it had all really been. In the wake of 1927, not only did Russia's status as an object of longing and desire diminish, but the overt romanticism that had permeated Chinese conceptions of revolution also receded, including the more general conflation of love and revolution.[5]

New Arrivals, New Scene

Back in China, 1927 left the Communist Party scattered, isolated, demoralized, and discredited in the eyes of the public. It also left many revolutionaries even more socially and politically vulnerable. The movement fragmented, going underground in Shanghai and other cities and fleeing to various rural regions. In a supposedly non-fiction "bio-interview" of a Chinese student he met in Beijing in 1926 and who subsequently studied at Chinese University in Moscow, Soviet writer Sergei Tretiakov portrays the student as leaving Moscow as soon as he heard about Chiang Kaishek's coup. In reality, the Comintern rounded up as many rank-and-file party members as possible to bring to the Soviet Union for safe-keeping and military training.[6]

The new arrivals were the most dispirited group of Chinese who had yet come to the USSR to "study." One student remembers how desperate many revolutionaries back in China were:

They were forced to beg for their living on the streets and await arrest and execution. . . . One solution to this problem was to send some of us to Moscow. We were all very excited about the prospect of learning to use weapons. After the catastrophic defeat the Revolution had just suffered, the idea that armed force was the ultimately decisive factor in any situation was very appealing to us. . . . In less than six months we had watched one military man after another switch from leading the revolution to opposing it. In quick succession they had shamelessly and bloodily deceived us. We were like abandoned concubines, or pitiful and impotent old-fashioned scholars.[7]

Going all the way to Moscow just to learn how to shoot a gun or to save themselves implied that the trip was a necessity and reflected a very different mindset from that of students who had arrived to participate in Qu's "History of the Heart."

If the Chinese students arrived dispirited, they were met with suspicion. Soviet authorities required a peculiar, one-time physical exam in the fall of 1927, which one student recalled as a bad omen in retrospect: the Soviet secret police spent a week physically measuring all the Chinese at his school in great detail. "Would the Russians use this record to hound us for the rest of our lives? . . . Jokingly, we said that we had now given ourselves body and soul to the Russians." The warm attitudes of ordinary Russians on the streets had also changed dramatically after Chiang Kaishek's reversal in April 1927; a new arrival that fall remembers having a tomato thrown at him.[8]

Paranoia and ambivalence about the Chinese in Moscow may have reflected changes in Soviet politics and society, but they coincided with real changes in the Chinese student community itself. More numerous than ever, the Moscow Chinese band of would-be revolutionaries reflected a movement that had spun out of control. It consisted of a bewildering array of people: a few May Fourth holdovers from the early days who had stayed on to become teachers and translators; groups of intellectuals and party founders who had arrived from France in the early to mid-'20s; a wave of students who had come on the heels of China's patriotic May 30th Movement; large numbers of rank-and-file Nationalists and Communists who had been systematically recruited for Chinese University in its early years; relatives of high-ranking Chinese revolutionaries who studied only nominally; soldiers from Feng Yuxiang's warlord armies; ordinary students who had been sent specifically for military training; and the newest arrivals who clearly symbolized defeat. Because the Soviet Union was none too efficient in processing people for departure, these groups accumulated in a sedimentary fashion.[9]

Throughout the fall of 1927, students would hear news of a series of failed uprisings, which could only increase their overall disillusionment.[10] Toward the end of the year, Qu and others became convinced that fighting among warlord factions in Guangdong might be used to stage an urban uprising. On December 11, 1927, Communist forces took control of the post and telegraph, police stations, and army barracks in the city, much as the

Bolsheviks had done in Petrograd in 1917. Of course, Guangdong in 1927 was not Petrograd in 1917. Anti-communist forces reacted quickly, shooting not only workers and Communists but also Russian consular officials who had allowed the consulate to be used as headquarters for the uprising.[11] On the Russian Revolutionary calendar, the so-called Canton Commune was commemorated as an act of doomed revolutionary heroism along the lines of the Paris Commune of the nineteenth century. Students who had been chosen to come to Moscow for a military education, then, seemed to be training for a series of ill-fated gestures rather than a well-planned campaign where victory was possible.

Chaos in China coincided with increasing awareness of strife within the Bolshevik Party. Just as the Chinese revolution reached a decisive moment of conflict between Nationalists and ultra-radicals, the Soviet leadership was gripped by a struggle between those who would have "socialism in one country" and those who would have "permanent revolution," those who would continue the New Economic Policy and those who would force rapid industrialization and collectivization, those who backed Stalin and those inclined toward his ever-shifting opposition. Stalin had more or less defeated Trotsky by April 1927, but Trotsky nevertheless seized on the defeat of the United Front as evidence that Stalin's foreign policy was fundamentally misguided. Suddenly China assumed unprecedented prominence in public debates about the Soviet revolution.

Trotsky and the Chinese

Nobody was as conscious of the way one revolution could be deliberately read onto another as Trotsky. In July of 1927, he was called before the Bolshevik Central Committee to answer charges of factionalism, and he responded by reframing the accusations against him in terms of the French Revolution:

> During the Great French Revolution many were guillotined. We, too, brought many people before the firing squad. But there were two great chapters in the French Revolution: one went like this (the speaker points upwards); the other like that (he points downwards).... In the first chapter, when the revolution moved upwards, the Jacobins, the Bolsheviks of that time, guillotined the Royalists and the Girondists. We, too, have gone through a similar great chapter when we, the Oppositionists, together with you shot the White Guards and

exiled our Girondists. But then another chapter opened in France when . . . the Thermidoreans and the Bonapartists, who had emerged from the right wing of the Jacobin Party, began to exile and shoot the left Jacobins. . . . I would like Comrade Solz to think out his analogy to the end and to answer for himself first of all this question: Which chapter is it in which Solz is preparing to have us shot?[12]

It took Trotsky some time to map the Russian Revolution onto the Chinese one—that is, to formulate his full critique of Stalin's China policy—but he had the essence of it already in early 1927, before Chiang Kaishek's reversal: "We have turned the Chinese Communist Party into a variety of Menshevism."[13]

In his polemics about both the French and Chinese revolutions, Trotsky was using other revolutions as mirrors for the Soviet one. And yet, there was a difference: the French Revolution was long over and therefore open for critical interpretation. The Chinese and Russian ones, however, were unfolding simultaneously, so any attempt to change one narrative would inevitably alter both.

In late 1927, some students at Chinese University and elsewhere decided that they, too, were Trotskyists. Blaming Stalin for the misfortunes of the Chinese revolution, they began scavenging for Trotskyist literature and making contacts with Soviet oppositionists. Various students, including Jiang Jingguo, flirted with Trotskyism, but the group seems to have had an inner core that was responsible for most of its organized activities. The most sensational of these occurred in November 1927, when a Chinese Trotskyist student marching in a ten-year anniversary demonstration suddenly jumped out of the crowd in Red Square and unfurled a banner with a pro-Trotsky message, as recorded by at least two American journalists.[14]

None were arrested at the time, but some were expelled and eventually arrested or shot. The campaign against Chinese Trotskyists in the Soviet Union continued off and on for years. The Chinese Communist Party took a more tolerant view of Trotskyists, allowing a small movement to form there. Husband and wife team Peng Shuzhi and Chen Bilan joined this movement, and one-time Party founder Chen Duxiu was sympathetic to it. Yet this small splinter group had even less organizational cohesion with which to survive Chiang Kaishek's repression, and Peng Shuzhi and others ended up in prison.[15]

Qu's Audience with Stalin

Just as the Chinese Communist Party and the Comintern had rounded up as many rank-and-file party members as they could to bring to the Soviet Union after Chiang's betrayal, so too many party higher-ups found themselves seeking refuge in Moscow after months of hiding out in China. Like ordinary students, many had mixed feelings and considered their journeys a flight from danger rather than a pilgrimage.[16] As summer of 1928 approached, plans were afoot for a Sixth Congress of the Chinese Communist Party in Moscow, on the grounds that there was no safe place for such a meeting to be held in all of China, and this drew even more of the top leadership to Moscow.

Qu had stolen across the border in late 1927; his wife, Yang Zhihua, came to the Soviet Union by train in May of 1928 as a participant in the Sixth Party Congress in her own right. Yang made her first journey to Moscow from Shanghai disguised as a peasant woman, in a coarse Chinese-style coat, her hair coiled in a bun. She pretended to be the wife of several different male traveling companions in succession, and she instructed her daughter to call each one daddy. She also sewed some of her travel funds into a pair of her daughter's pants, which then somehow she could not find, so they arrived in Soviet Russia hungry. When they got to Moscow they joined Qu at the Lux Hotel, where Comintern operatives stayed and even lived.[17]

Qu, now the general secretary of the Chinese Communist Party, had technically reached the peak of his political influence. He was the highest-ranking Chinese party member able to communicate effectively in both Chinese and Russian—at a time of true political crisis on both sides. Engulfed in disagreement and obsessed by accusation, neither party could convincingly present a unified front. The increasingly urgent desire to speak with and read about each other created enormous pressure on translators at all levels. The translators, Qu above all, often had stakes in the conversations, and, in the heat of the moment, received few concessions to the actual process and requirements of translation.[18]

The summer of 1928 saw a series of conferences in which debates over the future of the Chinese revolution captured the attention of the Soviet and international communist parties at the highest levels, and Qu, of course, played a major role. First came the Sixth Congress of the Chinese Communist Party in June and July, on the outskirts of Moscow in the vicinity of Zvenigorod—the last party congress until 1945. The Sixth Congress was a moment of real synthesis, when projections and reflections gave way to live, high-level engagement. Nearly all of the top party leaders from China who were invited attended, numbering eighty-four voting delegates and thirty-four non-voting delegates; notable exceptions included Mao and Zhu De.[19] Bukharin represented the Soviet side, at a time when he was widely seen as Stalin's right-hand man. The Chinese present were aware that because they were in Moscow they needed to pass some resolutions of which the Comintern approved. Yet they were deeply divided in their interpretations of what had happened in 1927 and what to do about it.[20]

Although Qu was the General Secretary of the Party, there were a number of delegates whose status was higher and power greater. And the events of the past year, when Qu had been at the helm, had been terrible: a series of defeated uprisings, harsh repression, and steeply declining party membership. As one Chinese University student put it,

> Qu's policy seemed rather like that of a frantic man betting everything he had on one last, desperate gamble, which failed. What was called for, surely, was an organized, disciplined, and patient retreat in order to preserve such forces as remained and to sustain morale. But this minor scholar, whose chief claim to fame was his ability to read and write, through his leadership hastened and deepened the crisis of the CCP.[21]

At least some historians have argued that it would have been hard, at that point, to craft a "good" agenda for the Chinese Communists.[22] But the Chinese in Moscow for the Congress were not so fatalistic: they had been deeply involved in and affected by the defeats of 1927. Qu, always associated with Soviet Russia, was an easy scapegoat.

One example of a powerful Chinese delegate skeptical about Qu was Zhang Guotao. A founding Party member whose political power was probably greater than Qu's, Zhang reported that when the Congress opened, Qu put forward an initial slate of committee chairs—and the Congress rejected it. Qu took this as a vote of no confidence and left the room. Only when Comintern officials intervened did the slate pass, with amendments.[23]

Bukharin gave a speech that reportedly lasted nine hours; one Chinese remembers that he often had a falcon on his shoulder, carried a hunting rifle, and sometimes left the congress to go hunting. Here, to the Chinese, was a Russian character whose charisma matched that of the now-discredited

Radek and Borodin. Moreover, they perceived Bukharin's authority as equal to Stalin's, so eventually the delegates decided to put their disagreements aside and pass a series of resolutions.[24]

Qu emerged from the Congress no longer general secretary—that honor went to a worker from Hubei whom everyone believed they could control—but still a member of the Politburo and one of two permanent Chinese representatives to the Comintern. The other representative was Zhang Guotao, who claimed not to understand Russian at all. So there Qu remained, dead center between two highly contested revolutions. Right on the heels of the Sixth Chinese Party Congress that summer in Moscow came the Sixth Comintern Congress, where Qu was one of the Chinese delegates and tried to regain his lost prestige. Once the Stalin-Bukharin split went public, he quickly came out against Bukharin and called the results of the Chinese Party Congress into question on that basis.[25]

In late 1928, when debates about China were raging, Stalin decided to investigate the matter himself. Qu had been demoted politically, but he remained the highest-level Chinese proficient in Russian, and so he along with Zhang Guotao was invited for a personal conversation with Stalin.[26]

Qu had first arrived in Moscow in 1921 enchanted with the Russian Revolution as he had conceived it and determined to bring elite Chinese radicals into contact with it. At that time a friendship with Tolstoy's granddaughter represented, to him, the ultimate human connection between the Russian and Chinese revolutions. Now he had an audience with the highest-ranking Soviet communist, to whom he would personally represent the Chinese revolution. It was a revolution that Qu himself had helped coax into the consciousness of both the Chinese radical elite and many Soviet leaders.

Qu did not record his encounter with Stalin, but Zhang Guotao did:

In early November, two weeks after the establishment of this three-man commission on the China problem, Stalin invited Qu Qiubai and me for a discussion, the first time we ever discussed the China problem directly with Stalin. On that particular day, at 9 PM, we were seated opposite Stalin, who was sitting behind a large desk in his austere office. Puffing at his pipe incessantly, he started off by asking about our lives in Moscow. He treated us in a friendly manner, reflecting his worldliness.[27]

According to Zhang, Stalin then asked two very peculiar questions: first, whether Sun Yatsen's widow Soong Ching Ling would call a policeman to arrest a Chinese communist in the street, and second, whether ousted Chinese Party founder Chen Duxiu could publish a newspaper in China. Qu continued to interpret as Stalin discussed the importance of Marxist-Leninist theory.

But then, Stalin began to talk about his own life, telling stories from his childhood and youth. At this point Qu stopped interpreting and, according to Zhang, just listened, "so raptly that he forgot to translate them for my benefit at the time."[28] Only later did Zhang hear from Qu the scraps of Stalin's stories. In this moment of unmediated connection to Stalin, Qu had closed the gap between the Russian and Chinese revolutions at the highest level in personal terms. But according to Zhang, it wasn't a real conversation.

Perhaps more important was the fact that Qu could no longer roam through the space between the two revolutions in exalted isolation. That space was collapsing as more and more Chinese came into direct contact with Soviet politics and as competitors emerged to challenge his interpretive authority.

The 28 Bolsheviks and the Soviet Purge

In 1925 the rector of the Eastern University had boasted to the Comintern that, through the alumni of his school, he could overthrow the leadership of any communist party in the Far East. On the sidelines of the Sixth Congress of the Chinese Communist Party was a young man who would put that claim to the test. This was a student from Chinese University named Chen Shaoyu, a "pleasant-faced, intelligent young man whose command of the Russian language was noteworthy and whose knowledge of the teachings of Lenin and Stalin was impressive."[29] Chen—also called Wang Ming—had excellent Russian and grasped the essence of Soviet politics very quickly.

While many students at Chinese University were inclined toward Trotsky, Wang picked the winner, siding with the unpopular Stalinist rector, Pavel Mif, who had replaced the Trotskyist Radek and was determined to become Stalin's new "man in China." Just as Qu had once become translator to the now-discredited Borodin, Wang linked up with Mif. Wang and several other students (including Qu's younger brother) attended the Sixth Congress of the Comintern as translators and observers. For the big-time Chinese communists, Mif was an irritant and Wang was a polite young administrative facilitator.[30] But together Wang and Mif sought to redefine the Sino-Soviet relationship.

The two men began with the Chinese student community in Moscow. They agitated among the students, teaching them how to express their dissatisfactions in political terms that resonated with concurrent Soviet developments. They were, of course, completely against anyone they saw as "remnants of the Rafailovshchina," as well as Trotskyists and, once the Stalin-Bukharin clash went public, rightists.[31]

But their truly ingenious move was to spread invented tales of a supposedly clandestine organization of Chinese oppositionists who were so antirevolutionary as to form a group based on the members' place of birth: the "Zhejiang-Jiangsu *zemliachestvo*." Zhejiang and Jiangsu were among the wealthiest provinces in China. *Zemliachestvo* was the Russian word for "native place organization," a phenomenon that dated back to the prerevolutionary era when large groups of peasants from a particular village or area would arrive in cities to work in factories. Chinese migrants also had native place organizations, *tongxianghui*, which eventually came to be seen as a major impediment to labor organization in the cities. By referring to a "Zhejiang-Jiangsu *zemliachestvo*" Wang and Mif played on Russian fears of inscrutable Chinese alliance patterns, as well as on natural geographic differences among the Chinese students in Moscow.[32]

Supposedly these rich revolutionaries (including Jiang Jingguo, who was from Jiangsu) would take their fellow provincials out for lavish dinners in a Chinese restaurant in some Moscow back alley and fill their minds just as they filled their stomachs. In fact, Jiang and others would occasionally treat their fellow students to Chinese food with money they got from home, and some Chinese in Moscow had turned against the Russian revolution they saw around them, but the Zhejiang-Jiangsu *zemliachestvo* was a figment created to exaggerate cross-cultural tensions in daily life and connect them with larger political issues.[33] It was a creative but sinister act of Sino-Soviet synthesis.

Soon the entire student body at Chinese University was in conflict. Leading the campaign was a group that came to be known as the "28 Bolsheviks," though at the time nobody called this small minority of highly political Russian speakers anything in particular. Connected to larger Soviet trends through Mif, they were impervious to the hostility and incomprehension of their fellow students. They succeeded in having several students expelled and sent to Siberia, which was unprecedented in the Chinese student community and caused real fear.[34]

Some students tried to circumvent Mif, going directly to the Bolshevik Party, which created an investigative committee, as well as to the Chinese Comintern delegation in Moscow. As the highest-ranking member of the delegation, Qu tried hard to stay out of these disputes. But the students managed to capture the attention of other members, who sided with them against Mif. This only enflamed the controversy, giving Mif, a relative nobody, grounds to argue that the current Chinese leadership in Moscow was not loyal to the Soviet Union.[35]

At the end of the 1928–1929 school year, Chinese University arranged one of its epic, end-of-year student meetings and invited Qu to speak. Although he was a Stalinist and perfectly aware that becoming involved could do him no good, Qu, according to Zhang, got carried away by the uproar among the students, spoke out on their behalf, and called on the rest of the delegation to do the same. The meeting dragged on, as hundreds of Chinese in a Moscow suburb fought for days with a Soviet schoolmaster. The Comintern declined to intervene, and Qu was trapped in a deadlock with Mif.[36]

At this point, Mif invited to the meeting the secretary of the Moscow district Party Committee (to which Chinese University technically belonged), essentially bringing straight Soviet politics into the mediated Sino-Soviet space. Zhang described this city party official as "a rowdy cadre of the country-bumpkin type, ignorant of Communist parties in foreign countries and personifying the chauvinism and power outlook of the CPSU [Communist Party of the Soviet Union]." The official got up and ranted against the entire Chinese delegation to the Comintern, at which point some students "leapt onto the rostrum and tried to drag [him] away." Zhang took the stage and coaxed the Chinese students down.[37]

This incident, apparently, sent Qu over the edge. Qu "became rather panicky when he saw this development of events" and went to speak with the city party official alone, calming him and convincing him to issue a joint statement that "a misunderstanding had cropped up as a result of the language barrier, that, in fact, there had been no conflict at all." This conversation temporarily restored the space between the revolutions.[38] Qu may have been able to finesse this particular student meeting but he could not prevent Chinese students in Moscow from becoming increasingly implicated in

Soviet politics, which magnified their disagreements onto a larger political backdrop.

In 1929, the Bolshevik Party launched a purge that ultimately expelled 10 percent of its membership and spawned purge committees in numerous organization, including Chinese University. The Soviet secret police enlisted the help of the 28 Bolsheviks not only to select possible purge candidates but also to participate in interrogations.

Both interrogated and interrogating students left memoirs of the experience. "Automatically," wrote an interrogating student of his interactions with a fellow student in a room at the Lubianka headquarters of the secret police, "we extended our arms to shake hands. As we did so, a powerful hand abruptly forced my arm down, while another hand struck the prisoner's wrist."[39] An interrogated (and then imprisoned) student recalls how in the early part of his interrogation, "a Chinese person came in. I saw that it was Wang Renda, in the past I'd heard he was a Soviet government agent . . . the Russian said that if my Russian in places wasn't clear he could ask Wang Renda to translate. I said whatever, for now we don't need him. In the evening he sent Wang to get us three dinner, we all ate together."[40] These anecdotes paint a picture of automatic Chinese solidarity, sundered by brute Russian force. The first Chinese student to lose his life in the purges was actually a Trotskyist who was pressured by Mif's faction to inform on his friends and then committed suicide.[41]

The Chinese students in Moscow, all of whom were now enrolled at Chinese University, were already so engulfed in controversy that the effort to determine who ought to be purged brought the entire institution into question—and it was closed. Lists of students were drawn up to share various fates: prison, labor camps, or hard labor in Moscow or provincial cities. Twenty-eight Chinese students were transferred to the Moscow Lenin School, which had opened a Chinese section in 1928 under the leadership of Old Bolshevik Klavdia Ivanovna Kirsanova. The Lenin School operated a small, regular Chinese group and functioned as a holding pen for higher-ups like Zhang Guotao and Jiang Jingguo. It appears that the one documented case of a Chinese sentenced to death in connection with the 1929 purge was not a student.[42]

The 28 Bolsheviks had already launched a full-scale assault on Qu. His younger brother responded by turning in his party card—at which point he disappeared, assumed either to have been arrested or to have killed himself.

Included on the list of students sent to work in Moscow factories was Qu's wife, Yang Zhihua.[43] Whereas in 1925 Qu had enjoyed seeing Yang dress up like a worker to agitate among female textile laborers, this was now inflicted as a punishment for Qu. In 1930, Qu and Yang applied to return to China, his History of the Heart in the Red Capital finally over.

The 28 Bolsheviks in China

Qu's political power was much reduced upon his return to China. Leadership of the Communist Party was highly contested, and the Comintern was eager to retain control. For a time, the party was led by the prominent labor agitator Li Lisan, who continued to push for armed insurrections against all odds. As the cities became more dangerous, communists fled to the countryside, trying to find places where they would be supported and defended by local populations. The most famous was the Jiangxi Soviet, which was founded in 1931 in the capital of Ruijin with Mao at its head, and eventually expanded over territory with a population of about three million.[44]

Just as the Chinese Communist Party had to go underground in the aftermath of 1927, so too did Soviet involvement with the Chinese revolution become clandestine. Between 1928 and 1933, Shanghai was the foreign headquarters of the Comintern's Far Eastern Bureau. Among its agents was Richard Sorge, sometimes considered the greatest spy of all time. From Shanghai, Sorge directed intelligence operations in China as well as Japan, Formosa, Indochina, the Philippines, and Malaysia.[45] While his activities laid the groundwork for continued Comintern support for the communists, Sorge did not openly lead or organize anything. Nor were he and the other spies doing the dirty work for the communists, who during this period were developing their first serious internal police force, conducting the first purges of suspected Nationalist agents in their own ranks, and recruiting and developing new types of party members including gangsters in a brutal effort to shield remaining loyal party members from discovery.[46]

During this period of secrecy and confusion, the Comintern made its most overt attempt at dominating the communists. In 1930, Pavel Mif went to China to take control of the Chinese Communist Party through his Moscow-educated protégés. For a time, Mif's loyalists were successful: Wang Ming became the general secretary of the Communist Party and so-called Russian returned students were de facto in control of the Jiangxi Soviet. But the Jiangxi Soviet was increasingly in danger of Nationalist attack. The scene was set for the emergence of some kind of purely Chinese revolutionary protagonist to take over, put an end to China's Russian revolution, and save the Chinese revolution for the Chinese.

Yet for Chinese revolutionaries at the time, there was no real binary between "international" and "national" revolution. So long as they could control territory and foment revolution within it, they did; when they had to abandon that territory, they did. If the Comintern offered training and resources, they took everything they could get; when communications and supply routes were broken, they survived independently and kept hoping for future Soviet assistance. The Russian returned students and Comintern advisors who planned the break out of the Jiangxi Soviet that led to the Long March certainly did not view themselves as abandoning their hopes for a Russian-style revolution in China. On the contrary, they were simply trying to preserve what forces they could for a more favorable future. Nor were they somehow miraculously converted or duped or coerced by Mao on the March. They kept fighting to control the revolution, with or without Mao, all the way to the bitter end. Mao himself allied with some Russian returned students against others and was always eager for Moscow's endorsement and aid.

Many of the 28 Bolsheviks and other Russian returned students made the entire March, despite enduring some criticism for their pre-March leadership. Some had no problem with Mao, settled down comfortably with his forces in Yan'an, held key positions in his new 1945 Central Committee, and emerged to assume major leadership positions in the People's Repubic of China.[47] Education in the Soviet Union was a common element in the formation of the first-generation Chinese communist elite rather than the basis for an unsuccessful foreign-backed coup within the Chinese Communist Party.

What the Long March did change was the story that the CCP could tell about its own development: it was an entirely Chinese odyssey that could eclipse the Soviet one. In this story of the Long March as the end of the Sino-Soviet affair, Qu Qiubai, the founder of the Sino-Soviet romance, is also eclipsed.

Qu's Death

After his return to China in 1930, Qu immersed himself in the leftist literary movement. Even as he left Russia, Qu was involved in a campaign to Latinize

Chinese and had created an alphabet, a cause he continued to champion back in China, where he could be seen scribbling Chinese words written in English letters in his notebooks during meetings. He was named commissar of education for the Jiangxi Soviet but remained in Shanghai. He quickly emerged as a key figure in the League of Left-wing Writers, a loose group of communist writers and fellow travelers that had begun about six months before Qu's return. The League debated the position of leftist literature in the post-1927 environment. Qu advocated "proletarianization," which he explained in a proliferation of jargon-packed articles, even as he undertook his own translation of Pushkin's narrative poem, "The Gypsies."[48]

As a prominent communist, however, Qu was a wanted man in Shanghai, and he had to move several times. He spent several extended stays in the home of Lu Xun, with whom he engaged in a protracted, philosophical conversation that returned to the early questions about translation and the Chinese language that had earlier animated them.[49] In December 1933, Qu got a telegram calling him to communist headquarters in Ruijin, Jiangxi province. When he arrived in early 1934, he was surrounded not by Shanghai's multilingual intellectual elite but by the illiterate masses city intellectuals like Qu spent all their time discussing. Qu's stream of literary articles dried up; later he wrote that he twice tried to make peasant inspection tours in Jiangxi, but that his "findings amounted to very little. There was no common language between me and the peasants."[50]

Qu had scarcely arrived in Jiangxi when preparations began for the Long March in early 1934. At this point the top decision makers in the Party were Zhou Enlai, who was always deeply implicated in structuring and disciplining the Party, and two of the 28 Bolsheviks, Bo Gu and Zhang Wentian.[51] It was hardly guaranteed that Mao, who was out of favor in the early 1930s, would make the march. In 1934, Zhang Wentian replaced Mao as "premier" of the Jiangxi Soviet, and Bo Gu was said to have chuckled that "Old Mao is going to be just a Kalinin now," referencing the figurehead Soviet president.

Decisions about who could come on the March were both political and pragmatic. Some were left behind to coordinate underground activities in southeastern China, and most sick or old comrades were excluded, too.[52] Qu was both politically out of favor and sick with his worsening tuberculosis. It was his romantic writing about his *Journey to the Land of Hunger* and his *History of the Heart in the Red Capital* that had inspired subsequent waves of young Chinese radicals to make the trip to Moscow, and nobody was more associated with radical Chinese Russophilia than Qu. The communists were about to march their revolution into the heart of China, but it was a trek the ailing Qu, who liked to be comfortable, was not suited to make.

Left behind, Qu was captured by the Nationalists. A journalist who visited him in June 1935 described him as puttering about his prison cell, writing classical poetry and carving little stone seals as he had done with his first wife. He occupied himself by writing one last autobiographical statement, *Superfluous Words*—his first piece of introspective writing since *History of the Heart*—in which he concluded: "That a mediocre man of letters, who may even be described as silly, should bear the burden of the tasks of a political leader, is indeed ridiculous, but it is a fact." And yet: "If you want to discuss any political problem with me, I have no approach to it except what I can deduce from my imperfect knowledge of Marxism."[53]

Qu ended *Superfluous Words* by making a list of the things for which he felt nostalgia, which began with his wife (whom he felt he had let down) and his adopted daughter (in Russia at this point), and included books he wished he had time to read again: Gorky's *Klim Samgin*, Turgenev's *Rudin*, Tolstoy's *Anna Karenina*, Lu Xun's "Ah Q," Mao Dun's *Dongyao*, and Cao Xueqin's *Dream of the Red Chamber*. Qu ended his final essay: "Chinese tofu is a really good thing to eat too, the best in the world. Goodbye forever."[54]

Neither Qu nor the people who wrote about him could leave it at that. According to newspaper reports of his death, on the morning of his execution he composed a poem in one of the most traditional of all Chinese forms, consisting of four lines from three different poets.

Setting sun, in ragged ridges, now bright, now dim;
Falling leaves and cold stream, in two tunes sing requiem
Ten years' solitude was mine to endure
Ties all dissolved, my heart clinging to half a hymn.

According to the reporter who witnessed the scene, Qu had been drinking as he wrote the poem. When called for execution, he was observed walking in some way that did not conform to expectations of how one ought to walk to one's death. Then, he sang the Internationale—in Russian—before the firing squad.[55] This story—in tune with the public persona Qu had always tried to project and perfectly symbolic of the history of Chinese communism—has been told again and again.[56]

The journalist's interview with Qu, the newspaper report of his death, and *Superfluous Words* have all been questioned as inauthentic. For Chinese communists trying to defend Qu as a true party hero, *Superfluous Words* had to have been written by Nationalist propagandists; a more cynical interpretation is that Qu wrote it in an attempt to gain his own release. Or perhaps, as one Chinese émigré historian has argued, *Superfluous Words* was an authentic renunciation of politics and a return to the sort of sentimentalism that had inspired his leftism in the first place, though his inclusion of a sincere discussion of Li Lisan's mistaken policies would then be out of place.[57] Qu's wife, Yang, never recorded her own opinion of his last testament.

The historical relevance of Qu's final recorded acts and words is separate from the questions of authenticity. The story reveals a historical plot line that was assumed to exist either by Qu, or some Nationalist propagandists, or some journalists, or even historians, or some combination of all four: departing for the Long March, the Chinese revolution left Qu behind to die; China's Russian revolution was a big mistake or misunderstanding; sentimental Russophilia could only continue to exist in a prison, walled off from the political realities of China; internationalism was for disease-ridden drunkards doomed to death; even the most internationalist of Chinese love tofu and write classical poetry.

Whatever the case, Qu died in 1935 and did not participate in the Long March.

Part III

LOVE AFFAIRS, 1930S–1940S

9

Kolia the Chinese

NOBODY COULD HAVE been more surprised than Jiang Jingguo when his father betrayed his communist allies in April 1927.

Ever since Jiang had left China for the Soviet Union, he and Chiang Kaishek had corresponded somewhat regularly. Jiang sent his father a letter en route to Moscow, and his father answered right away, urging him to "concentrate more on studying Russian and meeting and chatting with Russians and less on speaking Chinese with Chinese."[1] When Chiang received no reply to this letter, he wrote another, overflowing with questions about his son's life in Russia, advising him to study the language by reading newspapers and novels, and admonishing him to master theories of international revolution. When Jiang wrote shortly after his arrival to tell his father he'd joined the Komsomol, his father wrote back to say that as long as Jiang was a revolutionary, he could choose any party he liked.[2]

Jiang and his father likely knew that their letters were read carefully by the Russians who delivered them but how, exactly, this knowledge affected the contents is unknown. Father and son were not close before Jiang left for Moscow. Yet Chiang seemed to enjoy advising his son about his studies, even if he occasionally became irked by Jiang's questions. Once, after Jiang asked about his views on the role of common people in the Chinese revolution and the relationship between the Chinese and world revolution, Chiang replied: "I don't know whether these are questions you are asking me from your own research, or are other comrades asking me based on their research? I want you to answer me." Yet Chiang was also apparently proud of Jiang. "Revolution is my life's work," Chiang wrote. "So we are both, father and son, dedicated to revolutionary struggle from beginning to end."[3] Perhaps father and son were performing for their Russian audience. But they could have refrained from correspondence or written about strictly private matters.

These letters were the only communication Chiang and Jiang had, and they constituted their father-son relationship.

That Russia would play this role, connecting a Chinese revolutionary father and son, was something new: previously Russia had been a divisive factor among conservative fathers and revolutionary sons. It was Borodin back in Guangdong who most directly engineered the shift, by selecting children of high-ranking Nationalist officials to study in Moscow.[4]

But the most famous Chinese revolutionary family affair unfolded a bit differently than might have been expected in Moscow.

News of Chiang Kaishek's coup reached Moscow the day it happened, April 12, 1927. Chinese University students, including Jiang Jingguo, converged on the school assembly hall tense in anger and dread. They drafted a furious telegram to send to Chiang's government. Student after student stood to denounce Chiang's action, including several children of Nationalist officials, many of whom felt they had no choice. But Jiang came to the platform with a commanding presence and spoke with great emotion, outperforming them all. "I speak here not as the son of Chiang Kaishek, but as the son of the Chinese Komsomol." When he was done, the hall broke out in deafening applause.[5]

Subsequently, Jiang made an official statement that was distributed by the Soviet news agency TASS. "Chiang Kaishek was my father and a friend of the revolution. He has gone over to the counterrevolutionary camp. Now he is my enemy." Historians have speculated about the authenticity of Jiang's statement, wondering if he really wrote it or if he was pressured to sign it. A Russian military historian who published documents from Jiang's personal files in the Russian archives in 2004 believes that the message was phony. But the Taiwanese historian who performed extensive archival research in Moscow and who has carefully analyzed many of Jiang's letters, including his correspondence with his father, believes that whether or not he personally wrote the TASS statement, it accurately reflected his emotional state. Jiang, she argues convincingly, felt personally betrayed by his father.[6]

On another level, the historical significance of Jiang's actions and statements lies in their expression of a concept. The international socialist family drama that Jiang so vividly enacted may or may not have reflected his "true" feelings about his father, but his performance of it shows that it was in circulation. Jiang was not the only student to denounce his Nationalist father in the wake of the April coup; in June of that year the elder brother of Jiang's girlfriend wrote a *Pravda* denunciation of his warlord father Feng Yuxiang, after Feng had also turned on his erstwhile communist allies.[7]

In one sense, the idea was a classic one: revolution created an international "family" that transcended nation, race, and biology. In another, Jiang's dilemma showed how something that had been strictly a metaphor might come to define an individual's parameters of action. Such symbolically resonant behavior was nothing new to Russian or Soviet intellectual culture, nor was it new to Chinese culture, ancient or modern. But the international socialist family drama was something new: it was a transnational metaphor of radical politics that could be personified in very concrete terms by specific individuals, and thereby could define an otherwise difficult to imagine international community.

The problem with people personifying metaphors is the people themselves, who refuse to stay put in their categories and often don't like to play the same role again and again. Jiang himself was hardly consistent: he was neither a loyal son of Chiang Kaishek nor a puppet of the Comintern, neither a devoted boyfriend to Feng Funeng nor a single-minded Komsomol member.

But the Soviet authorities who decided Jiang's fate were relatively consistent in their implementation of the metaphor: for all practical purposes, it seemed they really did intend to make Jiang into a New Soviet Man, to prove that revolution trumped family and nation. Whether by accident or design, after 1927 Jiang embarked on a decade-long "Soviet experience."

Jiang Jingguo Becomes *Kolia-kitaets*

Jiang Jingguo, finding himself in the Soviet Union during the intense revolutionary transformation that accompanied Stalin's First Five-Year plan beginning in 1928, decided to throw himself into it as a direct participant. In this he did the thing that Chinese communists would later applaud and endorse most enthusiastically: he went among the so-called masses and became one with them, a long and complex process that eventually culminated in his marriage to a Belorussian worker.

Like many other Chinese communists in the early years of the initial Five-Year Plan, Jiang Jingguo spent some time in limbo. After leaving Chinese University he attended Tolmachev Military School along with a handful of other Chinese students. Judging by what Jiang had to say—he chose to describe October 3 at Tolmachev for his representative day in 1928—studying there imparted a different level of understanding than studying at Chinese University. Jiang reproduced several pages of his Tolmachev lecture notes in his diary as evidence of the meaty content he absorbed there. At the same time, he introduced, for the first time, a Russian character inflected with the contradictions of a real person.

This (unnamed) person was his teacher for battle tactics, the son of a tsarist aristocrat who had graduated from military school and had been a leader of the Eighth Army during World War I. After the revolution he had fought with the Whites, but in 1919, he had been captured by the Red Army and convinced to advise them. There he saw how "people who had received no military training could be officers and people who had no battle experience could wage war and he thought it was really strange." Eventually he became the leader of a Red Army division, where he served until he learned, one day, that his army was supposed to attack a White division that contained his own younger brother. At this point, Jiang's teacher deserted the Reds but was nevertheless captured along with his brother's troops and jailed, subsequently becoming a teacher. Jiang asked him whether or not he believed in communism and his teacher answered, "Hard to say, but whoever wants to topple Soviet power is hoping in vain."[8]

At Tolmachev, then, Jiang found a Russian he could describe with empathy—somebody who had been "captured" by revolution, whose family had been torn by civil war, and whose politics had wavered and retained ambiguity. Jiang related the teacher's conclusion—that there was something inexorable about Soviet power—without comment.

When his stint at Tolmachev was over, Jiang was neither allowed to join the Soviet Red Army nor to go back to China. Instead, he, like other high-ranking Chinese, spent his time on tourist jaunts, in Black Sea resorts and hospitals (he was actually sick for a time), and at the Moscow Lenin School. Later, in his anti-communist memoir, Jiang would claim that he was desperate to return to China, and some historians have concluded that Stalin personally decided to keep Jiang in the Soviet Union to use him at some future critical moment in his relationship with Jiang's father.[9] If Jiang was, implicitly, a captive, nothing about his actions suggested that he was passive, bored, or simply awaiting release. He kept himself busy, drawn ever more deeply, and apparently earnestly, into Soviet life.

Jiang describes this process himself in his memoirs. In 1931, he was working at the Moscow factory Dinamo and living in a dorm near the Moscow Lenin School. He took a streetcar to work every day and, in contrast to his fairy-tale description of a Moscow bus ride in 1925, he sketched a more familiar moment in Moscow life:

> Every day I wait for an electric car but when it comes it's full, I can't get on. It's so cold I can't move my hands. After another five minutes another number 16 bus comes and even though it's too full I still have to get on otherwise I'll be late for work. The people who open the doors say, 'The bus isn't made out of rubber!' But I still go all out to push on. Inside it's so crowded you can't move.

In his description of this day, Jiang also waited in bread lines, discussed the first Five-Year Plan and socialist competition in a factory meeting, and got a voucher permitting him to buy shoes, which he reluctantly had to give up because he didn't have the money to use the voucher.[10]

In this 1931 collage, we see Jiang leaving the culturally mediated Moscow Lenin School dorm and pressed up against the so-called Soviet masses on all sides. He traveled on this jam-packed tram from an international environment that was saturated with geopolitical debates and high-level Chinese party politics to a Soviet space where politics and even geopolitics were defined very differently and articulated in Russian by ordinary Soviet people. The special, for-Chinese-only "Soviet" stage, always a flimsy construction, was gone, along with the idea that Chinese in the Soviet Union were somehow being trained or preparing for a special Chinese revolution back "home." No more special spaces, no more special food, no translators.

There was still a Chinese Communist Party delegation in Moscow to which the Chinese could write letters by the dozen. But in practice there were only a handful of these intermediaries and they too were caught up in the "Soviet experience" as well as in the "Chinese revolution." What's more, sometimes the petitioners, in historical terms, were of far greater import than the recipients of their pleas.[11] In Jiang's case, Soviet-backed Chinese communist leader Wang Ming, currently presiding in Moscow, would have loved to see Jiang in jail.[12]

But that didn't happen. What happened instead was one of the most peculiar events in the entire history of personal relations between the

Russian and Chinese revolutions: Jiang Jingguo was sent to help collec-
tivize a recalcitrant Russian village, Bol'shoe Zhokovo, in the Bol'she-
Korovinskii district of Moscow province. In his Chinese-language memoir,
Jiang wrote about October 20, the day he left the district, to organize his
story about the year 1932. The villagers threw a farewell party that seems
to have genuinely touched Jiang, who had faced skepticism and scrutiny
upon his arrival.

> When I first got here because I was a foreigner nobody would give me
> a bed. So the first night I slept in the garage of a church. . . . The second
> day I went to the village square early. The villagers said a lot of things
> to make fun of me. But I still said to them very politely, "Good morn-
> ing!" Later an old villager said to me "You should work the fields with
> us!" I said, "OK!" So I did the winter ploughing with them. At first
> I thought ploughing was a really difficult thing, but later it didn't seem
> so hard. You just have to use a lot of physical power that's all. The hardest
> was turning at corners, at first I wasn't used to it and in the place where
> I turned the corner I left a small empty space. After the villagers saw this
> they told me to plough a little softer there. On this day I didn't return
> to eat any lunch, ploughed all the way until night, my body felt awful.
> When I returned to the church garage I felt ill. I ate a little something,
> and fell asleep. I slept half the night and then I heard somebody call
> me, "Friend, This is no place to sleep! Come to my hut to sleep!" This
> was a little old village woman, called Sofia (Shadiya), she was 68 years
> old. I thanked her but was also afraid. . . . I thought about everything
> I had with me, not even 30 rubles, a couple of shirts, a few books, so
> I agreed to go with her. . . . I barely slept until 4 am when it got light,
> I got up and went to the village square. "Whoa, it's early, ploughing is
> harder than eating huh?" the villagers all asked me. On the third day
> I ploughed again. I ploughed for five days, got the villagers' sympathy.
> On the sixth day they asked me to their meeting . . . this village, at that
> time, they didn't have a collective organization. . . . So in order to reach
> the goal I worked hard at propaganda and organization work.[13]

Remarkably, unlike other places where Jiang's pro- and anti-communist
memoirs diverge, here they are the same. Moreover, the report that the Soviet
district party secretary wrote about Jiang's performance in November 1931
called Jiang's work "absolutely exemplary." He "single-handedly created party

leadership," and under his leadership all four of the collective farms in the district were "fundamentally consolidated."[14]

Whether or not the peasants Jiang collectivized really felt the sort of goodwill implied by the good-bye party they gave him, no one can say. But if they did, it might have had something to do with another of Jiang's claims: that he used his connections in Moscow to get the peasants preferential treatment in terms of credit and procurement.

When the district party secretary wrote his report about Jiang, he referred to him only by his Russian pseudonym. During his months in Bol'she-Korovinskii Jiang was exclusively called Elizarov, and the story he tells of this time is a tale not only of Bolshevization of Soviet society but also of his own Russification. Isolated from his Chinese friends and only occasionally in contact with higher authorities in Moscow, in a purely Russian-language environment, surrounded by hostile peasants, Jiang relates a quintessential Soviet experience: achieving personal and social integration through collectivization, described as the back-breaking process of transforming the most basic methods of everyday interaction and organization. For Jiang, the transformation included a physical change: he learned to plough. Finally, it involved a cultural transformation, from son of a Chinese national leader to grandson of a Russian peasant *babushka*.

The way Jiang tells his story, even in his anti-communist diatribe, absolutely belies any claim that Jiang Jingguo did not become a New Soviet Man. Historians have identified the creation of exactly such autobiographical narratives about integration of self and society under communism as a key component of the "Soviet experience."[15] Regardless of its veracity, the story itself and its appearance in both memoirs suggests not only that Jiang believed that his experience in the Russian village had transformed him, but also that he had learned how to interpret his experiences in Soviet terms. But what, exactly, was a "New Soviet Man," if Chiang Kaishek's son could become one?

Kolia and Faina

It was in his new mode, as Kolia Elizarov, that Jiang showed up at the great Soviet industrial complex Uralmash in 1933, where he remained until his departure from the Soviet Union in 1937. His diary entries for the next four years describe the process by which Nikolai Elizarov managed to become *Kolia-kitaets*, or "Chinese Kolia," accepted as a regular functioning member at a Soviet flagship factory, and contributing to the production of the precast fortifications for the Moscow metro. He recalled worrying over lack of spare parts; watching the oil for machines turning to ice; seeing a Ukrainian dance group in the factory club. He also wrote about a worker in the factory who was expelled from the Party for lying about his origins: he claimed to be an orphan but really his father had served in the White army and had been arrested. Here Jiang related another story of family rupture in revolution—so resonant with his own—without comment.[16]

By 1935, he was sufficiently integrated into Soviet society to throw a small New Year's Eve party for close Soviet friends. In 1936, he was working on the factory newspaper and reported increasing difficulty in getting his articles past the censors. While all accounts of Jiang's experience of rural collectivization more or less agree, here Jiang's two narratives of his years at Uralmash diverge and are complicated by additional context that both omit. In the anti-communist narrative, Jiang claims to have spent several months at hard labor in the gold mines of Altai before arriving at Uralmash—an incident the Russian historian who has seen Jiang's personal files claims cannot be corroborated by the documents, but which Jiang describes rather convincingly.[17]

This narrative also relates his tortured relations with the Chinese Communist Party in Moscow, which was planning to go after him as a Trotksyist in 1937. Jiang visited Moscow several times, tried to write to his family through various channels, and was pressured to sign letters written for him to his parents to dispel rumors he was in prison. Archival records show that he had to denounce his father and his origins when writing party autobiographies, including the one he wrote for his application to join the Soviet Communist Party; he was accepted on December 7, 1936.[18] He claimed to have been shadowed by the secret police for several months in 1934, and he did, in fact, lose his job at the Uralmash newspaper and face expulsion from the Party on the eve of his departure. Kolia would surely have suffered during Stalin's Great Purge of 1937 when so many foreign communists were targeted. However, because he also happened to be Jiang Jingguo, when the Chinese Communists and Nationalists rejoined in a United Front against Japan in 1937, *Kolia-kitaets* was able to leave the Soviet Union at the exact moment when, without his other identity, he might have perished in Stalin's purge.

But political repression is not all that Jiang's pro-Soviet narrative overlooked. Just as this version of his story omitted sex in the 1920s, so also it left out love in the 1930s. Paradoxically, the anti-communist memoir explains

away Kolia's marriage to a Belorussian woman named Faina Vakhreva as further evidence of his complete estrangement from Russian society. "During
these years at the Ural Heavy Machinery Plant, the only person who
befriended me was Faina, an orphan, whom I met in 1933. . . . She understood my situation best and was always there to sympathize and help me
whenever I had difficulties."[19] Faina, the daughter of two workers, went to
work at age fifteen at the same factory as her parents had and joined the Party
at twenty. For the son of Chiang Kaishek, operating in a Soviet environment
where working-class origins were everything, it was "marrying up."

The tale of woe that Jiang tells about his life in his anti-communist memoirs leaves out his 1934 Black Sea honeymoon. A photo captured a smiling
Faina in a dark and white swimsuit, posing on her side in the water with one
shapely leg extended, her right arm supporting her torso and exagerrating the
curve of her waist.[20]

On March 25, 1937, Jiang was back in what he called "new Moscow,"
with Faina and their two children. In a single page, he sketched the physical
changes to Moscow—and his own departure. He got a passport, bought a

Faina Vakhreva at Yalta in 1933. Courtesy of the KMT Party Archives Library,
Culture and Communications Committee, Central Committee of the Kuomintang.

train ticket, boarded the train, and left Moscow with his new Sino-Soviet family. "Goodbye, Soviet Union."[21] There the Chinese language diary of twelve entries for twelve years ends.

Jiang Jingguo's English-language account describes it differently:

On March 25, 1937, my family and I left Moscow and thus ended my twelve years' nightmare, held as hostage while the Chinese Communists and the Russian Communists completely reversed their positions in

Jiang Jingguo, Faina, and their two younger sons in Taipei. Courtesy of the KMT Party Archives Library, Culture and Communications Committee, Central Committee of the Kuomintang.

Jiang and Faina at Faina's thirty-fifth birthday in Taipei in 1950. Courtesy of the KMT Party Archives Library, Culture and Communications Committee, Central Committee of the Kuomintang.

regard to control of China. During this part of my life, although I suffered deeply, spiritually and physically, yet I perceived clearly the true nature of the Communist International and the genuine face of the Russian Communist Party and the Chinese Communist Party. These twelve years taught me a lesson which is engraved on my mind and will never fade throughout my life.[22]

Yet Jiang's Soviet period also indelibly shaped his private life, a fact that he was careful not to emphasize. Faina Vakhreva went on to become First Lady of Taiwan, and as such she remained a model of discretion, never telling her story in public. She wrote entirely quotidian letters to her family in the Soviet Union, which were, naturally, read and kept in Soviet archives. Over the years, she and Jiang produced a series of highly performative photographs that are today in the public domain in one way or another, such as their honeymoon photos at the sea. But Faina never granted a serious interview nor did she leave behind any public memoir.

10

Liza/Li

The Agitator and the Aristocrat

AT SIX O'CLOCK on a weekend morning in 1931 in Khabarovsk, Liza
Kishkina is already awake, ready to leap out of bed and go play tennis. This
could be because she's an energetic teenager, or it might be because she has a
crush on her boss, who plays tennis. He's elegant, almost aristocratic in bearing, easy to talk to—and he happens to be Chinese.[1]

"Aunt Shurochka said that the Chinese are a hideous people (which by the
way is now considered *chauvinism*)," she had written home to her mother in
Moscow, ". . . but it's the opposite, they're lovely! Of course I'm not talking
about street traders, I'm talking about the ones who work with us as editors
of the Chinese literature section. They are so very refined, they've graduated
from universities, sometimes more than one. . . . We have such a good time
with them, they come over all the time, and we go swimming and play vol-
leyball and they are teaching us to play tennis. It's a wonderful game!"[2]

Liza Kishkina was born in 1914 to the second wife of a landowner on an
estate in Saratov province, not far from the Volga River. The Kishkins were
part of a sprawling noble clan that had been in the service of Russian tsars
since before Peter. According to family lore, some branches had dark features
and curly hair because of an ancestor who had taken a Turkish girl captive
during the Russo-Turkish wars of Catherine the Great. Liza's first cousin was
Nikolai Mikhailovich Kishkin, a member of the Provisional Government
in 1917, important enough to inspire the Bolshevik slogan, "Down with
Kishkin-Buryshkins." Liza's father possessed a law degree and 2,800 acres of
land in Tambov and Saratov.[3]

Liza's mother, Praskovia, came to care for her cousin after the death of
his first wife. She was sent to the Kishkins as a housekeeper, but she found

herself frequently pregnant out of wedlock by her cousin, who was thirty years her senior. After aborting or giving several children up to homes for noble orphans, she secretly sent a son to live in a nearby village. When she found herself pregnant once again at age thirty-seven, she gave her cousin an ultimatum: marry her or else she would leave, even though she had nowhere to go. He did, and so Liza, his last child, was born legitimate. And he was quite fond of her.[4]

Straight from a Book

Liza's memories of the estate where she lived until she was six dwell on the places where she spent her time: its enormous garden, the balcony overlooking it, the empty hall behind the balcony, and the bedroom off the hall where she slept with her parents. In summer she ran around the garden, which was nearly thirty acres and full of apple and pear and cherry and plum trees, plus gooseberry and raspberry and currant bushes, and a hothouse for apricots and peaches. Off the balcony, which ran the full length of the house, was a shady alley formed by lilac bushes. "When I read descriptions of noble estates in the Russian classics, in Turgenev or Bunin, scenes from my early childhood appear in my mind's eye," Liza says in her memoirs. All the women in the family gathered to make jam and candy from the fruit in the garden. "It was no coincidence," she writes, "that a scene depicting this sacred ritual of summer played out in Pushkin's *Eugene Onegin*." With few memories of her father, she resurrects him by combining details gleaned from her mother with literature. "I think my father might have belonged to that category of landowner such as Levin, described by Tolstoy."[5]

Perhaps it was no coincidence that this heroine of the Sino-Soviet romance located her homeland in nineteenth-century Russian literature. Many of the Chinese communists among whom she spent her adult life had formed their first impressions of Russia from books by Tolstoy and Turgenev. With her unstudied grace, family pedigree, and fluent French, it's not hard to see why the Chinese would have read Tolstoy into Liza, or why she, in turn, would have borrowed scenes from Pushkin to describe her childhood. But how did she get from Bunin's garden to Beijing?

In 1918, when the Bolsheviks came for her father, he took cyanide. After the village burned the following year, some villagers came to live in the Kishkin house. Liza and her mother kept their bedroom and a few acres of land, which her mother rented out. She also took on sewing, kept bees, and made honey. Praskovia was a hard-working, god-fearing, practical woman, who had treated the villagers well when she had the chance, and they repaid her with small kindnesses—a dozen eggs here, a bottle of milk there. Still, by the summer of 1920, she was making preparations to leave. In Moscow she and her daughter moved into a communal apartment in a building that housed many newly impoverished noble or merchant families. Praskovia got a job in a sewing factory, and Liza went to a Soviet school.[6]

Liza was an active, sociable, curious girl and as a child didn't process loss and upheaval as tragedy. She hadn't known her father too well and was told he simply died. When villagers moved into her house, she was happy to have playmates. In the new communal apartment in Moscow she made all sorts of friends.[7]

Liza loved to be a part of things—families, festivities, activities—and she wasn't fussy so long as there was fun to be had. In primary school she was an enthusiastic performer in the human pyramids that she remembers were popular among children at that time, and she played the role of the boy radical Gavroche in the school performance of *Les Misérables*. She was proud to sing the Internationale and earn her Pioneer kerchief, but she also loved to decorate Easter eggs and go to church with her mother.[8]

When she graduated from middle school in 1928, Liza was determined to find paid work because her mother had lost her job in the sewing factory and had become a common cleaning woman. A neighbor recommended her for a brand new school founded by the State Publishing House to train proofreaders. Liza was happy to land a position where she could simultaneously continue her studies and bring home a paycheck. Plus, she was part of a close-knit group of classmates who danced tango on weekends, went to Leningrad together in summer, and skied in the Moscow suburbs in winter. Her one regret was that because of her aristocratic father, she was not allowed to join the Komsomol. "In my soul I was always tormented by my 'shameful origins.' And I always wanted to keep up with the times, to be included in the ranks of the 'youthful avant-garde.'"[9]

Far Eastern Adventure

Liza skillfully combined a genuine enthusiasm for adventure with a firm desire for upward mobility in the new Soviet system. In 1931, when she graduated from the technical editing school, the Komsomol had launched a big campaign to attract educated people to work in the Soviet periphery, and so Liza and her best friend Klava applied to go to the Far East. The girls were swiftly on a train to Khabarovsk—where salaries were high and the doors of the Komsomol open to her.[10]

In Khabarovsk, seventeen year old Liza went to work for the Soviet Far Eastern Press, where she met her tennis-playing Chinese editor. But he was thirty, and when he came back from a business trip he brought her a doll—a clear indicator that his kindness to her was paternal, not romantic. Liza was crestfallen, but he soon left Khabarovsk for good. She quickly forgot about him in the novelty of life in the Soviet Far East, the long hours she put in at the press, and her growing circle of Chinese and Russian friends.[11] Yet in retrospect, Liza's Chinese crush seems to have sent her off in a slightly different direction than she might have taken otherwise.

In the story she tells of her life, she sifts through her early years, carefully accumulating even small exposures to things Chinese. She remembers a Hans Christian Andersen story she read as a child, "The Nightingale," which begins with the lines, "In China, you know, the emperor is a Chinese, and all those around him are Chinamen also." She remembers the first time she saw real Chinese people, street traders and laundry workers in Moscow. She also remembers 1920s news coverage of the endless struggles among warlords, quoting Mayakovsky to express the difficulty she had in keeping them straight: "Zhang Zuolin and Wu Peifu, and then a Sui, and a Fui too . . ." On the other hand, international revolutionary struggle was constantly emphasized in school, and she remembers paying more careful attention to reports of striking workers in China. In all of this, Liza was like other young Muscovites—though in retrospect she felt that even then, "a mysterious thing was quietly present, pulling my thoughts past the boundaries of everyday existence and calling somewhere into the romantic unknown: China."[12]

After a year in Khabarovsk, she and Klava were transferred to Vladivostok, where Liza's social life revolved more and more around Chinese people and culture. She and Klava ventured into the city's infamous Chinese quarter, with its gambling halls, opium dens, and brothels. And she became friends with two Chinese men married to Russian women: a professor at the Vladivostok Lenin School and the director, Zhang Xizhou, whose wife was the daughter of the famous Sinologist Dmitrii Pozdneev, the founder of the Beijing Russian Language Institute.[13]

Mysterious Suitor

In 1933, Liza returned to Moscow to work as a technical editor for a large science publishing house and entered night school. She and Klava kept up with their friends from the Far East and as a result were always meeting interesting Chinese. One night, a Chinese-Russian couple invited the two of them over with the intention of setting Klava up with a friend of theirs called Li Min. According to Liza, Klava was "a real Russian beauty. Men just fell at her feet. Next to her I felt like a plain thing."[14]

Perhaps she felt plain but Liza had inherited her mother's piercing, clear blue eyes, framed by perfect brows. She had her father's curly hair, ringlets that had earned her the nickname "Pushkin" in school—and his strong nose. Liza was not thin, nor fine-boned, nor especially curvy, but she had excellent posture and regal carriage. She took horseback riding lessons and volunteered for weekend construction of the Moscow metro. She lacked pretension and was an easy conversationalist, the sort of person who can make a room full of disparate individuals feel like a comfortable group. Klava may have been pretty, but Liza had presence.[15]

After the party was over, Li Min told his hosts that he preferred Liza. But Liza had barely noticed him. Although his looks were striking, he hardly said a word—actually he couldn't speak much Russian. Liza dismissed him as a taciturn type and paid him no mind. He became a regular, quiet feature at gatherings of her friends. If he was courting her, it was subtle. Once, though, when they went out to the former Sheremetyevo estate at Kuskino and found a long line for boating on the pond, Li went up to the window and flashed some sort of identification in a little red cover. They got a boat immediately. "I didn't really understand what it was," Liza recalls, "but it made an impression."[16] At that point, however, Li Min stopped attending gatherings. Her curiosity piqued, Liza got Klava to come with her to visit him. When they arrived they found him with open suitcases and a room strewn with things. He said he was going to Crimea . . . although he also had out winter boots. They assumed he was returning to China.

After his mysterious disappearance, Liza found out who Li Min really was. In passing a friend mentioned the name of the infamous Chinese labor agitator, Li Lisan, as if he were a close friend. If he was such a good friend, Liza remembers asking, "Why haven't I seen him?" "What do you mean you

Elizaveta Pavlovna Kishkina. Courtesy of Inna Li.

haven't seen him? What, don't you know Li Min?" "Of course I know him."
"Well that's Li Lisan."[17]

Liza had first seen a photo of Li Lisan in the pages of *Ogonek*, a weekly
magazine her brother subscribed to, published in 1925.[18] In this widely reproduced picture, a young Li—wearing simple worker's clothing, with a sun-
tanned face and a wild shock of hair that stood up as if electrified, slightly
elevated and in sharp focus against the background blur of a demonstration—
leans forward, into the crowd, his hands flung out wide behind him, palms
outstretched, shouting passionately. It is one of the most expressive images
the Chinese revolution ever produced.

If the demeanor of the man in the picture was completely at odds with
the reserved person Liza had come to know, so too was the impression
that the name "Li Lisan" had given her. In Khabarovsk, Liza had come
across a brochure called "The fight against Li Lisan"—Li was blamed for
the failures of 1927—from which she had formed a vague impression of

him as an old, gray-haired man. But Li Min seemed to her no older than twenty-five. When Liza connected the fiery photo, the strident brochure, and the polite man who mysteriously left, "I was shocked to the depths of my soul."[19]

About a year later, the telephone in the hall of her communal apartment rang, and Li was on the other end. He was back in town, and he began pursuing her in earnest—perfume, chocolates, theater tickets, and all. Once, they went to see Chekhov's *Cherry Orchard* at the Moscow Art Theater. Liza was surprised to see Li watch intently to the end. He explained that the play depicted a historical development that had occurred in China as well—the breakdown of aristocratic estates.[20] In fact Li, like Qu Qiubai and many other early Chinese revolutionaries, had come from an impoverished gentry family. But he did not mention this then, nor did Liza tell him about her father. By Soviet standards, noble origins made a potential partner less attractive.

What won Liza over was an evening in November 1935 when she finally saw Li with his Chinese friends. Even though she couldn't understand a word he said, she finally understood him. "He sat at the head of an enormous table, and offered toasts, which everyone seconded. . . . It was noisy and fun around the table, and the ringleader, the 'life of the party,' turned out, to my amazement, to be Li Min. Here, in his own circle, there was no trace of that reserve that marked him off in our mixed company— there was no language barrier here." And when Li laughed, his serious features gave way to a no-holds-barred buck-toothed grin. For Liza, who so loved happy groups, seeing Li at the head of that table changed everything.[21]

"Gradually my interest in him grew," she remembers, "it seemed he had come from another world, full of revolutionary romance in contrast to my monotonous days." He told her about his studies in France, the strikes he had organized in 1921 in the Anyuan coal mines, and how, after the May 30th Movement of 1925, he had narrowly escaped the police by running across rooftops. "To me it seemed like a high risk adventure, just like in the movies. . . . These stories placed a romantic halo around Li Min, and I looked to him with ever more respect and sympathy. The aura of this person enveloped me and held me. Unnoticed, all on its own, a special feeling was born, which, probably, is what people call love."[22]

Li Lisan and Liza, 1940. Courtesy of Inna Li.

A Russo-Chinese Marriage

Li asked Liza to marry him—but she still had reservations. It wasn't that he turned out to be fifteen years older than she was, or that he was Chinese. She began to realize that his romantic past was every bit as colorful as his political one. He had left an arranged marriage and son to join the army; later he fell for a woman who happened to be married to Mao Zedong's brother-in-law. She left her husband for Li—and then left Li. Her sister came to comfort him, and they married. He left her behind in 1930 to go to Russia, where he married yet again—to a woman who already had a son by another man. That marriage was short-lived; she returned to China and disappeared. While in Russia, Li treated her son, whom she left there, as his own.[23]

Though Liza claims that Li's four previous Chinese wives did not deter her, his reputation as a passionate man who fell in and out of love frequently and did not hesitate to leave a woman behind in the name of revolution was worrisome. One of the Russian women she had befriended in Vladivostok had already seen her Chinese husband disappear back to China.[24]

Actually, Liza most likely did not know how politically risky her relationship with Li Lisan could be. Li, who had been born in Hunan in 1899, attended school in Changsha where he briefly met Mao, went to France as part of the Work-Study movement, and learned about communism from a French communist who worked with him in a steel mill in the mining town of Le Creusot. In 1921, the French authorities put him on a boat back to China. Upon his return he went to Anyuan where he organized a miners' strike along with Liu Shaoqi, who had just returned from the Soviet Union. Li took a leadership role in the May 30th Movement in Shanghai, then moved on to Wuhan where he was active in the United Front. But, when Chiang Kaishek turned on the communists, Li, by now a top party leader, wanted to fight back. His strong advocacy of continued urban uprisings could be interpreted as either obeying or disobeying the Comintern, which issued a flood of contradictory statements and policies in the years after 1927. Ultimately, because his uprisings all failed miserably, the verdict came down: Li had disobeyed, and the whole mess was even named after him. Hence the brochure Liza had read, "Against Li Lisan-ism."

Thus Li ended up in Moscow, where he was technically enrolled in the Moscow Lenin School but in reality spent much of his time on written and oral self-denunciations in front of the other students. Yet even when denouncing himself, he was spellbinding. And he was still useful even to the Comintern. His brief trip to "Sochi" was allegedly to a Red Army Base in Kazakhstan on the border with China, where Soviets were trying to re-establish radio communications with the Chinese who were on the Long March. They needed a voice that would be easily recognizable over the radio waves and they chose Li. It wasn't Sochi, but at least it was a reprieve from useless denunciations and a chance to take action. When he returned, he was given a new job, as head of the Chinese section of the Foreign Workers' Press.

As Liza's feelings for Li grew, she "had the feeling of being drawn to dive head first into a pool. But I knew that Li Min had had a hard time, and that he was alone in Russia. I didn't want to give him another blow. Let no one think that I also was afraid to link my life to an 'opportunist.'" So she agreed to marry him. Their wedding in February of 1936 was a modest affair at the Lux—attended by Qu's wife and daughter, among others. Later in life, when asked which wife of Li Lisan's she was, she would always say, "The fifth. And the last."[25]

With the official ceremony over, it was time to introduce Li to her family. When her relatives arrived, Li was in the kitchen, busy dumbfounding Praskovia by sautéing cucumbers and tomatoes, which Russians typically eat raw. Li won Praskovia over with his respect and attention to her. "Such behavior to an old person surprised even me—I still didn't know about this element of Chinese custom, one of the best. Li Min surrounded my mother with steadfast care not only when he was courting me, but to the very end of her life." When Li first told Praskovia of his intention to marry her daughter, Liza remembers that her mother clasped her hands together and said, "You realize that my daughter has absolutely nothing? She has no dowry!"[26]

Liza had invited one other Chinese person with his Russian wife to the family celebration of the wedding, and this man was short with a rather ordinary face that somehow seemed wrinkled even though he wasn't old. When her relatives arrived, one of them saw him and shot her a look of disbelief— had she really married such a shabby guy? Just then the dashing Li came out of the kitchen. "I looked at my relative, 'Well?' In answer to my silent question he nodded his approval, 'That's a different story.'" Kishkins, Liza reasoned, had married Poles and Austrians and French before. What difference would a Chinese make? Her sister summed it up: "I've seen a lot of people in my time, but I can tell you Liza, that Li Min is no ordinary person. He's somebody."[27]

After a Sochi honeymoon, Liza and Li settled into married life in a single room at the Lux, which had a cafeteria where they ate dinner, sparing Liza cooking. Li encouraged Liza to go back to school, so she went to see about studying Chinese at the Far Eastern Institute, but it turned out only members of the Party or Komsomol were accepted there. Instead she applied to the Institute of Foreign Languages, where she hoped to study English, also helpful in China. Again she was denied: only those with a complete secondary education were allowed to study English; people like her who had graduated from factory schools were sent to the French section. And so this daughter of an aristocrat who had had her first French lessons under Russia's old regime learned it anyway, according to the logic of the new one.

In general, their marriage was harmonious—except that Li turned out to have a jealous streak, and Liza, for her part, was always worried about Li being sent back to China. Instead, he was given a new job, editing a publication called *Save the Homeland* written in Moscow, published in Paris, and then sent back to China, as well as circulated in the United States and Europe.[28] Li's assistant was a man named Zhang Bao, who was also married to a Russian woman, Nadya. Liza and Nadya became friends and the two couples rented dachas near each other in the summer. For just an instant, in 1936, Liza and Li lived their Sino-Soviet romance in harmony.

In recent years, the Liza-Li relationship has inspired several semifictionalized accounts, and this brief moment of marital bliss is a highlight in all of them. China Youth Press published *Transnational Love: Two Chinese Men and Two Soviet Women* in 1996. To the authors of *Transnational Love*, the marriages of their Chinese heroes to Russian women were empowering.[29] By including Zhang Bao, *Transnational Love* added an interesting twist: a Sino-Russian-American love triangle. Before he came to Russia, Zhang Bao had studied in the United States, become involved in the activities of the American Communist Party, and served as the head of its China Bureau.[30] There, he had met and married a woman named Molly. He narrowly escaped arrest and left for Moscow to study at the Lenin School, where he befriended Li. But Zhang's American wife eventually showed up in Moscow, where she got pregnant by Zhang. She did not take to her living conditions, however, and was afraid of giving birth there. So she returned to the United States, leaving behind a lovelorn Zhang and finding romance with a new man even as she gave birth to Zhang's child. Heartbroken, Zhang fell into the welcoming arms of Russian Nadya, or at least, this is the transparently symbolic story of geopolitics writ small told in *Transnational Love*: an ever-loyal China, betrayed by a finicky bourgeois America, turning for solace to a warm and accepting Russia.[31]

China's officially sanctioned publishing scions weren't the only ones to see the appeal of the Li-Liza romance. Perhaps intrigued by the French connection between a Chinese who had worked in Le Creusot and a Russian who had learned her first words of French almost simultaneously on a Volga estate, in the 1990s a French journalist named Patrick Lescot decided to write a book of his own about it based on extensive interviews with Liza. On the night Li first met Liza, Lescot imagines: "A ravishing young woman, gay, innocent, observant. Li plunged into the blue of her eyes, cursing his timidity in the language of Tolstoy." As for Liza: "June 1936. Stretched out in the grass, a sprig of dill between her teeth, Lisa smiled as she watched her husband out of the corner of her eyes.... Five months since she'd married him and she was still stunned by her own daring." And on the two couples: "The four of them, Nadya and Zhang Bao, Lisa and Li Lisan, were easier on the eyes than the other Russians seated on the benches of the Elektrichka they rode morning and evening. In town, on Gorky Street, the two pretty Russian women on the arms of these Chinese men intrigued more than one passerby." Liza herself remembers not so much lying on the grass as battling mosquitos that summer—and encounters with ordinary people on the bus could be deeply problematic. [32]

The Briefcase

One summer night in 1937 when Li left work at the publishing house to go to the Moscow suburban village of Kosino where the dachas were located, he took some work home with him in his briefcase. The train was crowded and somehow in the crush to board, he lost the briefcase.[33] The briefcase landed in the hands of some regular Muscovites who also had a dacha at Kosino. Liza remembers that the briefcase was stolen; according to the story the thieves told, when they "found" the briefcase they were afraid to call over a policeman, and they took it home instead.

When they opened it up they were stunned to find letters to France, some Chinese newspapers, and a personal letter in Russian from somebody named Li Min that talked about playing tennis. They also found the address of the Foreign Languages Publishing house where Li was working and his identification card. They tried to return the briefcase there but somehow that attempt failed. They debated whether to turn the briefcase over to the regular or secret police, but decided to give it to the lost and found in the train station instead.[34]

About a week later, once again the Muscovite couple was on the train traveling to their dacha when all of a sudden they saw a Chinese man holding a tennis racket. It was not Li but Zhang. They watched him carefully, and he noticed that they were watching him. Then they came and sat down next to him and began to question him: did he or did he not work at the Foreign Language Publishing House? What was his name?[35]

At this point Zhang Bao himself became suspicious and refused to answer further questions. Finally, the Russians asked him, "Were you or were you not carrying a leather briefcase?" At that point Zhang began to explain very nicely that it was his friend Li Min who had been carrying it. But the Soviet person got out Li's photo identity card that he had kept from the briefcase and pointed to it and to Zhang, explaining how the picture proved Zhang was Li. The two men looked nothing alike, but perhaps they were the only Chinese people he had ever seen, and perhaps they looked the same to him. Now all parties involved were truly agitated, and Zhang followed the Muscovites back to their Kosino dacha where a conversation about the briefcase lasted until 11 PM. The next morning on his way to play tennis at the dacha, Zhang tried to call Li in Moscow, but couldn't get through. Only when Li got back to the dacha late that night was Zhang able to give him the information on the briefcase.[36]

A weary letter several months later from Zhang Bao dated February 26—presumably three days after the arrest of Li on February 23, 1938—suggests all that had changed in the intervening months, and not only because of a lost briefcase. Zhang, apparently in an effort to stave off his own arrest, wrote to the Chinese delegation to the Comintern. "By now," he wrote, "most of the people who worked in the Chinese section of the publishing house have been arrested." He went on to explain that in the course of work, he had interacted with all these people, meaning that he too was under suspicion. Moreover "in such a stressful time, it was impossible for the people working in the Chinese section not to go together from time to time to have some fun."[37]

Liza recalls, "Really, the matter of the briefcase turned out to be fatal for Li Min." Kang Sheng and Wang Ming used Li's loss of the briefcase as a pretext for a new round of denunciations, including accusations of embezzling party funds years before in China. Li's case was turned over to the Comintern in early 1938—just at the moment when Liza and Li's neighbors in the Lux were disappearing right and left. The People's Commissariat for Internal Affairs (NKVD) came for Li on February 23, 1938. Liza was told to pack her suitcases, then move to an annex of the Lux that was located in its courtyard. There she roomed with two German women whose husbands had also been arrested.

As soon as she had met her new roommates, Liza went to see her mother in their old communal apartment.

I threw myself on the floor and buried my head in her lap like a child and let myself cry out the tears I had been holding back for so long. . . . I cried for a long time, and my mother waited patiently. Having calmed down a little bit, I told her that I was going to look for Li Min in all the prisons, and that I wasn't going to give up on him. "Of course. Of course, you have to look. How could you abandon a person in need!" said my mother supportively. What enormous moral support these words were for me! In my eyes my mother had always been an honest, just person. Now I was even more convinced of it. After all, so many acquaintances and even relatives advised me to turn my back on my foreigner-husband! "Well one way or another he's got ties abroad— there's probably something there"; "Why should you ruin yourself, you're still young. Find yourself a good Russian guy and make a life of your own," they advised me.[38]

But Liza listened to her mother and after months of searching found out that Li was being held at the Taganka prison and that she could give him 50 rubles a month. Later, Li told her that when he received the first 50 rubles, he cried. His cellmates were shocked: how could it be that this foreigner was getting money from his wife when so many natives had been forgotten by their families? He bought soap, cigarettes, onions, and carrots. "But the happiness came not from the smokes and the nutrients, but from the knowledge that he wasn't alone and abandoned, that here, far from his homeland, he had people who remembered and loved him."[39]

Release

One day when she went to the prison Liza was told that she could bring Li warm clothing—a sure sign, in her mind, that he was being sent to Siberia. Among his clothes she found a fine woolen shirt he had brought from China, which was riddled with holes. She worked all night to mend them, and, on the appointed day, brought it with his other things to the prison. When he saw that shirt, he told her, again he cried. Yet Li was never sent to Siberia. On November 4, 1939, after twenty months in prison, he was released. He went to live with Liza and her mother in the communal apartment, and in 1940 was restored to his old job at the publishing house.[40]

In 1941, after the German invasion, Li stayed behind in Moscow for a time after Liza was evacuated, but eventually he joined her and others from his office. In June of 1942 he was called back to Moscow, and soon after was able to bring her as well and get her a job in the French section of the publishing

Liza, Li, and their daughter Inna, in 1946, before Li's return to China. Courtesy of Inna Li.

house. In the winter of 1942, she fainted—and then discovered she was pregnant. Not long after the birth of their daughter, Inna, Soviet victories in the West became regular events. For Liza, the war was over.[41]

Only when the first Soviet victories over Japan in Manchuria were reported did Li get excited. Suddenly the Chinese writer Guo Moruo appeared in Moscow. Li had been officially excluded from the Chinese Communist Party, but Guo wasn't a member of it either, and so Li was able to meet with him. On December 31, 1945, Li was called to the Central Committee of the Soviet Communist Party. At midnight he came home with big news: he had been reinstated as a member of the Central Committee of the Chinese Communist Party and would be returning to China. It was unbelievable. Liza was happy for a moment—until she realized that her old fear might be coming true. Li might return to China without her, maybe forever. Two weeks later, she saw him off at the train station.[42]

11

Emi/Eva

The Love Affairs of a Sino-Soviet Poet

"I'M BORED IN the Louvre," declares the Mona Lisa in a whimsical poem. "Days, centuries rush by, but for me it's boredom, only boredom." To amuse herself, she keeps a diary, scrawled on the back of her own canvas, with a Parker pen she filched from a drunk American. Mostly she writes catty comments about the other paintings, until one day, she falls in love. "A simple Chinese man came to the Louvre and looked at me for a long, long time," she writes in her diary. This Chinese, named Si Ia-u, visits her every day, and over time, the Mona Lisa comes to feel that they share a silent but deep connection. She begins to scoff at the European paintings around her and to dream about Chinese watercolors. Suddenly her reverie is interrupted by a broadcast from the Eiffel Tower: anti-imperial rebellion has broken out in China. Si Ia-u is thrown out of France for demonstrating in front of the Chinese embassy in Paris. The Mona Lisa becomes suicidal with worry.

The Turkish poet Nazim Hikmet wrote his poem, "The Giaconda and Si Ia-u," about his old Eastern University classmate Emi Siao (Si Ia-u), in 1928.[1] After Chiang Kaishek began arresting and killing communists in 1927, Hikmet began to fear that perhaps Emi had been a victim. And so he wrote a poem in honor of his friend and the Chinese revolution—and, in the process, created Emi's first public love affair.

In part two of the poem, "the poet speaks." Concerned about the Mona Lisa, Hikmet explains, he took action, landing a plane on the roof of the museum at night to rescue her. He throws a rope down to her window, and the Giaconda hoists herself out of her frame. They fly together across the globe to Shanghai, where Giaconda searches frantically for Emi. She has just passed a knife juggler when suddenly the crowd "sways like a Chinese lantern" and she hears a shout, "Get back!" Chiang Kaishek's police are pursuing their communist suspect. From a distance she spots two Chinese, one chasing the other with a sword, running straight toward her, closer and closer. Then she sees: it's Emi! He is three steps from her when the sword flashes and his head rolls. It is the last of the Mona Lisa's smile.

Liberated by her fury, the Mona Lisa joins the forces of Chinese rebellion, puts on boots and a leather jacket, marches across Tibet, strangles British officers, is captured by French Congolese soldiers, and receives her sentence of death by burning. She goes up in flames, red and laughing.

Hikmet's poem, with its garbled history, could be read in many ways, but in personal terms the implication was clear. When Hikmet wrote the poem, he was caught up in the international frenzy of leftist indignation that accompanied Chiang's 1927 reversal. That he would conceive a political poem about the failure of the Chinese revolution in terms of a lovelorn Mona Lisa galvanized by revolution says something not only about European romanticization of the Chinese revolution but also something about Emi. If ever a Chinese revolutionary could have seduced the most beautiful woman in Europe, it would have to have been him.

Emi and Vassa

Emi was not dead, as Hikmet imagined, but active in both love and revolution. He left the Soviet Union in 1924 having graduated from Eastern University, where he had befriended Hikmet. He went home to Hunan, where he took a leadership position in Hunan's Komsomol branch—just at the moment when his childhood friend Mao Zedong was more or less excluded from Shanghai politics and had returned to his home village in Hunan. Here are two, completely opposite homecomings: Emi, the glamorous, trilingual veteran of international revolution returning home from the Red Capital, and Mao, kicked out of the Communist Party's Central Committee with no official party position at all. After brief stints in Beijing and Zhangjiakou, in the summer of 1926 Emi went to Shanghai, where he became a leader of the city's Komsomol, along with his old friend Ren Bishi. He also joined the Party's eight-person Shanghai strike committee, which included his mentor Qu. Of the eight, all but two—Zhou Enlai and Chen Duxiu—were returned students from Russia. Together they fomented the series of armed rebellions that constituted the heart of the Chinese revolution of 1927.[2]

In the midst of his political activities, Emi somehow managed to start an affair with a Russian woman in Beijing, where he spent time in 1925 and 1926 between assignments. Vassa Starodubova, according to Emi's Chinese biographer, was "a beautiful Russian girl" with "a pair of big bright eyes." In a photograph taken later, Vassa has a thick fringe of long dark bangs framing an oval face, shapely eyebrows drawing attention to eyes that were indeed large and bright, and an expression that suggested a certain fearless resolve. Like many men his age, Emi had already been married once, by the arrangement of his family, but this first wife had died before he left for France.[3] So Emi was unencumbered when he met Vassa.

The most vivid image of Vassa comes from Emi's third wife, named Eva Sandberg. According to Eva, who was eight years younger than Vassa, she was utterly formidable. Vassa had been born in 1902 in Vladivostok to a large "urban petty bourgeois family" that stayed close throughout her life. Fifteen years old in 1917, she had received her higher education entirely in Soviet institutions. She was, according to Eva, a product of the "new Soviet intelligentsia," incredibly well read with daunting cultural credentials. In the 1920s, she set out for Beijing to become a Russian language teacher—the epitome of a New Soviet Woman. When Emi was transferred to Shanghai, Vassa also moved there for a new teaching position, evidently quite taken with Emi, who was remembered by Liza Kishkina and other Russian women who met him as a ladies' man. Eva said Emi and Vassa had truly been in love—who knows?—but what is clear is that at the height of the Chinese revolution, Vassa got pregnant.[4]

In late April 1927, the Party leadership met for its Fifth Congress in Wuhan, which was still controlled by left-wing Nationalists. On the agenda was a discussion of the Shanghai strike committee's actions and a change in Party leadership. When the conference ended, the Party sent Emi back to Shanghai with a briefcase full of documents from the Congress. In Emi's first preserved Party autobiography, dated January 10, 1930, he explained:

> Upon my arrival in Shanghai I was arrested, and a lot of documents in my possession were lost. After this, I had a nervous breakdown, and the Komsomol Central Committee, having removed me from the leadership, allowed me to leave for Vladivostok to rest and get treatment.[5]

Unlike most of the subsequent autobiographies in Emi's personal file in the Comintern, he didn't sign this one. Instead, his name is typed at the bottom. Moreover, later, signed autobiographies omit this episode, calling its authenticity into question.

This 1930 autobiography is Emi's most tentative piece of writing about himself, and it suggests that whatever did happen in 1927 had a profound effect on his identity as a revolutionary. After a month's rest in Vladivostok he went to the local Comintern headquarters to learn whether he could return to China, but was told he would be starting work as a teacher for Chinese students at Vladivostok's Far Eastern University. Vassa was given a job as a Russian language instructor. They married officially and on December 24, she gave birth to a son, Allan.[6]

Whatever calm the new family might have enjoyed was shattered in February of 1928 when Emi took a fall on an icy street. He went into a coma and was hospitalized, and though he awakened a week later, he slipped in and out of consciousness and only gradually regained his ability to speak and move. His doctor released him after two months, but pronounced him disabled. Although Emi attempted to return to work he found he could not. Vassa worked hard to feed and care for Emi and Allan. Since he was absent from the Sixth Congress of the Chinese Communist Party held outside of Moscow in the summer of 1928, Emi's friends assumed he had died and held a memorial service for him.[7]

Once word got out that Emi was in fact alive, the Chinese delegation to the Comintern—including his old patron Qu—called him to Moscow. In December 1928, Emi traveled to Moscow for the second time in his life—this time with a Russian wife and child. Emi knew exactly where to go: downtown to the campus of Chinese University. He enrolled as a graduate student and got his old Bolshevik Party card back from his student days at Eastern University in 1922–1924.[8]

Yet chronic headaches made study impossible. He had to be re-hospitalized, at which point the Chinese delegation to the Comintern "handed me over to the Revolutionary Aid Organization."[9] The Revolutionary Aid Organization (Mezhdunarodnaia Organizatsiia Pomoshchi Revoliutsioneram/MOPR) had been founded to help foreign revolutionaries who had suffered in some way in the course of their political activities. The organization was led by Old Bolshevik and pre-revolutionary friend of Lenin Elena Stasova and had branches all over the world, including in China.

Stasova arranged first a stay for Emi in a sanatorium and then light employment giving informational talks and ceremonial greetings, with a stipend and lodging in a dormitory for political emigrants. Emi's physical and emotional health seemed to recover, and he began asking around among his Chinese friends about real employment. Finally in the fall of 1930, he was able to return to regular work, as a Chinese language teacher in the Narimonov Institute for the Study of the Far East.[10]

Emi Becomes a Poet

At this point Emi and Vassa's standard of living rose and Emi's health improved. Emi spent a few hours a day in class, teaching Chinese language and literature, and for this he obtained official professor status, with all the benefits it conferred. This job was a stroke of luck, not just financially but also because it pulled Emi out of his doldrums and into Moscow's thriving international language and literature communities.

One day Emi paid a visit to the offices of a new journal, *Literature of World Revolution*. The editorial staff was planning a congress of international revolutionary writers and asked Emi to contact authors back in China about attending. Emi duly wrote to Lu Xun at the League of Left Wing Writers in Shanghai. But the letter he got in return explained that nobody was available for the trip and that he should attend the conference in their stead. In the fall of 1930 he traveled to Kharkov as a representative of Chinese leftist literature, despite the fact that he was not a writer himself. However, he gave a speech about the League and the challenges it faced in Nationalist China. In the aftermath of the conference, the editorial board of *Literature of World Revolution* asked him again to write to China to request works of literature for translation and publication in the journal. Once again Emi wrote—but this time, he got no response at all. Faced with a dilemma, Emi wrote a poem himself.[11]

To translate Emi's first poem, the editorial board of the magazine enlisted Alexander Romm, a poet and well-known translator, who played a crucial role in launching and sustaining Emi's new career. Romm had been born in St. Petersburg in 1898 and had studied in the Department of History and Philology at Moscow State University. In 1919, he became involved in the Moscow Linguistics Circle, which originated among philology students at Moscow State and grew to include major figures such as Mayakovsky,

Pasternak, Bakhtin, and Shklovskii. The circle's interests ranged from poetic language to the study of folklore and dialects. Romm made a timely contribution to the group: he translated the work of Ferdinand de Saussure, sometimes considered the father of twentieth-century linguistics, from French to Russian. He went on to translate fiction to and from several European languages, as well as among various languages of the Soviet republics. Romm didn't necessarily read all the languages from which he translated, sometimes working with French, English, or German renditions supplied by others.[12] But Romm was no hack.

The rendition Romm produced of Emi's first poem appeared in *Literature of World Revolution* in early 1931. Titled "Such Is life," the poem told a straightforward story of a boy who grows up in a village ruled by an oppressive landlord but no matter what happens is always told by his father "such is life"—until one day the boy decides life should be different and joins the Red Army. From Emi's description of the translation process, the timeliness of the technique and topic was responsible for its success. At first he used the form of an old Chinese folk song for his poem and translated it into Russian. When Emi brought it to Romm, Romm had him read it aloud in Chinese, asked numerous questions about Chinese poetry, and had him recite some of the famously melodious Tang Dynasty poems. Romm took whatever gist and feeling Emi's poem and recitation gave him and mixed it with Russian folk songs to produce the final Russian rendition of "Such Is life." Encouraged by a positive review from a well-known literary critic, Emi continued drafting poems, corresponding with Romm even as he was pulled away to attend a conference on the Latinization of Chinese in the Far East.[13]

In addition to producing translations, Romm also placed them with mainstream publications like *Komsomol'skaia Pravda* and *Molodaia Gvardiia*. Clearly excited with this quick success, in September 1931 he wrote to Emi:

> You know, at first they [*Molodaia Gvardiia*] were going to start their issue with the political piece, but then they changed their minds, and instead of the article they began with your poem. See how we distinguish ourselves! The issue with [your poem] "Cotton" already came out. . . . *Literature of World Revolution* asked me for it, even though it's already been published in *Molodaia Gvardiia*. In a word, we're a colossal success. I'm waiting for you to come to Moscow as soon as possible,

we'll do a book together. But reading your article, I see what enormous work you've got ahead of you in the Far East, and I'm afraid you won't come back as soon as I'd like. In that case, don't wait for your return, send me the literal translations from Khabarovsk.[14]

In the final months of 1931 and early part of 1932, Emi continued to send Romm verses, culminating in the 1932 publication of a short pamphlet of poems. "Because of this," Emi recalls, "I came to be known as 'a poet.' "[15]

The majority of Emi's early poetry was intended to incite sympathy for the Chinese revolution among Soviet readers and to express Chinese enthusiasm about international revolution and Soviet culture. One of Emi's first and most famous poems was called "Nanjing Road," about a Chinese uprising in the foreign settlements of Shanghai:

It's quiet on Nanjing Road/In the shadows lanterns glow/It's cold and raining/Chilling rickshaw drivers to the bone/The wet walls shine/ Ladies and gentlemen sleep/The walls slumber/The shadows are in darkness/One slips ahead/Others by twos—you can hardly see them— Silently they have gone to march . . . And Zhang has come. And Li has come. And Wang has come . . .[16]

Other poems have titles such as "A Letter in Blood," "In Memory of the Guangdong Commune," "For Soviet China," "Red Square," "Lenin," and "For the Martyrs of the Spanish Civil War." "Whatever he wrote," his third wife recalled of the mid-1930s, "they published."[17]

Alexander Romm translated the majority of these poems. Memoirs and biographies describe a process by which Emi would sit down with Romm, reading out a Chinese original and verbally offering a rough translation. Certainly Emi wrote poems and sent them to Romm; this much is clear from their correspondence. Yet when a major Chinese publisher compiled Emi's collected works for publication, it omitted twenty-odd poems that had been published in Russian periodicals in the 1930s for which no Chinese originals could be found. Emi's bilingual secretary in his later years explained that when he was asked to give Chinese originals for "Such Is life" and other poems, he suggested she simply translate them from the Russian.[18] She did, but only a few of these appeared in the collected works.

More intriguing than the provenance of Emi's poetry is the emergence of a persona called "Emi Siao" that came to be synonymous with romanticized notions of Sino-Soviet revolution. In 1928, a Chinese communist, who had been born Xiao Zizhang in a village not far from Mao Zedong and had lived a colorful life in some of twentieth-century China's most interesting international venues, reappeared in Moscow. Shut out of the top leadership of the Chinese Communist Party, whether for political or health reasons, and clearly looking for a way to reinvent himself, Xiao discovered that Moscow had a position vacant—or rather, a persona lacking. Regardless of the actual status of China's leftist literary movement, *Literature of World Revolution* needed a Chinese writer of some sort—a poet would do—anyone who could produce firsthand accounts about the Chinese revolution and its major heroes for Soviet audiences. The fact that no reliable supply of suitable stories could be secured from established Chinese writers did nothing to quash demand for them in the odd market place of Stalinist cultural internationalism. "Emi Siao," then, was the name of an idea as much as a person. However Emi was also a person, one who sometimes struggled to reconcile the cultural and political differences between the Chinese and Russian revolutions, no matter how creatively he interpreted them or how much he benefited or suffered from his role as go-between.

Once Emi was identified as a Chinese revolutionary poet and publicist, he began to receive invitations to attend conferences and participate in delegations all over the Soviet Union. He had already been invited to a conference on the "Latinization" of Chinese in the Far East in 1931. Determined to give national characteristics to each of the Soviet republics and at the same time to produce a language that could at least theoretically one day become global, Soviet ethnographers and linguists were busy ensuring that all the non-Russian peoples in the Soviet Union had Latinized alphabets, including the Chinese in the Soviet Far East.[19]

Emi's mentor Qu Qiubai had been working on a system to Latinize the Chinese language on the eve of his departure from the Soviet Union in 1928 and continued after returning to China. The Latin alphabet Qu drafted and a pamphlet he wrote about it became a foundation document in both the Soviet Union and China. Qu made a key intervention in an existing standardization campaign in China, pushing the movement further toward present-day *pinyin*. Emi, along with others who would subsequently be involved in language reform in the People's Republic of China, inherited both Qu's role and his position in the Soviet movement by making a strong (albeit futile) argument that tones weren't necessary.[20] In 1933, the Institute of Red Professors admitted him to its literature department, bolstering his position as a literary scholar.[21]

At this point, Emi's sheer presence in the Soviet Union, his revolutionary credentials, and his status as a poet led to an auspicious invitation to attend the First Congress of Soviet Writers in August 1934 as one of China's representatives. Emi wrote to left-wing writers back in China to invite them, but they declined to make the dangerous trip.[22] Emi's attendance helped make his career, not only in the Soviet Union but also later in China.

At the Congress, Emi introduced himself as a representative of the Soviet Far East, thus situating himself firmly as a Soviet writer, but he also spoke about China's League of Left Wing Writers and highlighted key figures like Lu Xun and Mao Dun. He lamented his colleagues' ignorance of Chinese life—not all Chinese men have a queue and not all Chinese women have bound feet, he pointed out—and literature. He suggested an evening of Chinese culture later on—a party—as a means of rectifying the situation.[23]

Emi Siao's Writer's Union card, 1934. RGASPI, f. 495, op. 225, d. 96, l. 97.

It was the same tactic he used in Marseilles when confronted with people whose understandings of China were outdated: throw a party and try to slip in a bit about contemporary Chinese culture.

Just as Qu had emerged onto Moscow's international revolutionary scene through his attendance at international congresses in the early 1920s, so too Emi's profile began to rise. At the conference he met famous Soviet and foreign writers and became friendly with some, most notably Isaac Babel. He was also invited to dinner at Gorky's house, along with numerous other writers including Sergei Tretiakov (author of *Roar, China!*) and the poetess Hu Lanqi. Since Hu did not speak Russian, Emi translated for her. Buoyed by the invitation, Emi asked Gorky to play the role of host at his gala evening of Chinese culture, but when Gorky could not make it André Malraux took his place. Malraux had won the prestigious Prix Goncourt in 1933 for *La condition humaine*, a novel about the Shanghai uprising of 1927 that Emi had helped to foment. Emi's party featured a keynote speech by Malraux and was attended by Fadeev, Ostrovsky, and numerous other Soviet luminaries. A Soviet actor read a translation of Lu Xun's famous "True Story of Ah Q," Emi read a few of his own poems, and Hu Lanqi sang in Chinese.[24]

Emi seems to have worked as an interpreter for Hu Lanqi on various occasions during her stay in Moscow. Hu was a radical young woman who had traveled to Germany in the 1920s, joined the German branch of the Chinese Communist Party, and been imprisoned there for several months. She wrote serialized reports of her time in prison for *Le Monde*, and her spirit of extreme dedication earned her fame in international radical circles. One day Emi accompanied Hu for a visit to a factory—"GPZ Factory Number One"—to discuss a new book about China written by the well-known German leftist journalist Egon Erwin Kisch.[25] According to their Party representatives, the workers at the meeting had read Kisch's book. But the workers themselves, when presented with a real, live Russian-speaking Chinese person, wanted a chance to ask direct questions about China, its revolution, and its revolutionary culture. Emi was somewhat taken aback, because he had been under the impression that the workers would have read some of his recent work.

Emi was no prima donna, so he not only answered queries about Chinese literature as best he could, but he also spun out some stories of the Chinese revolution that were bound to entertain his audience.

In 1930 when they [Chinese communist fighters] were partisans and not literate, when they captured some radios from the enemy, they didn't know what they were. They seized the radios, looked at them, and threw them away. They thought that if it had been a cannon, then it would be worth taking. Then a more literate commander came along and said, you have to take it. Even though he was literate he wasn't a radio specialist. But then in the city they captured a radio specialist. He had served the Whites, but himself was neutral. They asked him, will you work with us? He said no I can't. They said why not. He said because I am afraid. What are you afraid of, there is nothing to be afraid of. We'll pay you 100 rubles a month. It has to be said that in China that is a lot of money. He agreed and we used him. In fact during the third campaign of the Guomindang he captured all kinds of secret evidence. . . . Somehow we captured some White provisions, a lot of canned goods. The Red Army didn't know what it was and thought they were bombs and didn't want to take them. But one brave guy gave it a try, there was no explosion and then they stopped being afraid.[26]

At this point, the stenographer noted, there was laughter in the hall. Despite his obvious disappointment that the workers knew nothing of his poetry, then, Emi still played the part of a representative of the Chinese revolution who had witnessed and experienced it firsthand. He wove this tale to do the job as it was handed to him that night and leave his audience satisfied.

Emi/Eva and the "Love of the Century"

In the aftermath of the conference, Emi was rewarded with two weeks rest at the Soviet Writers' Union resort at the Black Sea, where he met the woman who decided to be the love of his life. His poetic affair with the Mona Lisa and his marriage to a Russian woman, it turned out, were but preludes to a more enduring relationship. Eva Sandberg was a young German Jewish woman who had just graduated from photography school in Munich. Her brother was the conductor of the Royal Swedish Orchestra, in Stockholm, and he arranged for her to visit the Soviet Union along with a translator who was familiar with Isaac Babel. Babel arranged for them to accompany his secretary to the Black Sea, and it was there that Eva met Emi.

Eva Sandberg. RGASPI, f. 495, op. 205, d. 749, l. 21.

Many years later Eva wrote her memoirs in German published as *China—My Love, My Trauma*. But the Chinese translation was titled quite differently: *The Love of the Century—Me and Xiao San*.

Fresh air and sunshine, red flags flying everywhere. At the resort, lunch was already on the table, it was facing the sea. She (Babel's secretary) led me to a table for four. At the table was a Chinese guy who seemed young and likeable. It was the Chinese writer San. We looked each other in the eyes and were lost for a moment. This was the love that would last a lifetime. I was 23 and he was 38 but he looked just 25. On my birthday at the table there was a red flower, this is how he expressed his love for me. This flower decided my whole life path.[27]

Emi spoke only a little German and Eva spoke no Russian but conversation was apparently beside the point.

The writer's resort was by the sea. We spent every day sunning ourselves and swimming. There was a collective farm nearby and every day they brought us fresh food. . . . There were flowers everywhere, kids were jumping and dancing and singing. Just that year, the Soviet Union started having Western dances. Xiao San quickly became a great dancer. There was a song, Chinese Marching Song, that had no Chinese flavor at all, and wasn't good for dancing but it became a symbol for Xiao San and I. For the rest of our lives we just had to hear that music to look at each other with meaning, to be lost in memories.[28]

Babel's secretary knew something about Emi and tried to tell Eva that he was married with a seven-year-old son, but Emi assured Eva that he and Vassa were divorcing.

According to Eva, the problem with Emi's Sino-Russian romance was Vassa. Russia's New Soviet Woman, it turns out, had a bad temper—at least according to the European fellow traveler who wrote about her years later. After graciously conceding Vassa's good qualities—she was wildly intelligent as well as kindhearted, generous in helping others, honest, and straightforward—Eva zeroed in on her flaws. "It was too bad her personality wasn't so great. She thought that whatever needed doing only she could do it, that everything happened because she willed it to, and the minute something wasn't right she'd start criticizing and never shut up, saying things that really hurt people." As Eva saw it, the overbearing Vassa harassed gentle Emi endlessly; he had no way to cope with her, and so, even though they loved each other, they simply could not live together, and eventually split up. Soon after, Vassa met a brilliant, sweet, younger Russian Jewish Sinologist, who "resolved her personality problems," and they lived happily, in Eva's telling.[29]

Eva and Emi had a whirlwind Moscow courtship. There was the time she went to see him on the day of Kirov's funeral, scaring him because she was late due to the crowds of mourners; there was her decisive overnight stay at the dorm for political emigrants where he lived; there were evening visits from Babel; and there was New Year's Eve, 1935, spent at the country house of one of Emi's Russian friends, Nikolai Virta:

That little villa in that snowed-in forest was a genuine Russian wood cottage, there was wood burning in the fire, it felt like the gingerbread house from Hansel and Gretel. It was warm and comfortable in the house, on the table there were all kinds of appetizers according to village custom . . . so much it seemed like the table might bend from the weight of it. I remember it like it was yesterday . . . at midnight they dimmed the lights. . . . This was also the first time Xiao San experienced a big Russian New Year's party.[30]

But Eva and Emi's Russian romance was soon interrupted when the Soviet government stopped extending Eva's tourist visa. Unlike Emi, Eva wasn't an official political emigrant. All their famous writer friends intervened, but nothing could be done: Eva had to leave in February 1935.

According to Eva, Emi was completely lost without her, writing to her almost constantly and even calling her on the phone, trying to convince her to give up her German citizenship and become a Soviet citizen so that she could return to Moscow and be with him. It was a big decision for Eva. She held out for a while, vexing Emi, according to the letters she quotes from him. Emi wrote:

Last night after we talked on the phone it was really hard for me. I was sad all night. It's obvious you haven't yet decided to join the Soviet nation. Maybe you don't love me as much as you think and as much as you write in your letters. I absolutely will not force you, and I won't demand and persuade you to join the Soviet nation. I just want to explain to you, why I don't approve of your attitude. I am just explaining the following points to you as a comrade: 1. If you become a Soviet citizen what are you losing? I know there are a lot of foreigners who dream about becoming Soviet citizens; becoming a Soviet citizen is a great joy, a great honor. . . . 2. After you become a Soviet citizen, do you really believe you'll never be able to leave the Soviet Union? Here you are entirely wrong. This is because you don't understand the international situation and the history of revolution. These questions are hard to explain clearly in two or three sentences. I am only really strictly telling you: pretty soon—in the end it's hard to say exactly when, of course it isn't completely decided, world revolution will come. At least in some countries, the working class will gain victory. This isn't optimism, this is concrete political party knowledge. Then who knows who will get sent abroad to work? But only you can decide whether or not to enter the Soviet nation; this has no connection to our love.[31]

Here life and fiction intersected perfectly paradoxically: Emi wrote a poem titled "Ia—sovetskii grazhdanin," ("I am a Soviet Citizen") in which he enthusiastically declared himself a Soviet citizen in spirit: "I raise my head high/I stretch out my chest/I breathe freely/I gaze proudly.... I'm climbing the Urals/One leg remains in Asia/The other—in Europe. There it is, the Union! Where are its shores?" Even in this unambiguously titled poem, Emi states clearly that his destination is still China: the final stanzas place the author on top of the Kunlun mountains in China, observing the country, leading its people to enlightenment with his songs. For Emi, who did not have to make any actual decisions about his own citizenship, Soviet citizenship seems to have been a symbolic thing.[32]

While haranguing Eva with polemical diatribes, Emi simultaneously peppered his biggest supporter, Romm, with a very different set of messages: a series of love poems that were every bit as anathema to Romm as Emi's political arguments were to Eva. Judging from a handwritten letter Romm composed, Emi was embarrassing himself:

I want to write something that's unpleasant and hard for me to tell you, but tell you I must. Maybe you got the impression that I don't want to work with you. It's not true. I want to work with you and I will work with you, if you want that too. But there is something that I can't and won't do, at least in the coming months: I really am not in a position to translate your love poems. I honestly tried to do it, but either I couldn't do it at all, or else I did it badly ("Ostrich," "The Black Sea"). Notice that I translated all the political poems you sent me, and translated them successfully. And will continue to. Of the love ones I was really only able to do "By the waves of the Black Sea." The very idea of "Ostrich" seems false to me now: you can compare the one you love to whatever or whomever you want, but to call all other people geese—that's not the imagery of a socialist poet. Even in "Black Sea" there is some kind of exaltation and deification that is not part of our relationship to women. And "Waiting for your call"—it's comical, yet also neurasthenic.... Here's my conclusion: it's not worth it for me to force myself, and there's no reason for you to hesitate, you just need to find another translator for the love poems.... Maybe Svetlov would agree, he's very lyrical and soft, it would suit him. In any case, I can't.[33]

Romm's refusal to translate these poems did not end their professional relationship; the two continued to collaborate on publications through the 1930s.

Emi did not accept Romm's denial of the suitability of his love poems in the socialist context, however. In February of 1936, Emi was invited to speak at a meeting of the Soviet Writers' Union in Minsk, and his speech mingled the internationalist political themes he had been expressing to Eva with a rebuttal of the sensibility that made lyrical poems so distasteful to Romm.

> When a lover wants to prove fidelity to the one she loves, or on the contrary, a lover to the one he loves, they often say I am yours twice over, and so I would also like to say that I am twice Soviet. Why? Because I am a citizen of the Soviet Union, but I'm also a citizen of soviet China.[34]

At this point in Emi's speech, the stenographer noted, the entire hall jumped up in a roar of applause. Emi continued by emphasizing the significance of Soviet literature in China, and vice versa. He also made a case for the importance of songs and the people who wrote them, mentioning by name the "lyrical and soft" Svetlov who Romm had recommended. He continued:

> I would also like to talk about lyric poetry. My comrades and I all question so-called purely lyrical poetry. But not long ago I went to a Moscow kolkhoz [collective farm], and was reading lots of poetry, when suddenly one young guy stood up and said, "Read something lyrical." I told him that I question strictly lyrical poems, because personal life isn't separate from the life of society.... Then I thought about it. It's true, we're always singing about the revolution, the Comintern, socialism, the Red Army, we always need these songs, but people have moments when it's not the Comintern you're thinking about, it's not socialism you're thinking about, you're thinking about something else entirely. And it's exactly "about this other thing" that we have to write songs. In *Pravda* there was an article by Chukovskii about how schoolgirls are gathering entire albums of bad poetry. Everywhere people are singing "Me and my Masha at the Samovar." I think that we have to create a true Soviet lyricism, a real Soviet romance.[35]

To this there was no thundering applause, just a lone voice from somewhere in the hall, "Right." Yet Emi's speech was timely, coming just after criticism of avant-gardists like Meyerhold and Shostakovich and just before an attack against "formalism" in literature.[36]

In describing himself as a "lover" of the Soviet Union and calling for a "Soviet romance," Emi was in tune with a more general emphasis on passion in Soviet high culture of the late 1930s. These were the years of the Spanish Civil War, which incited great emotion in people all over the Soviet Union—and the years of the purges. Soviet intellectuals were busy reading the *Sorrows of Young Werther* and going to a new theater production of Anna Karenina—stories that had captured the imaginations of young Chinese a decade earlier and were now attracting the attention of a Soviet culture preoccupied by what one literary historian has called "fatal passion."[37] It wasn't just Emi's speeches that put him in tune with the times; it was also his very biography. He had experienced one of the great, fatal moments of revolutionary passion in recent memory— Shanghai, 1927—and had built his career as a poet writing about it, even as he embraced the contemporary Soviet attraction to Spain. With his divorce and remarriage involving two foreign women, he epitomized both a revolutionary and a lover whose emotions crossed national and racial boundaries.

A Happy Family

In August of 1935, six months after her departure, Eva returned to Moscow as a photographer for a travel magazine and moved into the dorm for political emigrants with Emi. Her recollections of life inside Moscow's international revolution are par for the course: the Hungarian and Chinese neighbors squabbled, she was taken aback by the poverty of the Soviet Union, she shopped in special stores for foreigners and felt guilty about it.[38]

Emi's Russian friends had mixed reactions to Eva, and vice versa. On one hand, as Hikmet's poem suggested, a love affair between a Chinese revolutionary and a European woman had a certain romantic appeal. Eva and Emi were friendly with the writer Nikolai Virta, who wrote an unpublished story inspired by their romance called "The Girl from Norway," in which Emi became an African and Eva a Norwegian. Eva, pleased to be fictionalized, drew a mock cover for the book: Devushka iz Norvegii in girlish Cyrillic cursive at the top left of the page, a map of the Soviet Union with a hammer and sickle superimposed on it in the middle, and a cut-out picture of her and

Emi at the bottom, she smiling like an awkward but satisfied newlywed, Emi peeking over her shoulder looking all-too-knowing.[39]

On the other hand, it seems some could be a bit catty. Emi's friendship with Isaac Babel predated his relationship with Eva, and because Babel lived near Emi's dorm and often hosted political emigrants, Emi came to be a regular visitor. Emi, whom Babel's wife remembered as "short, slender, good-looking," would read his poems to Babel in Chinese, because Babel liked to hear how they sounded.

> One day at dinner Babel asked him, "Tell me, Siao, what's the ideal woman like for Chinese men?" And Emi Siao answered, "She should be so elegant and weak that she'd fall over from a breeze." I remember it well. In the summer of 1937 [sic] Emi Siao went to vacation on the Black Sea. Returning in the fall he came to visit with a full-figured girl named Eva and introduced her as his wife. She had a lovely face with dark blue eyes and a short boyish haircut on a rather heavy body. When they left, Babel said, "Ideals are one thing, reality's another."[40]

Eva wasn't above a bit of cattiness either. Nikolai Virta, she thought, lacked taste, noting that he spent the money from his successful novel, *Alone*, on an expensive furnished apartment that was nevertheless "a little tacky."[41]

Ironically, Eva and Emi's closest Russian friends turned out to be Emi's ex-wife Vassa and her husband. Vassa came to Moscow soon after Eva's arrival and stayed with them. Emi—and all the neighbors—braced for the moment Eva and Vassa would start screaming, but Eva claims it never happened. According to Eva she was extremely patient with Vassa, who got very sick in Moscow and whom Eva nursed, overlooking her terrible temper. But there is another Vassa between Eva's lines: Vassa (whose Russian was crystal clear) teaching Eva to speak Russian; Vassa showing Eva how to cook to Emi's tastes ("so weird I was stupefied"); Vassa, on the day Eva and Emi officially got married, rushing out to buy food, and arranging an impromptu wedding celebration.[42]

In November, Emi was called to Khabarovsk for an extended stay to participate in a special commission on Chinese language reform. Vassa and her new husband lived in Khabarovsk with Allan, and they invited Eva and Emi to stay with them in their three-bedroom apartment. Vassa's Sinologist

Eva and Emi. Courtesy of the Siao Family.

husband was also part of the language reform initiative, while Vassa worked in an orphanage for Chinese children. They had a maid to help with cleaning and laundry, but Vassa did the cooking. Vassa's husband found Eva some work as a freelance photographer and set up a makeshift darkroom for her. "We were a very harmonious family of five," remembers Eva. Emi's secretary and translator speculates that two of the love poems Emi wrote that year were actually inspired by Vassa, for whom he still had feelings.[43]

In April, Eva gave birth to a son and in May they returned to Moscow, where Emi had been allotted a brand new three-room apartment on the tenth floor of a Soviet Writers' Union building. In retrospect, it was a brief

moment of calm amid the inevitable centrifugal forces socialist internation-
alism exerted on families. That summer, the baby got sick with dysentery
and died; a Japanese attack at the Marco Polo Bridge began the Second
Sino-Japanese War; and Stalin's purge expanded to mass repression. While
Eva quickly became pregnant again and gave birth to a healthy boy named
Leon, political pressure on the family only intensified. Like so many others
Emi at first believed that purge victims were true traitors to the socialist
cause—until Vassa's husband was arrested, at which point he began to have
his doubts.[44]

Emi had already come under pressure from Wang Ming and Kang
Sheng, ringleaders of the purge inside the Chinese community in Moscow.
They wanted Emi to write a letter to Lu Xun instructing him to close the
League of Left Wing Writers. Emi had spent considerable energy build-
ing up the literary reputations of Lu Xun and other writers from the
League inside the Soviet Union. At first, Emi recalled, he ignored them.
But Wang and Kang were firmly in control of the Chinese Communist
Party in Moscow, deciding who would be allowed to return to China, who
would be left alone, and who might be sent to a Soviet camp or worse. Emi
wrote the letter.[45]

Soon Emi found himself in a worse predicament. In June of 1937—a time
when fear and suspicion particularly crippled the moral sensibilities of the
Soviet elite—Emi wrote an extensive denunciation of numerous Chinese
with whom he had worked in the Far East.[46] Whatever his calculations upon
writing this letter, however, Emi's position only worsened. In the fracas, one
of the accused, whose Russian wasn't very good, had asked Vassa's husband
to help him write a letter defending himself, which he did—before being
arrested himself. When Emi learned of this from Vassa, he wrote a new letter, denouncing the Chinese who had asked for help with the letter. He neither defended nor directly denounced Vassa's husband, but simply stated the
nature of their relationship: "The wife of Liubin [Vassa's husband's Chinese
name] was in the past my wife." Emi's careful wording painted Vassa's husband as a simple translator for a person whom even the most politically vigi-
lant communists (such as himself) had not known was a traitor.[47] The letter
suggests that Emi was worried about guilt by association, but he refrained
from denouncing her husband.

Under these circumstances anybody would have been anxious to leave the
Soviet Union.

Escape

In the spring of 1938, Ren Bishi appeared in Moscow, straight from Yan'an. Ren was a close ally of Mao and was sent to Moscow to secure Mao's image as undisputed leader of the Chinese Communist Party.[48] Ren was also a good friend of Emi's from his youth in Hunan and at Eastern University in Moscow in the 1920s. Here, finally, was Emi's chance to use his Soviet status to regain his place in the Chinese revolution—and perhaps escape the increasingly dangerous Soviet purge. Emi had been working on a biography of Mao's early days, and he shared this with Ren, along with his sincere wish to return to China. He began a campaign to publish as much of his writing as possible and to build a case for himself.

Emi prepared a new and lengthy autobiography designed to show how his time in the Soviet Union had enhanced his revolutionary credentials. Gone was the tentative tone of his 1930 statement, replaced by a far more coherent and confident presentation of his identity as a Sino-Soviet revolutionary writer with a unique perspective to contribute to the Chinese revolution.

> For a long time I, like a lot of our comrades, was under the mistaken influence, the influence of Confucianism that sees literature and art as petty and worthless occupations. I didn't think about becoming a professional writer. But participating in the literary life of the U.S.S.R., seeing ... the development of Soviet literature, paying serious attention to how the party of Lenin and Stalin sees literature, I again began my literary work.[49]

Similarly, in a letter to the Chinese delegation to the Comintern, he explained,

> I have understood that "literary affairs are part of general proletarian affairs" (Lenin) and recognized the great responsibility of "the writer— as the engineer of the human soul" (Stalin). ... It's been 11 years that I have lived in the U.S.S.R. I saw the completion of two Stalinist five-year plans for the building of socialism. I have become acquainted with a variety of the best Soviet people and have seen the happy life of the Soviet nation. I understand that this is all thanks most of all to the proper leadership of ... the great Stalin.[50]

By that point Emi could boast publication of two volumes of his poetry, an edited volume of translations of Chinese literature published in Kiev, and two biographies—of Zhu De and of Mao. While his later public writings were a bit reticent about his early ties with Mao, in his official but private correspondence inside the Soviet Union at this time he played up his childhood relationship with the leader of the Chinese Communist Party. Ren Bishi read Emi's biography of Mao and felt it would be useful; later it was approved for translation into foreign languages in the People's Republic. A flurry of correspondence among Comintern officials repeatedly summarized Emi's qualifications. On January 2, 1939, Comintern chief Dimitrov wrote to secret police chief Beria asking that Emi, along with two other Chinese, be allowed to leave for China. [51]

In December 1938, Emi traveled to Novorossiysk on the Black Sea to visit Allan and Vassa, who had gone there to live with her sister after her husband's arrest. He returned in time to spend New Year's with Eva. Once they received official permission for Emi to return to China, Eva was allowed to leave with Leon for Stockholm, where she would live with her brother.[52]

With Eva safely in Sweden, Emi contacted influential friends to advocate the release of Vassa's husband—which occurred in April of that year. He also arranged for proceeds of his literary endeavors in the Soviet Union to be transferred to Vassa, and the Chinese delegation to the Comintern requested that the Revolutionary Aid Organization send assistance to her and Allan. Emi was writing poems and corresponding with Romm regarding their publication in a collection titled "Flutes of Hunan" up to the eve of his departure. He dashed off a hasty foreword to the book, thanking Romm for his work as translator. "You could say that we often had some friendly co-creation in the best sense of the word. I hereby express my thanks." But, he concluded, "Let no one say, as some try to claim, that it's Romm, not Siao."[53]

On March 5, 1939, Emi visited Comintern headquarters in Moscow one last time, turned in both his Bolshevik Party card and his Writers' Union membership card, returned to his apartment, and called Eva in Stockholm. The next morning, he boarded a train headed for Kazakhstan. After arriving on the border of Xinjiang and Soviet Kyrgyzstan, he traveled by car across rough roads to a tiny border town at the foot of the spectacular Tianshan Mountains. There he caught a ride with a convoy of forty jeeps carrying Soviet weaponry for the communists in Yan'an, where Emi would soon reunite with his childhood friend, Mao Zedong.[54]

12

The Legend of He Zizhen, Mao's Wife in Moscow

EVEN THOUGH MAO himself did not travel to Russia until 1949, his family has its own place in the Sino-Soviet affair. Mao's brother, third wife, two sons, and daughter spent considerable time in the Soviet Union. Taken together, their Russian experiences add up to a very different Sino-Soviet symbolism.

In fact, the Mao family produced the great anti-heroine of the Sino-Soviet romance. Her name was He Zizhen.[1] In 1927, at the age of eighteen, Zizhen met Mao when he came to her hometown in the mountains east of Changsha, the capital of Mao's native Hunan. She accompanied him on the Long March and bore their six children. In 1938, she left Mao, Yan'an, and the Chinese revolution to go to Moscow, to study.

Like Chinese revolutionaries in years past, she found that there was a new school there, designed just for people like her. The Chinese Communist Party, which was said to have severed its ties to Moscow, turns out to have been operating in Moscow (and Manchuria, and Xinjiang, and Siberia, and France, and a great many other places as well) all along. Mao's brother trekked back and forth between Moscow and Xinjiang, working to open a corridor from Yan'an to the Soviet Union, through which radio communications, people, planes, money, and—he hoped—arms could eventually flow. Mao's two sons by his second wife Yang Kaihui were already in Moscow. Zizhen and her daughter by Mao wouldn't leave Russia for a decade.

Whatever aliases Zizhen may have acquired in Russia didn't stick. She couldn't, or wouldn't, learn Russian. If she had a friend, much less a lover, nobody knew about it. In the dystopia that was Mao's Russia, she lost her remaining children and was designated insane.

A Woman with Two Spears

Mao's first marriage had been arranged and like other male communists he abandoned it. His second marriage (1920–1930) was a reflection of an earlier revolutionary period: Yang Kaihui was the daughter of a favorite teacher among radical students at Hunan First Normal. Mao had two surviving sons by this second wife; after he abandoned her, she was arrested by Nationalists and killed. Supposedly, before she died she wrote a series of letters to Mao (some of which were published in 1984 and others that have come to light since) that give Yang some sort of public personality.[2]

Zizhen, on the other hand, left behind no published or unpublished voice to the public; if her daughter (still alive) and granddaughter (educated in the United States) have any of her personal writings, they have not granted access to them. Therefore written material about Zizhen fits into the category of lore or legend and must be taken as such. But the legend of He Zizhen became a part of the Sino-Soviet romance.

Zizhen was supposedly born in 1909 in a small village at the foot of a mountain known as Jinggangshan. Her childhood name was Guiyuan but she renamed herself Zizhen (which literally means "self-value") when she went to school. She was the second of five children in a family of provincial scholars who owned a tea house. She learned to read and write from her older brother's tutor, and her parents allowed her to go to a local missionary school for girls run by two Finnish women—but Zizhen had no patience for their type of instruction.[3]

As girls, she and her two sisters were so tall that somebody dubbed them the "three flower branches of Yongxin." Photos show that she had thick, dark eyebrows, big shining eyes, a full mouth, and a wide nose. Later, among communists, she was considered attractive—she is often listed among a small handful of early female party members who were known for their beauty, despite their unisex self-presentation.[4]

Along with this prettiness was a rebellious nature and a preternaturally early interest in politics. Zizhen was inspired by the passage of Chiang Kaishek's forces through her province in 1926 and was said to have been one of the earliest and youngest members of her local communist party. She made fiery speeches and was involved, along with her older brother, in local rebellions. Zizhen got a reputation for being able to shoot a gun. According to one story, somebody once teased her that they had heard that two officers had been felled by her gun the day before. She replied that yes, she had shot two officers, but not with one gun. At this point, the story goes, she became known as a "woman with two spears."[5]

The tales told about Zizhen—of a tall, beautiful, rebellious young girl in outlaw territory, too smart to stay home, too restless to study, keen to engage in political action, a crack shot—these are really the only natural or even appropriate stories, considering how things turned out for her, and for the Chinese revolution. It would have been odd had she been portrayed as an educated, romantic girl, like some female radicals a decade older than her, including Mao's first wife.

Zizhen's brother was close to a local bandit leader, to whom Mao and his ragtag band of would-be revolutionaries appealed upon entering Zizhen's county. According to one local historian, the bandit introduced Mao and Zizhen as a way of resolving his own personal dilemma: his concubine was jealous of Zizhen, whose passion, youth, and engagement with revolution made her a natural object of attraction for the men around her.[6] However their meeting happened, when Mao left Zizhen's territory a year later, she went with him, to what would become the seat of China's "Soviet" territory, the city of Ruijin in Jiangxi Province. According to a counter-myth, Zizhen actually never really fell in love with Mao but simply gravitated to him for physical protection. Once she got to know him, she wanted to leave, but Mao prevented her from doing so.

Whether in bliss or discord, Zizhen and Mao lived together in Ruijin until the beginning of the Long March. Mao was hardly the leader of the Chinese Communist Party—his fortunes rose and fell—and he spent a considerable amount of time at home. Zizhen was said to have been pregnant three times before the March even began. Mao miscarried the revolution, Zizhen lost their children.[7]

Zizhen on the Long March

And so a young pregnant woman set out on the Long March as Mao's wife, one of the roughly thirty-five women among 80,000 men to take part in the journey that became the quintessential experience of twentieth-century Chinese communism.

The course of the March, traced on a map, shows that it moved first west and then north, punctuated by strange loops, unlike the relatively logical arcs and lines that led most Chinese communists to Moscow on boats and trains. Early sojourners to Moscow made much of the dangerous, under-ground nature of their exit from China and the long and uncomfortable train ride to Moscow, but they weren't subjected to enemy fire nor did their journey have an immediate military objective. A large majority of people on the Long March either deserted or died en route, from exhaustion, hun-ger, cold, and disease. The Chinese, so the story goes, walked all the way to utopia.

The women on the March played a particular role in changing the rela-tionship between love and revolution, Chinese style. For the men on the March, having a woman along was an obvious privilege, and this implied that a woman's status on the March was closely tethered to that of her male companion. Whereas in Moscow, according to Chinese Communist Party lore, the relative imbalance between Chinese male and female students gave women power and led to wild promiscuity, on the March the scarcity of women led to new ideals of chastity. The stories that women themselves tell of their March experiences suggest a certain logic: pregnancy was a disaster. How could a woman recover from a difficult labor or a botched abortion on the March? Horror stories abounded. When a baby was born, who could carry it?[8]

Pregnant at the outset, Zizhen gave birth in February 1935 to a girl. She refused to name her daughter before leaving her with peasants; it is said that on her deathbed, out of the blue she asked a visitor and fellow Marcher, "Where, but where was it that I had that baby, do you remember?" She might have forgotten because she was hit by a bomb two months later; others died but Zizhen just had her skull and back filled with shrapnel. Among the many legends about her, one says that you could feel the metal if you ran your hand across her back. Most of the journey she had a horse and when she was in really bad shape, she was carried on a litter like Mao himself. She was so mis-erable that people say she begged to be shot.[9]

Of the alleged six children that Zizhen had with Mao—three before the March, two during, one after—only one survived and was officially recog-nized. She was named Li Min and nicknamed Chao Chao.

Later in life, spurred on by childhood friends, Chao Chao would attempt to piece together the story of her own birth to include in a book she called *My Father, Mao Zedong*. She wrote:

I was born in 1937 in the region of Baoan, in Northern Shanxi province. There are different versions about my birth date: some say I was born in

August 1936; others, that it was the winter of 1936, but my father said that it was the beginning of 1937 and my mother confirmed this too. In general for ordinary mortals, like me, the exact birth date doesn't have much meaning. What difference does it make, if you know it or you don't?... Really, if one more little being came into existence on the enormous plateau of the Yellow River, what difference did it make on what day it happened? For the daughter of Mao Zedong it was all the less important, because my father was focused on the birth of an entire nation.[10]

Chao Chao tracked down the midwife present at her birth, the wife of another party member, who recalled: "Far away I heard the groans of He Zizhen carrying all the way from the artillery turrets.... I went in and saw He Zizhen: pale and emaciated, she was lying on a mattress right on the floor and was shivering from the cold. The walls of the turrets were made of stone, and the roof was made from straw puttied with clay. Gun barrels stuck out of all the crevices." It was Chao Chao's lot to have been born at the very end of the Long March. Like the other children, she was given to a local woman to nurse and hardly saw her parents in Yan'an, but she survived.[11]

The Moscow-Yan'an Connection

The Long March was supposed to have caused the Chinese Communist Party to finally turn inward, toward the needs of the Chinese peasantry. Yet, now free to create their own little revolutionary state, one of the first things the Communists did in Yan'an was to tell their story to the world—most famously through the journalist Edgar Snow.[12]

Anybody who knew anything about real Soviet politics in these years knew that the Russian party was killing itself and taking as many foreign communists with it as it could. Fellow travelers could, and did, go to the Soviet Union and report only good things, but it was a distinct public relations coup that there was an exotic new red utopia where the leaders actually lived in caves and cared about the peasants. Foreigners began visiting Yan'an, from Agnes Smedley, a Midwestern girl who became a fellow traveler and went to Moscow before heading to Yan'an as a Comintern agent, to the Soviet documentary filmmaker Roman Karmen, and many more.[13]

Yan'an, then, was not only a Chinese communist base in the heartland but also the kind of international socialist entrepot where people like Emi might thrive. In Yan'an, Emi translated for Roman Karmen, corresponded with the Soviet literary establishment, talked poetry with Zhu De, reminisced about Paris with Zhou Enlai, and visited almost the entire party elite. He also reconnected with Mao, who saw to it that Emi was named the rector of Lu Xun Academy under Kang Sheng and invited Emi to his cave for late night chats.[14]

Emi also resumed his womanizing, taking up with a friend of his younger sister, even as he stayed in touch with his foreign wives. Vassa fretted over Emi's health and wrote to Union of Soviet Writers chairman Alexander Fadeev about his life in Yan'an:

Comrade Fadeev!

Although we are not acquainted I appeal to you with a request for help in a serious matter.

I recently received a letter from Emi Siao from which I can tell that Emi has had to endure great financial difficulties there. Despite the fact that he is rector of the Lu Xun Literary Academy, he eats as poorly as any student. (Twice daily gruel with a small amount of vegetables.) He doesn't always have money for tobacco.

Knowing all too well how poor Emi's health is (after all we lived together for eight years) I think with horror that after a year of such living he'll get tuberculosis. He himself no matter what does not complain, and his letters are full of enthusiasm and vigor. (after all, he never knew how to take care of himself). When he left he gave me and our son all his author's rights and honorariums. From time to time we receive (from E. Wolf in Moscow) small amounts. In Goslitizdat there are about five thousand [rubles] in fees for a book of Emi's poems, a collection of prose, as well as some articles. . . . And this is my request. Help get permission for Goslitizdat to transfer some money [to Emi], at least a small amount, to hard currency. . . . I would like for Emi not to know that it was me who asked for the money to be sent. Let it be as if from the Soviet Writers' Union.

All the best,
V. Starodub.[15]

Meanwhile, Eva began a serious campaign to join Emi in Yan'an. As Hitler's grip on Europe tightened, Eva scanned the Soviet papers for news of Yan'an, her heart jumping when an article by Roman Karmen mentioned Emi in

July of 1939. She wrote to Emi, who in turn asked Mao for permission to bring her to Yan'an.

In August of 1940, Eva left with Leon for Leningrad, where she visited Vassa. She then traveled to Moscow and boarded a train for Kazakhstan. By now Soviet planes were flying between Almaty and Lanzhou, so Eva and Leon were placed aboard a diplomatic flight and thereby avoided the long drive across Xinjiang. A Soviet military truck took them to Xian, where Emi met them for the final trip to Yan'an.[16]

After Eva arrived, Emi left the cave he had been assigned by the Party and used his own money to pay for a different one for the two of them and Leon. Leon remembers that the adults treated him very well. "When I was little I was especially cute, and when grown-ups would take me to the market, small traders would give me things to eat. So my father, afraid of the effect on revolutionary discipline, very humorously put a sign on my back that said 'Please don't feed him.'"[17]

One day, Eva and Emi visited Mao, who—according to Emi's biographer—asked Emi, "So you're living on your own now?" Emi side-stepped the reference to his living quarters with a joke, "No, I got married and got a job." Mao played along: "What job?" Emi: "Homeless vagrant." Mao: "Having no job is also work. For example, people with no property are still a class. . . . Basically, you're a petit bourgeois." "Basically," answered Emi, "not a very good type."[18]

Not many people in Yan'an would put a funny sign on their child's back or joke with Mao about their class backgrounds, but these stories signal that Emi's position in Yan'an was a bit precarious and that his personal relationship with Mao both safeguarded him and opened him up to criticism. Some considered Emi dissolute and a bad influence on Mao.

Others didn't like the way Emi championed Soviet literature, which intellectuals at Lu Xun Academy and elsewhere considered aesthetically impoverished. Mao and Emi spent hours discussing the role of literature in the Soviet Union—including the First Soviet Writer's Congress, where socialist realism was introduced and art was subjugated to politics—before Mao's famous "Talks on Literature and Art" in 1942.[19] These talks were part of a larger Party purge that served to consolidate Mao's power and sideline his Soviet-backed rival Wang Ming. If his biographer is correct, Emi was a conduit through whom information about Stalin's methods of handling intellectuals reached Mao at a crucial moment.

Whatever the nature of Emi's friendship with Mao, it was not enough to smooth the way for Eva. She was unhappy in Yan'an, not just because she had interrupted Emi's affair with a younger woman. She was not allowed to take pictures, could not speak Chinese, and was essentially isolated while Emi was immersed in party and cultural work. She left for the Soviet Union, where she spent several difficult wartime years in Shymkent, Kazakhstan, eking out a living for herself and her two sons.[20]

After Eva left Yan'an, Emi resumed his affair with his sister's friend, with whom he proceeded to have two sons.[21]

Zizhen Departs for Moscow

Not only did foreigners come to Yan'an, but so too did young Chinese radicals, a new crop of communists and potential communists who had come of age under siege by Japan or else under Nationalist rule, and who were curious about the new communist haven. Among these radicals were women—young women who had not been worn out on the March.

Mao's promiscuity in power is well known, but He Zizhen was allegedly the one woman who stood up to him, the woman who propelled him to the top and wouldn't back down even when he got there. What exactly happened between Mao and Zizhen is a matter of pure hearsay, but the most frequently told story came from Agnes Smedley, who said that one night Zizhen walked in on Mao and a girl.

The best rendition of what Zizhen screamed is: "Son of a pig, turtle's egg, whoremongering no-good! How dare you sneak in here to sleep with the little bourgeois bitch!" Then, Smedley came on the scene and found Zizhen beating Mao with a flashlight. Mao didn't resist but told her to be quiet, which exacerbated the situation. Zizhen scratched the girlfriend and hit Smedley, who hit her back. What kind of husband, Zizhen wanted to know, let some foreign woman beat up his wife? Multiple bodyguards were needed to drag Zizhen away. Whether or not any of this happened, scandal erupted. Smedley was kicked out of Yan'an.[22] Within six months, in late summer of 1937, Zizhen was pregnant again.

Whether Mao sent Zizhen packing because of a Shanghai actress or she left of her own accord, she departed with several wounded party leaders, the first of several groups of high-profile people who would leave Yan'an for

He Zizhen and Mao Zedong in Yan'an. Courtesy of Li Duoli.

Moscow. What is known is that by January 1938, Zizhen was in a top Kremlin hospital being treated for her shrapnel wounds.[23]

Mao's Russian-Born Son

On April 6, 1938, Zizhen gave birth to her last child with Mao. Here, in Moscow, she had proper care in a special *roddom* (birthing home), the type of place where many women gave birth in the Soviet Union.[24] The healthy boy was given a Russian name—Tolstoy's name—Lev. She stayed in the medical center for six days. Here was a male heir for Mao, born in Russia no less.

Mao's older sons, Anying and Anqing, had recently arrived in Moscow, where a peculiar family reunion took place. They remembered their first meeting with Zizhen:

> She was tall, thin, with big eyes, an awkward smile, as if she wanted to say something but was shy. She looked tired and sad. How to break the awkward silence? Finally she asked: Is this Anying and Anqing? She said our father missed us. . . . [Zizhen] saw our dirty room and started to clean, she put fruit and plates on the table. Then she saw our dirty clothes and brought them to a river to wash them and hung them out to dry, we felt awkward about how she was bustling around, and we tried to help her. . . . She came to see us on weekends, bringing gifts. She spent her entire 70 ruble a month stipend on us, gradually she became an irreplaceable person for us. If she didn't come we missed her.

According to the Mao brothers, Zizhen's sadness evaporated after Lev's birth.

> We went to her house and saw the newborn. She smiled and her smile was so soft and sweet. We had rarely seen such an expression on her face before. This little room became our home, here we heard stories about the Long March, helped teach her Russian, she told us about our father, herself, her wounds. She sang to us in her clear voice folk songs that brought us back to our homeland. This home was full of happiness, laughter and songs.[25]

But Lev succumbed to pneumonia and Zizhen's spirit, at least according to Mao's son Anying, died with him. She became "an entirely different person."

After the death of her son, Zizhen was first sent to study—by now the default option for high-ranking Chinese communists who arrived in Moscow.

Secret School

The school where Zizhen matriculated, which had already been operating for several years when she arrived, was one of the most peculiar places in the history of Soviet international education. A far cry from the schools of the 1920s, Zizhen's school reflected a new, sordid desperation in Sino-Soviet revolutionary relations.

By 1933, the Japanese invasion of Manchuria had started a murmur in the Comintern: wouldn't it be a good idea to bring some young Manchurian communists (or at least, anti-Japanese activists) to Moscow for some serious education?[26] After the Comintern lost touch with the Long Marchers, Wang Ming, as leader of the Chinese delegation in Moscow, focused his efforts on Manchuria. The number of local radicals and anti-Japanese partisans was growing there, and a Manchurian Communist Party was developing independently of the Long March. Wang started bringing Manchurian party members to Moscow. With Chinese University closed and the capacity at the Moscow Lenin School limited, Communist Eastern University—which had been in continuous operation as an international revolutionary school since Qu and Emi's days there—was given the task of organizing a new set of Chinese courses.

In the 1933–1934 school year, Eastern University had twenty students in its new Chinese section; by December of 1935, there were seventy, and plans were in the works to double the size of the student body, which included mostly partisans from Manchuria, a handful of Chinese from the Soviet Far East, and a "special short-term group of six people." Reflecting the 1930s Soviet ethos of conspiracy, these three groups were housed in three different locations. The school had six teachers who taught in Chinese, like Wu Yuzhang, one of the leaders of the Latinization campaign who later headed the PRC's first committee on language reform, and Guo Shaotan (also called Krymov), who later spent time in the gulag before emerging as a prominent Soviet Sinologist. There were also courses "on China" taught by members of the current Chinese delegation to the Comintern in Moscow. [27] In the years 1934–1939, the delegation included not only the leader of the so-called 28 Bolsheviks and sometime general secretary of the Chinese Communist Party Wang Ming, but also a person far more significant in the later lives of many Chinese communists: Kang Sheng.

One of the more detested people in twentieth-century Chinese history, Kang Sheng possessed immense creativity for devising ways to make people suffer both physically and emotionally. His English-language biographers write that he spent his years in Moscow "completing his political education and earning postgraduate degrees in every aspect of political terror." This statement echoes a theme that runs throughout histories of Chinese students in the Soviet Union: perhaps the most important thing they learned was the art of political repression. Chinese students in Moscow are portrayed as experiencing political terror themselves, participating in it, and then importing it back to China. This implies that the Chinese did not already understand enough about torture or methods of political control, and—at the other end of the logical spectrum—that the French had not already clearly demonstrated that terror often accompanied violent overthrow of an existing order and forcible creation of a new one.[28]

However important Chinese experiences of Soviet terror may have been, the activities of most Chinese in Moscow, even at the height of the purges, were rather diverse. As for Kang Sheng, Wang Ming brought him to Moscow, where he lived at the Lux and made speeches in the Comintern supporting Wang's leadership of the Chinese Communist Party. He also helped to organize cavalry forces in Outer Mongolia to support the Chinese Communist Party in case it ever reached there. And it seems that he spent a considerable amount of time on what might be called basic revolutionary pedagogy. Kang was seriously involved in the Chinese sector at Eastern University, where he gave lectures.[29]

Similarly, students in this underground school did not simply study Stalin's speeches. They were also supposed to visit an orphanage and the airport and factories and the metro and even a meteorological station; go to the zoo, the planetarium, and the Museum of the Red Army; and see movies (*Love and Envy, Under the Rooftops of Paris, Chapaev*) and plays (*Intervention, Mother*). Ironically, there is no evidence that they attended the one performance they might have understood best—the appearance on Moscow stages of the Chinese opera star Mei Lanfang during a much feted visit in 1935. Mei was in Russia as part of the cultural diplomacy between Chinese Nationalists and the Soviet government that preceded their political alliance against the Japanese—and therefore the appearance of a large group of Chinese communist students at a performance would perhaps have been undesirable.[30]

Starting in August of 1934, Old Bolshevik Boris Izrailovich Kraevskii was brought to give a series of lectures in the methods of underground work. But these lectures were about evading arrest or what to do upon arrest or under torture—if lectures were given on how to do the arresting and torturing, those weren't transcribed and preserved. Kraevskii explained how he would force himself at night, when he had just dropped off to sleep, to wake up and recall every last detail of his fake passport; how once when he was arrested and imprisoned for two years, he was able to surprise the police by giving the exact same story upon interrogation at the end as at the beginning, because he had remembered everything so precisely; how ordinary people, when asked to close their eyes and recall the details of a room, can't even remember how many windows it has, but how Asians have better memories, a fact he backed up with an example from Kipling's *Kim*; how the police even used children to follow suspects, so it was wise to be suspicious of children; how the police play on love, luring scorned women into betraying their unloving husbands; how if an illiterate comrade was forced to put a fingerprint on a document, he should somehow move his hand so that it would be clear in court that the print had been forced.

Kraevskii ended one of his lectures to the students with a little pep talk on what to do if they were arrested and tortured by the police:

> It's important not to underestimate them. It's true that village police sometimes aren't that experienced, but still you have to look at them as if they know what they're doing. And don't fool yourself into thinking that if they arrest and interrogate you you'll be able to fool them. Also the police are more and more internationalized, they communicate with the police from other countries, share experience. . . . You have to remember, if they arrest you, you're alone and they have the whole power of their apparatus behind them. . . . But on the other hand, you shouldn't be too afraid of your opponent, we shouldn't think they are all-powerful. You have to remember the weakness of the bourgeoisie. We are the stronger class, and one way or another we will win and we'll win in the near future. . . . Our strength lies in the fact that whatever they do, in any case death awaits them in the near future. . . . His weakness is in the fact that he's historically powerless. Practically he's very powerful at the given moment, but historically it's a powerless political class. He can't do anything against us. We'll beat him.[31]

Finally, Soviet teachers of revolution stopped trying to get the Chinese to read Lenin and started just talking in an accessible way about something practical and relevant. The students asked all kinds of questions.

Perhaps to make a point, a year after the Eastern University students heard Kraevskii lecture on how to operate in secret, they went on a field trip to a special museum in Moscow, called "Hard Labor and Exile," which included

model cells and other relics from the days when the Bolsheviks had to operate illegally in pre-revolutionary Russia. The students loved it, according to
their schoolmaster, who noted a particular fascination with the methods by
which communists communicated with each other in prison by knocking.
They were intent on understanding the composition of the Bolshevik Party
and its mechanisms of purging itself. They were also wildly enthusiastic about
the Spanish Civil War and had to be restrained from donating too much of
their monthly stipend to the cause.[32]

During this second period of educating Chinese at Eastern University
during the 1930s, Kang Sheng presided over the pedagogical sessions that
the school's teachers and Comintern representatives held jointly to discuss
how to improve the education of Manchurian communists. They worried
about not having enough specialists in Manchurian geography and military
matters. Kang Sheng insisted that the main objective of the courses was to
tell the students "what concretely they must do in Manchuria." Instead of
physical geography, for example, they should be taught military geography
so that students would understand the strategic importance of Manchuria
in the battle against Japan. Not so much time should be spent talking about
history; too much had changed since then in China.[33]

By early 1936, the Comintern was dreaming, once again, about a larger
Chinese student body. By April, a scout had gone to Manchuria to find new
recruits.[34] Interest in fomenting revolution abroad by bringing foreign radicals to Moscow clearly remained even as the Soviet Union headed into the
purge. But ideas of educating foreign and domestic easterners together in
one big, open institution that symbolized internationalism and fostered
ties among revolutionaries from different places had given way to pressure
for greater secrecy. In the name of keeping the foreigners isolated from the
domestic students, Eastern University had split itself in two. From May on,
foreigners would be at a separate place called the Scientific Research Institute
for National and Colonial Issues, or Colonial Research Institute, directed
by Pavel Mif. The institute began dispersing its various national groups to
different locations in central and suburban Moscow, with the idea that none
would even know the others were there.

The school for the Manchurian operatives was supposed to be a complete
secret and in fact existed, in the Soviet context, in what its own officials called
an "illegal" state, which meant it had no official existence in Soviet party or
bureaucratic circles.

We have an abnormal situation with the military section, in fact it exists illegally. So there is a whole array of abnormalities with provisioning all sorts of materials we need, and with teachers. So the question came up about military equipment, here we have a military section but we can't get military equipment. We have to decide the question of whether or not we need to legalize our military section, if this is necessary, then where and with whom can we get in contact on this question, whom do we need to approach with this question.[35]

In fact, they said, what weapons they had were small-caliber pistols that they had bought themselves in stores whenever had been able to do so. They conducted training in the countryside where ordinary peasants sometimes happened upon them, causing further anxiety; yet they were unsure whether they could obtain permission to use a more secluded spot. From this discussion, it's clear that the Chinese courses at Colonial Research Institute after 1938 were in a precarious position, without clear patronage in powerful places that would provide them with a direct source of necessary supplies. The anxiety associated with running an illegal school—full of people who had just come from Japanese-occupied Manchuria and were therefore, in the Soviet Union of 1938, prime suspects of espionage—might explain why school officials were so determined to keep the students isolated and how upset they got when that was impossible.

Coercive Intimacy

The problem was that the more the authorities tried to isolate the Chinese students, the closer and more intimate the young people's contact with regular Russians seemed to get, no matter where officials put them. For a time, the graduate students remained at the original Eastern University, which had established habits and rituals of interaction between students and the people around them since its opening in 1921. But in the summer of 1936, some Chinese and Koreans went to a short summer course that was located in or near some dachas at Udel'naia station in suburban Moscow, and Soviet vacationers were always around, making noise and interrupting things.

Increased exposure to Soviet people during the summer had been a regular part of Chinese experiences in Moscow educational institutions from the very beginning. What was unusual was the extent to which, in the mid-1930s, some Chinese who were supposed to be completely sealed off from Soviet life during the normal academic year were right in the middle of it, all the time. In the fall of 1936, there were about fifteen Chinese students in sector "11" whose entire life and education was being conducted out of two rooms in a building where the regular employees of Eastern University lived on Neglinka street, which ran from behind the Bolshoi Theater in the center of Moscow out toward Tsvetnoi Boulevard.[36]

One of the rooms served as both the dining hall and a classroom, which would have been fine except that it was a hallway between the living quarters of all the Eastern University employees and the kitchen and washroom they used, so people were constantly passing through this room, day and night. The employees heckled the students for being "foreigners," "not one of us." On top of this, the room was located above a restaurant that got really noisy in the wee hours of the night.[37]

The second room for these Chinese students was actually part of the *masterskaia* [workshop] for the school's employees that had been sectioned off by a piece of plywood. In the workshop the radio played all day and people talked loudly; there was also a glass door in this room which opened onto a passage between the workshop and the employees' living quarters, so people would often open the door or peer through the glass. Despite repeated appeals to find this group a new location, in early 1938 they were still there. By that point, at least one Russian girl had become pregnant by one of the Manchurian partisans.[38]

The head of section 11 wrote in his rector's report that under these conditions, all the talk about the need to keep this educational effort a secret was pointless:

The students, in reality, find themselves in an open situation, all the more since the residents of this building and workers of Eastern University don't answer for the students to anyone, they often carry on conversations among themselves about the students. I can't get anyone to take responsibility for this. This leads to a situation in which among the students there is a tendency to carry on with women, and this can't help but impair the students' discipline. For example, on the night of September 30, 1936 the students Tin Tao and Chzhan" vun

went to Udel'naia station without any permission whatsoever to meet
with Niura (an employee of Eastern University) and Tasia (a worker on
the state farm at Udel'naia station). This all was made possible by the
sickroom at Eastern University (this was a place for meetings and for
passing letters) and also by the employees of Eastern University, that is,
the employees of Eastern University played a catalyzing role . . . even
telling the students the locations of the other sectors.[39]

School officials were also dismayed that the students were rude to the staff,
prideful of whatever meager education they had already received elsewhere,
or passive. Only a few seemed to perform acceptably. One of the biggest
problems was with a student who had been the head of a partisan detach-
ment in Manchuria and had been brought to Moscow with his parents, wife,
children, and a group of bodyguards who were loyal to him, which made
teaching him anything difficult. But the worst was when he beat his wife.
Kang Sheng personally raised a big fuss about this, riling up the partisan's
own bodyguards to condemn him for it.[40]

If these Manchurian partisans were fraternizing with ordinary Muscovites
and running amok more generally, the graduate students, in sector 7, had
problems of their own. More educated and with more experience in the
Manchurian Party, this group of relatively elite students experienced a level
of intimate coercion that created a bizarre educational environment. The students quickly paired off and started having babies.

The unusual situation attracted the attention of higher-ups. In February
of 1938, the head of the graduate student section made a report on the
group which was followed by an active question-and-answer session by
someone named Kotel'nikov. The very first question this overseer asked was
about the students' emotional state and relationships with each other. The
head of the section launched into a long explanation about how relations
between the sexes were problematic, and while he assured the investigator
that nothing too untoward was going on, there was at least one situation
where a couple had gotten together and been permitted to marry.[41]

In reality, there was a much larger number of couples among the graduate students and Chinese teaching staff. By 1937–1938, marriage among
students was being reported as a general phenomenon. The marriages were
discussed in some detail, with some seen as legitimate and others not. School

authorities paid special attention to the students' private lives and relationships, encouraging some couples and breaking up others.[42]

The Chinese Woman, Betrayed

Controversies over sex among the Chinese in Moscow not only continued through the Soviet terror but also became implicated in it.[43] This was true both among students and the Chinese Communist Party leadership in Moscow, from Wang Ming on down. The result was that by the time Zizhen arrived in Moscow as the jilted wife of a major party leader, she would find other women with similar stories.

One of the more tragic Moscow cases was that of a Chinese woman who had been convinced to come to Moscow to keep her husband company there while he served on the Chinese Delegation to the Comintern. His name was Zhang Hao and hers was Su Keqin. Su was Zhang's second wife and, according to her own account, had been steadfast in her support for her husband over the course of many long and difficult years. But once she arrived in Moscow at her husband's insistence, she discovered that he was conducting an open affair with a German woman. The rest of the Chinese delegation intervened and made Zhang promise to end his affair since it was embarrassing everyone. But he did not. Fed up, Su, who had a daughter by Zhang, decided to write an open letter, using an alias for her husband, to the committee asking for its intervention in her private life:

> Members of the Representative Committee,
>   My problem with Comrade Fu Sheng is not, I don't think, a personal problem or a freedom of marriage or divorce issue. My problem with Comrade Fu Sheng is a comrade cheating a comrade problem, it's a comrade because of love coming up with all sorts of traps to embarrass another comrade problem. It's a problem of a comrade using politics as an excuse to attack another comrade because of love. . . . A party member should behave, because in all the world it's only the CP that doesn't oppress women. All over the world if a man has position and money, he can bully his wife with three wives and four concubines, he can leave his wife anytime he wants. . . . [Fu Sheng] used Comrade Wang Ming and Comrade Luo Xue as excuses to tell me forcefully that "girlfriends are necessary, here social interaction is important, if

Luo Xue didn't allow Wang Ming to have a girlfriend, relations wouldn't be secure." True he didn't want to get rid of me, he just wants me to stay at home and take care of him and let him go out with the German woman and sometimes I can even come along and walk behind them and maybe if I want to have sex do it after her, only in that way can I be a good wife, it's too bad Fu Sheng forgot that I am a comrade, forgot that I am a party member with a spirit of protest.[44]

Su seemed to have an impressive case against Zhang, and she might have emerged victorious, except for one unfortunate misstep: she mentioned Luo Xue's acceptance of her husband's extramarital relationships. And so Su was condemned for her "feudal" attitude toward male-female relations and sent to work in a Moscow factory and then to a labor camp in 1937.[45] At the height of the purges in the Soviet Union, within the small Chinese community in Moscow, sex and politics were just as hopelessly entangled as ever.

It seems there was something in the air: Lin Biao, who came to Moscow a bit later than He Zizhen, became completely enamored of the Shanghai film actress Sun Weishi, who had been studying in Moscow drama schools and was the adopted daughter of Zhou Enlai and his wife Deng Yingchao. Lin is said to have chased Sun unsuccessfully throughout his entire time in Moscow.[46] He then left his wife behind in Moscow when he went back to China, and she spent years—like Su Keqin and He Zizhen—in the backwaters of provincial Russia.

Other Chinese were not so lucky. A systematic accounting of all Chinese sentenced to death or years in labor camps has not yet appeared, but archival documents suggest that by 1939, at least 1,700 Chinese citizens were officially acknowledged in Soviet camps—not including Soviet citizens who were ethnically Chinese. Anecdotal evidence suggests that Chinese were also as likely as anyone else to be sentenced to death. Data gathered on the 20,000 people shot at Butovo outside Moscow includes dozens of Chinese—some laundry or factory workers, some intellectuals—and a database kept at the Sakharov Center in Moscow contains similar evidence.[47]

Zizhen and the Nadir of the Sino-Soviet Romance

When, exactly, Zizhen signed on as a student at the Colonial Research Institute is unclear, but she is listed, under her Russian pseudonym Ven Iun, on a student roster generated in December 1938, just months after the death of her son Lev.[48]

Soon after this, the Colonial Research Institute was officially closed. Nevertheless, a small group of Chinese comrades, Zizhen included, continued to receive an education of sorts in a remote Moscow suburb called Kuchino, in a group of dachas very isolated from the Soviet population. At the time, it took two and a half hours to get to Kuchino from Moscow on the *elektrichka*, the electric trains connecting Moscow to its suburbs. This school was run from the fall of 1938 under the auspices of the Revolutionary Aid Organization, the same organization that had helped Emi in the early 1930s.[49]

Despite or perhaps because of its remote location, the school had problems, both from the point of view of the Chinese who attended it and according to the Soviet authorities. The single Chinese memoir that discusses this school in any detail recalls it as being poorly provisioned. In January 1940 on a visit to the Soviet Union, Zhou Enlai wrote directly to Comintern chief Georgii Dimitrov, detailing the nature of the school and its students, mostly "sick comrades," survivors of the Long March who genuinely needed medical care. In the summer of 1940, the Russian director of the school wrote a report suggesting that few of their needs were being met: in the winter the temperatures in their buildings had dropped below zero; some of the comrades had neither boots nor winter coats; and students weren't getting the medical care they needed.[50] This is what it came down to: the Chinese revolution sending its cast-offs to Moscow, and Moscow hiding them away in some remote, frigid dacha, with little of the material or spiritual sustenance they had come to find.

In the summer of 1940, Zizhen was sent, along with several dozen other Chinese comrades, to a special sanatorium for rest, but few of the Chinese sent there registered substantial improvement. The "school" was then disbanded by the Revolutionary Aid Organization and its students were dispersed to other places and institutions, as so many other Chinese students had been in the past when the educational experiments designed for them had failed.[51] And so ended, for a period of eight years during the war and the postwar period, the Soviet Union's effort to educate adult Chinese communists. When, in 1948, the Soviet Union once again opened its doors to foreign communists, including first and foremost the Chinese, assumptions about international socialist education had completely shifted.

The Sino-Soviet romance had begun when a flighty, neurotic writer traveled to Moscow, imagined himself in love with Tolstoy's granddaughter, and wrote a *History in the Heart of the Red Capital*. Now, it seemed, it had ended, with Mao Zedong's cast-off, wrecked wife mourning the death of her Russian-born son by Mao, unable or unwilling to articulate her own heart's history in any language at all, reflecting a grim vision of the Sino-Soviet relationship.

13

Sino-Soviet Love Children

IN A CHILDREN'S home in a little village seventy-five kilometers south of Moscow, in 1932 an old carpenter pried apart the planks of a barrel in order to make skis for a particularly rambunctious five-year-old boy known as Yura. Yura was the sort of boy who had to get tired out, every day, or he would torment the other children with his shenanigans. At bedtime when he was hungry, the old nanny who worked the night shift gathered the children who couldn't sleep and told them stories; her voice, reciting the opening lines of Pushkin's fable of the golden fish, is one of the first sounds Yura remembers: "There once was an old man who lived with his old woman right near the deep blue sea . . ."[1]

The scene was common enough in the early 1930s, when Soviet homes were full of children orphaned by the great upheaval of the first five-year plan.[2] What was unusual about it was the children themselves, who were not Soviet but foreign—in Yura's case, Chinese—and whose parents were not necessarily deceased. Yura's father had studied at Eastern University in 1923 at the same time as Emi and then had returned to Moscow with his wife and infant in tow in 1928, along with Qu and other top party cadres. He left Yura tucked away in this tiny, obscure Russian village called Vaskino, along with Emi's son, Qu's daughter, and a handful of other Chinese or Chinese-Russian children, each, in one way or another, a child of the Sino-Soviet romance.

Qu's daughter was called Tuya, the Russian word for an East Asian cypress tree that is not usually a name but sounds a bit like her Chinese name, Duyi, which meant lonely. While Yura was too young to remember his parents or his trip to Moscow, Tuya was six years old in 1928 when her mother, Yang Zhihua, brought her to Russia, and she had vivid memories of the journey. On the boat from Shanghai to Dalian, her mother dressed as a peasant woman to avoid scrutiny, covering her bob with a wig of long hair coiled in a bun. She also sewed some US dollars into the hems of Tuya's pants, but the pants got lost and so their train ride to Russia turned out to be much hungrier than Qu's own Journey to the Land of Hunger had been seven years before. Once in Moscow, Tuya stayed with Qu and Yang in room number 12 at the Lux Hotel. She remembers being the only child at the Sixth Congress of the Chinese Communist Party, held outside of Moscow in July. "I was there the whole time. Why? Because they had nowhere to put me. . . . [D]uring breaks I danced and sang for the delegates. . . . Kids my age joked, 'Hey, you're our delegate.'"[3]

After the Congress was over, Qu and Yang were given tickets for a vacation in Crimea, without Tuya, so they put her in an ordinary Russian orphanage. "These were kids picked up off the street. They were little hooligans, guys, rotten boys. When they sent me there I didn't know how I'd survive. I was little. Smaller than the others. . . . The director there was a Bolshevik, an Old Bolshevik, and she had real sympathy for the Chinese. And she said, 'OK, I'll keep this little girl with me.' And I slept in her room." But this was no permanent solution; after they returned from Crimea, Tuya lived with her mother in the Eastern University dorm until 1930, when her parents returned to China, leaving her behind at Vaskino, in a new, special home for children of foreign revolutionaries located in one of Eastern University's former summer houses.[4] Tuya has fond memories of the place, perhaps because it was so much better than the previous orphanage where she was left.

By then she was eight, a few years older than Allan, Emi's son by his first, Russian wife Vassa, who arrived at the home in 1932. Emi wrote a poem called "Vaskino" about dropping Allan off there.

Little Allan my son
Today I am taking you to Vaskino
My heart so very happy
My heart endlessly sad

I remember in 1923
"Eastern University" students vacationed here
Wang, Luo, Chen and Shiyan
Not one is still alive!
Vaskino! You have become a historical place
You could say you're my second hometown!

I think of so many close brothers
who were sacrificed, who shed blood for Soviet power.
Here we sang songs of revolution together
Each more fervent and rousing than the next . . .[5]

Actually, Allan stayed only a few months, unlike Yura and many other Chinese children who grew up entirely in a series of Russian orphanages for the children of international revolutionaries. Some arrived in Moscow along with both of their parents; some came with one after the other had been killed, as did the two sons of the fallen comrade [Zhao] "Shiyan" mentioned in Emi's poem.[6]

Others, however, were born not in China but in the Soviet Union while their parents were studying there in the passionate 1920s. Yura's closest childhood Chinese friend, a gentle, quiet boy named Vova, was born of a fleeting love affair. After his parents split up, Vova's mother got together with Li Lisan. Li treated Vova so well even after marrying Liza Kishkina that for a while he simply assumed he was Li's son.[7] As Vova understood it, he wasn't exactly abandoned; his parents were just too busy for him and had never really been a family in the first place.

They split up not because of a problem in their relationship, but because they graduated from the university at different times. There was no time to take care of a son. So they sent me to a nursery at the university. Because all the students there were young—23, 24, 25 years old. Lots of them met and got married there, or whatnot. And then there were children.[8]

Vova's mother graduated in 1929 and was sent to work in Khabarovsk, where Liza once caught a glimpse of her and was told she was the wife of the famous Li Lisan. Vova's father, who had been recommended for the Chinese Communist Party by Qu Qiubai and went by the name of Borodin in Moscow, stayed on at the university as a translator until 1930.[9] Before returning to China, he brought Vova to Vaskino, where there were a dozen other Chinese children, including several born in Moscow just like him. In this way, Karl Radek's joke came true—that children born to students at Sun Yatsen University could be raised in nurseries for baby revolutionaries.

A Home in the Sun

In 1933, Tuya, Yura, Vova, and several other Chinese children were taken from Vaskino to Ivanovo, a textile city about 250 kilometers northeast of Moscow, to live in a brand new home that had just been built by the Comintern's Organization for Assistance to Revolutionaries. The home was officially called the Internatstional'nyi Detskii Dom im. Stasova, or the International Children's Home, named after the Old Bolshevik Elena Dmitrievna Stasovoi, but known to this day simply as the Interdom. Throughout the 1930s, two dozen more Chinese children came to the Interdom. They lived in relatively privileged conditions, in a home meant to showcase the Soviet Union's commitment to international revolutionary families.[10]

Before the Second World War, the Interdom's student body included the children of Matyas Rakosi, Josip Broz Tito, Boleslaw Bierut, Dolores Ibarruri, Eugene Dennis, Sen Katayama, Pak Hon-yong, Fernando de Lacerda, and Georgii Dimitrov. Not all Interdom students had such prominent parents; a fair number were children of rank-and-file party workers. But in between the super-elite and the rank and file, there were many children like Yura whose parents were not internationally famous, but who nonetheless played key roles in the Comintern or in their national parties.[11] According to the school's records, between 1933 and 1950, 763 students of 40 different nationalities passed through it. At 15 percent of the total, the Chinese were the largest single group; 12 percent were German. Bulgarians, Poles, Spaniards, Latvians, Jews, and Italians each comprised between 4 percent and 6 percent of the school's population in these years. Small handfuls of students from other exotic locations, such as Brazil, Korea, the United States, or Japan, were also important, both to the culture of the school and to its reputation as an internationalist institution.[12]

In a parallel drawn by Emi himself in his poem about Vaskino, the Interdom in the 1930s and beyond, like Eastern University in the 1920s, was a concrete aggregation of exotic foreigners and an inspirational space. Thousands upon thousands of pictures were taken of the children and the home and many were disseminated broadly via postcard subscriptions and articles in internationalist periodicals.[13] The large population of Chinese children ensured that any given photomontage included conspicuously non-European faces.

1934 Cover of a Communist International magazine, featuring children from the Interdom. Qu Qiubai's daughter Tuya on far right. *Internatsional'nyi Maiak.*

In the years before World War II, by all accounts life in the home was a lot of fun for many of the children. While some suffered miserably when they were separated from their parents, many others had never really known their parents, or had lived such difficult lives as children of revolutionaries that the regularity of the home, the boisterous student body, the rigorous education, and the rich set of extracurricular activities made the Interdom the best, and sometimes only, home they had ever had. The building itself had been designed by a futurist architect from Moscow and was situated on an idyllic piece of land owned by a wealthy merchant before the revolution.[14]

In its early days, the home had many unusual playthings for the children. One Chinese who transferred from Vaskino remembers how someone brought the children a pair of bear cubs to play with—which they did, until the bears got too big and a bit dangerous, at which point they were shot, stuffed, and placed at the entrance to the school. So Russian bears rearing up on hind legs greeted the children, startled visitors, and added interest to photographs. For a time the children also had toy cars big enough to ride in outside, as well as miniature ones to play with inside, along with numerous other games and toys. [15]

More important than any toys were extracurricular activities and the handful of caring people who led them. The Interdom had a well-equipped gym and a good track and field, cameras and a well-supplied darkroom, a movie theater, a swimming pool, and a rich library with a kind librarian whom many remember as a surrogate mother figure, along with the school's beloved female doctor. The children went to a local school, where they were treated well by their classmates who held them, respectfully, at arm's length. They were strongly encouraged to perform academically by being given supervised homework hours.

This motley crew of foreign children also learned to dance Ukrainian folk dances, sing all sorts of songs, and play all sorts of instruments, and they put on numerous pageants inside and outside the school. In winter they went skiing and ice skating; in summer they went to camps or just camped out in the woods by the school. They rambled on long walks through the forest and swam in the river. There were groups of girls, including Tuya, who made up informal music groups and gathered wreaths of flowers for their hair as they walked alongside the river; and there were bands of troublemakers who skirmished in the forest.[16]

Yura, the little Chinese boy who got his first pair of skis at Vaskino, was one of these rowdy boys, if not the rowdiest. "The thing is," Yura remembered, "that in the children's home I was always in the ranks of the most 'difficult children.' They were constantly punishing me for boyish fights, poor discipline, monkey business every single day, often causing my caregivers to lose their composure. They were always depriving me of the privilege of watching the weekly movies or going to the city circus for my boyish 'anarchism.'"[17]

Among other things, Yura led a gang of boys in an ongoing battle against a rival group led by the school's only Cuban student.

Yet Yura, like so many other children at the Interdom, was ultimately "saved" by a caring adult who led an extracurricular activity:

> Comrade Bragin, who worked as our P.E. teacher, had enormous enthusiasm for his work. He really loved children and, even though he wasn't a professional pedagogue-psychiatrist, he understood the souls of little boys better than many other teachers. He was the one who was able to take a bully-troublemaker who had discipline problems almost every day, find some kind of leverage points, and use them skillfully to fashion out of me what he considered a real, useful guy. First and foremost, he quickly made a scallywag-ringleader of wild boys into a zealous P.E. assistant. For me there was no worse punishment than the deprivation of my right to play soccer, to do gymnastics, or in the winter to ski or skate.[18]

Yura's physical education teacher also convinced him to stop smoking and taught him the fundamentals of sportsmanship. Once his troublemaking was in check, another Interdom caretaker chided him into studying.[19] Yura's story—of some type of difficulty smoothed out and turned to advantage by the activities and the staff of the Interdom—played out repeatedly for a wide range of children, sometimes with lifelong effects.

While some of the children in the Interdom, like Yura, never really knew their "native" languages at all, those who did learned Russian quickly—and often forgot their mother tongue. Qu's daughter Tuya described the process, which for her had occurred already in Vaskino. "Because everyone spoke Russian to each other and memorized things really quickly . . . [w]e also quickly forgot Chinese. Within a year we already spoke entirely in Russian. I only remembered the children's songs that they taught me at the Sixth Congress." In fact, Tuya began communicating even with her father in Russian; after her parents left the Soviet Union, letters and postcards from her mother came for her through Mikhail Borodin, written in Russian in her father's hand. Only when her mother returned to Moscow in 1935 after Qu's death and Tuya left the Interdom to live with her did she encounter Chinese on a daily basis again.[20]

The home hired "foreign" language teachers for large national groups such as the Germans, Bulgarians, and Chinese. And yet, except in cases where

Chinese teacher at the Interdom. Courtesy of her son, Han Moning, also called Monia Kibalchik.

children were a bit older—adolescents who had perhaps already had some schooling when they came to the home—"native/foreign" language instruction was largely ineffective, which caused no end of consternation on the part of officials who occasionally came from Moscow to inspect.[21]

Yet the Chinese children were not left in that relatively nurturing Interdom environment for long. Even before the upheaval of purge and war, in the mid-1930s the Comintern and the Chinese Communist Party were envisioning and creating institutional settings for them with very different objectives.

A School in the Dark

On November 19, 1936, Wang Ming sent a proposal to Dmitry Manuilsky, the Russian Communist Party's official representative to the Comintern. In addition to the top-secret sections that Eastern University was currently operating for adult revolutionaries from Manchuria and other parts of China, Wang was intent on forming another, very special section for Chinese children, ages ten to seventeen. At Eastern University, he explained, the children could learn Chinese properly and receive a solid revolutionary education. Wang made a list of children he intended to bring to the school—mostly orphans of prominent revolutionaries or children like Tuya already in Moscow with a parent. But it also included the two sons of Mao Zedong, who were en route to Moscow with Wang's protégé Kang Sheng.[22]

The inclusion of the Mao brothers shows that Wang's goals in creating the children's section were complex. Some sources suggest that Stalin himself was directly involved in bringing Mao's sons to Moscow, as pawns in a game to control their father. If so, Stalin was overestimating Mao's commitment to his children; the boys had already been left behind in Shanghai after the Nationalists executed their mother, Yang Kaihui, in 1930. Mao had never made an effort to find them; his brother, Zemin, finally tracked them down in 1936. Their names in Chinese were Anying and Anqing, but in Russia they went by the pseudonyms Serezha Iun-Fu and Nikolai Iun-Shu. Like Chiang Kaishek's son before them, the boys ended up staying in the Soviet Union for years. Later on, Anqing/Kolia would write his autobiography in Russian, describing his early life in the following way:

> I, Iun-Shu Nikolai was born in 1925 near the city of Changsha. My father Mao Zedong abandoned me because of his revolutionary activities when I was around five or six years old. My mother, Yang Kaihui, the daughter of a professor, was shot by the Guomindang in the city of Changsha. . . . After the death of my mother my grandmother took me and my brother and placed us in some sort of children's institution, organized by communists. After the destruction of this institution by the police, a "communist" who later turned out to be an agent of the Guomindang took me and my older brother Anying (my younger brother Anlong had died in the hospital) in. In the summer of 1936, taking advantage of the absence of our host, the communists were able to make a deal with his oldest wife, who saw us as "spongers" and who didn't know about the money the communists sent her husband for our upbringing, and sent us to the Soviet Union.[23]

Written expressly for the Russian authorities and now kept in a Russian archive, Anqing's autobiography is as much a legend as anything else about the Mao family and may reflect what he was told about himself as much as what he remembered. Other sources suggest that the Mao brothers spent some time fending for themselves in Shanghai. [24]

What is certain, however, is that the boys had had no formal education before arriving in Moscow and no ties to their father. Emotionally and intellectually, they were orphans, street children, the kind of kids Tuya had encountered in her first stay at a regular Russian orphanage. Wang Ming wanted to try to turn them into young Comintern operatives. In theory, one can imagine that the children of famous revolutionaries—especially orphaned or abandoned ones—would be good candidates for training as underground party workers, whose primary loyalty would be to the revolution and whose entire upbringing could be oriented toward that future career. But the reality was much more complicated, as school records showed.

One day in January 1937, Eastern university officials showed up at Yang Zhihua's house and took fifteen-year-old Tuya to join the new, top-secret section. They also rounded up the son and daughter of martyred Hong Kong labor organizer Su Zhaozheng, whose widow had come to Moscow and brought her children back from the Interdom to live with her. In March, two other Chinese girls were taken directly from the Interdom—Ni-ni, the thirteen-year-old daughter of Cai Hesen and Xiang Jingyu, and Fi-fi, the eleven-year-old daughter of a Russian woman and an unnamed Chinese man. Another former Interdom student called I Fu, the son of an unnamed operative of the highly secretive International Liaison Department of the Communist International [OMS], was also brought to the new section. In this way, Chinese youngsters with radically different life experiences and linguistic abilities were united in a single class as part of an underground school for seasoned revolutionaries—with rather disastrous consequences.

At this point, the Chinese sections of Eastern University were completely secret, and the youngsters were not supposed to maintain any ties with their former Interdom classmates or any family members in Moscow. When the school's overseers gathered to discuss its problems, ongoing relations between students and the outside world were at the top of the list. On the one hand, these young teenagers were trying hard to follow their instructions and stay hidden; they were, for example, learning to remind each other to close the window curtains in cars on trips through Moscow and not to look out the windows, and they didn't talk much to each other about their past lives before coming to the school. In fact, schoolmasters noted that Tuya told them that she thought it would be better if she never went home to her mother at all because she was not accustomed to remaining silent to her mother's questions. On the other hand, on their visits home the students also heard things the school didn't want them to hear, such as the fact that many people were being arrested.[25]

Beyond the obvious problem of how to keep a diverse group of teenagers cut off from the outside world, what really bothered the school officials and their overseers was the lack of clarity and/or realism in their educational mission. While some of the young people, like Tuya, I-Fu, and Mao's older son, were considered to have good potential for future political work, others were considered "immature" and not cut out to be serious revolutionaries.

> The biggest abnormality lies in the fact that we have seven people who because of their age we just can't look at these people as people, as cadres, whom we'll eventually be able to use for work. It means that either we take upon ourselves the responsibility for their general upbringing and then after several years send them to [regular] work, or we simply warp these people. Take the girls, Nini and Fifi. They have no ties to China whatsoever, they were taken from a children's home, they were just born sometime to Chinese parents. And these are the children we have brought to a serious political Chinese school.[26]

In fact some of the girls were said to be "floozies," and one gave birth to a child in 1938. While I Fu, the son of the OMS operative, was considered a strong student, he behaved inappropriately with girls.

The school's overseers repeatedly raised questions about its basic mission: "Is it really appropriate to have these young people there, where adults are living?" "Shouldn't they be studying the things that children their age usually study?" "With this group of young people we face a question about their future: what are we making of them, what will become of them in the end?"[27] A lifetime later, Tuya herself answered their questions: "You know, in my opinion, now that I think about it, it was a mistake. . . . The other students who were sent there had practical revolutionary experience, and were sent to increase their theoretical knowledge. But we had no practical experience. . . . We were still kids. And the others were adults." At Eastern University Tuya became pregnant and gave birth in 1939 to a boy named Karl whom she sent in 1944 to be raised at the Interdom.[28]

Tuya, also called Qu Duyi, at her home in 2004. Behind her, memorabilia and photos of her parents, Yang Zhihua and Qu Qiubai. Photo from the author's personal collection.

Segregating the Children of the Sino-Soviet Romance

On December 31, 1938, a decision was finally reached about what to do with these Chinese teenagers: they were to be sent to yet another home for the children of international revolutionaries that had opened in late 1936 in a suburb thirty kilometers east of Moscow called Monino. But less than a year later this school closed due to poor management.[29] In 1939, Monino was converted into a "rest house" exclusively for Chinese communists—and their children.[30]

Neither the Chinese Communist Party nor the Comintern could give up the idea of some sort of special institution just for children of Chinese revolutionaries. After all, an entire network of homes was taking shape to house hundreds of Spanish children, and China was engaged in an equally serious battle against the Japanese.[31] Whereas most Chinese children in Moscow up to this point had been born there or brought there with their parents, the arrival of the Mao brothers was the harbinger of a new trend: children would soon be scooped up from villages all over China, brought to Yan'an, then to Moscow, then tucked away in the suburbs or provinces. While some were children of top leaders with name recognition in Moscow, others were orphans.

Combing through the list of Chinese children sent from China to be educated in Russia shows that the one thing nearly all had in common was a parent or parents who had studied in Moscow. Whether intentionally or not, by sending these children, the Chinese communists marked certain families as Sino-Soviet and ensured that a second generation reflected the vision that had inspired the first. Moreover, while their parents had conceived them at a past moment of intense interest in a Russian revolution for China, these children also represented a potential future for the party.

Shi Zhe, one of Mao Zedong's future translators, was placed in charge of running a new school just for Chinese children at Monino. Shi had originally been sent by the nationalists to attend a Soviet military academy in the 1920s; in 1929 the Soviet secret police tapped him for work in the Soviet Far East. He returned to Moscow in 1938 and was given the job of running the school for children, which he claimed to enjoy very much. Lists of future students were compiled of all the Chinese children who were currently with their parents or in nurseries connected to the soon-to-be-closed Chinese sections of Eastern University.[32] At that point, all of the Chinese children from the Interdom were also brought to Monino, which relieved the Interdom's administration of the problem of having no language teacher for them.

In 1937, the Interdom was shaken by the arrest of the school's Chinese teacher, Li Zhangfu. Li's "crime" was that he had helped a student in the school, named Oktiabrina, send a letter to her father, who had been arrested as a Trotskyist and exiled to Siberia. Some of the children, at least, were aware of his arrest. In the larger atmosphere of terror and obsession with the possible presence of foreign spies spreading across the Soviet Union, the school administrators were beside themselves, and began writing frantic letters to Elena Dmitrievna Stasova. Stasova wrote back unequivocally: "The children cannot answer for their parents, especially since it's been so long since they lived with them." At the same time, she unambiguously upheld the teaching of students' native languages.[33] With the logic of this letter, perhaps Stasova saved her namesake school. All the same, once the school no longer had a Chinese teacher, the chance to send the large Chinese contingent to a special school just for them came at a good time for the Interdom.

New Arrivals and Famous Visitors

Back in Yan'an, the Chinese Communist Party set about locating displaced children of top leaders, bringing them to Yan'an, and then sending small groups of them to the new school for Chinese children in the Soviet Union. The first group traveled from Yan'an through Xinjiang with one of the Party's leading women, Cai Chang, and included the remaining orphaned children of her brother, Cai Hesen. The second group was more glamorous, flying directly from Yan'an to Moscow by plane with Zhou Enlai himself. This was in the early phases of the second United Front, and so Chiang Kaishek sent his personal plane to Yan'an to ferry Zhou Enlai to Moscow for negotiations. Included on the plane were the children of Liu Shaoqi and Gao Gang, among others.[34]

One of these children, Liu's daughter Aiqin, remembers how abrupt and improbable her departure was. After her mother was killed by Nationalists, Aiqin had been entrusted to a family who received some sort of support from the Communist Party, but they sold her, at age eight, as a child bride. The mother of this family beat her and subjected her to all manner of abuse. After the Long March was over, Aiqin was located by the Chinese Communist Party and brought to Yan'an, where she saw her father for the first time. "Say Papa!" her caretaker whispered in her ear. She ran forward but couldn't say a word. One day in 1939, her father asked her and her brother whether they knew the name of the country to the north. "You're going there tomorrow," he said, "So go get ready."[35]

Nobody in Yan'an knew how big Chiang Kaishek's plane would be or how many people could come. When it arrived, everyone was surprised to find that it had twenty-five seats and was hardly full. Seeing this, Zhou Enlai and his wife Deng Yingchao, who had no children of their own but had adopted

Chinese children at Interdom under portrait of Mao Zedong. Courtesy of Roza Yubin.

the beautiful young Shanghai actress Sun Weishi, decided on the spur of the moment to take her along—but knew they had to get Mao's permission first. Sun jumped on a horse and galloped off to find Mao, was back in a snap with his approval, and hopped on the plane. As the plane was preparing for take-off, a number of people came on board to say goodbye to those departing, including a couple with a four-year-old son. The child was having such fun playing on the airplane that, when it came time to leave, he threw a tantrum and didn't want to get off. Another version has the child overlooked as the plane departed and discovered only when it was too late to go back. Zhou Enlai, the story goes, just shrugged his shoulders and said, "Well, I guess that means he's coming." Not only did he come, but he stayed in the Soviet Union until 1951.[36]

Once in Moscow, Zhou and his wife took the time to travel to Monino to inspect the school and speak with the children. By then, all the Chinese children knew of Zhou. As Yura the athlete put it, "The word Homeland was embodied for me then in fiery words like 'Mao Zedong, Zhou Enlai,

Liu Shaoqi, the 8th Route Army, the Long March, Jinggangshan!'" Many children recalled Zhou's visit for the rest of their lives, for he brought the first news many had heard of their parents. But perhaps no Russian-speaking Chinese child was more influenced by Zhou's visit than Yura. In his memoirs he wrote:

> Zhou greeted each of us Chinese students warmly, was actively interested in our life and schoolwork, and was very satisfied that the Soviet people had created such excellent conditions for us. Then Uncle Zhou carried on a lively, spontaneous conversation with us. He asked each of us what we wanted to be when we grew up. Several answered things like doctor, pilot, engineer, etc. Finally, it was my turn. But I stood there, the cat had my tongue, I didn't know what to answer. Then everyone started yelling out, "Yura's our jock! He loves sports!" I blushed all over with shame, since I thought that sports wasn't a serious thing. But Uncle Zhou said approvingly, "Oh! That's really great. The Homeland needs strong and healthy revolutionaries. I'll tell you a really interesting story from my own life: When I was working in the underground, enemies happened upon me by chance and began to follow me. I ran for my life. The chase went on forever. Finally, the enemies gave up hope. Why did I beat them? Because I always practiced sports and had a lot more endurance and ran a lot faster than them." Then Uncle Zhou raised both hands in the air and said with a smile: "You must not only study well, but also do sports, so that our arms and legs are strong like steel . . ." That night I couldn't fall asleep for a long time. It was the first time I understood that sports isn't just for fun, but a really necessary and important thing for my people. And this is exactly why I signed up without hesitation at the physical education training college in Ivanovo.[37]

When a distant hero swoops in and, with a few magical sentences, turns an embarrassing predilection into a heroic quest, any thirteen-year-old boy would feel himself transformed. On some level, though, Zhou's special encouragement—singling Yura out for praise and a personal story—had to have been connected to his relationship to Yura's father, Huang Ping, who had personally saved his life.

Zhou Enlai and his wife Deng Yingchao visiting with Interdom children. Courtesy of Roza Yubin.

Back to the Interdom

In the fall of 1940, the brief experiment with a Chinese-only school for children came to an end, and the entire group was transferred back to the Interdom. For some, who had grown up there, it was a relief. For others it was a challenge. It was said that Liu Shaoqi's son Yunbin had such trouble learning Russian that he got up at 5 AM every day and went outside with a friend and practiced Russian, memorizing letters, then words, then phrases, then short poems, which they recited in the schoolyard. After a year, the story goes, Yunbin could recite his favorite Pushkin poem—"Monument"—by heart. He did so the following summer at camp to impress a Russian girl.[38] For many of the children who had been gathered up and brought to Yan'an, the Interdom provided the first systematic, formal education they had ever experienced, and academically gifted children like Yunbin flourished.

His sister Aiqin has happy memories of her time in Russia for different reasons: "I learned to ice skate, I wasn't afraid to fall, and quickly picked up the skill. I had snowball fights with the boys, I didn't take anything lying down. The boys played with slingshots, I asked them to make me one, the boys laughed and said what kind of girls play with slingshots, forget it! But I made myself one, and once I used it to hit a big boy who hated girls."[39] This was a significant improvement, for sure, from her life as a child bride.

Meanwhile, there were a number of mothers of children at the school, ostensibly there as caretakers, who were in fact more or less ignored by the children themselves. The most sensational example was He Zizhen. After the special school for the Chinese in Kuchino closed, Zizhen ended up as a nanny at the Interdom, along with Lin Biao's spurned wife Zhang Mei. Zizhen had been with Mao all through the Long March, and if anyone was qualified to convey an appreciation of China and the Chinese revolution to the large group of Chinese students there, it was she. But few of the students who were in the school with her at the time remember her at all.

Those who do remember a woman crazed by her isolation and irrelevance in Ivanovo, taking her frustration out on Chao Chao, who lived with her and attended the Interdom. Some children recall passing by Zizhen's apartment and hearing her beating Chao Chao repeatedly. Finally one day they staged a bit of a kidnapping, bringing Chao Chao to the director of the school and telling him what was going on. The director had Zizhen committed for beating Chao Chao. Chao Chao has her own version of what happened to her mother in Ivanovo. In her memoir of her father, Chao Chao recalls that she herself got sick, and her mother wanted to take her back to her own living quarters to care for her. Makarov refused this request, whereupon Zizhen flew into a rage. Makarov used this incident as an excuse to have her committed to an insane asylum in Ivanovo, where she spent the remainder of the war.[40]

Either way, this is a strange kind of Sino-Soviet romance: a small-time Russian schoolmaster, a sorry stand-in for Stalin, as Russian father; the cast-off wife of Mao Zedong, vituperative yet mute, abusive yet powerless, as mother. The corrupt, arbitrary Russian man deemed the raging, abandoned Chinese woman insane.

The Lost Children of International Socialism

In early 1941, Chinese children continued to arrive in Ivanovo from China. A last group of toddlers was transferred from a Moscow home to the Interdom—babies that had been born to students in the underground sections of Eastern University, whose parents had long since gone back to China, or to the gulag—in late March, on the eve of the Nazi invasion of the Soviet Union.

In June, the Interdom was preparing for summer as it always did, sending youngsters to a variety of camps and sanatoria and preparing to accept new arrivals. One group went to Artek, a famous camp for foreigners, while a smaller group, including children in need of special medical care, was sent to a rest house in Belarus. In a twist of fate so strange that it became the basis for a 1995 hit movie in China, this group included none other than the daughter of the commander in chief of the Chinese Red Army, Zhu De.[41] His daughter, Zhu Min, was one of the last Chinese children to come to the Soviet Union before the German invasion, and she was asthmatic. She and a couple dozen other Interdom children had just arrived at their summer destination in Belarus when the German invasion swept through the territory. Zhu Min and the other children who had been to Belarus were lost, some for the duration of the war, and some for good.

When word of the Nazi invasion reached the Interdom children in Belarus, several children, including one half-Chinese half-Russian boy, immediately broke off from the group, headed east toward Minsk, and were never found. Some wounded Red Army men took three other children with them, also traveling toward Minsk. The rest were present when Nazi troops arrived. When the Germans discovered that two of the children were Jewish, they took them away and shot them. A bit later, they took two German boys out of the home to work as Russian translators for the police. In 1943, three of the older girls, including Zhu Min, were sent to work in German factories in Koenigsberg (present-day Kaliningrad).[42]

In 1944, toward the end of the war, several Interdom children from the original group remained. But on July 8, one day before the arrival of the Red Army, German troops took the children and headed west. They were never seen again, despite a desperate, personal search by one of their mothers and a systematic, institutionalized one by the Soviet secret police. Zhu Min, however, survived and returned to Moscow along with Red Army troops in 1945.[43] The fact that the commander in chief of the Chinese Red Army would send his daughter to the Soviet Union for safekeeping only to have her fall into Nazi hands is ironic, but also accidental.

The children who remained behind in the Interdom fared much better, but they faced wartime upheaval as well. In the fall of 1941, the Comintern was planning to evacuate the Interdom children to Central Asia, but those plans were scuttled at the last minute. In the meantime, much of the equipment and supplies that the school needed to care for the children disappeared from the home, local officials siphoned off funds intended for the home, some children fell ill from hunger and cold, and ultimately a new director was chosen. The school the children had attended before the war was converted to a hospital, so they had to walk several kilometers to attend a different school, and their formal education slowed considerably. The nighttime air raids were deeply unsettling to the Chinese toddlers who had arrived in the home only months before.[44]

Mao's Son as Sino-Soviet Patriot

The stories the Chinese tell of their wartime experiences are striking, but perhaps the most famous is that of Mao Zedong's older son, Anying, who went by the name of Serezha at the Interdom. Serezha arrived at the school in September of 1940, and he quickly became friends with a German boy named Fritz, who was born in Leipzig in 1924 to a working-class couple who became active in the opposition to Hitler. Fritz's father worked in the communist underground in Czechoslovakia, and when the Gestapo arrested his mother, Fritz slipped across the border to his father. Then a German communist going to Moscow took him along under a false name. He lived in Moscow in a house for German political emigrants (adults) and was paraded around collective farms and factories, where he recounted his story over and over again for several months. He remembers feeling enormous relief when he was finally sent to the Interdom, so he could be among people his own age and no longer had to publicly relive his flight from home night after night.[45] Like Anying/Serezha, Fritz symbolized something important to the adults around him, and he was always aware of it.

Serezha and Fritz did the things most boys would do: Serezha taught Fritz Chinese swear words, which he could still pronounce with startling accuracy as an old man, and they spent hours playing chess. Fritz also tells a sly story about discovering Serezha's crush on the daughter of Brazilian communist Fernando Lacerda, named Fernanda, who spent her entire childhood in the home. One day the two boys were deep in conversation when Fernanda momentarily breezed into the room and interrupted them. After she left, Fritz noticed that Serezha had lost his composure. "You're in love with her right?" asked Fritz. Serezha just nodded his head. Today, Fernanda explains that she could not return his feelings since her heart already belonged to someone else.[46]

Serezha was also obsessed with the war in China, and, like many other Interdom boys, wanted to enlist in the Soviet army. When he arrived at the home, Serezha was already eighteen and had not only received some military training at Wang Ming's underground school but was also street savvy from a childhood spent fending for himself in Shanghai. Serezha was determined to see battle, and his classmates remember that he wrote a letter directly to Stalin, pleading to be allowed to enter the army, to no avail. Fritz recalls Serezha standing by a map of China and jabbing in little pins to mark the territory held by the Japanese, the Chinese Communist Party, and the Nationalist Party.

Restless, Serezha became the secretary of the Interdom's Komsomol organization. He made numerous speeches designed to raise the morale of ordinary Soviet people. Once, he was sent, along with Fritz and a Bulgarian girl named Petra, to a textile factory to speak to some female workers, who told them that "Batiushka Gitler" would take good care of them. The three were subsequently called to a secret meeting and instructed not to tell anyone what they had heard. Serezha also became embroiled in the petty politics of the school. When one of the students' favorite teachers was dismissed, Serezha confronted local officials and, dissatisfied with their answer, subsequently held a "conspiratorial" Komsomol meeting to discuss the matter. When the meeting was discovered, Serezha and his "co-conspirators" were forced to back down and accept their mistakes.[47]

Serezha also received criticism from his famous father, whom he had not even seen since he was five. Probably encouraged by the staff of the home, Serezha wrote to Mao, but because his education back in China was practically nonexistent, he was not terribly literate in Chinese. Both he and his brother had made quick progress in Russian, so much so that one of his brother's essays won a local writing contest and was read out over the radio. But Mao responded to his son's letter with reproach for the poor quality of his Chinese writing and then personally sent the Interdom some books in Chinese. The school did resume Chinese language instruction when a pair of Chinese Comintern workers were sent to the school with their son, Monia, to act as Chinese teachers. There were several Chinese women on hand as nannies for the toddlers, but these women were barely noticed by the children. Even Monia says that he rarely saw his parents and hardly spoke Chinese at all, even with them.[48]

The Interdom appears to have been a remarkable illustration of the well-known potential for peer groups to outstrip parents as sources of authority and affection for children. The large contingent of Chinese children who had been born in the Soviet Union and therefore spoke Russian as their native language, and the fact that subsequent arrivals were staggered in small groups hindered the development of a separate, Chinese-speaking contingent. There was little social incentive to speak Chinese—a fact noted even by inspectors sent from Moscow. On the contrary, one needed to speak Russian to make friends with Fritz or Fernanda. Anying did work on his Chinese and in subsequent letters Mao noted—in Russian translation—that his Chinese had improved: "I am very happy that you are moving forward there. Iun Fu's writing isn't bad and it's obvious he's learning something."[49]

Yet Serezha also found a more proximate father figure—the director of the school, Timofei Makarov—as is evident in a series of letters he wrote after he had received permission to leave the home to attend a military academy. His behavior there apparently left something to be desired—he had trouble because of a woman—and in his letters to Makarov, Serezha is alternately boastful and contrite, reporting his victories and defeats as to a father, even requesting money, clothing, and school supplies. He became clearly uncomfortable and unhappy when a letter went unanswered, especially if he thought the silence indicated reprobation: "You, as a pedagogue, as a mentor, as the director of the home from which I came, having found out that your former charge has become 'such an unsuitable person' should have scolded me well and truly, pointing out my mistake to me. But you didn't say a single word to me, you didn't even answer my letters, am I really so hopeless that it wasn't worth wasting your time?"[50] Fritz remembers Serezha (as confirmed by the one letter he still has from him) at this time as deeply conflicted, searching his soul for the ability to be a true communist, not always

Mao Anying, also called Serezha Iunfu, in a Soviet military uniform. Courtesy of Li Duoli.

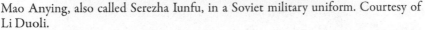

finding what he was looking for, and imploring his German friend to write a complete evaluation of his character, so that he could "compare the Interdom Sergei with Sergei today."[51]

What is so striking about the story of Serezha/Anying is how fervently and self-consciously he threw himself into Soviet life. There are echoes of Kolia/Jingguo in the stories people tell of him: here was revolution-ary China's number one son, falling in love with a Brazilian girl, riling up his fellow students as a Komsomol leader, and chafing to fight Nazi Germany. For him—and for many other Chinese students—the war created a blended identity. They felt equally Soviet and Chinese by virtue of the fact that during the war both peoples could be defined first and foremost as warriors against fascism, be it German or Japanese. And while the Chinese were not allowed to enlist, many tell stories of working in the local hospital, putting on pageants, and participating in wartime construction projects in Ivanovo. As they tell it, before the war they were foreign children, somewhat privileged and isolated. But the war, however difficult it was, broke down the barriers between themselves and ordinary Soviet people.

A Russian Chinese

Serezha's experience was somewhat exceptional for Chinese teenagers, for, no matter what, nobody was ever going to treat him as anything other than Chinese. More typical is that of Yura, the athletic ne'er do well, who, along with other Chinese boys his age, was actually kicked out of the home by Makarov during the war and had to make his way in Soviet society on his own. When the war broke out, the Interdom quickly found itself bursting at the seams as large numbers of children, including many Russians, were sent there. Makarov, the figurative patriarch of this little international socialist family, arrived in the school to find a group of teenagers who had grown up in the home in the 1930s and for whom obedience did not come naturally. Even as an old man, the son of "Shiyan" mentioned in Emi's poem was still aggrieved by the fact that Makarov forced some of the older children out. "Because of so-called bad behavior or poor studies some kids had to leave the home. We thought that was wrong. The Interdom wasn't a school, it was a big family, they shouldn't make a child leave the family. When kids were kicked out it put our hearts in our throats."[52]

As the leading black sheep of the Interdom family, Yura was turned out of the school promptly after he finished seventh grade in 1941. After leaving, he enrolled in the Ivanovo College of Physical Training, and then, after he had finished that program in 1943, he got a job as a coach at the local agricultural institute, where he lived in the student dorm. To supplement his student rations, he helped out as a farmhand for women whose husbands were at the front and, more important to him, "I gave blood for three and a half years. Every month. 430 grams every month. . . . They paid a little bit, but more important was they gave you a potato. And cards to buy meat and butter, to keep up the blood." What else could a person do, to become part of a nation, than give blood—even or especially if the reward was food?

Actually, there was something else he could do. "Russians never treated me as a foreigner," he said. "They accepted me. They knew that I was Chinese. Fine. But I was also Soviet. I hung out with the other students and they were a lot of fun. One . . . two girls were in love with me . . . one helped me with my homework . . . and when I got sick and was in the hospital suddenly this other girl started visiting and bringing me pastries."[53] Eventually Yura himself fell in love with a Russian girl named Tamara. He and his roommates took turns cleaning up, and one day he couldn't find a broom, so he went knocking on doors.

> Finally someone answered, a female voice called out, 'Come in!' Well I opened that door and there was this girl sitting there, I remember it perfectly. . . . The sun was falling like this from behind her, so that her face was dark, but she had blond hair, and so shining on fire from the sun. It just hit me! I stood there like an idiot and couldn't say a word. I forgot why I came. . . . After a while it got to be a joke, I could never find a broom.[54]

Tamara and Yura started going dancing as often as they could at the cheap city dance hall. "It was so innocent," he remembers. "We were so young." "There was nothing profane about it." But eventually his Interdom connections helped him to secure admission to college in Moscow and, in 1947, to the elite Moscow Institute of Physical Education. Tamara got a job in Siberia. They wrote to each other regularly.[55]

Chinese Students in Moscow Universities in the 1940s

Yura was far from the only Chinese Interdom student to make it into elite higher education institutions in Moscow. In fact, as the war ended and entrance exams were given, many Interdom Chinese scored remarkably well and earned admission into elite schools like Moscow Energy, Moscow Steel, Moscow State University, and a host of other top engineering institutes. In some ways they were ordinary Soviet students, in part because many spoke native Russian. Compared to Ivanovo, Moscow was cosmopolitan, and it seemed like everyone there was from somewhere else anyway. So they didn't

feel different. Yet as the 1940s wore on, geopolitical shifts created new pressures on them, marking them off even from other foreign students, whether
they liked it or not.

As the son of "Shiyan" explained it, when Interdom students reached sixteen or perhaps eighteen, they were given a choice: they could accept a Soviet
passport, which they could easily obtain with two sponsoring letters and official approval, and which would allow them to move freely around the Soviet
Union and work where they wanted—but might make leaving hard. All
Chinese Interdom students, even those who were born in the Soviet Union
and did not remember their parents, had been told as long as they could
remember that China was their homeland—in Russian, their "rodina"—and
that someday they would grow up and go "back" to that homeland. Because
many had never seen it, they tried to read about it or daydreamed about it.
One little girl imagined China as a place where so much fruit grew that one
could eat as much one wanted. As a boy, Yura had convinced an Arab friend
of his to cook up some frog legs over a fire by the river with him, because he
had heard that Chinese ate frog legs.

During the war, they had watched Soviet citizens fight and die for this
thing called "rodina," so they knew it was important, and that, because they
weren't allowed to fight for it, they weren't part of the Soviet "rodina." Later
in life many decided to call Russia their "second homeland," even if, in the
hearts of many, it was their first. And yet, if they declined Soviet citizenship so that they could leave the Soviet Union whenever they wanted, their
mobility was limited and getting a job would be harder. And, though nobody
said this, implied was that the Soviet Union could or would not protect them
if China decided they had to leave.[56]

As the 1940s wore on, more and more Chinese graduated and came
to Moscow. The oldest, who had been born in 1921, was already twelve
when he arrived at the Interdom, had subsequently attended the underground school at Eastern University, had gone straight from there to film
school, and spent the war years in Moscow. Cai Hesen's son was the first
to attend Moscow Steel, where he matriculated in 1944, won a Stalin prize
for his studies, joined the Soviet Communist Party, and began encouraging other Chinese Interdom students to come. Li Fuchun and Cai
Chang's daughter (who went by the name Roza) tested into the prestigious
Bauman Polytechnical School—Russia's second university, founded under
Catherine the Great.[57]

Liu Shaoqi's son and daughter threw themselves into Soviet life with particular gusto. Klim, the Russian name of the boy Yunbin, first attended Moscow Steel and then transferred to Moscow State University. Klim had become obsessed with the idea of developing a nuclear bomb for China, and though he could not attend Moscow State's new nuclear science program, he got as close as he could—the chemistry department. (Another boy, the son of Zhang Tailei, was admitted to the nuclear department in 1947.) He also met a Soviet woman, married her, and became the father of a little boy. Meanwhile, his sister Aiqin attended a communications technology institute—where she fell in love with and married a Spanish classmate Fernando, a nephew of Dolores Ibarruri, whom she had first met in the Interdom and by whom she was pregnant. Other Interdom students had boyfriends or girlfriends, and some even married, but the Liu children were among the few to start families.[58]

On one hand, then, many Chinese were fully integrated into postwar Moscow life. On the other hand, their common Interdom background and continued ties to China gave them a reason to stay in touch and help each other out. Before the Soviet economy picked up, stipends even at top universities didn't meet all their needs. Many of the young men went down to the river docks at night to unload boats in exchange for dinner and a cup of vodka, or else worked nights in construction or at factories. Roza came down with typhoid in 1947, and unexpected help came from the Borodin family, who nursed her back to health for months after she got out of the hospital. But this was exceptional; most of the Chinese had no family or support network inside the Soviet Union. So they started a little informal association— at that time small communities of foreign students in Moscow were allowed to start so-called native place groups—that generally got together on Sundays at the Lux Hotel, where Mao Anqing, the younger son, lived.[59]

As Chinese students began to graduate from top Soviet schools with valuable skills, they came under increasing pressure to make decisions about their future. While a couple of Interdom children, including Tuya, had returned to China with their parents in 1941, Serezha/Mao Anying had been the first to leave after the war, in 1945, at his father's request. That same year, the oldest Chinese Interdom student also returned to China, applying his Moscow film school training to shooting live footage of Red Army battles, while a handful of other students were sent by the Soviets to Manchuria to help with the underground struggle against the Japanese as radio technicians and broadcasters. In 1947, one boy who had graduated from a naval academy returned to China, presumably to put his military skills to use.

But generally speaking, most Chinese students who graduated from colleges in the late 1940s stayed in the Soviet Union to attend graduate school. The Nationalists were still in charge in China, and the students were the children of communists—sent to the Soviet Union not for military training but to receive an education that would prepare them to "build socialism" in China when the time came. The time hadn't come quite yet.

Part IV

FAMILIES, 1950s

14

Male Metaphors

IN THE SUMMER of 1949, Liu Shaoqi was in Moscow. He was looking at dresses, specifically, his daughter's dresses. And he was shaking his head.[1]

Liu Shaoqi, soon to be named vice chairman of the PRC, went to Moscow in May for a secret three-month summer visit. Two days before Liu left, Mao announced his "lean to one side" policy, a public declaration of pro-Soviet inclinations. In Moscow, Liu held wide-ranging talks with Stalin, who apologized for not helping the Chinese Communist Party more during its long civil war with the Nationalists. He urged the Chinese Communists to proclaim a new government as quickly as possible and told Liu that China would henceforth be in charge of communism in the East. But Liu averred that the Soviet Union was and would always be the leader of world communism—and brought up specifics of immediate military assistance.[2]

For decades the relationship between the Russian and Chinese communist parties had been carried on behind the scenes, through Comintern operatives. As a government, the Soviet Union dealt with the Nationalist regime. Top Chinese communists often interacted with men who, in the relative hierarchies of the Bolshevik and Chinese systems, were lower ranking than they were. Some of their most intimate relationships in the Soviet context were with women. Now, however, communist leaders like Liu would be dealing publicly with their Soviet, male counterparts—people who were older and had decades of experience running a government, fighting a war, and transforming a culture. Personal experiences and power dynamics were about to shift and, along with them, the metaphors.

The Soviet-PRC relationship that Liu was in Moscow to discuss would require the involvement of hundreds of thousands of people and the support of millions more, particularly in China. The message the two governments transmitted about the nature of the relationship needed to be simple.

For the individual Chinese communists whose emotional involvement had helped make this geopolitical engagement possible in the first place, feelings about Soviet Russia had been passionate, shifting, and complex. Metaphors were latent—enacted privately and implicitly, flashing openly and explicitly, then receding to the inchoate and confused—never requiring official definition.

Now, however, the two regimes attempted to define metaphors that ought to govern the emotional reactions of the masses to this new relationship. While older brother/younger brother emerged as the most popular, it competed or combined with teacher/student, friend/friend, a miscellany of other occasional formulations—and a strong romantic undertow. What all the explicit public metaphors had in common was exclusion of women. And yet, however focused the two regimes were on keeping their relationship symbolically platonic, romance still permeated many of the most popular representations of Soviet Russia in China.

Now as much as ever, metaphors of socialist fraternity or friendship fell short of useful or accurate description of the continuing experiences of the many top-level Chinese communists who had some sort of biographical investment in the Soviet Union. Of the fourteen Politburo members between 1945 and 1969, nine had spent time studying or working in Moscow, and seven had biological or adopted children in Russia; only two of the fourteen had no association.[3] For these leaders and many other senior Chinese communists with personal ties to Soviet Russia, the metaphors they publicly promoted of brotherhood and friendship left out the mixed and sometimes bitter memories, the love, the sex, the children—and now, the families: families made and lost, broken and reunited, coherent and disjointed.

In reclaiming their Soviet-educated children, Liu and other individual Chinese communists not only faced their own prior selves, but they also recreated Sino-Soviet families in a new context. These private families—and their emotional workings were hidden from the public view—were far messier and less harmonious than the socialist fraternity was supposed to be.

Liu's Daughter and the New World Order

A person who has to meet with Stalin and his cronies day after day and negotiate the terms of a new world order is not a person who could be expected to care about his daughter's dresses—unless, somehow, those dresses had something to do, in this person's mind, with that new world order. According to Liu Shaoqi's daughter, they did.[4]

Liu Shaoqi had been in the first group to make the treacherous journey to the Soviet Union in 1921 to study at Communist Eastern University. He also chose to send his two children by his second wife to be educated in the Soviet Union. Soviet Russia was, therefore, an indelible part of Liu's family biography. By the time he got to Moscow in 1949, his children's Russian was better than their Chinese.[5]

However aware they were that their futures most likely lay in China, their lives were unfolding alongside those of others in their Soviet generation. Both had finished or nearly finished college and gotten married. In 1949, as she was ready to graduate, Aiqin wrote to her father to explain her plans. She was pregnant with the child of her Spanish classmate at the time. She recalls that while she always assumed she would eventually return to China, she didn't know how soon the Chinese Communist Party would actually take over and assumed it was further in the future. Looking back, she viewed her decision to marry in Russia a bit naive, but at the time China had seemed far away. In any event, she heard nothing back from her father, until he suddenly showed up.[6]

Aiqin was a living, breathing, fully fledged New Soviet Chinese Person. So was her brother Yunbin. So were dozens of other children of Chinese revolutionaries who had grown up in the Soviet Union, sent by the Party to receive a true revolutionary education in a safe environment. They spoke excellent Russian and were on their way toward achieving exactly the sort of higher education and technical expertise that the new People's Republic of China needed so badly. They also felt sincere, if abstract, patriotism toward China and respect for their revolutionary parents, as the Soviet Union had taught them to.

Yet on a deeper level—the level of posture and gesture, bathing and eating, courting and dancing, hairdos and, yes, dresses—they were Soviet. This is what their revolutionary parents had had in mind when they sent them off to the Soviet Union. What the parents didn't realize was how much the Soviet Union was going to change while their own children—and their own revolution—matured.

Negotiating with Stalin by day and getting to know his grown daughter by night, Liu Shaoqi was caught right where the personal meets the geopolitical, and where symbolism can be so important. When Aiqin showed him her dresses, his biological daughter, a New Sino-Soviet Woman with a Spanish husband, displayed clothing that reflected the fashions of postwar Moscow, not revolutionary Beijing. The Aiqin who stood in front of him was the living product of his own past. And he could hardly understand her. All he did was shake his head about the dresses.

Eva Reclaims Emi; Emi Promotes Sino-Soviet Friendship

It's June of 1949. Eva takes a candid shot. A large, bald man in a rumpled shirt slouches comfortably in his seat, his elbow perched on the frame of a riverboat window. Behind Chilean poet Pablo Neruda sits Emi, propped up on the back of Neruda's seat, shirtsleeves rolled up to his elbows, his right arm hanging down into the empty seat next to Neruda, the white of his cigarette jumping out from the dark of the seat cushion.[7]

In Moscow a few days earlier, Emi had spoken to a crowd composed of premier poets of the postwar socialist internationalist literary milieu. Standing on a makeshift platform in front of Pushkin's grave, left hand behind his back as if to hold himself upright, Emi gave a speech he had prepared for the celebration of the poet's 150th birthday, the characteristic lock of hair brushing his temple as he looked down, reading from the paper.[8]

It was a privilege to be there—Emi was China's representative to the event, personifying what was soon to be the largest, most geopolitically significant new communist country in the postwar world. If Emi looked at ease with Neruda it may have had more to do with politics than poetry. After the Pushkin commemoration the poets embarked on a Soviet junket, first to Stalingrad and then down the Volga River. Back in Moscow they celebrated the eightieth birthday of the Danish communist author Martin Anderson Nexo with a blowout party, where Paul Robeson sang Chinese songs in honor of Emi.[9] His presence symbolized China's acceptance into the international socialist culture club.

Before 1949, there certainly had been high-profile cross-cultural moments between Nationalist China and Soviet Russia—such as the famous tour of the renowned female impersonator Mei Lanfan in the Soviet Union in the 1930s. But for early Chinese communists "culture" and "politics" weren't separate. Qu Qiubai, after all, who had written the *History of the Heart in the Red Capital*, also served a term as general secretary of the Chinese Communist

Party. Emi shifted seamlessly from underground agitator in Shanghai to Sino-Soviet poet and lover in Moscow.

The postwar era saw the rejuvenation and reinvigoration of international socialist cultural communities. China needed to mingle in the general flow of international socialism. But that meant that China had to have people to send to participate in international cultural events, and those people had to know how to operate in those circles. Emi was a good person for the job: not primarily a poet or an administrator, not a leader or a follower, but rather a connector, a person who moved easily in elite circles without holding any real power of his own.

When Emi arrived in Moscow for the Pushkin celebration, Eva was waiting for him—in the very same Moscow apartment where they had lived so long ago and where she had been instructed to return to wait for him. The two had not seen each other since Eva had departed Yan'an in 1943. Eva had spent the war in Kazakhstan; when it was over she placed her two sons in the Interdom and went to live with Vassa in Ukraine, writing repeatedly to Emi expressing her desire to return to China. In April 1949, the Chinese authorities contacted her to let her know that Emi would be coming to Moscow. As Eva tells it, the five years they had been separated simply fell away when they saw each other, and they vowed never to part again. He invited her to accompany him on the Pushkin junket, and then she and the children would go back to China with Emi. Unreal, she thought.[10]

After some travel around the Soviet Union, Emi, Eva, Leon, and Vitya flew together to Chita, where they boarded the train to China. Emi made frantic phone calls along the way in an effort to ensure that Eva had a place to stay in Beijing, but when they arrived in Beijing, nobody was there to greet them. Finally Ding Ling, the leftist writer who had been so in love with Qu Qiubai in the 1920s, showed up in the pouring rain.[11]

Despite Emi's efforts, nobody had found a place for his Soviet family to live. Normally, of course, they would have simply moved in with him, but for a glaring problem. After Eva left Yan'an, Emi had resumed his relationship with a Chinese woman, with whom he had two sons. Eva knew this and was ready to forgive and forget—but the Chinese leadership, apparently, was not. Eva and her children spent their first night in Beijing in the apartment Emi shared with his Chinese wife and children.

The next day, Zhou Enlai visited to communicate the fact that no Chinese revolutionary could possibly have a German wife, Soviet children, and a Chinese family, or whatever else Emi might have had in mind. Zhou declared a six-month hold on the Eva-Emi relationship, during which time they would live separately and Emi would consider his choice of wife. Zhou arranged a nice apartment in Soviet-controlled Dalian for Eva, right near the ocean, where she and her boys went swimming nearly every day. Technically, Eva worked for the Dalian branch of the Sino-Soviet Friendship Association, but she spent most of her time studying Chinese and resting on the beach. [12] She and her children had washed up on that shore like a little band of German-Jewish-Chinese-Russian-Soviet refugees from one of history's greatest storms.

Emi, on the other hand, found himself on the front lines of China's campaign to become best friends with the Soviet Union, part of the manic preparations for a new Sino-Soviet Friendship Association in Beijing to promote the alliance. A brand new building was under construction in the heart of Beijing to house the headquarters of the envisioned national-level organization.

The association had its work cut out for it. Despite the many books produced later in the 1950s about the long history of friendly Russian-Chinese relations and cultural ties, in reality, Russia's people and culture were virtually unknown to the vast majority of the Chinese population. People did know, however, that the Soviet Union had not returned the Changchun Railroad nor the naval base at Lushun, both of which had been promised, let alone the northeastern territories annexed by Imperial Russia, including even Lake Baikal. When Soviet troops entered cities in the northeast in 1945, they engaged in weeks of rape and looting before settling down. They also dismantled as much industrial equipment as they could for transport back to the Soviet Union, thereby earning the population's mistrust. [13]

In this context, the first "Friendship Associations" were founded in 1945 in Port Arthur, Dalian, and Harbin. Changing Chinese public opinion was an uphill battle. It was fought with movies and summer camps for children and propaganda about Soviet doctors saving Chinese lives, floods of popularized Russian culture, and waves of information about Soviet life. Even so, actual skirmishes between Soviets and the local population continued into the early 1950s. [14]

As deputy general secretary and director of the Liaison Department of the new Beijing-based Sino-Soviet Friendship Association, Emi was part of the human interface between the organization and its Soviet counterparts and visitors. At fifty-five years of age, he was working the hours of a twenty-five-year old. He spent most days in the temporary offices of the association. As the 1950s wore on, China's "Friendship" production process became routine and was delegated to other mass organizations, but in the first months after the Soviet Union officially recognized the People's Republic, the Beijing Association was all-important.[15]

In late summer and early fall of 1949, Emi was writing an endless stream of pamphlets like "Marx, the Great Leader," as well as numerous "first-hand accounts" of Soviet culture and education for the new Sino-Soviet Friendship Magazine. In mid-September, his Mao biography, *Mao Zedong: His Childhood and Youth*, was finally published in Beijing. Emi ruminated over a letter to Mao, but he hardly had time to write anything at all, let alone promote a major publication. In mid-August, a major exhibition of Soviet photography opened in Zhongshan Park, right next to the Forbidden City; Emi made a speech before 6,000 people. On September 12, he gave a key speech detailing the development of culture under Stalin's five-year plans—a subject that he, after all, knew firsthand—which was reprinted in full in the *People's Daily*.[16]

If, in the early 1930s a thirty-something Emi had written Eva a flood of love letters mingling political and personal passion, his frequent missives now told of his exhaustion and sometimes the tedium of Sino-Soviet Friendship. Parties stopped being parties, books stopped being books, music stopped being music, and everything melted together into a constant din of work. "I am so busy. . . there is so much work . . . I have to write so much . . . everything has to be done yesterday." Emi drew the line at visiting local schools: "My body just can't take it," he wrote.[17]

On October 1, 1949, Mao Zedong stood up in Tiananmen Square to announce the creation of the People's Republic. A Soviet "Cultural, Artistic, and Scientific Delegation" arrived to participate in the celebrations—no political officials were included because the Soviet Union had not yet severed ties with the Nationalists. The delegation included major cultural figures such as Alexander Fadeev, Alexander Gerasimov, and Konstantin Simonov, who all sat on the ceremonial platform when Mao made his announcement.[18]

Five days later, on October 5, the Beijing-based Sino-Soviet Friendship Association was officially founded with Liu Shaoqi as the chairman. During the opening ceremonies he made a speech pointing out the educational elements of the pre-1949 relationship without a trace of romanticism:

> In the past our Chinese people's revolution was carried on "with Russia as a teacher," and that is why it could attain the success of today. From now on in our national reconstruction, we must likewise proceed "with Russia as a teacher" and learn the Soviet people's experience of national reconstruction.[19]

Liu's speech expressed a basic intention: the past experience of the tiny Chinese Communist Party was now to be replicated—sanitized and simplified—on a mass scale for the People's Republic as a whole.

After the ceremonies, the Soviet delegation set off on a tour of China, with Emi in tow. In the course of three weeks, the delegation attended 29 mass meetings with more than half a million Chinese, gave 57 lectures to over 70,000 people, and offered music and dance recitals to nearly 600,000.[20] In late October, the delegation reached Harbin, at which point Eva came from Dalian to join it. Perhaps coincidentally, at this point the six months of separation got shortened to three, just at the moment when this cross-cultural family was most symbolically useful.

Eva and Emi were allotted an apartment right near the new Sino-Soviet Friendship headquarters, in the diplomatic section of Beijing where the Soviet embassy and consulate were located. There was also a Soviet school that Emi's two sons attended. Emi continued in his role at the Sino-Soviet Friendship Association, an organization that had grown to two million members and was quickly becoming the largest mass organization in China. Eva got pregnant with a third child, TASS gave her work as a photographer, and the PRC's Xinhua followed suit.[21]

Man to Man: Mao, Stalin, and the Experts

In December 1949, the Sino-Soviet Friendship Association engineered a massive celebration of Stalin's seventieth birthday—just as Mao was about to leave for a visit to Moscow, the first foreign trip of his entire life. This visit, the first personal encounter between Stalin and Mao, is one of the most mesmerizing meetings in twentieth-century history. As the historians who chronicled the visit put it, it was a "summit of communist titans, men whose absolute control of hundreds of millions gave them a historical stature, larger and harsher than anything we have seen before or since."[22]

The purpose was relatively straightforward: Mao wanted major technological and military assistance, and Stalin wanted territory and natural resources—and both sought reassurances that the other would not align with their enemies. China should not become a renegade communist state like Yugoslavia; the Soviet Union had to quit its relationship with the Chinese Nationalists. And both sides had to stand firm against the West.[23]

When all was said and done, these objectives were accomplished, or at least discussed seriously, during the meetings, which were devoid of fireworks, as the transcripts of the first conversation on December 16 show:

> *Mao Zedong*: We would like to decide on the question of Soviet credit to China, that is to draw up a credit agreement for 300,000,000 dollars between the governments of the USSR and China.
> *Stalin*: This can be done. If you would like to formalize this agreement now, we can.[24]

On February 14, 1950, Mao and Stalin signed a new Sino-Soviet Treaty of Friendship and Mutual Aid, which defined the terms of the communist bloc's most crucial alliance. China would receive—and pay dearly for—Soviet military and industrial expertise; Mongolia would retain its independence; the Soviet Union would relinquish the China Eastern Railroad and would depart Manchuria by 1955. This treaty was the express purpose of Mao's trip to meet Stalin.[25]

Yet on another level—the gossip that accompanies and enlivens the serious business of geopolitical history—the Stalin-Mao exchange was also about birthday parties and hurt feelings. Ever since, in the words of two historians who have tracked emerging records of the meetings, scholars have been trying to figure out "what went wrong in the Mao-Stalin relationship and how it affected the whole course of Sino-Soviet relations thereafter."[26]

Mao had wanted to visit Stalin since 1947, but Stalin had put him off. In 1948, Mao sent a telegram saying that he would leave for Moscow in ten days, which Stalin rebuffed. When Mao announced the creation of the PRC in October of 1949—in line with the advice Stalin had given Liu that summer—Stalin still issued no invitation for a visit. Zhou Enlai finally told the

Soviet ambassador that Mao wanted to be invited to Stalin's seventieth birthday party in Moscow on December 21.[27]

Mao left on December 6 by train, and upon his arrival, he immediately met with Stalin. But then, Mao was sent to stay in one of Stalin's dachas outside Moscow, isolated from the elaborate goings-on in the city and prevented from meeting with leaders of other communist parties.[28] Though his material conditions were much better, there is some irony in the fact that his own wife, He Zizhen, had spent a similarly frustrating period of time in a dacha outside Moscow a decade earlier.

Here was the birthday extravaganza of the communist century, and there was Mao, off in the dacha. The memoirs of people involved in the visit contain scintillating tidbits that are hard to confirm or deny. Mao didn't like the fish he was served. He demanded that his bed be replaced by wooden planks and that his pillow be filled with buckwheat. He was constipated and actually complained about it. Meanwhile, his own fifty-sixth birthday came and went.[29]

When Mao finally got to the birthday celebration, he was seated next to Stalin and got a standing ovation from the crowd, who chanted the two leaders' names together. An iconic picture shows the two seated and clapping—sternly—among an array of other leaders. After the party, however, Mao was whisked back to the dacha. He tried to call Stalin at home but was told he was out. Stalin called Mao a couple of times, but the conversations were empty. Stalin sent Molotov to visit Mao and "see what sort of fellow he is," and Molotov reported back that Mao was "a clever man, a peasant leader, a kind of Chinese Pugachev."[30] For his part, Mao refused to go sightseeing.

Only when Beijing received official recognition from Great Britain did Stalin agree to meet with Mao again—the second and last face-to-face encounter between the two—to finish their negotiations. Stalin extracted enormous concessions, including the right to continued Soviet presence and influence in Manchuria, but Mao did get promises of funding and technical support without which he could not run the industrial, urban parts of his country.[31]

It's almost unthinkable that just two months into his leadership of a giant new country, Mao would have spent three whole months far from Beijing, in a Moscow dacha. However frustrated Mao reportedly was, the fact that he stuck it out suggests just how important he considered his new country's relationship with Moscow.

At the same time, his physical presence in Moscow and his personal meetings with Stalin established him as the major protagonist of the Sino-Soviet relationship of the early 1950s. Mao held a party and invited Stalin, who finally showed up as Mao's guest, with a bottle, some say. And yet, historians conclude, "The actual experience of Russia and Russians does not really seem to have been to Mao's taste. He and Stalin were never able to find the right foot from which to start their partnership, nor did they succeed in having a single moment of informal connection, the only hope for confidence building."[32]

With or without "informal connection," the Mao-Stalin talks opened the way for an alliance that scholars have called a "marriage," complete with a "honeymoon."[33] Regardless of the "delicate matter" of their personal relationship, their exchange began the largest technology transfer in the history of communism. The Friendship Alliance, the outbreak of the Korean War, and the subsequent launch of China's first five-year plan would ultimately send more than 20,000 experts from the Soviet Union and Eastern Europe to China. Sino-Soviet propaganda depicted the experts as a massive donation of precious expertise from one socialist people to another; in reality, the Chinese paid dearly for each expert's time.[34]

The Soviet experts were nearly all men working with Chinese male counterparts on projects in industry and defense. While eventually some were allowed to bring wives and families, the vast majority came alone. Their attitudes toward their China assignment varied: some viewed it as an adventure, others as an opportunity to enjoy luxuries not allowed at home, and yet others as a chance to participate in a massive socialist construction project on par with prewar Soviet industrialization.[35] China began a large-scale textbook translation initiative and sought to import Soviet technology not only for heavy industry but also for primitive forced labor camps.[36] Although historians have uncovered serious problems with the Sino-Soviet technology transfer, the presence of Soviet men in factories and schools all over China personified (and sometimes problematized) notions of brotherhood and friendship that otherwise would have remained entirely abstract.

Along with the public relationship between Mao and Stalin and the growing interactions between male experts and hosts came a wave of new Sino-Soviet propaganda featuring exclusively men. Perhaps the most incredible visualization of the new Sino-Soviet male metaphor was a poster of two generically handsome men—nearly identical, even in coloring, save a minor difference in eye shape—each standing with an arm around the other's shoulder—and one hand on the shoulder of one of two young boys in front of them. A blond boy stands in front of the Chinese man; a black-haired child stands in front of the Russian man. Above the Russian man is the Soviet hammer and sickle; above the Chinese man are the five stars of the People's Republic of China.[37]

It's a perfect portrait of the Sino-Soviet family, seemingly able to reproduce without women at all.

15

Wang, Dasha, and Nastya
Russian Romance Redux

WANG MENG WAS just twelve years old when he encountered his first Russian woman. Her name was Dasha, and, in his mind's eye she was

> wearing a red turban, healthy, strong like a ballerina, sexy, steaming hot, filled with a huge bitterness and a deep hatred, a spirit without limits. . . . [S]he was my revolutionary idol, you could also say she was a sort of imaginary sex symbol that I got from reading. . . . Dasha's attitudes toward sex weren't communist nor were they mainstream in China, but reading *Cement* gave me a vague yet violent feeling, like a field on fire.[1]

Wang had gotten his hands on a Chinese translation of the Soviet socialist realist novel *Cement*, whose Chinese title was a transliteration—"Shimintu"—rather than a translation. First published in the Soviet Union in 1925, *Cement* is about a Red Army soldier, Gleb, who returns home to his village in the early 1920s only to find that his wife—Dasha—no longer wants to act like his wife, while the villagers have no idea how to act like communists. A cement factory has been built in the village but it sits idle, and on one level the novel is about Gleb's quest to get the factory—and thereby socialism—up and running in his hometown, after years of war and famine have left the population too exhausted and hungry to envision the future, much less work for it. On another level, Gleb must untangle an emotional mystery: what happened to his beautiful, loving wife Dasha while he was away to cause her to be, as Wang observed, "filled with a huge bitterness and a deep hatred."[2]

Reading *Cement* and fantasizing about Dasha in Beijing in 1946, Wang Meng was committing a complex transcultural act that felt deeply personal, secret, even transgressive at the time, yet turned out to be exemplary for left-leaning intellectuals of his generation. Wang had been born in 1934 and had spent his entire youth under the Japanese occupation. In 1946, the Japanese had just left Beijing, China's civil war was raging, and the Communist Party underground was busy setting up front organizations in Nationalist territory. Although the communists had made their global public relations debut in Yan'an as a rural party of guerrilla warriors, its leaders knew that the coastal cities and industrial centers of the northeast would be crucial to taking and maintaining power.[3]

Starting Over

In the late 1940s and early 1950s, students continued to be just as central to urban communism in China as workers, despite Marxist dogma. In the early 1930s, Nationalists had decimated the Beijing Communist Party such that, by 1935, the leadership could only locate seven members in the entire city. As late as 1948, there were only about 3,000 members of the Communist Party underground in all of Beijing, and over 40 percent of them were students— compared to 25 percent workers.[4]

In retrospect, it almost seems as if the Communist Party had to "start over" in the cities. It didn't matter that veteran communists in their forties and fifties had already helped to organize major urban strikes in the 1920s. Anyone born in a city later than 1930 would have had no personal memories or associations with communism at all. So older, seasoned communists had to begin with young people if they wanted to take territory, even in the imaginations of Chinese urban dwellers.

Wang Meng was typical of the sort of young person the communists knew they needed to win over. He was a top student, brimming with enthusiasm and idealism, and longing for a future in a China that could use his talents. Wang was an avid reader, and fiction was his entree to politics. In the months after the Japanese surrender in August 1945, while Nationalist and American troops were moving into Beijing, Wang was reading leftist literature from the 1920s and 1930s, such as Ba Jin's *Destruction*, Cao Yu's *Sunrise*, and Mao Dun's *Corrosion* and *Midnight*, as well as a 1924 Russian civil war novel, Serafimovich's *Iron Flood*. "These books told me that society was already decayed, China was already endangered, what China needed was a big change, a storm, a baptism by iron and blood." Yet, like many precocious young readers, along with books written for adults, Wang continued reading children's literature. He was entranced by European fairy tales, such as Hans Christian Andersen's "Little Match Girl" and the Grimm Brothers' "Cinderella." These stories told Wang that there were many "beautiful, honest, kind-hearted people in the world who suffered injustice." [5]

Thinking back on that time, Wang later recalled the kind of youthful logic that attracted him to revolution:

> How does a revolution come? Revolution comes from practicing geometry. Revolution comes from singing and dancing. Revolution comes from reading everything, from being dissatisfied with everything, from every kind of social conflict, class conflict, family conflict, interpersonal conflict, from everyone fantasizing about a new life. When my parents argued, I thought that only a revolution could solve their differences. When I heard my neighbor playing the violin at night and he played badly—again!—the noise made me tired and confused and I thought that only a revolution could end this awful racket. If a book was written really badly, I believed that only a revolution would get rid of these low-brow shitty books. If a book was moving, I believed that only revolution would stop the characters' tears, so that lovers could become families. [6]

In retrospect, Wang may seem naive, but how else could "revolution" appeal to an entire generation that had no experience with radical politics?

Wang became disillusioned with the Nationalists after they took control of Beijing. Their propaganda recycled themes from the "New Life Movement" of the 1930s, which had emphasized the creation of a morally strong nation via campaigns against petty vices—ideas that seemed stale in the chaotic aftermath of the brutal Japanese invasion. [7] In school, Wang befriended a popular tennis player who turned out to be an underground worker for the communist party. He took Wang under his wing, bringing him home for talks about politics and to a bookstore on North Xinhua Street that carried radical literature and works translated from Russian. [8]

Wang began reading Soviet novels whose very availability in Chinese was a reflection of two decades of translation work that had somehow continued through civil war and foreign occupation. Whereas China's first generation of revolutionaries had found inspiration in Tolstoy and Turgenev, by the late 1940s, translators had moved on to the Soviet period.

While Wang mentions a variety of Soviet stories and novels that he read before 1949, he insists *Cement* made the deepest impression on him. He dismissed some Soviet novels that were better known in China at the time, such as the 1927 civil war story *The Rout*, whose author had fought against Japanese troops in the Russian Civil War and which had been mentioned by Mao himself in his famous Yan'an "Talks on Literature and Art." Wang found it depressing. He did like other works focused on the dilemmas of foreign occupation and partisan warfare, including Valentin Kataev's 1937 *I Am the Son of the Working People*, about the fate of a demobilized Red Army soldier, and Wanda Wasilewska's 1944 "Rainbow," about a Ukrainian village under Nazi occupation. The latter had been turned into an unusual, pioneering film in that same year. *Cement*, on the other hand, focused on what happened after the battle was won. "Of course," Wang recalled, "at 12 I couldn't really understand the Soviet October Revolution or the New Economic Policy," but he was fascinated by the vivid characters, with their passionate natures and conflicts, as well as the urgency the novel conveyed about the need to jumpstart a war-torn economy. *Cement* was rewritten several times in the Soviet Union; by 1946, when a later edition was published in China, some of the bawdier language and flawed characters had been whitewashed.[9]

All editions, however, contained sexy Dasha, renouncing the roles of wife and mother and giving herself to the cause of the Red partisans body and soul. For a boy who had grown up under Japanese occupation, Dasha was a timely heroine. Whatever Wang had experienced, she had overcome worse, and the book also delivered a powerful message—that it was both possible and necessary to rebuild a ravaged society on an entirely new basis and that there was hope for the future. In 1946, while he was reading *Cement*, Wang recalls seeing banners up around Beijing that said "Down with the Soviet Union" and asking his father what they were all about. His father simply answered, "The Soviet Union is the most powerful country in the world." Wang himself fantasized about Dasha and kept up his friendship with the communist elements in his school.[10]

Wang felt incredibly proud of his ideas about communism and his casual ties with the front organizations, but he kept them secret. He describes himself as a somewhat arrogant boy, who did in one hour the homework that took his classmates five. What happened next, though, took him by surprise: the communists in his new high school were arrested and his erstwhile communist contact asked him and a friend to join the party and carry on its activities at the school themselves.[11]

> I thought that becoming a Communist was out of my reach, that Communist Party members had been tempered by steel, Pavel Korchagin style, were people with truly lofty ideals, big fearless heroes, veteran fighters, leading the way for the masses, standard-bearers for the people who held their torches high. Yet I knew deep down that I was naive and weak. I felt a little apprehensive, even disappointed. If even I could be a Communist Party member, wasn't the Communist Party a little too common?[12]

Yet Wang joined and duly took part in the organization of the communist cell in his school in the winter of 1948, which he remembers as exceedingly cold and hungry. He and his comrades hid out in the boiler room writing propaganda; it felt "more like child's play than a grim struggle."

Soon he and his young friends were given real assignments: they were to pass out leaflets in advance of the arrival of the Red Army in Beijing and were given the responsibility of guarding the shops and residents on a specific street as the Red Army approached the city to prevent rioting and looting. Wang was entrusted with a revolver for his night shifts as a guard, and by day he participated in student meetings and rallies, singing the Internationale and greeting his fellow students with a "Bolshevik Salute," the title he gave to a later, semi-autobiographical novel. Thinking back on it decades hence, Wang wondered whether, for him personally, the revolution hadn't been a bit too easy.[13]

Thus swept into Beijing's rapidly growing Communist Party on the eve of the communist takeover, Wang was perfectly positioned to enjoy the fruits of a victory that wasn't his, yet in a larger sense had been won for his generation as a whole. In the early period after the People's Republic was formally established, Wang spent eight months at a top Communist Youth League school and was given his first official position coordinating activities in the middle schools of a district in Beijing.[14]

He also met his future wife. As Wang and other left-leaning intellectuals of his generation remembered it, the early years of China's communist regime were a golden age of romance.

> Those years were particularly unfettered. So many boys and girls were in love, we just felt so happy. There was none of that "students shouldn't make love" kind of thinking. So later I called it the "Season of Love." From 1949 to 1957, China was a kingdom where love reigned free.[15]

For Wang, the subtext and soundtrack for that season was Soviet. Liu Shaoqi could talk all he wanted about Soviet teachers and friends and brothers, but Wang and his friends were too busy doing just as first-generation communists had done in the 1920s—falling in love, reading translations of Soviet fiction, and getting Russia and romance hopelessly mixed up.

The Tonya Phenomenon

The 1950s saw an explosion of translations of Russian literature, broadcasts of Russian music, and screenings of Russian movies in China. Pre-1917 classics were republished and refined, and new translations of contemporary literature proliferated. Along with the large number of translations from Russian came smaller numbers from other languages of the Eastern bloc—including a re-issue of Guo Moruo's 1922 translation of *The Sorrows of Young Werther*, featuring the very hero whose romanticism had been so hotly debated by young Chinese radicals in the 1920s. Between 1949 and 1958, approximately 3,500 new translations of Russian literature appeared, not including those published in magazines.[16] Altogether, nearly 82 million copies of Russian novels and collections were sold in China during this period.

One book crowded out all the others—a book that came to define the Chinese literary imagination into the 1970s. That book was Nikolai Ostrovsky's *How the Steel Was Tempered*, which sold a million copies through the People's Liberation Publishing House alone.[17]

A brave Chinese Red Army partisan makes a cameo appearance in the novel, but this could hardly explain the book's appeal in China. It was no literary masterpiece, but many of the storylines most central to socialist culture were encoded in this novel, and, it would appear, the Chinese recognized this.[18] *How the Steel Was Tempered* was an engaging story of a poor young man (Pavel) who falls in love with a girl (Tonya) of a higher socioeconomic rank. She returns his love, but then, Pavel becomes caught up in the drama of the ongoing Soviet revolution. Tonya is staunchly opposed to Pavel's new values—to Chinese, she was exactly the sort of "love above all" romantic who had been so passionately discussed in the 1920s, including by Chinese in Moscow. In the novel, Pavel rejects Tonya, joins the army, and becomes involved with politically correct women. Eventually he falls ill but continues to serve the Soviet cause by writing his autobiography as a didactic tale. The title of the book entwines the actual tempering of steel—an integral part of Soviet industrialization—with a revolutionary transformation of human emotions and aspirations.

The People's Republic Ministry of Education decreed that this book be prominent in education from grade school up through university, with emphasis on memorization of key passages and public, collective recitation of them. Wang Meng wrote about these events in *Season of Love* in scenes described by one scholar of Chinese literature:

> Although it is referred to as a discussion, there is no discussion at all—not even a rhetorical "devil's advocate" approach. Questions such as "Why should Pavel Korchagin break up with Tonya?" are directly answered in Pavel Korchagin's voice—his decision to choose revolution over love. . . . Speaking in his voice, the participants imagined themselves merging with Pavel Korchagin. Rejection of Tonya in chorus served as the ligament binding the collective.[19]

If anyone misquoted the text or expressed doubts about the rejection of the old order, fellow students hounded them until they caved in.

And yet, all the criticism heaped upon the soft, feminine Tonya led readers to worry about her quite a bit. As this was ostensibly an autobiography, it was assumed that there was a real Tonya. In 1958, Ostrovsky's wife—who had written a preface for the Chinese translation of the book in 1952—actually visited China. She reassured the audience that the model for Tonya was alive and well and worked as a teacher in provincial Russia. According to a student present at the talk, the audience "lived in the ecstasy and excitement brought by this revelation for a long time."[20]

Russian women also featured prominently in the many Soviet films imported by China in the early 1950s, offering even illiterate or apolitical

Chinese viewers an entire collection of heroines who lured and lulled viewers into consideration of socialist values. By 1957, 660 Soviet movies had been imported to China and were seen by hundreds of millions of viewers. Major Soviet actresses starred in multiple films, thereby acquiring status just as iconic in China as in the Soviet Union. Some Soviet actresses went on tour in China and spoke before thousands of fans in dozens of cities.[21]

Altogether, the films expressed mixed messages about love and revolution. Some Soviet movies featured beautiful actresses engaged in carefree romances, like Marina Ladynina in the major Sino-Soviet hits *Tractor Drivers* and *Kuban Cossacks*. Other actresses—also beautiful and also engaged in romantic relationships—were shown in more serious roles, fighting in the Russian Civil War or against the Germans in World War II, for example. Yet even these films could feature moments of passion, such as a famous scene in *The Fall of Berlin*, in which the hero and heroine kiss right in front of Stalin himself who was giving a (fictional) speech in Berlin. One expert on Sino-Soviet film exchange points out that Chinese films of the early 1950s were kiss-less, so this image of two Soviet people locked in a passionate embrace was a rare kiss the Chinese population experienced collectively on film.[22]

If the mix of films betrayed some confusion about the proper role of women in a socialist society, there appeared to be no confusion whatsoever that Soviet Russian women were beautiful and that socialist societies did in fact have room for glamorous starlets. Whatever layers of propaganda, explanation, or exhortation the Chinese Communist Party wrapped around these Soviet films, once the film reel starting spinning, viewers were enveloped in a Soviet world where women were pretty and people kissed in public. In this context, the idea that "the Soviet Union's today is our tomorrow" had romantic overtones that could appeal to even the most apolitical viewer.

Chinese Realities and Russian Dreams

Wang Meng remembered seeing some of the most popular Soviet movies several times in the early 1950s, along with audiences who shouted and applauded with genuine enthusiasm. But it was *The Fall of Berlin* that moved him most—so much that he saw it "at least" seven times. "I firmly believed that beautiful scenes like the one in Battle for Berlin of the lovely teacher Natasha in the flowers really were China's tomorrow."[23]

Wang went to the movies to find inspiration, and not only in the abstract. He remembers how a scene from a Soviet movie inspired him to reimagine the celebration of the New Year—a major event in both cultures.

The film "Zoya" described the deeds of the Soviet girl hero Zoya as an anti-fascist partisan. Zoya was famous not only in the Soviet Union, she was also a household name in China. My favorite scene in the movie was Zoya's high school New Year's party.[24]

In 1951, at age seventeen, Wang was in charge of organizing his district's New Year's parties for students, and he was eager that the parties be the best anyone had ever seen. "There was no countdown or bell like in the Soviet movie, but just before midnight, in order to 'check on the progress' of the different parties, I got on my bike and just rode around, passing from sixteen to seventeen, from 1951 to 1952, from old to new with such excitement. . . . I was so happy."[25]

If ever Wang's immediate surroundings dampened his spirits, he turned to Russian culture for a lift. Yes, he had Party work to do. Yes, the Korean War began. Yes, his parents divorced. Yes, his application to engineering school was rejected. But what did that matter? He committed to memory and frequently recited aloud a Chinese translation of a poem by Pushkin that went, "If life deceives you, don't grieve or seethe! Make peace with melancholy days; believe: a day of fun will come. The heart lives in the future; the present may be gloomy, but everything is fleeting, everything will pass; And what's past is pleasing." Wang's girlfriend shared his love of Russian literature. He gave her a copy of a Soviet novel translated into Chinese as *Shao nian ri ji*, or *Diaries of Youth*, which, she later told him, offended her, because it seemed like a book for a child, and she was already reading *Anna Karenina*.[26]

Wang had read *Anna Karenina* too, and among the scenes he best remembers from the novel was an early one when two young lovers meet at an ice rink. The characters in question are not the doomed Anna and Vronsky, but rather their happy foils, Levin and Kitty. Levin is a master ice skater and the much younger Kitty an unsteady one, yet somehow it is Kitty who controls the tempo of their interactions on the ice and Levin is constantly off balance, veering between bold declarations and terrified insecurity as the two weave toward and away from each other.[27]

Wang had first met his wife in 1950 when he was sixteen, but she was three years younger and still in junior high. Wang had a terrible crush on her, but "One minute she was wonderful to me, and the next minute she was telling me that I didn't understand her and we should just forget everything that had happened." Still, in fits and starts, he kept courting her. And in the winter of 1952, he became an ice-skating fanatic.

> Almost every Saturday night, I went to the Shichahai skating rink. At that time, the rink was pretty primitive. But first of all, the canteen sold a cold soup made of red berries, and to get soup that red in winter was a super human miracle. Second of all, they sharpened your skates with an electric grinder for free, and watching them sharpen and sharpen them until sparks flew everywhere was fascinating. Third and most important were the loudspeakers that blared Soviet music. The song that touched me most was "Who Knows?" sung by the Piatnitsky Choir, the many voices of an all-female chorus singing with the throaty sound of a folk melody, rich and blazing, charming and innocent, it was enough to make a person cry.[28]

Written in 1938, "Who Knows?" is a timeless, simple, flirtatious song, sung by a girl guessing at the intentions of a mysterious man who may or may not be a suitor. Kitty and Levin in the form of a Soviet-era song brought tears to the eyes of an ice-staking, Tolstoy reading, Chinese communist in the Beijing of 1952.

Wang Meng was hardly the only young Chinese person listening to Soviet music in the 1950s; it was through music that Russian culture reached the most people in China. As early as June of 1949, Beijing radio was broadcasting a Russian music program nightly, including singing lessons. Since Yan'an, the Chinese Communist Party had been interested in developing "new" music to replace "yellow" or "old" music—and after 1949 it went to great lengths to promote the composition of ideologically correct songs. But the population as a whole rejected much of the new music; when people received a new edition of *Song* magazine where new music was published, they would immediately flip to the Chinese folk or foreign section.[29]

Soviet music had the double advantage of being both politically correct and, at times, hopelessly romantic. Wang Meng remembers that when he first heard the wartime classic "Katyusha," about a girl missing her soldier boy-friend, he couldn't figure out what was revolutionary about it. The answer was nothing. An odd double standard applied: Chinese composers stuck to marches and ideologically correct lyrics, while Russian songs enjoyed much greater leeway. As in literature and film, this meant that themes of love and beauty were over-represented in the Soviet music that Chinese people lis-tened to and learned to sing. And so, if a young communist wanted to sing about love, chances are he would sing a song translated from Russian. "Why was it," Wang Meng asked, "that the human beauty, passion, and spiritual life rendered so carefully in Soviet novels was considered 'unhealthy' or 'petit-bourgeois' if done in China?"[30] Whether intentionally or not, the tight grip the middle-aged Communist Party leadership kept on Chinese cultural production, and the more permissive stance it took toward Soviet content, served to conflate Russia and romance in the imaginations of a second gen-eration, just as it had in their own.

Wang and Nastya

Unfortunately for Wang Meng, being a young communist in Beijing of the 1950s wasn't all New Year's parties and ice skating. He also had to lead cam-paigns against superstition and religion and do the tedious logistical and propaganda work that would spread and strengthen the new regime's youth organizations. By 1954, Wang had decided to try his hand at writing. Among his early efforts was a poem called "Stalin Will Return," which he wrote after Stalin's death and which got published rather easily, along with a couple of other short pieces. Then he set to work on his first novel, *Long Live Youth*, a contemporary story about an idealistic group of young people and their romantic dilemmas.[31]

At that point, Wang was picked to participate in a special seminar for promising young writers, where he heard lectures by authors like Mao Dun—an empowering experience. Just then, the Chinese Youth League issued a national directive for educated young cadres to study a 1954 Soviet novel called *The Newcomer*, about a young woman named Nastya who arrives at a dysfunctional agricultural collective and bravely confronts her lazy, corrupt superiors to get the tractors running again.[32] The Chinese authorities meant that young people should bring Nastya's fearlessness to their own work in factories and farms, but Wang took the directive a bit differently. He decided to write a parallel story about a young Party member—and to write Nastya directly into his book. The result was the semi-autobiographical *A Young Man Comes to the Organizational Department*.

Wang's hero, Lin, is a primary school teacher whose energy and enthusiasm earn him a "promotion" to the Chinese Communist Party organizational department. Lin shows up on the first day at his new job with a book in his pocket—*The Newcomer*. Lin's cynical boss asks him:

> "Well then, young Lin, have you got yourself a girlfriend?"
> "No . . ." Lin blushed.
> "Blushing at your age?" Liu laughed. "You're only twenty-two. You've
>   still got plenty of time. By the way, what's that book in your pocket?"
> Lin took out the book and showed him. Its title was *The Tractor Station*
>   *Manager and the Chief Agronomist.* [*The Newcomer*]
> Taking the book, Liu scanned a few lines before asking: "This is the
>   kind of thing that the Youth League recommends you young people
>   to read, isn't it?"
> Lin nodded
> "Can I borrow it?"[33]

In Wang's story, the boss does in fact read the Soviet novel, but, when Lin tries to bring up problems in the factory whose party work he's managing, his boss shuts him down. Lin silently weighs his options: "He could either follow Nastya's principle of nipping transgressions in the bud or he could fall in line with Liu's policy of waiting until the time was ripe." He decides to speak out, only to be sharply reprimanded by the boss, who uses the Soviet novel against him explicitly: "Young people have a very high opinion of themselves and plenty of ambition. When they start a new job they think they can battle against all the shortcomings, like Nastya, the heroine in the novel. This is laudable and heartwarming but it's also based on wishful thinking."[34]

At this point in the story Wang introduces a romantic subplot: his dejected hero is seduced by an unhappily married co-worker, while Tchaikovsky plays in the background. Actually, Wang's original version featured a much tamer flirtation; it was the editors of the story who added the actual sex to what was otherwise a sublimated romance. The co-worker invites Lin back to her apartment, where her child is sleeping. The story ends when he returns to his co-worker's apartment to ask her whether or not she loves him. Her answer is yes, and no . . . as she stands in front of a new painting of Moscow on her wall, titled "Spring."[35]

A German scholar of Chinese literature who has done a close reading of *A Young Man* characterizes the depiction of the Soviet Union in Wang's story in the following way:

> It is not Soviet socialism that enchants the fictional heroes in this story; Tchaikovsky lived long before the Revolution, and so did Turgenev. . . . The feeling that Nikolayeva's Chalikov has when listening to the Tchaikovsky waltz, that there is some great and exhilarating emotion lacking in his own life, and that he yearns for it, is the very feeling evoked by these Russian and Soviet works in China. Russia is the land of grand emotions, of lofty aspirations, of ideal love under the full moon, and enthusiastic production drives, of fiction that makes you weep, and eternal spring weather with buds of joy and energy sprouting all over the place. It is not a utopia where all houses are painted pink and all human relations are harmonious, but rather a place where one can live fully. This foreign land is so far out in space that we know of it only through films and novels, music scores and paintings; it exists as a work of art and can be appreciated only in this way.[36]

This passage is part of a specific and nuanced literary analysis yet captures perfectly the weary skepticism that scholars sometimes bring to their treatments of Sino-Soviet relations in the 1950s more generally.

As literature, Wang Meng's *A Young Man Comes to the Organizational Department* is hardly a stand-out, but as transcultural politics, it was brilliant. Like so much of Qu Qiubai's work, it was the sheer timeliness of his message and the way he leveraged Soviet cultural capital to deliver it that caused the story to take off. Wang was immediately criticized only to have Mao Zedong himself intervene. "I don't know Wang Meng," Mao said in a Central Committee meeting, "but his critics don't convince me." "Bureaucracy doesn't exist in Beijing? I support *anti*-bureaucracy. Wang Meng has literary talent."[37] And so Wang became an overnight literary sensation.

He did not, however, attain one thing he had been secretly hoping for: a ticket to Moscow. When he first contemplated writing a book, he remembered thinking, "If my novel is successful, maybe I'll be selected to participate in . . . the World Youth Festival, maybe take a trip, and after a trip to the Soviet Union, my life would have been worthwhile."[38] His fictional alter-ego may have been content to contemplate the Soviet Union "as a work of art," but Wang would not be satisfied until he had experienced it firsthand.

16

Legitimate Offspring

Chinese Students in 1950s Moscow

IN MAY OF 1951, China's new ambassador to the Soviet Union took some embassy officials and went to a bookstore to buy two full sets of Soviet tenth grade textbooks. Back at the embassy, they sat down and took a look. The ambassador himself skimmed through history, geography, logic, biology, and literature.[1] Didn't the ambassador, Zhang Wentian, have more pressing things to do? Clearly he didn't think so.

Zhang was one of several senior Chinese officials who was focused on the massive initiative to send thousands of young Chinese to Soviet universities and graduate schools in the 1950s. Zhang created a special section of the Chinese embassy in Moscow dedicated to managing the educational exchange, in close cooperation with a three-person commission created in 1950 to oversee Chinese students abroad at the highest level: Nie Rongzhen (chief of staff of the People's Liberation Army), Li Fuchun (northeast deputy to the Central Committee), and Lu Dingyi (Central Committee propaganda director)—all of whom had studied in the Soviet Union in the 1920s.[2] They reported directly to Zhou Enlai, and Liu Shaoqi was deeply involved as well. Given that in the early 1950s China was rebuilding after decades of war, establishing a new government, and fighting the Korean War, it's remarkable that such high-ranking leaders were managing study abroad at all. Beneath the surface, a more complex story emerges.

First Generation Romantics Grown Up

Zhang Wentian—who went on to become vice-minister of Foreign Affairs— left no memoir, yet his basic biography shows a life as deeply embedded in the Sino-Soviet romance as any. He first went abroad to the United States in 1921, where he wrote articles for a Chinese language newspaper in San Francisco and crossed the bay to audit classes at the University of California at Berkeley. In 1923 he returned to China, where he wrote a novella about a Chinese student in the United States who falls in love with an American girl but eventually leaves her and throws himself into the Chinese revolution.

In 1925, Zhang joined the Chinese Communist Party and in 1926 he went to study at Chinese University in Moscow; there he learned Russian quickly and became embroiled in the personal politics of the school, chasing the popular female student Chen Bilan and joining the so-called 28 Bolsheviks. He then attended the Institute of Red Professors, where he met and moved in with a Russian woman named Anna. She had just given birth to a son when he left her to return to China in 1931.[3] Zhang became a member of the Central Committee, made the Long March, threw in his lot with Mao, married a Chinese woman, and held key positions in the northeast, before his appointment as ambassador in 1951.

Back in Moscow twenty years later, he made informal inquiries through a third party to find Anna—only to discover that their son was among the Interdom children who had been in Belarus when the Nazis invaded and had never been found. Anna herself had spent years looking.[4] Given how tumultuous his own student years in Moscow had been, never mind his Russian girlfriend and his lost son, his interest in the lives of the growing numbers of young Chinese in Moscow makes more sense. Zhang Wentian was one of any number of first-generation Russian returned students whose memories structured the experiences of a second generation.

In the 1950s and 1960s, the People's Republic sent more than 8,000 students to attend Soviet universities and another 7,500 for short-term training. These included future president Jiang Zemin, Premier Li Peng, and many others who would eventually form a second generation of Soviet-oriented Chinese leaders. Nearly 80 percent of all Chinese students abroad between 1948 and 1963 went to the Soviet Union, and by the late 1950s, Chinese students made up close to half of the Soviet Union's foreign student population.[5] In terms of sheer scale, the Sino-Soviet 1950s educational initiative was reminiscent of the 1920s.

Like so many parents who travel a rough road to create a smoother one for their children, the Chinese in charge of the Soviet educational initiative spent inordinate amounts of time and money preparing the young people for college and ensuring that they were both better cared for and better behaved than their predecessors had been themselves. Chinese students in the Soviet Union in the 1950s were the most visible and numerous representatives of "New China" in direct interaction with ordinary people, institutions, and landscapes of "Soviet socialism." They not only needed to learn Russian and absorb the intricacies of highly technical specialties desperately needed to rebuild the Chinese economy, but they also needed to enact Sino-Soviet "friendship" on a daily basis. Even their performance of trivial actions—kissing a girl, cramming for an exam, spending a summer in the country—could be held up as public reflections of the Sino-Soviet relationship, potentially disappointing not just their parents but also the leaders of the People's Republic, or, in the case of students whose parents actually were the leaders, both.

Protecting the Second Generation

When the first group of 375 Chinese students arrived in Moscow in August of 1951, representatives of the Chinese embassy and the Soviet Ministry of Education sat down to help them choose an appropriate major. Unlike the 1920s generation who studied in special, relatively insular political schools, the 1950s students were to attend regular Soviet institutes of higher education alongside Soviet students. The vast majority—roughly two-thirds—were to study science and engineering to enable large-scale technology transfer between the two countries.[6] But this first group consisted largely of so-called revolutionary intellectuals, people who decidedly had not had the sort of education implied in the tenth grade textbooks purchased by Ambassador Zhang before their arrival. Moreover, few were Russian speakers.

By February 1952, the Chinese Ministry of Education had instituted formal criteria for the selection of future students. Political vetting, a physical exam, and basic tests of cultural awareness were to precede four months of Russian language training in a brand new school. Conditions at this school were excellent, but the expenditure came with serious oversight. The Ministry of Education and the Foreign Ministry cooperated to generate a flood of increasingly strict regulations for the selection and preparation of the students down to the most intimate detail. In turn, city governments and provincial capitals created bureaucratic committees to implement them.[7]

It hardly mattered where the students were preparing to go, as the increasingly elaborate selection process served as a barometer for status in New China. The fact that top Chinese leaders were involved only heightened the effect. Li Fuchun—whose daughter had grown up in the Interdom, attended a Moscow agricultural institute and married a Russian before settling back in China—redlined lists of majors, blasting choices like nutrition, hygiene, pedagogy, and library sciences and demanding that students abandon majors that could be studied in China. Liu Shaoqi also intervened directly in minute decisions; one handwritten letter from the Ministry of Education archives shows him deliberating to Li Fuchun about whether the test scores of two specific Chinese students were high enough for the students to go to Russia.[8]

In 1952, Liu Shaoqi took time for a chat with one batch of students on the eve of their departure. He told them that they each cost China the equivalent of twenty-five village families' annual incomes and encouraged them to study as hard as possible. But he also reminisced a bit. Liu was hardly a romantic Russophile: he had spent much less time in the Soviet Union than Ambassador Zhang, rumors that he had had some kind of Russian girlfriend were never confirmed, and he had pulled his pregnant daughter back to China from Moscow in 1949. Yet he had allowed his oldest son, Yunbin, to remain there with his Russian girlfriend. Yunbin was studying hard in the Moscow University chemistry department, vowing to contribute to the construction of a Chinese atomic bomb.[9]

These facts suggest that Liu saw a trade-off to be made: some exposure to potentially corrupting influences could be managed in exchange for much-needed expertise. Liu reportedly told the young people that the Soviet Union still had serious class differences—"women wearing necklaces and rings with precious stones . . . they also have beggars, thieves, and drunkards"—and that not everything there was worth studying.[10] At a time when Chinese propaganda was spreading idealized images of Soviet life, his message was a striking departure. Perhaps he wanted to prepare the students for the gap between the ideal and the real they were about to experience and to keep their expectations and romantic imaginations in check.

Banning Love, Promoting Friendship

It's hard not to see Liu and Li as two dismayed fathers worrying about their children by collective proxy. Both had seen the wilder side of Moscow in the

1920s for themselves, and both had daughters who had fallen in love with foreigners while they were supposed to be studying. Liu's daughter Aiqin was broken-hearted when her father wouldn't let her bring her Spanish husband back to China with her; Li's daughter's Russian husband two-timed her with a half-Russian, half-Chinese woman.[11] It was easier to imagine in the abstract ways to avoid such messy situations altogether for future Chinese students in Moscow. The easiest was to ban love, and that is exactly what they did.

When the very first postwar group of twenty-one Chinese students departed from northeast China for the Soviet Union in 1948, they were told in no uncertain terms: "No making love until your studies are over." Each set of formally articulated rules for the behavior of Chinese students abroad contained some iteration of this restriction: "It's best not to fall in love or get married while studying," ran a mild version. "In order to concentrate your energies on completing your studies," another one read, "in regards to love you should restrain yourself, deal with it correctly, it's not permitted to marry during your time of study."[12] Whatever the language, all the students understood the rule. Most of them followed it, such that even romances among Chinese students were relatively rare.

Ironically, the explicit metaphor that was supposed to govern Sino-Soviet interpersonal relations—friendship—was perhaps more difficult to enact. In the presence of linguistic and cultural barriers, flirtation can be easier than friendship. Even if citizens of "friendly" countries had socialism in common, the reality on the ground was far more complex because the Eastern bloc was characterized not only by a wide variety of cultures, but also a multitude of socialisms. So when Chinese students departing for the Soviet Union were told to make friends with their classmates, they were given a complex task.

Liu Shaoqi learned this the hard way when he sent his eldest son, Yunruo, to study at the Moscow Aviation Institute in 1954. Unlike his younger brother Yunbin, who had spent years in the Interdom before going to an institute in Moscow, Yunruo had grown up entirely in China. Once in the Soviet Union he sent his father and stepmother a flood of letters detailing his complaints, starting with the food. Liu replied,

> You are now studying and living in a new environment, and you've got to get used to it. . . . The Soviet diet is good, and the nutritional value of the food is higher than in China. Most comrades who go to the Soviet Union gain weight. The last two times I went I gained several

kilos. Although in the beginning I couldn't get used to the milk and the fish, over time I got to liking them. You shouldn't keep on with this prejudice against Soviet food. . . . In the past when we sent you some Chinese food, that was OK because it was when you first got there, but we don't intend to send you any more, because it could have a negative effect. You need to understand that life is really happy now, your conditions for study are really good. In 1921 when I was studying in the Soviet Union, living conditions were actually pretty tough, and there was nobody sending us stuff, but we didn't complain. We just cheerfully went on studying and living.[13]

Liu senior appears to have been on solid ground until he claimed that they had not complained. Some complained; others tricked extra food out of the school administration. Liu hadn't lasted even a year under the tough conditions he said he braved so cheerfully.

Moreover, Liu's son was facing a social situation that was entirely unprecedented in the longer history of Sino-Soviet education: he was living in a dorm room with a Soviet roommate. It was one thing when Yunruo's older sister and brother had been sent off to the Russian-run Interdom to live among a motley group of foreign children in the 1930s, and quite another to be dropped down in the Aviation Institute dorm with a Soviet roommate in Thaw-era Moscow and told to make friends with him for the good of Sino-Soviet relations. Moreover, Liu senior's advice was most likely the opposite of what Yunruo might have done had he really wanted to make friends:

About the Soviet roommate of yours, if he's really like you say he is, staying up all night gambling and drinking and offering toasts, being so loud his roommates and schoolmates can't study or rest, then that's bad. That kind of behavior you shouldn't approve of, you should give him some advice, criticize him, try to get him to improve. But if he doesn't, then you shouldn't retaliate. Later on, you could go to the Dean, there's no mistake in that. But to deal with a disagreement between Soviet and Chinese classmates, you should follow a more organized procedure. You should go to the Chinese youth organization in your school, then they can go to the Soviet organization, and let them criticize and educate him. This would avoid harming Sino-Soviet relations among the students of your school, and could even rally Chinese and Soviet students together.[14]

Yunruo's problem, of course, was that if he listened to his father, he would be considered a goody two-shoes, not a friend. It's even conceivable that his roommate was toasting to Sino-Soviet friendship in an attempt at striking up the kind of unofficial camaraderie that was increasingly valued during the Soviet Thaw, a time when sincerity and informality were emphasized over the kind of official procedures Liu senior was suggesting. Liu went on to berate his son for not getting along with his peers.

Yunruo was not the only Chinese student who was having a hard time, just the only one unlucky enough to have China's vice-president for a father. The Soviet Komsomol repeatedly reported that Chinese students complained about Soviet students listening to the radio late into the night or playing jazz in the "red corners" where party work was supposed to be done, or getting drunk and bringing home boyfriends or even carrying on with girls right in front of them. Soviet and Eastern European students paired up and even married, provoking the ire of Soviet authorities. One Chinese student at Moscow Energy publicly stated that the behavior of certain Soviet students disqualified them as examples for the Chinese, with their bad grades, cheating, poor discipline, and truancy. The Chinese students reported for playing cards and fighting or skipping town to travel across the Soviet Union were the exceptions that proved the rule.[15]

Soviet authorities were empathetic to complaints of Chinese and other foreign students about dorms, food, and roommates, and the Soviets worried about them quite a bit. There was considerable tension between the priorities of acquainting foreign students with Soviet life and winning them over as proponents of that life. Initial postwar policy called for foreigners to live in regular dorms with Soviet students, but, as a result of complaints, an idea emerged that special, better dorms should be built where only foreign students lived, as well as special cafeterias for foreign students where they would be served their own national dishes on a regular basis. In fact, there was a special Chinese dining hall at Moscow Energy Institute where Chinese from schools close by would also eat.[16] Ultimately, the Soviet Union would return to a Communist Eastern University–style segregated solution, opening Lumumba University in 1960.

But partial segregation did not put an end to the central dilemma. Uncertain local officials inundated the Komsomol with questions: could foreign students participate in military training, attend Komsomol meetings, participate in social organizations like the Red Cross or sports clubs, go on excursions to other cities, have their own newspapers, or help with dorm construction projects? Could foreign students be criticized along with Soviet students, or be awarded prizes? What would happen if foreign students were subject to racism, came to harm, or even died in the Soviet Union? These questions were often answered unsystematically by local officials on the ground.[17] Even Liu Shaoqi was unsure how to advise his own son, and he turned his letters over to the Chinese embassy officials in charge of students.

The lack of clarity on all sides and levels over how, exactly, to implement "friendship" between Soviet and Chinese students in spontaneous situations did not prevent the organization of official friendship rituals, in which Chinese students were expected to participate no matter what. One student recalls the requests he and his classmates received to speak at community events in order to "propagandize Sino-Soviet friendship" were so frequent that they often didn't get home until 1 or 2 AM and had to ask school officials to intervene. If they refused, as did one student who attended an agriculture institute, they were written up by the Soviet Komsomol. This particular student reportedly stated that he didn't want to speak in public about his experiences in the USSR because none of them were good. He was the exception to the rule—records at the time and later reminiscences show the Chinese as cooperative symbols.[18]

Yet no matter how hard they or their Soviet counterparts tried to be friends in spontaneous, individual interactions, they quickly discovered that they did not even share the same assumptions about the one thing they were supposed to agree on: "socialism." Even before Khrushchev denounced Stalin or campaigned for a higher standard of living, Soviet university students were more likely to be listening to jazz than talking politics. "Socialism" in the Soviet Union was nearly "achieved," and all they had to do was keep it going. Liu Yunruo's roommate really just needed to learn how to fly a plane or build one; he didn't need to worry about eradicating capitalism and building a large-scale state-owned industrial avionics industry from scratch, the very tasks facing Yunruo when he returned to China. Once, a Chinese student asked a Russian friend why the Soviet students didn't do more political study, and the friend replied that, as far as he knew, the Soviet Union had gone through a similarly intense period just after the Russian Revolution but then had relaxed, and that the same thing would happen eventually in China. The Chinese student took offense, but years later came to believe his Russian friend had been right.[19]

Costs of Friendship

Given the dissonance about "socialism," Khrushchev's Virgin Lands campaign was a welcome surprise for many Chinese students, who were among the most enthusiastic volunteers. Launched in 1954, Virgin Lands was a flagship program that resettled thousands of Russians and other Soviet ethnic groups in Kazakhstan, where they put vast tracts of land under cultivation for the first time in order to increase Soviet production of wheat. Although not nearly as coercive or destructive as Stalin's collectivization had been, Virgin Lands was reminiscent of an earlier, maximalist phase of the Soviet revolution.[20] The sheer scope of its transformative vision appealed to young Chinese students, finally giving them a chance to see what "building socialism" really meant. Yet from the time they arrived, many Chinese discovered just how difficult it really was and how anathema to "friendship" the process could be.

One student named Chen Peixian remembered his own Virgin Lands experience with a sort of bemused pride. He and his three Chinese classmates rushed to sign up for a summer in Kazakhstan, only to be shocked by actual conditions upon their arrival. Kazakh mosquitos and flies were terrible, but by far the worst trial was the effect of the unrefrigerated, spoiled meat on their digestive systems. Their Soviet classmates were livid about the conditions and went on strike, creating a problem for the Chinese. Chen recalled years later,

> As far as the Soviet officials were concerned, since we had volunteered to go for labor training . . . naturally we shouldn't strike; as far as the Soviet students were concerned, since we wanted to be friends with them, we couldn't let them misunderstand us, to think that the Chinese students didn't support and sympathize with their battle to oppose bureaucratism. We four deeply understood that this matter had strong policy ramifications, dealing with it well could advance Sino-Soviet friendship, dealing with it poorly not only would influence

our relations with our Soviet classmates, it would even undermine the image of Chinese students.[21]

The four Chinese finally came up with a solution: they would offer to do all the work—their own plus that of the Soviet students—and thereby maintain good relations with both sides. From a policy angle it worked but physically, it was hell. The students were stationed at a delivery point where wheat was brought to dry in the sun. Their job was to unload wheat from trucks whenever it was delivered and turn it out to dry. They worked so hard they almost couldn't eat, each awful meal interrupted by multiple trips to unload trucks and to the restroom. The labor and the digestive issues brought them near physical collapse, but they survived and were nominated by the local government for a Virgin Lands gold medal, a keepsake that Chen treasures to this day.[22]

Mothers and Lovers

For the most part, Chinese students were too busy learning Russian, studying, and going to their own political meetings to actually make friends with the people around them. Memoirs are more likely to recall a special teacher, who sometimes doubled as a mother figure. Young Chinese found that among the older people who were sympathetic to them were a number of aging women, who perhaps harbored embers of nostalgia left over from the enthusiasm of the 1920s for the Chinese revolution.

Most often these were the Russian language teachers who were the Soviet Union's first line of defense when confronted with waves of Chinese students who at first could do nothing else in the Soviet Union besides learn Russian. Even a year of crash courses was not enough to support advanced, specialized study. The pressure to learn the language was overwhelming, much greater than it had been in the 1920s, when most Chinese students were taught through translators.

Chinese in the 1950s were faced with nearly impossible tasks. One supposedly advanced student of Russian literature was assigned a famous nineteenth-century novel, Nikolai Chernyshevsky's *What Is to Be Done?*, and told to write an essay of critical interpretation about it. Published in 1863, the novel is a complicated love story about young radicals.[23] In order for the Chinese student to understand the novel well enough to both express his own opinions and comment on contemporary Russian literary criticism, he enlisted the help of his Russian teacher, who happened to have the same name as the novel's heroine, Vera Pavlovna.

Vera spent hours tutoring this particular student, but also, he remembers, she took care of the Chinese students more generally. At holidays she invited them over to eat and made huge Russian salads—favorites among Chinese— and she continued to invite them even after her time teaching them was over. At her house, he said, students just chattered away and forgot all their worries. "She really was like a mother with her children." Years later, as an elderly man, the student was upset that he could not remember her last name and knew little about her, since she hardly talked about herself. Just once, when he was alone at her house and she was helping him to write his essay, she told him stories of the siege of Leningrad, in which she had lost all of her loved ones. She didn't know why she was still alive.[24]

While the story of Vera Pavlovna was remarkable, she was one of numerous similar maternal figures. There was the Russian film student who titled her brief memoir "My Russian Mother" and wrote about a teacher who had taken special care and who had left a deep and lasting impression on the students. Her teaching was formidable, but she was also kind in small ways— once she replaced pocket money that had been stolen from her Chinese protégé by other students in her dorm, the ones who were supposed to be her friends. Then there was the peasant woman a group of Chinese students met when they were on the Virgin Lands campaign. Bringing them some melon seeds, she asked them to describe Moscow because she had never been there. And she said she had lost her only son as a teenager in the war. The Chinese students piped up and said she could pick one of them as her son. She asked: is there one of you without a mother? No, they said. But many Chinese students stayed in Russia for the entire duration of their studies. You can still name one of us, they said. She did, he called her mother, and she cried. It had been so long, she said, since she had heard the word.[25]

Perhaps the strangest story was about a woman who was actually only twenty-seven years old but who, a student said, "looked much older." She was one of two translators chosen for a special group of nineteen Chinese students who attended the Central Komsomol Academy in Moscow, and her Chinese was excellent. From the student's account it appears as though this woman's age put her at the cusp between lover and mother. The student described her looks in detail and told of dancing with her at a holiday celebration. He gave a common Chinese compliment—that her personality made her "seem Chinese." She answered that she loved China so much that she hoped her daughter would marry a Chinese man. How can you decide that for her, the student asked. "I've hung pictures of China all around my home, and also pictures of Chinese boys. I am fostering her feelings for China." Years later she spent her own money to visit her former students in China several times.[26]

In fact, this woman also stood at the nexus between acceptable and unacceptable relationships—and metaphors—for Chinese students and the Russians they encountered. Mothers were acceptable, but lovers were not.[27] The kind of open, wild promiscuity that their parents' generation had experienced in Moscow thirty years before was off limits, from the point of view of both regimes. Whatever the two countries had was no longer a romance.

Yet legislating the emotions of large groups of young people far from home is impossible, especially when they are away for several years in their late teens and early twenties. It was inevitable that some would develop feelings for each other and their Russian classmates; romances between Russian and non-Chinese foreign students became more common as time went on. Rules aside, some Chinese married other Chinese students even while they were in the Soviet Union, obtaining Soviet marriage certificates and approval from the Chinese authorities, especially if they waited until near the end of their studies. But relationships with foreigners were more problematic. Chinese men found young Russian and Jewish women particularly beautiful—"like dolls"—and they believed that Soviet women were attracted to them because they were more loyal, diligent, and sober than the average Russian man.[28]

One student still remembers the Russian sweetheart he left behind when he returned to China. "I almost got married," he recalled. "A Russian girl, she really loved me, it's too bad I didn't dare bring her home [to China] . . . she was so good to me, not just in an ordinary way . . . she said she loved me, and I told her I loved her too, I just didn't have a way. She said what do you mean no way? . . . Later she went to my cousin's, and she cried, 'I love him, why doesn't he care about me?' And she [my cousin] explained it wasn't that I didn't care about her, it was that we Chinese had a rule, we couldn't. . . . In the end when it came time for me to graduate, she came to see me often, she held me, she kissed me, I wanted to move and I couldn't, I said no, I can't, don't . . ."[29]

Star-crossed lovers caught in the vortex of the Sino-Soviet affair were so symbolic that they attracted high-level attention. In August 1961, a note from the KGB to the Soviet Central Committee described the situation of a young male Russian student at Leningrad State University who had met and fallen in love there with a Chinese girl in 1956.

On the 24th of July, 1961 a Soviet citizen, B.M. Logachev, a young research assistant at Leningrad State University, arrived at the border station of Zabaikal'sk and announced that he had come there for a meeting with the PRC citizen Van Fen-si, who was in China, with whom he was preparing to enter into marriage. Logachev became acquainted with Van Fen-si in 1956 while she was studying at Leningrad University. Subsequently he repeatedly made requests for the entry of Van Fen-si to the USSR, but the Chinese authorities hindered this. In connection with this Logachev and Van Fen-si decided to meet by any means and join their fate. At the present time Van Fen-si has also arrived in the border town of Khailar and intends to cross the state border illegally, about which she informed Logachev through passengers of the Beijing-Moscow train. Logachev displays exceptional persistence in his attempts to meet with Van Fen-si and announced that he and Van Fen-si will kill themselves, if their plans aren't realized.[30]

Having related this tale, the KGB added that it "considers it possible to render Logachev assistance in the arrangement of his personal life" and suggested to the Central Committee that if Logachev could get Chinese permission to enter, the Soviet Union should allow him to depart, and the Central Committee concurred. The ultimate fate of these particular lovers is unknown, but given that even Liu Shaoqi's children weren't allowed their foreign spouses, it seems unlikely that they succeeded in convincing the Chinese government. However much Chinese were encouraged to make friends with Soviet citizens, or to consider them brothers, they were not to consider them lovers as their parents had done.[31]

17

Female Families

Liza's Home, Eva's Adventures

IN THE STORY of the Sino-Soviet relationship, any number of patterns occur in the peregrinations: the 1920s pilgrimages of fathers structured the 1950s sojourns of sons; thousands of Chinese students moved to Moscow while thousands of Soviet experts traveled to Beijing; Mao called on Stalin, and Khrushchev repaid the visit. Yet if the tale is told as a romance in which all journeys are symbolic and Qu Qiubai's was the beginning, with which journey does the story end?

When Liza Kishkina arrived in Harbin in 1946 at the request of her Chinese husband and the permission of the Soviet government, she was utterly disoriented. Nearly sixty years later she attempted to explain her confusion:

> At present the word "adaptation" is in fashion—in my time there was no such concept. We lived, locked in our own borders, thinking once and for always according to an established canon and sincerely supposing that the entire world was organized exactly as it was for us. Therefore when I went to China, in essence I knew nothing about this country, the Chinese, and their daily life. The world was turned upside down. The only thing I had read was a book by Agnes Smedley, "Land," in which the old patriarchal China was described, but it seemed so distant, so incomprehensible, that nothing from it stayed in my mind. And so, despite ten years of life with Li Lisan [in Russia], China remained for me a "terra incognita."[1]

Qu Qiubai had embarked on his quest filled with abstract yearning for an unknown land, hoping to turn his world upside down. In his seminal travelogue, the most romantic and alluring characters were the young aristocratic women whose determination to make their way in the rough new Russia of revolution did nothing to diminish their charm. Neither Qu nor his contemporaries could have dreamed up a more perfect heroine to bring back to China than Liza Kishkina—of noble birth, natural curiosity, Russian beauty, and Soviet convictions. Never could they have imagined what would happen to her once she got there and began, however unwittingly, to adapt.

Harbin Time Machine

Just as Qu's journey to Russia had begun with a long and dismaying delay in Harbin, so too Liza began her time in China with an extended stay there, bewildered from the instant she stepped off the train—to find an empty platform and a pale blue Ford. Her husband was in a meeting, she was told. What kind of meeting, she thought, could trump the arrival of a wife and child from so far away? Liza had not seen Li for months, and much of that time she had spent worrying they might never meet again. When the Ford finally pulled up to a brick house, there in front stood a man dressed like a Nationalist general who did not even kiss her when she got out out of the car.

> Since I was mad at him and then some, the meeting turned out entirely differently than I had pictured so many times in my mind. . . . Certain disturbing changes had taken place in my husband: a kind of imperiousness had appeared in him, an impetuousness, a habit of command. . . . Instead of the modest intellectual Li Min', before me was a completely different person—a party leader, a general, always followed by an entire army of bodyguards.[2]

Yet Liza quickly forgave Li, for he had not only procured children's furniture and bedding but had also hired a Russian housekeeper and cook from among the local émigré community to ease her way into her new life.

There was something especially liminal about Harbin of the late 1940s. Liza arrived a year after the Soviet army, but before it was clear that the Chinese communists would win the civil war. In late 1946, Nationalist troops were just sixty kilometers outside the city, across the Sungari River, and there was real fear that the river would freeze and they would cross it. But the Japanese were gone, leaving behind not just military and industrial equipment but also furniture and clothing and dishes. Liza remembers being taken to a huge warehouse full of everyday items where, as the wife of a high-ranking communist, she could take what she needed.[3] There was some irony in it, since the expropriation of her own family's estate by the Bolshevik Party was one of her earliest childhood memories.

Harbin's émigré community, a mixture of longtime employees of the rail-road, businessmen, and White refugees, offered a glimpse into a Russian past just beyond the reach of Liza's memory. White Russian émigrés there were determined to preserve Old Regime culture and saw their small communi-ties as "more" Russian than the Soviet-controlled territories to the north. Watching Orthodox rituals or hearing pre-revolutionary speech patterns, at times Liza felt that she had gone back fifty years in time. On Christmas, she marveled as women stayed home and men went visiting in a practice she had only read about in Chekhov's "Visitors." Yet there was nothing stable or pure about it: the Soviet government was in the process of wooing the émigré community "back," while local Russian girls found themselves the objects of the perennial attentions not only of wealthy Chinese, as Qu had noticed in the early 1920s, but also of an unruly band of Soviet soldiers. Liza's house-keeper had one daughter with a rich Chinese lover and another who was carried off illegally across the border by a Soviet officer in a boxcar with his own troops.[4]

However fascinating Russian Harbin was to Liza, she wasn't really free to participate in it. Li, the Chinese communists, and the Soviet consulate all viewed the émigré community as counterrevolutionary and discouraged her from attending its events. Although there was also a Soviet Russian presence in the city, Liza soon found its doors closed to her as well, as Li's 1930s inter-rogator from the People's Commissariat for Internal Affairs (the NKVD), in Harbin under a different name, cast doubts on Li in Soviet circles.[5] Thus, while it was pleasant to hear Russian spoken on the streets, to talk with her housekeeper, and to be able to speak Russian in the shops, she had no Russian social circle to speak of.

Instead, as Li's wife, Liza was called upon to socialize with his Chinese colleagues. For the first time in her life, she found herself among "real Chinese," as she put it, "not Europeanized ones." While her reactions varied, in her reminiscences she returns to themes of femininity and domesticity as markers of difference. Even the highest-ranking Chinese communist women dressed in loose dark trousers and wore their hair in a nondescript bob, while Liza sewed the first piece of navy cloth she was given into a dress with red trimming and later found a pair of Russian seamstresses to fashion her clothes. She was appalled when men at dinner parties looked at her as if she were a "blank space," though Li explained that she should not take it personally since flirting with another man's wife was absolutely taboo. Women helped men with their coats, walked behind them in public, and asked them to dance at parties—for which they did not dress up. So anathema was this that Liza preferred to stay home.[6]

Once Liza became pregnant with her second child, she faced a whole new culture clash. In Russia nobody mentioned a pregnancy at all, but in China women and men alike discussed it constantly; Lin Biao himself commented on her growing stomach. Yet soon after her baby was born, the Chinese were shocked when she appeared in public, for they were accustomed to new mothers staying in bed for at least a month with all sorts of postpartum restrictions and concessions. When the baby turned out to be a second girl, no one could understand why Liza did not continue bearing children until she had a boy. Liza, for her part, was critical of what she perceived as poor sanitation and nutrition for Chinese children.[7]

As time passed in Harbin, Liza did make a peculiar, close circle of Sino-Soviet friends. Chinese acquaintances who had been in Russia during the war began returning to China, many to Harbin, and some with Russian wives. Liza also befriended a singular Manchurian woman who went by the Russian name Ania. Ania's father was a banker with a European education who had been eager for his daughter to learn Russian and therefore had placed her with a Russian family as a child. She grew up both bilingual and bicultural, attended the Russian language Harbin Polytechnical Institute, went to work for TASS, the Russian news agency, in Shanghai before migrating to Yan'an, and in Harbin, she oversaw the day-to-day operations of a new Russian Language Institute. The Institute was specifically for Chinese communists, who found themselves in increasing interaction with Soviets in the northeast.[8]

Liza wanted very much to find a job. Ania hired her for the Institute to teach relatively advanced students who had already had learned some Russian in Yan'an or elsewhere. As the wife of a leading Chinese communist, Liza was considered a more politically trustworthy teacher than most members of the Harbin Russian community. When a Harbin Bureau of Translation opened, she worked there, too.[9] With two children, a handful of friends, and a lot of work, Liza's life in Harbin gradually filled out. When the time came to relocate to Beijing, she was sorry to leave.

In March of 1949, Li was transferred to Beijing, where he was soon to be appointed minister of labor. Mao himself stood up for Li in his May 1949 conversations with Ivan Kovalev, Stalin's representative in China, in terms that both acknowledged and dismissed Soviet doubts about Li:

> In the past Li Lisan committed big political mistakes . . . [and] was removed from [his] post and sent to the Soviet Union. . . . There he was arrested for Trotskyism, but was freed from confinement. . . . After the arrival of Li Lisan to China, we studied him carefully. Li Lisan behaves himself honestly. [He] takes active part in work. His attitude toward the Soviet Union and Soviet comrades is a good one.[10]

Kovalev added: "Li Lisan is from the same place as Mao Zedong, they know each other from childhood, and therefore . . . Mao Zedong consistently and insistently supports Li Lisan." Thus, with Mao's "consistent and insistent" support, Li entered the core of the impending communist government's ruling elite. The Li family relocated that summer, like other top Chinese communist families, to a cottage in the Fragrant Hills outside Beijing. In the fall they moved into a new house that would be their home for more than a decade.[11]

A Sino-Soviet Family

Whatever political and professional roles Liza and Li played in the early years of the People's Republic, as the mother and father of perhaps the most durable, visible, high-ranking Sino-Soviet family, together they created a noticeably syncretic home. To foreground this scene of intimate negotiation between the two great cultures of international communism is to watch a different sort of Sino-Soviet history unfold. The house, its occupants, their possessions and activities and routines and relationships, their comings and goings and visitors and invaders—in the story Liza tells—all moved together through time in a markedly feminine, somewhat defiant display of Sino-Soviet romance, family, and loyalty during a time of brotherhood, friendship, and eventual betrayal.

The cast of characters was the product of a deliberate set of decisions that Li made, beginning with the decision to bring Liza to China and to keep her there. After Li returned from the Soviet Union in 1946, he could have done as many others did and found a new wife or reunited with a former one. According to Liza, however, he politely declined opportunities to meet women and insisted directly to Zhou Enlai and others that Liza be allowed to join him. It's impossible to know what motivated him—love, obligation, nostalgia—but he told Liza that he explained his feelings to his communist peers in terms of her loyalty to him in prison. The Chinese communists who sized her up may not have known of the Russian legend of the Decembrist wives, aristocratic women who went with their rebel husbands to Siberian exile in the early nineteenth century. But they did know the high value their own traditional culture placed on loyalty in a wife, and some knew firsthand the agony of disloyalty in times of cultural uncertainty and political danger.

Just two days after Liza arrived in Beijing, she opened the door to her hotel room to see her own mother—for whom Li had sent months before. Li had been close to Liza's mother in Moscow, and Liza's mother had encouraged her to stand by him through his prison term. Now that Li was in a position of power and privilege, he returned the favor by including her in his family's new, well-appointed life. The result was that Li was the Chinese patriarch of a family in which the other four members were all female Russian speakers, including his daughters, who were cared for by an outspoken and maternal Russian nanny.[12] Unfortunately, Li left no memoir to record this experience.

Li's next move was to reckon with the many members of his extended Chinese family, starting with his own mother. In September 1949, after his home province of Hunan was under communist control, he called for his mother, who arrived in Beijing along with his oldest son, who had grown up with her. Liza recalls her impressions of Li and his mother in vivid detail.

> Li Lisan and I went to the train station to meet them. They allowed our
> car directly onto the platform, and we stopped directly across from the
> sleeper car. The conductor opened the door, and there in the vestibule

Liza with her mother and two daughters, Alla left and Inna right, in Beijing. Courtesy of Inna Li.

appeared a wizened old woman with a face wrinkled like a dried apple. Her grandson held her gently by the hand, and then carried her on his shoulders to the car. Specifically on his shoulders, not in his arms—this is how women were commonly carried in China. (Just try to hoist a Russian grandmother onto your back!)[13]

However surprising the physical image, Liza was downright shocked by the apparent lack of warmth between Li and his mother, with whom he had a deep attachment from childhood. "It was obvious," Liza decided, "that the traditional etiquette of behavior—not to show true feelings and emotional reactions—was deeply rooted in the subconscious of even such an emancipated Chinese as Li Lisan." Li installed his own mother at one end of their eight-room house and his mother-in-law at the other, from which positions they exerted what influence they could in the atmosphere of multicultural confusion, while maintaining a stance of respectful distance from each other.

At mealtimes the two women sat at opposite ends of the table where each enjoyed her "own" food. Pay rank in the Chinese Communist Party was according to seniority, and because Li had joined the party very early, his salary was relatively high and his food allowance generous. In her first years in China Liza gained twenty pounds, making up, she said, for a lifetime of deprivation. A wealthy Russian merchant in Beijing ran a milk business and a grocery store fully stocked with the numerous dairy products (sour cream, cheese, curds) so loved by Russians and so rarely consumed by Chinese. Although Liza's cook was Chinese, the Russian nanny tutored her until she was able to cook traditional Russian food. In front of the house was a garden with huge mulberry trees, and the nanny picked the berries each year to make Russian jams and cordials, thereby giving Liza's mother a taste of familiarity in an otherwise disorienting environment. At the other end of the table, Li's mother dined on Hunanese food so laced with hot red peppers that even Li couldn't really eat it. She refused the dairy products, but surprised everyone by trying and liking coffee, a cup of which she drank each morning.[14]

Though it was possible to accommodate a variety of tastes at the dinner table, mediating the priorities of two different traditional cultures at a time of great social change required constant effort. Li's mother commented with surprise on the fact that Liza and Li chatted freely at mealtimes; she herself had never been allowed to utter a word while her husband ate. She fretted incessantly over the fact that Liza and Li were unsuited according to the Chinese zodiac, and she strongly urged Liza to keep having children. At the other end of the house, Liza's mother plotted with the nanny to have her granddaughter Alla baptized, in secret and without even Liza's permission never mind Li's, by a Chinese priest at the Russian Orthodox church in the city.[15]

Adding to the tumult of the Li household were a number of relatives, including Li's children from previous marriages, who came to Beijing at his behest and stayed with the family while Li tried to rearrange their lives. Li took responsibility for a young niece and nephew, who learned Russian and became, as Liza put it, "one of us." More complicated were some older children, who had already married or made life plans. One son was a quiet veterinarian and the other an active Nationalist planning to study in the United States, but Li promptly shipped both off to Harbin to the Russian language school. When a daughter arrived, he sent her to the Soviet Union to study at the Moscow Steel Institute.[16]

From Liza's recollections, a picture gradually emerges of a man engaged in a careful, deeply personal process of cross-cultural negotiation and accommodation. At a time when many other Chinese with mixed families or children who had been raised in the Soviet Union were urging their children to learn Chinese and drop Russian, Li came down strongly on the side of a bilingual education for all of his children. At home he spoke Russian with Alla and Inna, his two daughters with Liza, fearing that his Hunan accent would "spoil" their Chinese. When it came time for Inna to go to school, Li sought the approval of both the Soviet consul and the Chinese authorities for her to attend a school for Russian émigré children.[17]

Whenever a symbolic question pertaining to identity arose, Li parsed it out. On one hand, he objected to Liza's expenditures on consumer goods out of a general disapproval of "private property." He refused to wear a Western suit; Liza said Mao himself had scolded Li for wearing foreign clothing. Upon the death in 1952 of Liza's mother, who had retained her Orthodox faith through not one but two revolutions, Liza sought his permission to have her buried in the Orthodox cemetery in Beijing. Li agreed—but said that the cross the old woman had wanted for her grave was impossible, so Liza suggested instead the star that marked the graves of soldiers back in the Soviet Union.[18]

The distinctions Li made suggested a complex sense of self—one that, at times, appeared almost bifurcated. In Liza's words,

> It must be noted that with his older, purely Chinese children, Li Lisan related as was required by Confucian tradition and the laws of the Mao era, that is, taught them, urged them, read notes—in general, carried out ideological-political upbringing. This was the style of family behavior belonging to all of the "ganbu"—nomenklatura circles. But this had nothing to do with Li Lisan's behavior to me and our girls—here he behaved like an attentive husband and a loving father, relaxed in his exchanges with us and not caught up in political lectures.[19]

The duality that Li apparently sustained inside himself was perhaps unusual among his peers. According to the stories told by Russian-educated children of high-ranking revolutionaries, it was far more common for parents to insist not only on Chinese language but also on Chinese ways on the home front—even as they enthusiastically advocated brotherhood and friendship with Soviet Russia in public. Public pressure to accept all things Russian was answered by a private rejection, suggesting just how difficult it was for Chinese communists to be mediators of foreign influence in a society so weary of imperial encroachments.

Russian Teacher for the Chinese

When Liza moved to Beijing, she left her Harbin teaching job behind but quickly found herself with an unexpected new batch of students. In the summer of 1949 she was asked to teach an advanced class for Central Committee staff members who had already studied some Russian. She had no teaching materials with her, but she had obtained a popular, Stalin-prize-winning novel, *Cavalier of the Gold Star* by Semen Babaevskii, and used it as a teaching text. The book paints a rosy picture of village modernization with heavy doses of the pastoral—and the eroticism of rural women. The protagonist is a World War II veteran who brings his military-style leadership to a collective farm, where he also seduces a shepherdess named Irina.[20] For Chinese communists just emerging from war and gearing up to transform an overwhelmingly rural society, Babaevskii's tale was timely. Political analogies aside, there is something striking about the image of a small group of elite Chinese communists on the outskirts of Beijing, poring over a novel with a strong romantic subplot, under the tutelage of a Russian woman.

Central Committee staff weren't the only ones interested in private lessons from Liza. In 1949 in the Fragrant Hills, Li had introduced Liza to Mao, who shook her hand and said, "Good comrade!" Subsequently, she was called back by Jiang Qing, who was hoping to accompany Mao on his upcoming trip to Moscow and was eager to learn basic Russian with proper pronunciation. Liza was trusted enough for regular visits to Mao's home, though not told the reason for the lessons, which continued even after Mao and Jiang had moved to Zhongnanhai. Several times a week a Soviet Pobeda (a special car produced to commemorate victory in World War II) would arrive to bring Liza to the Mao residence. While others complained about her, Liza recalled:

> Jiang Qing made a positive first impression on me. She wasn't bad looking. She was distinguished by an almost cat-like softness of movement and some sort of especially magnetic charm. . . . With me she was

nice. Sometimes if lessons ran over she had me stay to eat. A couple of times Mao sat with us, and a normal family atmosphere reigned at the table. Mao was tender with Li Na (Jiang Qing had given birth to her in Yan'an), and he smiled at [Liza's daughter] Innochka, whom I brought with me on several occasions, she played with Li Na.[21]

While the only material payment Liza received from Jiang was a floral table-cloth and napkins, this assignment clearly conferred honor. What other Russian woman in Beijing had tutored Mao's wife?

Later in 1949, Liza was offered a job at the Beijing School for Russian Language Specialists, an internal party organization to train translators for top cadres closed to the public. The head of the school was Shi Zhe, who had spent many years in the Soviet Union, had a Russian wife, and was to serve as Mao's translator during his first visit in Moscow. The deputy head of the school was an old friend of Liza's from Vladivostok, Zhang Xichou, who was married to Liuba Pozdneeva, daughter of the founder of the first Beijing Russian Language school at the turn of the century.[22]

Liza soon received another, highly prestigious job offer. Beijing University had just opened a Russian language department and the dean, Cao Jinghua, offered Liza twice the salary as the Beijing Russian Language school for the Chinese Communist Party elite. Cao had been one of the students at Communist Eastern University in Moscow in 1921, and his teacher there said they could study Russian their whole lives and never understand it. Cao had gone on to study for several years at Leningrad University, then became a famous translator and literary figure. Liza was impressed by Cao, yet the relaxed, open culture of the school was totally foreign. After less than a year she decided to return to the school open only to top cadres, "maybe small, but clean and exacting, where there were small groups, strict discipline, and closed windows without drafts."[23]

Liza loved her work and was rewarded by being given more of it. In the early 1950s, she was in the classroom twenty-four hours a week, "and at home—endless essays and tests that had to be corrected all the way to midnight, preparing my teaching materials, and on and on. Most of the Chinese teachers simply couldn't handle the work physically, but I never complained." The Beijing Russian Language School expanded rapidly to roughly 4,000 students by the mid-1950s.[24] "Every day early in the morning, in all the courtyards of the school, you could hear pure, pure voices reading aloud from every floor of every building, all merging together as one, like a bird song, or flowing water."[25]

Liza's career rose on a tidal wave of demand for Russian language instruction in the 1950s whose sources were both practical and philosophical. When the communists took power, English was still the most widespread foreign language in China, reflecting the broader intelligentsia's tendency to find inspiration and guidance from the science and culture of America and Europe. But, as Central Committee member Peng Zhen put it, the "majority of the technical intelligentsia received their education in the USA [and] formally agree with Soviet methods of work, but in fact do not support [these methods]."[26] To make dreams of Soviet-style socialism in China a reality, the communists believed Chinese people needed to learn Russian not only to understand Soviet technology but also to experience a major paradigm shift.

In the early days of the People's Republic, the government launched a large-scale campaign to teach Russian that can only be described as aspirational. By December of 1949, the Sino-Soviet Friendship Association was broadcasting Russian language lessons on the major Beijing radio station and distributing printed material to accompany them. The press proudly reported that by January 1950, 12,000 people were already listening to them. In 1950, Russian language schools were springing up throughout party, government, and military units though the quality of instruction was minimal and the results were paltry. In 1951, the Russian Language section of the Central Committee, along with the Ministry of Education, called a national meeting to decide how to meet the demand for high-quality, mass instruction. In 1952, serious schools dedicated only to Russian language instruction opened in seven major cities; eventually there were twelve such institutes. Russian was also taught in fifty-seven other institutes of higher education, as well as in some middle schools in the northeast and all middle schools in Beijing. By 1956, China had "produced" nearly two thousand Russian language teachers, and another thirteen thousand students had graduated from Russian language departments in universities throughout the country.[27]

If China had a First Lady of Russian Language, it was decidedly Liza: a Russian woman married to one of the new state's founding fathers; a visible human link between two revolutionary cultures; a teacher of teachers who would influence generations to come. Yet in the heyday of the 1950s, Liza felt marginalized—starved for exposure to the very culture she stood for and, perhaps most ironically of all, shunned by the growing colony of Soviet experts in Beijing, who acted as if they ran her workplace and reduced her status even in the eyes of her Chinese colleagues. She remembers one expert who was sent to run her own department:

> I really disliked his way of speaking and behaving—aloof and dismissive. It was obvious that this person strictly divided people into two categories: those sent from the Soviet Union were in one, and in the other was everyone else, including some kind of stray Russian woman, with no special education in Russian philology and what's more the wife of a Chinese.[28]

Liza felt sure her Soviet boss was preparing to accuse her of spreading religious ideas among her students after a Bible was found in a dorm room, but just then he was relieved of his position.

Yet the presence of the experts continued to exacerbate Liza's sense of isolation. "Against the background of the emphatically respectful behavior to the specialists my sense of being a second class citizen was especially acute. In the Soviet consulate they treated us, the wives of Chinese, coldly, and, in my opinion, even with contempt." In her memoirs she chides them for living in their special compounds and hewing to their ways, noting that as far as she knew, she had never heard of a single expert or spouse learning Chinese. Instead, she says, they peppered their Russian with butchered Chinese terms. Soviet ladies were using the Chinese word for "eat" in place of the Russian word for "banquet" and replacing "got drunk" with "cheers," for example, to create gibberish sentences that sounded to Liza like the height of ignorant snobbishness. To be fair she noted, correctly, that experts were under strict surveillance and were not normally allowed to visit Chinese homes as guests, a prohibition that extended even to her. Years later one expert remembered that in China it was as if between Russians and their hosts there was "some sort of estrangement (otchuzhdennost), like some kind of wall stood between us, transparent, invisible, but some kind of wall."[29]

With occasional exceptions, the closest Liza got to the hundreds of Soviet Russian women who thronged the shopping district of Beijing was when she visited the Russian hair salon, or, perhaps, her tailor. Pushed aside at work and excluded from Soviet cultural events in Beijing, she observed the poor cross-cultural "adaptation" of the women who might otherwise have been her friends.[30]

Peacemakers

In the course of a five-hundred-page memoir Liza scarcely mentions Eva Sandberg at all, which was curious because, of all the foreign women she knew in Beijing, Eva's fate was perhaps closest to her own. Liza was a friend of several Russian-speaking Chinese women, such as Ania from Harbin, and several Russian wives of Chinese men she and Li had known back in Russia, such as Nadya Rudenko, whose husband, Zhang Bao, returned to China in the 1950s after eighteen years in Soviet labor camps. Her best friend was a relatively uneducated woman named Grania, the wife of a Chinese they had also known back in Moscow. Sophisticated Chinese Ania was jealous of simple Russian Grania, asking Liza, "Whatever do you see in her? There's not even anything to talk about with her." Of course, Liza recalls, she could not discuss literature or theater with Grania, "but I liked her spontaneity, her good cheer, the expressiveness and pointedness of her language, which was peculiar to her. She carried within her true Russian soul, that Russianness that I was missing in China."[31]

Li and Liza with colleagues from the Bureau of Translation, 1954. Grania Gusakova, far left, and her husband, Cheng Changhao, far right. Courtesy of Inna Li.

Perhaps in Liza's description of Grania lies an explanation for her reti-
cence about Eva. Like Liza, Eva was a Soviet citizen and the wife of a prominent Chinese. She was also hard-working and determined to hold a job. As
fate would have it, she was one of the few foreign wives to stay in Beijing
long term. But Eva could offer Liza none of the "Russianness" she so craved.
Moreover, in the 1950s, the two women rarely crossed paths in daily life.
While Liza focused all her energy on her home, her family, and her students,
Eva traveled almost constantly, camera in hand, in China and abroad—
with or without Emi. If she was not homesick like Liza, it might have been
because she traveled to East Germany frequently, for long periods of time.
But it might also have been because she was a fundamentally restless soul,
who felt at home everywhere and nowhere. She relished the international
creative community she and Emi had inhabited in the 1950s, never stopping
to think much about her own identity.

In 1949, Emi had been busy with the Sino-Soviet Friendship Association,
but by 1950 his efforts were focused on China's participation in the Soviet-
funded World Peace Council. He traveled to Stockholm in March 1950 for
a council meeting and in early April brought Eva with him on a multi-city
tour to promote the peace movement in China. Eva shot candid photos of
peace demonstrations—in one, a brigade of young soldiers marches through
an arch in an old city wall, as a young pregnant woman gazes at the camera.
She is holding the hand of a small child who twists around to see the marchers. Eva herself was pregnant at the time, and when her third son was born
in October, she and Emi named him Heping—which means Peace. Eva had
already hired, on Liza's recommendation, a fifty-year-old Russian nanny. Emi
was then sent to Prague as China's permanent delegate to the council. Eva
and the children were to join him.[32]

It was almost as if Emi's promise to Eva in the 1930s when he was trying to convince her to become a citizen of the Soviet Union—"pretty
soon . . . world revolution will come. . . . Then who knows who will get sent
abroad to work?"—had come true. For the next two years, they would enjoy
a glamorous lifestyle, with a home in Prague and permission to travel all over
Europe.

Just after her son was born, Eva learned that some of the pictures she had
taken of Chinese peace rallies had been shown under her name in a Moscow
exhibit and published in numerous magazines. Thus she arrived in Europe as
a bona fide international socialist photographer, and, as such, was offered a

Eva and Emi, May 1952, in Sochi, on the veranda of the hotel where they first met in 1934. Courtesy of the Siao family.

job in the propaganda section of the World Peace Council. Between her salary and Emi's, which was paid in hard currency, their standard of living rose dramatically, and for the first time in decades, Eva felt financially secure.[33]

Eva's memories of those years glow with the names of cities and people who lit up the international socialist scene. Wherever the World Peace Council held a meeting—Vienna, Bucharest, Stockholm, Oslo, Berlin, Budapest, Sofia—Eva and Emi went. They brought their oldest son Leon to the World Youth Festival in East Berlin in 1951, the first time Eva had been in Berlin since 1933, when she had seen it festooned with Nazi propaganda. Not everything was perfect, but life was as good as it had ever been. They visited Eva's brother Herbert in Stockholm and hobnobbed with everyone from the famous Soviet journalist Ilya Ehrenburg to East German president Wilhelm Pieck. When Alexander Fadeev noticed that Emi wasn't well, he issued a personal invitation for a rest in a Moscow sanatorium in the summer of 1952, including an all-expense paid trip to the very resort in Sochi where Eva and Emi had met nearly two decades before.[34]

After the Peace conference in Budapest in June 1953, Eva and Emi returned to Beijing, though each would travel frequently for years to come and they continued their duties as China's informal ambassadors to the international socialist cultural community. They settled temporarily at the Beijing Hotel, right across from the rooms of Rewi Alley, one of the

Chinese Communist Party's most famous foreign "friends." Alley had been born in New Zealand, moved to Shanghai in the 1920s, became involved in the Chinese Communist Party, and adopted two Chinese children. He and Eva collaborated to produce an English language book on Peking Opera, published in Beijing in 1957.[35]

By April 1954, Eva and Emi had moved to a smaller hotel—"prettier and more comfortable, with a garden so Heping could be out in the fresh air"—where Eva befriended the German writer Bodo Uhse. Bodo, as Eva called him, had spent three years in the Nazi Party before leaving and joining the German Communist Party in 1930. He was a wanderer, living in Prague and Paris in the 1930s, fighting and writing in the Spanish Civil War, then moving to the United States and Mexico in the 1940s, before finally returning to East Germany in 1948. Eva and Emi and Bodo and his wife stayed up late at night talking about the Chinese revolution, and, by day, went sightseeing. Eva took them to the Ming Tombs, which made a deep impression on Bodo. Eva shot photos on the excursion, and after he returned to Berlin, Bodo made a concrete proposal to publish a book with her photos and his text in East Germany.[36]

Eva was ecstatic, feeling that this project had the potential to quiet her restlessness.

After our return from Prague, I gradually came to feel very conflicted. My dream was fulfilled, I was finally in China. I enjoyed my work, and I was overwhelmed by all the beautiful, the new, the strange. I had everything you could possibly wish for. Emi was good to me, read my every wish from my eyes and kissed me; the kids were sweet and nice. And yet I was overcome sometimes by an uncanny desire to go to Europe. [The writer] Stephan Hermlin once wrote to me that my case was unsolvable: "In Europe you wanted to go to China, in China, back to Europe."

And then Bodo came into my life. I talked a lot about myself to this unusual, sensitive person. Our common wordless experience of the [Ming] temple animals, Bodo's enthusiasm for China and my photos, his heartwarming friendship and desire to make a picture book with me helped me to cope with my conflict. I had to reconcile my love for Emi and China with my desire for Europe. On one hand I had to take China to Europe, on the other hand allow my European friends to see

China through my eyes, bring them close to China. Only then my life
and my work could make sense. Bodo showed me this path.[37]

There's no evidence of an affair, but Bodo had wandered farther and longer
than Eva, shared Eva's perspective—"our common wordless experience"—
and perhaps really did know how to calm her demons. A candid head shot
Eva took of Bodo captures him mid-drag on a cigarette, eyes crinkled in
laughter. Arrayed on a page with eight similar shots of other writers and artists, Bodo is the only subject who looks to be sharing a private joke with the
photographer.[38]

Emi, Eva notes, was "generous enough to let me have my freedom in
friendships, in my work and in my travels to Germany and other countries."
But also, "he had his personal friends, mostly Chinese, who gave him what
I could not give him, and with whom he talked about his work and things
Chinese." While Eva was beginning to know some Chinese, she could not
really read anything Emi wrote, and at home and with their children Eva and
Emi spoke Russian. They had coffee in the mornings together but spent their
days in different worlds. And so Eva set to work taking hundreds of photos
for Bodo's album, *Beijing: Impressions and Encounters*.[39]

In summer 1954, Emi left for Chile while Eva and the children vacationed
in Beihaide, where she set up a makeshift darkroom. That fall Emi returned
to Beijing with his eldest son Allan, who was a reporter for *Komsomolskaia
Pravda* and intended to stay in China and learn Chinese. But Emi had been in
a car accident in Chile and suffered another concussion, leaving him unwell.
Eva's brother Herbert was also sick, so the two planned a trip to Stockholm,
where the World Peace Council had a meeting scheduled for November. The
Chinese delegation was set to stop over in Prague, where Emi would spend
some time in the famous spa town of Karlový Vary while Eva went to Berlin
to complete her book with Bodo. In mid-December she left for Moscow,
where Emi had already gone for the second session of the Soviet Writer's
Congress.[40]

Here in Moscow Emi's star first began, ever so slightly, to fade. On
December 15, two decades after the First Congress of Soviet Writers in 1934,
a Second Congress was to be held, and Emi was not invited. The slight would
not have been so great had Emi not attended the First Congress. When
Fadeev learned that Emi was in Moscow, he asked that an invitation be sent
to Emi, and Ding Ling suggested he secure an invitation from the Chinese

delegation, but no invitation ever arrived. Eva speculates that the reason was certain powerful Chinese writers' dislike of Emi's work.[41]

The Second Writer's Congress was exactly the sort of cultural event that Chinese politicians desperately needed good intermediaries to understand. For one thing, almost nobody from the First Congress had survived the purges or the war; Ilya Ehrenburg was one of a handful of Soviet writers attending who had also been present in 1934. Yet it was Ehrenburg, not the younger writers, who had just published a novel, *The Thaw*, whose title came to define its epoch. An uninitiated observer at the Congress would have heard speech after stultifying speech repeating the formulas of Stalinist socialist realism almost exactly as they had been laid out two decades earlier. Only Ehrenburg and a few others made short comments gingerly questioning these tenets. The fact that Khrushchev himself was carefully watching the Congress is something few could have known at the time.[42]

The Second Congress would have seemed quite different to Emi, who was not only fluent in Russian but had also been at the First Congress, than to other members of the Chinese delegation. While Emi was a Stalinist and personally closer to Fadeev, his work on the Peace Council put him in contact with Ehrenburg. He knew the semiotics of Soviet behavior and had always, regardless of his politics, come down on the side of what was now being lauded by cutting-edge writers as "sincerity." In a 1936 speech to the Soviet Writer's Union Emi had remarked,

> It's true, we're always singing about the revolution, the Comintern, socialism, the Red Army, we always need these songs, but people have moments when it's not the Comintern you're thinking about, it's not socialism you're thinking about, you're thinking about something else entirely. And it's exactly "about this other thing" that we have to write songs.[43]

Had he spoken those words in 1954, no doubt he would have received the same applause as Ehrenburg. It was Emi who had frequented the raucous writers' nights at Isaac Babel's before his own return to China and Babel's arrest, and it was Emi who knew how to socialize with the likes of Pablo Neruda. Neruda held a huge banquet at the Metropole Hotel after the closing session of the conference and invited Emi and Eva as honored guests.

They sat at a special table, Eva between Emi and Ehrenburg, with Ding Ling and Lao She on Ehrenburg's other side.[44]

But Ding and Lao could have sat through ten more banquets next to Ehrenburg and a simultaneous translator without fathoming an iota of what Emi could likely gather without even having attended the conference. The political function of cultural gatherings was never more clear than at this Congress, and it was precisely the ideas behind *The Thaw* that would most undermine the Sino-Soviet alliance. Emi had the knowledge and connections necessary to interpret this key, early shift in Soviet politics for the Chinese, yet he wasn't invited to the Congress. One wonders just how many similar opportunities for nuanced communication the Sino-Soviet alliance missed.[45]

In retrospect, Neruda's banquet marked a turning point in Emi's life, for in 1955 his health took a turn for the worse, a harbinger of further difficulties to come. Back in Beijing, a Soviet doctor hospitalized him and recommended drawing some fluid from his brain for an examination, followed by an extended period of absolute quiet. Eva was hard at work on another series of photographs for Bodo and was planning another trip to Berlin. She felt guilty, but both Emi and the doctor told her to go, so he could recover undisturbed.[46] In hindsight it seems clear that what ailed Emi could not be healed by a doctor.

Part V

LAST KISSES, 1960s AND BEYOND

18

The Split Within

Sino-Soviet Families under Pressure

FROM THE 1950S to the mid-1960s, the People's Republic of China went from signing a Treaty of Friendship with the Soviet Union and publicly promoting all things Russian to breaking off diplomatic relations and demonizing Soviet Russia. Understanding the apparent speed and totality of these two shifts is the goal of a massive quantity of scholarly literature. However, if the Sino-Soviet story is told as a cross-cultural, interpersonal romance that began in the 1920s, this "long decade" of mercurial shifts could be seen as a single stage in the evolution of the relationship. Once the Communist Party was in power in China, the stakes for its relationship with the Soviet Union rose dramatically, and with that came pressure and volatility—particularly for the Chinese Communist Party elite. "The period of the 1950s is now called the 'honeymoon' of the Soviet-Chinese friendship," Liza Kishkina observed, "but in fact there never was a time without conflict."[1]

Home Alone

Some of the earliest memories of Sino-Soviet rupture come from a particular group of people who were barely teenagers in 1950—the Sino-Soviet "love children" of Chinese communists who had grown up in a Russian international children's home. In the late 1940s, some of the older children had graduated from the tenth grade and matriculated in Soviet institutes of higher education, but three dozen young teens remained in the Russian school. After the communists took power in China they decided that it was time for these children to come home. The children had been left in Russia for safekeeping while their parents fought for a communist China; the return of the children represented victory.

On July 30, 1950, thirty-two Russian-speaking Chinese left the children's home in Ivanovo where most had spent their entire lives. The Soviet Union made a short documentary about them, *Going Home*, in which they merrily board a bus in matching outfits and suitcases and wave affectionately to the classmates and teachers they were leaving behind. In reality, the children did not speak Chinese and were unprepared for their future in China. As far as they were concerned, they were "Leaving Home." After a brief stopover in Moscow they boarded the trans-Siberian railroad and arrived in Manchuria on August 6.[2]

The Chinese side had purchased tickets for the children to transfer to a particular Chinese train to Beijing and had arranged a special meal car for them. But to their chagrin the Russian train was late and all their careful preparation was wasted. When the children finally did arrive, they had to part with the Russian nannies who had accompanied them, and they cried so fiercely that the Chinese officials who met them mentioned their distress in a cable to Beijing. Grasping the vulnerability of these children, the Chinese got worried about sitting them in ordinary bench cars for the long trip to Beijing and instead purchased more expensive sleeper seats for them.[3]

In Beijing they were met on the platform by crowds of Chinese students from the Russian Language Institute waving welcome banners in Russian and carrying big bouquets of flowers, the school orchestra playing jauntily in the background. They were China's prodigal Russian children, the Chinese children of the Russian Revolution, the Russian Revolution as Chinese children, coming home to China. Lurking nervously behind the crowds of young people were clusters of adults, who turned out to be the long-lost parents. Children without relatives present were held back a bit on the train, and then let out at the end. The crowds of enthusiastic Russian language students rushed to surround them, and this is when they realized that nobody had come for them. A large group of the children were taken to a special hotel for guests of the Central Committee.[4]

What followed was a series of cross-cultural blunders, mischief, and mishaps that made the children, who had been used to thinking of themselves back in Russia as somehow at least nominally Chinese, realize just how Russian they really were. One day the children were invited to Zhongnanhai, the compound where Mao and other top leaders lived with their families. There they were treated to a special meal that the wives of the top leadership arranged for them. Soon after, they were invited to another, authentically Chinese meal—until then they had been rather cautiously fed on Russian food. The table was crowded with curious onlookers, who laughed with delight when the children could not cope with their chopsticks and could not manage to gulp down even one bite of the sea cucumber that was supposed to be a tasty delicacy. One of the girls broke down and yelled at the onlookers. The children bolted away from the table, ran into the street, and bought peanuts and sweet rolls for dinner.[5] What had been supposed to be a happy and highly symbolic homecoming had turned into an embarrassment.

Soon the children were packed quietly into a train for the still relatively Russian city of Harbin. At first they were placed in a school for other orphaned revolutionary offspring, but they were so enraged by the constant curious scrutiny of their Chinese classmates that they began to pick fights with them and to misbehave so badly that the province's governor, a Chinese general whose wife was a kindly, generous woman, took all twenty

Chinese Interdom children in the Zhongnanhai leadership compound with top Party officials Zhu De, left, and Ren Bishi, right. Jiang Qing, Mao Zedong's wife, back left in short sleeves. Courtesy of Roza Yubin.

children into their house. They cleared out all the furniture in their dining room, living room, and veranda, and packed the children in.[6] The children attended a Russian school and finally began to settle into this privileged milieu. When it was no longer possible for them to live with the governor, they were placed in a group home with a Chinese cook who knew how to prepare Russian food, a Russian nanny, and a Chinese language instructor. They stayed until the Soviet officials who ran their school protested this arrangement and insisted on moving them to a new location. They lived in this Sino-Russian twilight zone for nearly two years before being transitioned back to Beijing.

Love Children in the Era of Friendship

At first, a number of the teens were enrolled in Chinese language classes organized by Beijing University, but just as their parents had struggled to learn Russian in the 1920s and 1930s, they struggled to reverse the process. They felt all the desperate longing for "Russianness" that Liza Kishkina described, but because they were ethnically Chinese children rather than ethnically Russian adults, they enjoyed little of the leeway she was given to seek it out. Liza herself recalled how Mao's younger son Kolia/Anqing came over to her house so frequently that when he couldn't be found in Zhongnanhai it was assumed he was with Liza. Kolia would sit wistfully at the piano, picking out the notes to familiar Russian songs with one finger. During the 1950s, Mao allowed Kolia to return to Moscow for extended periods of hospitalization.[7]

Many of the teens dreamed of returning to Russia for college alongside other Chinese their age—and a few managed it. Kang Sheng's niece, for example, was allowed to return to the Soviet Union and was one of a small group of students to enroll in the Architectural Engineering Institute in Kiev. Unlike other Chinese students, she had no language or cultural barriers, found a Russian boyfriend, and thoroughly enjoyed student life.[8] Others weren't so lucky. According to a story told in hushed tones by his friends, one young man had such difficulty adjusting to life in Beijing that he somehow snuck back across the border and made his way to Moscow—only to be drugged and returned to China, where he lost his mind and was permanently committed to a psychiatric ward. Apocryphal or not, for some of his classmates his story seems to represent a fundamental truth: for all the

Mao Anqing/Kolia and Li Min/Chao Chao in Shenyang in 1949. Courtesy of Li Duoli.

talk of Sino-Soviet friendship, actually being Sino-Soviet in Beijing could be enough to drive a person mad.

Not all suffered so terribly. Some found niche careers that leveraged their native Russian language skills and allowed them to maintain daily contact with Russian speakers. A good example is a woman named Dora Liu Xia—born in Moscow during the Spanish Civil War to Manchurian partisans, who named her in honor of Dolores Ibarruri. Dora was among the teens studying Chinese at Beijing University in 1954 when one day a recruiter for Beijing Radio came to the school in search of native Russian speakers for a weekly new program that was to broadcast in Moscow. Dora had a particularly deep, distinctive voice with good diction, and she was happy to quit what seemed to be futile Chinese studies in favor of a solid job where her Russian was prized. Dora was only sixteen at the time, and at first the station was hesitant to put her on the air. But when a Soviet specialist arrived and listened to all the announcers, he chose her as the lead presenter. From 1955 through 1959, Dora's voice could be heard in Soviet apartments, broadcasting information about Russia's exotic ally in a voice at once familiar and distinct. Dora says that she received Russian fan mail during those years, addressed to her Chinese radio pseudonym: "China, Beijing, Beijing Radio, Liu Lang."[9]

Dora was also lucky in marrying a fellow Russified Chinese. Many of her classmates admit that at the time they dreamed of finding just such a person, since it was difficult to obtain permission to marry a Russian and romances with Soviet citizens often ran into trouble. One young woman moved in with a Russian pilot working in Harbin, but they did not marry. When she became pregnant, he refused to acknowledge paternity, and she had an abortion. On the other hand, several young men fell in love with a beautiful half-Chinese, half-German woman they called the Amazon ("Amazonka"). It was she who broke up a marriage between an older Interdom girl—Li Fuchun and Cai Chang's daughter—and her Russian husband.[10] While some of the Sino-Soviet children eventually found Chinese spouses and had happy marriages, just as many such marriages failed. A few still laugh when they tell the story of one classmate who divorced her husband the day after she married him—because he wouldn't let her go see her Russian-speaking childhood friends. Under these circumstances, then, Dora felt lucky when she met her own husband, a Chinese whose family had emigrated to Russia in 1940 and who was deployed back to Manchuria in 1945 as a radio specialist.[11]

Dora was not the only Russian-educated child of Chinese communists to find work that used her language skills. Her friend Roza, for example, went to work for the Russian language edition of the pictorial magazine *China*, while others were employed by the various publications of the Sino-Soviet Friendship Association. Still others found work in translation bureaus. Older classmates who finished college in Moscow and returned to work in industry sometimes became the liaisons with Soviet experts sent to their otherwise Chinese workplaces. Almost none found Russian-speaking spouses in the 1950s. And so the several dozen Sino-Soviet love children who found themselves in Beijing of the 1950s tried to get together as often as they could—preferably when someone's parents or spouse was out of town—for all-night carousing that served as a vital release from the pressures they faced, even at the height of so-called Sino-Soviet friendship.

"Just What Are You Right Now?"

The problem wasn't just that the Sino-Soviet love children were unaccustomed to Chinese daily life; also, some of their parents either refused to acknowledge them or put extraordinary pressure on them to "become Chinese." One elderly woman still vividly recalls being brought to see her biological mother—who, apparently unprepared for her arrival, ran into another room and refused to admit that the girl was her daughter at all. This woman had a new family and feared the reaction of her husband to the news that she had a Moscow love child with another man.

The most intimate window into the dynamics of a newly constituted Sino-Soviet family comes from the memoirs of a woman who calls herself Lena. Her parents had fallen in love at Communist Eastern University in the 1930s and given birth to her in 1937, but in 1938 her father had been purged and sent to a Soviet labor camp, while her mother had been allowed to return to China. At first her mother worked in the translation department in Yan'an and then, as a Russian-speaking Manchu woman, she was sent to help with the communist takeover of Manchuria in 1946. Her mother remarried and was given a series of leadership positions in key factories in the northeast, culminating in her appointment as a representative to the National People's Congress.[12]

As Lena describes it, even as China extolled the virtues of the Soviet "older brother" and encouraged Chinese people to learn Russian, her mother engaged in an all-out campaign to turn her into a "real Chinese girl." In 1951, at the end of Lena's first year in Harbin, her mother brought her home to the city of Benxi, a coal and metallurgy center in the northeastern province of Liaoning where she was working as a senior manager in 1951. At night, mother and daughter would sit down for Chinese lessons, and as the weeks passed Lena's mother became increasingly reluctant to send her back to Harbin. In her memoirs Lena gives the following approximation of an exchange with her mother:

> One day after our lessons, Mother said, "We need to have a serious talk.... We've been studying Chinese together, and I see what great progress you've made. But why are you doing this? If you go off to Harbin, you'll again be immersed in a Soviet environment, you'll become a Russian schoolgirl, and you'll forget everything we've studied.... I am thinking not only of Chinese. In Harbin you have no contact with the real China; you'll be living almost as if you were still in the Soviet Union. So what would be the point of your having returned to the motherland?"
>
>   I replied, "They told us we had to go, so we went. If they gave us the chance to return now to the Soviet Union, we would all gladly go.

What difference does it make where we live and work? After all, communism is international."

After my reply Mother pondered for a few moments, then asked, "Tell me, are you Russian or Chinese? Where is your motherland?"

I still did not grasp the criminal nature of my thoughts and I responded in the previous spirit, "Does it make any difference who I am? One can be a Communist and a revolutionary both in China and in the Soviet Union. In International House we were taught internationalism. . . .

"Do you know what you're saying? Everybody has their own motherland, they must be patriots of their motherland and think of it first— love, defend, and protect it. A Chinese is first of all a Chinese, not a foreigner. Serving one's motherland must always come first."

I resented listening to her lecture me like that, and I recalled everything I had learned about the history of the world revolution. "Didn't Chinese fight and die in the ranks of the Red Army after the October Revolution? Wasn't an International Brigade formed to aid the Spanish Republic in the struggle against Franco? Didn't the Soviet army help China smash the Japanese aggressors in Manchuria? Was all of this wrong?"

Mother angrily cut me off. "I know all of this better than you do. If necessary, we Chinese are ready to help the socialist revolution of any people, but as Chinese, not as foreigners, as we are doing now in Korea. Just what are you right now? Chinese? Russian? Nobody?"[13]

Actually, Lena's mother probably did "know all of this" better than Lena, for she had joined the Communist Party as an anti-Japanese partisan and had been among the Chinese group at Moscow's Eastern University that had once tried to send its entire monthly stipend to Spain. But to her daughter's surprise, she used exactly this experience to argue that Lena should stay in Benxi and attend a Chinese school rather than returning to Harbin. "You're already a big girl, fourteen and a half!" she said.

At your age I was already the leader of the Komsomol organization in a girl's school. In the unequal struggle against the Japanese aggressors we were ready to give our lives because we were defending our motherland.

Neither family, friends, habits, or feelings could stop me. My life was focused on just one goal—the anti-Japanese struggle. When the party decided to send me to the Soviet Union, I went without hesitation to an entirely unknown country with an alien language and alien traditions. But in a year and a half I was able to learn Russian and do my job to the best of my abilities. I was seventeen.[14]

Lena's mother got permission from the Organizational Committee to remove Lena from the Russian school in Harbin and enroll her in a Chinese school in Benxi. She also began bringing her daughter to the factory where she worked, where she introduced her to workers and showed her their poor living conditions.

Lena's mother gave her a new Chinese name and Chinese clothes.[15] Yet, despite her mother's hopes, Lena experienced no change of heart. Instead, she was miserable in the Chinese school, where, at assembly time, students would crowd around her clapping and shouting, "Soviet person, sing a Russian song!" By the end of the fall semester Lena suffered a kind of nervous breakdown—at which point her mother finally relented and agreed to send her back to Harbin for the spring term of 1952, and then to a school for Russian émigrés in Shenyang. Only in mid-1953 did Lena transfer to a Chinese middle school.[16]

Why, exactly, Lena's mother felt so compelled to effect a change in her daughter's linguistic and cultural identity is unclear. It is tempting to speculate that she observed Mao and read his behavior toward his own children as a better indicator of the status of Russia in China than the massive pro-Soviet propaganda campaigns. Yet plenty of people higher in party ranks than she was—Li Lisan and Emi Xiao, for example—drew very different conclusions and were less strict with their children. Even Liu Shaoqi allowed his son to bring his Soviet wife and children back to China. Or perhaps it was a generational difference. Lena's mother joined the Communist Party during the brutal, fiercely nationalistic anti-Japanese campaigns of the 1930s, not during the heady internationalism of the early 1920s. In any case, whatever the reason, as Lena remembers it, she and her mother rehearsed some of the basic arguments that drove the Sino-Soviet split long before it actually happened—indeed throughout some of the most optimistic early years of the alliance.

Becoming Chinese?

Lena and the other children her age faced the daunting proposition of finishing high school back in China and sometimes experienced cultural difference as family conflict. But some of their older classmates who had matriculated in Soviet universities before 1949 and returned to China as adults seem to have internalized the tension, which they often understood in professional terms.[17] The best example comes from Yura, the athlete whose father had been a friend of Zhou Enlai, who had fallen in love with a Russian girl, Tamara, only to leave her to "return" to a China he did not even remember. In some ways the stories that Yura and Lena told of their shifting identities were diametrically opposed: while Lena fiercely defended her Russian ways against her mother's attempts to Sinify her, Yura struggled to become Chinese.

When Yura first arrived in Manchuria in 1951, nobody was there to meet him at the station, a situation that left him quite nervous. Pacing the platform, he noticed an old man lying on a mat.

> I looked and there he was with two pigtails, such long pigtails! And a beard! Oh I got scared! Because I had read that in China under the Manchu dynasty all men had to have pigtails. And then I thought: they're not really going to make me grow pigtails!? I got frightened for real. What's more I had been waiting for two hours, and nobody had come for me. Then I got a little closer. It was clear that the old man was from the countryside, he was dressed so poorly. But on his feet he had sports shoes—tennies. New ones!! I never had anything like that. What a contrast! Here you have feudalism, and then the state-of-the-art. I breathed a little easier. Something related to sports. When I was a student we always envied anyone who had shoes like that. We tried any way we could to get some. And here, a simple old man. . . . It means that in China they sell sporting goods! That means, probably, there are sports . . . there's something.[18]

Yura had not been in China since his mother had brought him to Moscow in 1929 when he was a toddler and he hadn't seen or heard from his parents since. At twenty-three he had decided that helping to build New China was his destiny.

When Yura arrived in Beijing, to his surprise, he was feted as a major sports expert. He had studied at the elite Moscow Institute of Physical Culture under the legendary high-jumping coach, Vladimir Dyachkov. In Moscow he had been a regular, impoverished student, but in Beijing he was taken on VIP tours.[19]

In 1953, Yura was chosen as the coach for New China's first official track and field team hastily organized to send a token group to the World Youth Festival that summer. At first, there were only five athletes on the team; by the end of 1953, there were forty-three—but they ranged in age from fifteen to twenty-seven and they did not really coalesce by event. It would have been a tough job for any coach, but for Yura, whose Chinese was still basic, who was culturally completely Russian, and who was only twenty-six years old himself, it was a stretch. Moreover, he was at first completely beholden to some "foreign" expert who literally sent him written training plans to follow each month. Since these plans had nothing to do his actual team, they didn't work.[20]

His athletes and colleagues considered him a "foreign" Chinese. "It was really not nice to feel yourself so isolated for so long like a 'white crow,'" Yura recalled. "I wanted to yell, 'I am Chinese too! Why do you consider me foreign?'" And so Yura embarked on his own quixotic campaign to "become Chinese." For him, being Chinese was not only about speaking Chinese (hard) or eating Chinese food (easy), but also about respecting authority, being politically active, and working with unimaginable intensity to overcome natural weakness. Much as he admired these characteristics, his memories are shot through with ambivalence. Though he wanted to become Chinese, he did not necessarily want to cease to "be" Russian. Being Russian was about having a sense of humor, playing games, being professional first and political second, and being both naturally and technically superior. Ultimately, being Yura was about being a little bit of each—or being Sino-Soviet. He liked Chinese food, but retained the tastes of his youth and preferred Russian food in private. He did learn Chinese but spoke with a strong Russian accent. He worked back-breaking hours but never stopped cracking jokes and playing games with his athletes. [21] Yura claimed that he respected no authority—neither Chinese nor Soviet. Particularly repulsive to him were the endless political meetings of 1950s China. Early on he simply refused to attend, announcing,

I grew up and was educated in the U.S.S.R.—the first socialist state in the world. I studied Marx's "Das Kapital" for several years in college and passed all tests on this subject with distinction. In the Soviet Union, besides in the movies, I never once even saw a live capitalist, landowner, or kulak. So, in my consciousness there can't be any bourgeois remnants and I don't need to re-forge myself.[22]

Ignoring the political campaigns, Yura focused on his athletes, doing everything he could to adapt his expertise to their capabilities—and failing. Yura recalls a particularly comical conversation he had with one of his most talented protégés, a fifteen-year-old girl named Zhen Fengrong. From a poor family in Shandong province, Zhen was recruited for Yura's team after placing third in a competition for school-age high-jumpers.

During one of our trainings I was teaching [her] high jumping techniques. I told her the theory of it in detail. I was so pleased with myself, such a good teacher. But then I noticed she was acting strange: looking around, even, my god, picking her nose. Then there was a short dialog. "Aren't you ashamed of yourself? Why aren't you listening to anything?" "Trainer Huan, I'm telling you, no need to drag it out. I don't understand any of it anyway. You'd be better off to show me how to do this stuff."[23]

Deeply competitive, Yura did not like the fact that many foreign coaches dismissed Chinese athletes as naturally inferior. Though his athletes were uneducated, he quickly discovered that they shared the extreme enthusiasm of their generation, and they could work harder than the competition. At the time, most jumpers practiced only five or six times a week. Yura increased the number and duration of practices and began including a wide variety of activities, from weight-lifting to gymnastics, considered risky at the time. In fact, Yura's zealotry cost him some of his best athletes, who were overworked and injured. At first he trained Zhen so hard she broke down and had to rest for an entire year healing from her injuries before she could start again.[24]

Even after Zhen had recovered from the injury, she was still Yura's most promising athlete and so he continued raising the bar. Zhen never complained about practice—when she didn't jump high enough, she would cry, but then she would dust herself off and try again, continuing until all the other athletes had gone home. Sometimes Yura would hang up a white flag to tell her to surrender, but she'd just keep jumping. "We broke all the rules of safety in training," Yura remembers. "But friends, don't forget, these were the 1950s, the romantic years in our sport."[25]

As he strayed further from his Moscow training in professional terms and became closer personally to his Chinese athletes, Yura found himself increasingly alienated from his Soviet colleagues. For Yura, the biggest psychological hurdle was a decision to abandon the Dyachkov method in favor of an old-fashioned "scissors-kick" that seemed better suited to Chinese bodies. Ironically, given how hard it was for him to turn his back on Dyachkov's teachings, doing so also exposed him to criticism—not only from the Soviet coaches who arrived in Beijing along with other experts, but also from the Chinese. "Imagine my position: in the 1950s, when the country was making its first small steps in the building of socialism after the liberation of the country, the word of the Soviet 'older brothers' was unspoken law for us— Chinese."[26] In fact, in the summer of 1957, Yura was training Zhen at Dinamo stadium in Moscow when Dyachkov came over to tell him that if she didn't change her "scissor-jump" technique, she'd never win. Yura agonized over this advice for weeks, but stuck to his own plan.[27]

On November 17, 1957, in Beijing, Zhen Fengrong became the first Chinese woman to break a world sporting record, jumping 1.77 meters with a scissors kick.[28] It was a great leap before the Great Leap—a perfect metaphor for what China was trying to do on the world stage. And it had been accomplished by a tough young Chinese woman and a Russian-trained coach who had incorporated the best of Soviet theory, then abandoned it in favor of intensive training and less "advanced" techniques that he perceived as more suited to China.

Parents under Pressure—Eva, Emi, and Professional Politics

Whereas "children" felt tension in the Sino-Soviet "family" even in the early 1950s, some "parents" recall their first real experiences of personal or professional conflict only later in the decade. Eva and Emi, both employed in high visibility cultural realms, for example, first found themselves at odds with their employers in the late 1950s. Eva had departed for Germany in 1955 to work on her most recent photo album, leaving Emi in the care of a Soviet doctor in Beijing. Two months later, she returned, determined to bring

Emi and their children for a restful summer at the Communist Party resort Beidaihe on the coast of Hebei province. But very quickly she heard whispered criticism of herself and her husband. Emi was said to be lazy, not sick, and "covered with foreign flavor"—an accusation that particularly upset Eva. Entertaining China's foreign friends at home and abroad as Emi did was important work, she argued. And though she did not say it, wasn't she part of the foreign flavor "covering" Emi?[29]

Emi, on the other hand, tried to comfort Eva. Although most of her photographs were going into East German publications, she was still nominally an employee of Xinhua, and as such, was subject to its criticism. Eva saw photography as an intuitive method of spontaneous expression. When shooting the Peking Opera, she captured the actors not only during performances but also when they were putting on their makeup or were sweaty and exhausted after the show.[30] But, though her direct boss at Xinhua encouraged her, she clashed with the editor.

> He wanted only posed pictures, like what they often saw in Soviet magazines. The people had to be dressed neatly in all walks of life and above all always be laughing. An artist who is carving a jade figure does not laugh; the image must on the contrary show his concentration, his intense inner participation. The earnestness on the faces of the worker or children playing and learning was not "optimistic" enough, while I believed on the contrary (and still believe) that it is precisely those pictures that showed the optimistic will to build a new China.[31]

Artistically, Eva was applying principles of spontaneity and authenticity akin to those of Ehrenburg and others in the Soviet Union.

Eva was also politically in step with de-Stalinization—and therefore out of step with major currents in Chinese politics. In July 1957, Mao launched the Anti-Rightist Campaign, targeting intellectuals in particular. When the movement hit the Chinese Writer's Union, Emi was conveniently scheduled to go to Moscow for the International Youth Festival. While he was in the Soviet Union—still a politically correct place to be—Ding Ling and many other friends were labeled rightists. The contrast between the euphoria and wonder of the Moscow youth festival and the situation Emi faced upon his return to China could not have been greater. He was reassured that everyone knew that any mistakes he had made were likely the result of his friendship with Ding Ling and that he needed to make a public self-criticism as quickly as possible. When his own draft was unacceptable, it was edited. Emi stood up in the writer's congress, and read out the approved text, and escaped relatively unscathed. In October of that year, when a delegation of Indian writers arrived, Emi was chosen to introduce them to Mao, whom he had not seen in person since Yan'an, and who now gave him a warm reception.[32]

Eva recalls that at the time of the Anti-Rightist campaign, Emi told her few details; she was only aware that he was having some difficulty with higher-ups. Emi himself published nothing in his memoirs about this moment. Yet his travels all the way up to the 1960s repeatedly exposed him to the radical difference between the increasingly tense political climate in Beijing and the relatively more relaxed situation in Russia—never mind Chile or India. Emi was under no illusions—he served at the pleasure of the Chinese leadership, his childhood friend Mao first and foremost. That his Stalinist friend Fadeev had recently killed himself and the relatively open-minded Ding Ling was expelled from the Chinese Communist Party showed just how far apart Moscow and Beijing were in zeitgeist. On some level, the Sino-Soviet split was the product of a growing gap between two increasingly different cultures of communism—a gap that could easily be tapped and exploited.

Estrangement

What had been a difference in sensibility that had been possible to finesse, misunderstand, or ignore in 1957 turned into a serious difference in policy in 1958. When China launched the Great Leap Forward, with its extreme grain requisitioning, backyard furnaces to melt domestic metals ostensibly for industrialization, and collective kitchens to manage food consumption, the country embarked on a program reminiscent of Stalin's First Five Year Plan. Soviet experts in China were skeptical, as were key members of the leadership. Even urban dwellers were not entirely shielded from the massive famine that resulted in 1959, and eventually food shortages affected at least some members of the party elite.[33] In 1959, Marshal Peng Dehuai famously challenged Mao, seconded by one-time member of the 28 Bolsheviks and now Vice Minister of Foreign Affairs Zhang Wentian. Contemporary Soviet economic policy emphasized achievements in advanced science and technology and improvements in standard of living. Just as de-Stalinization was used as a critique against Mao's growing cult of personality, so too Soviet economic policy was leveraged by domestic critics of the Great Leap Forward.

Meanwhile, a series of geopolitical disagreements between China and the Soviet Union in the final years of the decade brought the two countries to the brink of diplomatic rupture. These included Mao's apparent willingness to involve the Soviet Union in a conflict with the United States over Taiwan in 1958, Khrushchev's meeting with Eisenhower in 1959, a rocky meeting between Khrushchev and Mao in 1959, and disagreements over China's policy toward India and in Tibet. By 1960, Mao and Khrushchev were engulfed in mutual recriminations; Khrushchev lost his cool and recalled all experts in China back to the Soviet Union. In 1960, China and the Soviet Union compromised, pulling back from aggressive rhetoric and gestures. The early 1960s saw the two sides repeatedly attempting reconciliation, only to see hostilities flare up again.[34] This train of events is well known among historians of the Sino-Soviet split and global communism, though at the time it was hardly clear, even to elite politicians, that the two sides were headed toward such a deep and long-lasting break.

Liza Kishkina paints a nuanced portrait of the emotional and political split in her description of a period of estrangement she experienced with Li Lisan in late 1961. As she understood it, in the aftermath of Peng Dehuai's critique of the Great Leap Forward in 1959, there was a general perception that Peng had been in separate communication with Khrushchev. "From here rose a wave of suspicions regarding secret relations with foreign countries," she recalls in hindsight. At the time, all she knew was that her husband was pulling away from her.[35]

After Peng Dehuai's disagreement with Mao in 1959, Kang Sheng had suggested to Li that he ask Liza to change her citizenship. Li had fought off that pressure and had not even mentioned it to Liza. In her memoirs, Liza quotes a letter she says Li wrote to Kang, which she obtained much later. In it, Li reasons with Kang:

I thought about it, and is this politically necessary? If she were really politically unreliable, then changing to Chinese citizenship wouldn't change anything. But I can vouch for the fact that there is nothing wrong with her politically. On the other hand, she's really tied to her people. She's Russian, she grew up in Moscow, her national habits are second nature. Therefore she's often homesick, and always wants to go for a trip there. She has relatives there (simple people, not one among them is in a leadership position), and now she only writes with her sister-in-law and sister. She misses them and is really happy when she gets a letter from them. Therefore I think that asking her to break with her country and change her citizenship to China, she will never agree to it. If I try to make her, there will be a terrible argument, which might even lead to divorce. If this were necessary politically, then I'd do it, no matter what, but I think that there is no such political necessity.[36]

Li also wrote to a close friend, Foreign Minister Chen Yi.

In matters of daily life I give in to Liza, but I follow my own way in politics. When they put me in prison in the Soviet Union, in such extremely difficult circumstances she didn't leave me because she trusted me. And I believe that she never did nor ever would do anything bad for our party behind my back.[37]

He sent similar missives to Deng Xiaoping and even "directly to Zhongnanhai," meaning to Mao. Apparently, when Mao heard Kang's accusations against Liza, who had, after all, been Jiang Qing's Russian tutor and dined with Mao on more than one occasion, Mao simply asked, "Is there proof?" And in 1959 for Liza and Li, that was enough to temporarily end suspicion.[38]

Yet as tensions worsened between Russia and China, many Russian wives simply left China. Liza's circle of Russian female friends dwindled, until finally only her closest friend Grania was left. And the reaction of Grania's husband, Chen Changhao, was very different from Li's. While Chinese Ania warned Liza not to confide so much in Grania for fear she would naively share damaging information with Chen, Liza dismissed Ania's caution as jealousy. Grania was the friend to whom she felt she could tell everything, the only person apart from Li in whom she could confide unconditionally. As the toll of the Great Leap Forward became evident, Liza shared her doubts about it with Grania, who duly reported to Chen. Chen had been one of the original 28 Bolsheviks; subsequently, he also took Zhang Guotao's side against Mao on the Long March. In the PRC he had been placed in charge of the Central Committee's Bureau of Translation—not a top-tier ministry position, but also not political oblivion. In short, he had something to lose.[39] And Chen did use the information to maximum advantage. He wrote a letter to the Central Committee with all kinds of accusations against Liza and Li. According to Liza, Chen said that she regularly visited the Soviet embassy with secret messages and that she prearranged meetings with the wife of the ambassador at the tailor frequented by so many Russian women in Beijing.[40]

The letter caused a scandal, and Li was called repeatedly to the Central Committee. There Li Fuchun (whose daughter had been married to a Russian), Kang Sheng (who had personally brought Mao's sons to Russia and who had spent a fair amount of time in Moscow himself), and Zhou Enlai (whose adopted daughter had Russian theater training and ran a children's theater popular with Soviet people in Beijing) tried to convince Li to divorce Liza. During this time Li explained nothing to Liza, but she fretted that he was pulling away from her.

> The general situation had an impact on my relationship with my hus-
> band. He retreated into himself, didn't have much to do with me, and
> I felt as if a wall of estrangement was growing between us. In my heart
> I was confused and worried. Once he even moved to live in the Higher
> party school near the Summer Gardens. His old friend, the director of
> the school, gave him a small apartment there. It was in winter 1961–
> 1962. He didn't give a reason and I didn't ask though it was painful for
> me. I told myself he just wanted to be alone for a while. Maybe there was
> too much "foreign influence" in his family, which had become more
> and more reprehensible? But there wasn't anything I could do about
> that—it's not so easy to change habits you've had since childhood.[41]

In fact, Li's absence from home coincided with a critical moment of tension inside the Chinese Communist Party. In January 1962, the Party held a broad meeting open to a large cross-section of provincial officials. Though the Great Leap Forward had been reversed a year before, the economy had not improved; the conference was an occasion to revisit the Party's program. Liu Shaoqi, generally considered a friend of Li Lisan's since their days together in Anyuan in the 1920s, gave the crucial speech at the Conference. Liu ever so cautiously reopened the question of blame for the famine, and Mao offered what was generally perceived as an apology. Yet Liu also reaffirmed China's critical stance toward Soviet revisionism, and Mao stated that although "the numerous Party members and cadres of the Soviet Union are good," in Moscow power was in the hands of revisionists. One can only imagine the deep suspense with which Conference participants in general—and Li Lisan in particular—would have listened to these speeches.[42]

Ultimately the Conference resulted in a relaxation of economic policy and a surge in Liu Shaoqi's status. This relieved some pressure on Li, who returned home, albeit with a new demand. Li explained the intense pressure he had been under to divorce Liza and told her he had fought for her. When Zhou Enlai pressured Li to divorce her, he told her, he had refused, saying that Liza was "incapable of espionage" and that if they didn't believe him they could exclude him from the party. As Liza tells it, he told Zhou, "Mostly the Soviet people are a good people . . . we mustn't think that every Soviet person is a scoundrel." Finally, Li explained, the Central Committee made its decision: Li would not have to divorce Liza, but she would have to become a Chinese citizen. Liza responded as Li had believed she would; she feared she would not be able to return to Moscow, would never see her family again, and perhaps would even be considered a traitor. But Li reassured her time and again that "the current conflict is temporary, Soviet-Chinese relations will improve in the end, and you'll be able to go home again. Your countrymen will understand you."[43]

Liza was, in fact, in a difficult position. Her oldest daughter Inna had been studying in Moscow until 1960, when she returned home and, without telling her mother and to the great relief of her father, handed in her Soviet passport in exchange for a Chinese one. With Inna's permanent return, Liza reasoned that what awaited her in Russia was "a lonely old age, without husband, children, work. The way back had closed." Moreover, "I understood that for Li Lisan in the current political circumstances to have a wife with a Soviet passport was political suicide." And, "I believed that among the Soviet leadership there were revisionists, though I had only a fuzzy understanding of what revisionism was." At first Liza and Li agreed that when her current passport was up she simply would not renew it, but that she would think about a permanent switch to Chinese citizenship.

Looking beyond the story of loyalty in the face of political pressure that Liza tells, it's striking that the person who crystallized ambient pressure on the Li marriage was a man who himself had a Russian wife. Chen Changhao, however, according to Liza, acted just the reverse of Li. He "made a big public scandal out of wanting to divorce [Grania] because she was politically unreliable, supports Soviet revisionism, is bourgeois in her lifestyle, has a revisionist influence on her son, etc." Yet when Grania and Chen went to court, their divorce was granted on the basis of personal, not political, differences, and Grania was given half their property and the right to raise their son.[44] Obviously Chen had overplayed his hand. The Chen-Kang-Li-Zhou process ultimately suggests that the xenophobic insecurity of the 1960s might have begun at least in part with the leadership's own doubts about its Soviet Russian origins and ties. It also shows how one person could project self-doubt onto another, magnifying collective insecurity and rendering geopolitics personal all over again.

Breakdown

As tensions in the socialist camp rose, Eva and Emi continued to travel as privileged members within it and found themselves absorbing and processing those contradictions personally. In early 1958, East Germany offered Eva a position as a China correspondent, brought her to Berlin for training, and equipped her with a movie camera for documentary footage. She therefore no longer worked for Xinhua but rather was one of a number of foreign journalists whose activities were managed by the Information Department of the Chinese Foreign Ministry. This new status gave her greater artistic freedom and access than she might otherwise have enjoyed at this time.[45]

Eva recalls that in the early days of the Great Leap, the country as a whole, herself included, was gripped by a sense of excitement. Emi met up with Mao again that summer in Beihaide, their oldest son Leon was admitted to the Beijing Film Academy, and Eva was allowed to travel to Tibet in August 1959 to shoot footage in the aftermath of the uprising there. Eva was also on hand for Khrushchev's arrival in the Soviet Union, as the East German government had made a special request that she film it. When the Chinese prevented her from shooting, she exploded in anger. Later at home, she began to fear the consequences of her reaction; Emi advised her to apologize, which she did. Yet she still felt that blocking her access was exactly the kind of bureaucratism that all of Mao's movements were designed to combat.[46]

Eva's perspective gradually shifted in the course of her travels back and forth to Berlin. Once, she stopped to see Vassa and Allan in Leningrad, and the visit quickly bogged down with political conversations. In Berlin, the length of her contract was shortened due, she was told, to political uncertainty. "The conflicts between China, the Soviet Union, and East Germany tormented me, because I felt connected to these three countries and had worked for so many years for friendship between their peoples."[47] Eva and Emi invited two guests from the Soviet embassy to Emi's sixty-fifth birthday party in October 1961. When the couple was asked to attend the opening of Soviet Film Week, Emi was discouraged from going. In retrospect, it seemed to Eva that she and Emi were willfully ignoring signs that the Sino-Soviet conflict was indeed serious and were carrying on with their lives as if the disagreement was temporary and would soon resolve.[48]

Curiously, Eva describes a period of estrangement from Emi in late 1961 very similar to the one that Liza had experienced with Li at the same time.

> Our crisis was mostly of a personal nature, but of course it was also related to politics. I do not know what caused the estrangement between us. Xiao San wrapped himself up tightly in layers, he wouldn't talk to me, he was often depressed, frustrated, and moreover seriously ill. Leon and Vitya complained that their father didn't take the time to be with them, whereas the father of their Spanish friend spent a lot of time and energy on them. But Xiao San of course was a completely different type of person. I could see he was suffering, but I was also annoyed. We still talked about the news and politics, but there were a lot of things he was hiding from me and our sons. Once Vitya wrote him a letter pouring out all his thoughts. After that I wrote him a letter too. I always felt like it was easier to write the words I held in my heart than to speak them. When Xiao San got the two letters, he took them seriously. He was happy we were so honest with him. But still he was hiding something.[49]

Eva thought back on her life with Emi, asking what had happened. But it was only in mid-1962 on the family vacation at Beihaide—around the same time that Li returned home and came clean to Liza—that Emi explained himself. People had been calling him a revisionist and spreading all kinds of rumors about him, he said. These conversations reduced family tensions a bit, but Emi continued to face pressures in the Party and the Writer's Association that he rarely shared at the time.[50]

Remarkably, Eva carried on with her work and her travels until late 1963. Then, upon returning from a trip to Berlin and Stockholm, she suffered a nervous breakdown.

Eva, Emi, and their three sons, Leon, far left, Victor, above, and Heping, below.
Courtesy of the Siao Family.

> I cried constantly, without having a specific reason, and somehow stood
> outside myself. Of course, it had a lot to do with the political tensions
> between China and the Soviet Union. . . . I stood in the middle of this
> dispute, conveying the Chinese people in detail to the peoples on the
> other side through my movies and photos.[51]

Her son Vitya came to the rescue by beginning to teach her Chinese so she
could read the works of Mao—which was, after all, becoming a litmus test
of sorts—and by May she reports her crisis had ended. But the family's woes
continued. Despite the fact that Emi's poems were being published and he
was in good standing at the Writer's Association, by 1964 he confessed to Eva
that having a foreign wife was costing him—at which point Eva agreed to
become a Chinese citizen.[52]

Liza Kishkina too capitulated in 1964, agreeing to change her citizenship while walking in a park that summer with Li. In September they received a letter approving the switch signed by Zhou Enlai himself. Thus, at a time when China was drawing ever stricter distinctions between friend and foe, self and other, these two women occupying high-profile positions at the nexus of communist cultures were slipped "in," rather than pushed "out." Liza, who symbolized China's most literal attempts at understanding Russia, continued to teach. Eva, whose images offered the rest of the Eastern Bloc a visual window onto a China that was increasingly incomprehensible, continued to film. From a cross-cultural perspective, these two women had nearly eclipsed their once-formidable but now aging, sidelined husbands. And their husbands stood by them—almost as if aware that, at a time when direct political expression was so limited, this act of personal loyalty was a political statement after all.

19

Defiant Romantics

Ironies of Cultural Revolution

HOWEVER OBVIOUS IT may seem that the formal split between the Soviet Union and China in 1963 should have spelled the end of the Sino-Soviet romance, the reality wasn't so simple. For first-generation Chinese communists who had spent some youthful years in Moscow or dreamed of a Russian-style revolution for China, disillusion with the Bolshevik-dominated Comintern before World War II had done nothing to prevent them from attempting to implement a Soviet-style transformation in China after the war. For their Russian-born or educated children, the Sino-Soviet split only intensified a deep longing for home. And for some newly minted Russophiles in the People's Republic, radical suppression of Russian language and culture during the brutal years of the Cultural Revolution could not help but strengthen the association between Russia and a happier time in their own lives. Nobody was exactly sure how long the Sino-Soviet split would last, and many hoped it was a temporary separation. Even as the Cultural Revolution seemed to sweep anyone who harbored a shred of sympathy for Russia into a cauldron of physical and emotional torture, it could not necessarily extinguish those feelings for good.

Calm before the Storm

Once the Sino-Soviet split went public in 1963, the Russian and Chinese Communist Parties exchanged open letters to each other that were reprinted in the press and broadcast over the radio in China. Liza Kishkina remembers how riveting these broadcasts were and how earnestly she listened to them:

> At the appointed hour, exactly at 8 pm, the entire country sat down before loudspeakers to listen to the harsh, measured voice of the

announcer for the all-China radio news program, reading out these devastating texts. When these broadcasts came over the radio, my daughters and I also sat breathlessly at the radio. For us at the time they were revelations of Marxist thought. We sincerely believed in the truth of what was written in these articles; we were frightened by the syndromes of doom for socialism uncovered in them. We wanted China to avoid such a fate.[1]

Liza remembers a moment of hope after Khrushchev was deposed in 1964 and Zhou Enlai flew to Moscow to meet Brezhnev at the annual celebration of the October Revolution. The Soviet leadership was gripped with a similar sense of hope, bolstered by a temporary halt to Chinese propaganda for several weeks after Khrushchev's ouster. Even Mao seemed to believe that the Soviet leadership might finally be coming around. And yet, whatever slim chance for renewal of the Sino-Soviet relationship there might have been was squandered in one drunken evening at the Kremlin, when Defense Minister Malinovskii managed to imply to Zhou that the Chinese ought to overthrow Mao. One historian of the Sino-Soviet split wonders whether "Malinovskii got drunk and blurted out what everyone in the Kremlin actually thought but would not say publicly, at least when sober." Zhou and his delegation departed with exactly what they came for—proof that the Soviet Union was indeed "revisionist." Anti-Soviet propaganda resumed in China in the spring of 1965.[2]

For a time, some remember, work proceeded normally. Liza continued to teach at the Foreign Languages Institute; ironically, Russian language was still vital in China. After the Soviet experts had departed, Chinese engineers struggled to piece together what information they could find to complete the large-scale projects—including the atomic weapons program—they had left behind. Meanwhile, a new "Provisional Committee for the Translation of the Works of Mao Zedong and Important Documents of the Central Committee of the Chinese Communist Party" gathered a wide range of Russian language experts to live and work in a special hotel owned by the Party's Organization Department.[3]

This group was an odd haven for a collection of Russophiles. Remarkably, Liu Zerong, the young student Qu Qiubai had encountered on his way to Moscow in 1921, was included. So was Qu's daughter Tuya. Tuya, following in her father's footsteps, had worked briefly as one of Xinhua's first foreign

Liza and Li, 1965. Courtesy of Inna Li.

correspondents in Moscow in the 1950s. Now, she and other members of this privileged translation bureau, including several of the younger "love children," were well fed despite the famine and free to be the "half-Russian" versions of themselves that many had felt pressure to repress in the 1950s. One young woman known as Fifi, who had studied in the underground school at Communist Eastern University in the 1930s, was, according to Lena, "the chief instigator of various amusements. Of all the others she was the most attached to Russian customs. She loved Russian food, sang Russian songs, dressed in dresses and skirts, read a lot in Russian, and almost always spoke Russian to our Chinese translators, those who were native Chinese and had learned Russian in Chinese institutions." The sole ethnic Russian (born in Harbin) argued with the other members that translations should accurately reflect the quality of the original rather than improve it, a non-starter, Lena remembers, since the group was primarily occupied with translating the works of Mao.[4] This little group—tucked away in a comfortable hotel, giving Mao a touched-up Russian voice—was perhaps willfully unaware of the ironies of its existence.

Yet not even this group was unaffected by the Socialist Education Movement that swept through China in the mid-1960s. This was the brainchild of leaders like Liu Shaoqi, whose rural inspection tours had helped to end the Great Leap Forward. Liu and others were appalled by the corruption of local party bosses, on one hand, and the oblivion of urban intellectuals about the true poverty of the peasantry, on the other. The Socialist Education Movement sent groups of city cadres into the countryside to simultaneously "root out corruption" and "learn from the peasantry." Yet the process was often chaotic and ineffective. The fact that a group of Russian translators from the Committee on Translation of Mao was sent in June of 1964 to a rural area outside Beijing where they were ill equipped to understand local politics, much less combat corruption, is indicative of the general inefficacy of the project.[5]

Liza Kishkina recalls how "Socialist Education" affected her family:

Inna left for the countryside with the students and teachers of our institute. Soon after Li Lisan was sent to Hebei Province to lead the [Socialist Education] campaign. He lived in a peasant home and slept on a *kang*. He went around in a padded green army coat and coarse shoes. . . . After several months in the countryside, Li Lisan returned home in a downcast mood. The situation in the country made such a deep impression on him, he hadn't imagined that people lived so badly. . . . It seemed to me that my husband began to suffer a crisis of conscience since our family lived so comfortably, though we didn't go beyond the limits of the acceptable—Li Lisan strictly saw to that.[6]

According to Liza, it was not only Li's party stipend that allowed them to eat and dress and furnish their house so well. It was also the 400 yuan per month salary that she continued to earn as a teacher for the Foreign Languages Institute and her access to a special store for foreigners, where she had been able to purchase sausage even at the height of the Great Leap Forward.

Though Li had defended Liza's ways to his comrades and though Liza had taken Chinese citizenship, divergent experiences meant differing perspectives. Echoing Soviet critics, Liza remembers that the idea of going to the countryside to learn from poor peasants "went against my understanding, taken from my Soviet political education: why was it necessary to study the peasantry, which was fomenting capitalism by the hour, and not from the working class, the leader of revolution?"[7] Li had been a labor organizer, not a rural communist, but months in the countryside gave him an experience that contrasted sharply with Liza's work as a Russian language teacher at an elite Beijing college.

In the 1960s, cleavages inside families were exacerbated by increasing social isolation that pervaded even the most tightly knit communities of Beijing Russophiles. Liza recalls a "spy mania" gripping the capital, with rumors swirling that various people had been arrested for espionage. Mao's personal Russian-language interpreter and director of the Central Committee's Translation Bureau, Shi Zhe, disappeared, stoking rumors that he had been a

The last complete photo of the Li family, 1966. Alla, far left; Inna, far right. Courtesy of Inna Li.

Soviet spy. As the 1960s wore on, the phone in the Li house rang less and less, and only a few close friends continued to visit. Chen Yi—foreign minister, nominal head of the Foreign Languages Institute, and a friend of Li's from their time as work-study students in France—still came over occasionally, as did Russian Grania and Liza's Harbin Chinese friends Ania and Olia.[8]

Liza was also in touch with Eva, who had been grounded in Beijing and whose life was perhaps more similar to Liza's than when she had been jetting around Europe in the 1950s. Once she became a Chinese citizen, Eva lost her East German employment and could not find anyone to hire her in China. Emi and the children took trips to the countryside, leaving her behind. She took out her rising frustration by doing heavy work around the house and going for long bike rides—before suffering a heart attack. Try as they might to continue their active social life, Eva and Emi soon found themselves prime suspects in the "spy mania" sweeping the city.[9]

When Li told Liza not to see Eva so much, Liza shot back, "Don't you think they're saying the same thing about us?" Similarly, Lena recalled her mother telling her to stop going to parties with her Russian-speaking childhood friends. Lena replied, "Think, where will I hide from them? I have to associate with them at work. Moreover, the children of Mao Zedong, Zhu De, Liu Shaoqi, and other leaders come to these gatherings. What are you afraid of?" But her mother just waved her away. Indeed, in 1963, Kang Sheng's niece and Mao's daughter stopped attending the gatherings, which by that point were held mostly at Emi and Eva's. One of Lena's friends with a highly placed father took her aside and explained that Emi and Eva were "under secret political surveillance; therefore, one should avoid contact with their family." Despite these warnings, most attended a May 1, 1963, party at Eva and Emi's—the last time they would dare to gather so openly in such a large group.[10]

A Sino-Soviet Family Sundered

Liza remembers that the Cultural Revolution came to her house innocuously enough. One of her daughters' friends, a half-Chinese/half-German girl named Sonia, arrived to "do away with old superstitions" in their house—which largely meant taking down Liza's porcelain Buddha statues. Curiously she made no reference to her own domestic implementation of the Soviet anti-religious campaign in her youth, when she had taken away her mother's much-loved religious icons. In mid-1966 Li was told he could no longer attend the meetings of the Northern Bureau of the Central Committee, while her daughters began participating in student raids on the homes of so-called capitalists. One day while Liza and Grania were sitting in Liza's courtyard, protected from the street by a wall, a mob arrived on the street, throwing the furniture out of her neighbor's house and breaking the windows. The two women sat silently, waiting for it to pass.[11]

Soon "big character posters" in which Cultural Revolutionaries expressed criticism were plastered around Beijing denouncing Li, Liza, and their lifestyle. One day they got a phone call asking whether it was true that their dog slept on a mattress and drank milk. It was, unfortunately. Li drove the dog outside the city and let her go. After that he began to roam the streets on foot, his driver following him as a bodyguard, to read the posters. Their daughters went away with the Red Guards, which left Liza at home alone. Even when the girls returned, Liza remembers, the family no longer talked much, retreating to their rooms alone. At one point, a friend of Li's who taught in a military academy and had served in the Soviet Red Army invited him to come and live there for a time to keep him safe—which he did. But Liza, with her obviously foreign face, could not possibly accompany him, so Li returned home. Feeling stir crazy, one day Liza decided to go to the Foreign Languages Institute, where a colleague helped her to read big character posters, including those making outlandish accusations against her.[12]

On February 1, 1967, Li Lisan was called for the first of many struggle sessions, the mass meetings Cultural Revolutionaries convened to harass and torture targets of their campaigns. There Li was accused of any number of things, including being a Soviet spy. At first people from his own office brought him to and from the sessions, which were closed. But one day Red Guards showed up and carried him off to the Railway Institute, where he was subjected to his first mass struggle session. "When they brought him home," Liza remembered, "he could no longer stand up. The Red Guards dragged him down the hall by the arms and threw him on the bed. I sat near him, asking nothing—I didn't want to exacerbate his psychological wounds." Soon Red Guards were interrogating Li at home. Then, they began attacking the house itself.

One night for some reason I came home at eleven. The evening was already stifling, it was the hot and dusty month of May. I came through the gate into the yard and stopped short: our house was brightly lit, all the lights were on. What on earth? Why this illumination? In the yard, next to our outdoor terrace, was a minivan, with people bustling around it. I went up and saw that one of them was holding an old doll that one of our friends a long time ago brought my daughters as a gift from abroad. The doll's linen hair was disheveled, its face was smeared, but the blue eyes were still opening and closing along with the movements of the Red Guard. Angrily shaking the doll he turned to the wife of our gatekeeper. "Look what this is! Did you play with such a doll when you were a child?!" The elderly woman, at a loss, stayed silent, and the Red Guards stuck another doll under her nose, a black girl doll. "So this is the kind of stuff these bourgeois kids play with!" Now I understood: our house was being searched, they were looking for evidence of our bourgeois corruption. Of course, it was there: toys, thin nylon stockings, which they poked under my nose, harmless trinkets, photo albums, and other nonsense. All this the Red Guards and rebels piled up in a heap in the van and drove away.[13]

Liza went inside and found her house ransacked and her husband lying in his bed. The next day she put her home back together, but the searches and harassment continued. One night a group of Red Guards arrived and announced they were from Tianjin and intended to take Li there. When Liza asked Li a question in Russian they became enraged, and only after a group of soldiers in uniform arrived—called by the neighbors—did they depart.[14]

But things got worse. One day, Li told Liza that he had seen Alla writing at her desk in a notebook, and asked her to go find it and read it. Liza remembers feeling guilty, but doing it anyway.

I opened the first page and sat down in a state of shock. My daughter had written that she had just learned of the contents of the presentations by Tsi Ben'iuia, a member of the Cultural Revolution Committee, who had announced at a meeting with rebels and Red Guards that Li Lisan is not a "paper tiger," but a real counterrevolutionary, who maintains secret contacts abroad, and that Li Sha [Liza] is a major Soviet spy and that there was no need to stand on ceremony with her because she was a Chinese citizen, not a foreigner. Then in the diary came the words that made my heart bleed: "Is it possible that my mom, whom I trusted absolutely, is actually so vile, so wretched?! Tsi Ben'iuia said it openly, which means it's true. Who can I even trust after this?" My poor daughter! It was hard not to cry. How easy it was to cast seeds of doubt in such a pure, artless soul.[15]

When Liza told Li what she had read, he sank even deeper into silence. She felt he was thinking the political ramifications through, while she was reacting as a worried mother.

Big character posters now appeared accusing Liza and Li of espionage— and particularly accusing Liza of ties not only with the Soviet embassy but with other embassies as well, which she supposedly visited with her daughters acting as her helpers. According to the posters, an all-China organization for the struggle against Li Lisan had been created. Liza was called to the Foreign Language Institute for a meeting, where she was accused of spying and told to prepare a confession. When she got home, she exclaimed to Li, "If all this were happening in the Soviet Union, we'd have been arrested long ago." Li gave her a long searching look and said nothing.[16]

Soon Liza was summoned along with Li for a struggle session.

The hall was so full even an apple would have nowhere to fall, it was a sea of black heads. Thousands of eyes were fixed on the stage, at the center of which was Li, flanked on each side by three people who were also being criticized. These were the heads of the Northern Bureau [of the Central Committee.] And I was among them, on the far left. Each of us had a placard on our chests describing a variety of "crimes." On mine in big characters was written "Soviet revisionist spy Li Sha."[17]

Liza looked into the audience and saw that most were students, including some from her institute. She and the others stood perfectly still for hours and it was terrible, yet in the end there were no really sensational revelations. People began getting up and leaving, and the session ended with a half-empty hall. When they got home, Li collapsed in his bed, but, summoning some energy made a joke: "Your rank has risen, Liza, they put you right next to the secretaries of the Central Committee Bureau!"[18]

After this the so-called Center for Struggle against Li Lisan moved to their house. Liza recalls how Red Guards found the electric mixer in her kitchen and seized it, convinced that it was the radio equipment by which she communicated with the Soviet Union. The cook tried to explain that it was for making cakes and that Liza had no idea how to use it, but to no avail. The family was forbidden to leave, their telephone was disconnected, and a Red Guard from the Russian Language Institute was dispatched for the sole purpose of educating Liza, which he did by reading her Mao quotations in Russian. Li too had such a "tutor."[19]

On June 19, 1967, both were taken to a struggle session. When it was over the couple had a moment alone in a room. Liza had just enough time to pour Li a drink from a thermos on the table there before she had to go. "Take care of yourself," Li said in Russian—his last words to her. Two days later Liza was taken from home to her own institute and told to confess her crimes or face a mass struggle session with its threat of physical violence. But the next day she was arrested instead and taken to the infamous Qincheng Prison where high-priority political prisoners were kept. She was given black prison clothing and a number, 77. When finally the doors of her solitary confinement cell shut behind her, she remembers feeling instinctive relief at the sheer quiet after all the months of noisy turmoil. She faced the deceptively simple task of surviving in prison, walled off from the complex and dangerous world outside it.[20]

Complexities

The Cultural Revolution affected millions in China. While Sino-Soviet families, people with life experience in Russia, or Russophiles were certainly targeted, so were many other categories of people for a bewildering number of reasons. The strong anti-Soviet premise of the movement held particular complexities and paradoxes for people with Russian ties. Of countless ironies, one of the most striking is how indiscriminately it swept people together who had only recently been arguing and drawing distinctions among themselves.

The movement also generated an entirely new set of stories about Sino-Soviet experiences, full of surprising narrative twists that often left the supposed protagonists themselves dumbfounded. That some of the victims had, in fact, undergone espionage training in the Soviet Union only complicated matters. While the Cultural Revolution produced identifiable types of suffering—loss of work, house arrest, labor camp, exile, struggle sessions, torture, prison, illness, death—victims and their families processed similar experiences differently and reached different conclusions and fates.

The stated objective of the Cultural Revolution was to ensure that China did not betray the goal of radical egalitarian transformation as the Soviet Union allegedly had after Stalin's death. Under Khrushchev, the Chinese public had been told repeatedly, class struggle had given way to bureaucratic stasis and confrontation with global capitalism to a defeatist policy of peaceful coexistence. The Chinese revolution was in danger of a similar fate—that is, of abandoning the core mission of social justice before it was achieved—unless young people identified, ousted, and punished powerful elders who were entrenched in privileged lifestyles and actively working against beneficial economic and political change at home and abroad.

Mao and a handful of cronies may have originally conceived of the movement as a way of getting rid of rivals who had become too powerful in the aftermath of the Great Leap Forward, and who did indeed espouse more moderate policies in line with postwar Soviet socialism. But it also tapped into pent-up emotions within the broader population—ranging from hostile fury toward the new elite to desperate longing among young people for a revolutionary adventure of their own—that eventually fueled a mass uprising of "Red Guards" whose scope surpassed the vision of its creators. Given that the goal was to combat Soviet-style "revisionism," people with Soviet experience or ties were natural targets. By allowing public denunciation of Deng Xiaoping and Liu Shaoqi as "Chinese Khrushchevs" in January of 1967, Mao and his co-conspirators signaled open season on even the most senior party elites.[21] Li Lisan had his first struggle sessions in February, culminating in his arrest and (unbeknownst to Liza) murder in June.

A few short months of mayhem rendered years of qualms and arguments and divisions quaint and even a bit ridiculous. What had it mattered that Liu Shaoqi had been skeptical about Soviet Russia from his very first visit in 1921 and had denied his children their Russian spouses in his efforts to show they were first and foremost Chinese revolutionaries—if his was the very first head to roll? Actually, Liu was never struggled against; he was simply denied medical care and died in 1969. His son, Yunbin, threw himself under a train.[22] Chen Changhao divorced Grania and did everything he could to distance himself from her, while Li Lisan stood by Liza and did all he could to defend her. Both men were killed in 1967, and both women landed in the same prison. What had it mattered that Li had allowed his Russian Orthodox mother-in-law to be buried by a priest but had denied a cross for her grave, or that he allowed his wife to wear dresses but refused her the use of his car? He was swept away along with people who had much more and much less to answer for.

However indiscriminate it was, the Cultural Revolution nevertheless generated fantastically specific narratives about the Soviet treason of its victims. Liza recalls her utter surprise upon being called for her first interrogation in Qincheng to learn that the fifty-person tribunal she faced, headed by the minister of public security himself, was absolutely fixated on a dinner party she had forgotten she had even given. The guest of honor had been a man known as Krymov who had studied and taught off and on in Moscow between 1925 and his arrest in 1938. Freed under Khrushchev's amnesty, Krymov was treated to numerous reunion banquets when he arrived in China. Liza and Li had invited him over for dinner one night, and apparently the tribunal had decided that this dinner party had been the birthplace of a formidable ring of Soviet revisionist spies under Li's leadership. Ironically, Krymov had been imprisoned in the Soviet Union on similarly bizarre charges—including having attended a conspiratorial dinner party.[23] The fact that one person could be accused of fomenting so much counterrevolution at dinner parties all across Eurasia would be funny if he had not suffered unbearable torture and lengthy Soviet imprisonment before his release, and if the Chinese dinner parties he attended had not been a pretext for similar treatment of others during the Cultural Revolution.

While this dinner with Krymov was apparently the lynchpin of Liza's repeated interrogations, she was also accused of hiding secret documents in the suitcase of her daughter Inna when she went to Moscow to study, and other improbable acts.[24] Even if Liza somehow had been working for the Soviet secret police, the narratives that the tribunal constructed were unlikely and hence in some way creative. How would a Russian woman married to a Chinese communist go about undermining the Chinese revolution, anyway?

The curious truth about Cultural Revolution–era espionage charges is that on some level, in some cases, there was some kind of reality behind the outlandish narratives—a reality that the accusations only served to further obscure. As far back as 1924, the rector of Communist Eastern University had boasted that its graduates could overthrow the leadership of any communist party in Asia, and historians have since shown how dedicated the Comintern was not only to fomenting but also to controlling world revolution more generally. Many young Chinese who came to the Soviet Union before World War II were exposed to a variety of training programs and drawn into assignments that could be construed as espionage—in the name of (Soviet-led) world revolution. When China was ruled by Chiang Kaishek and Moscow trained Chinese for underground work in Nationalist territory—including liaison skills to keep lines of communication open to Moscow—was this training in pro-Soviet espionage, or survival skills for a nearly extinct organization dedicated to Chinese communism, or both? Without such training, would the Chinese Communist Party have survived the Nationalist decade or the Japanese occupation? When Red Guards made accusations of pro-Soviet espionage against Soviet-educated Chinese, they were obscuring the more general truth that such training was not necessarily detrimental.

Yet this was only the first and most general layer of complexity; underneath was a bewildering tangle of individual circumstances woven into the tapestry of Cultural Revolution, connecting people to its story with some thread of truth that made extrication difficult. The fact that, in the 1930s, Kang Sheng and Wang Ming had organized a special group of Chinese teenagers, including Mao's own sons, Qu's daughter, and several others for training in a Soviet underground school, meant that any time any one of these former trainees was accused of being a Soviet spy (and several were), the accusers unwittingly referenced an ambiguous experience. Red Guards did not know about the school; its existence was only uncovered after the collapse of the Soviet Union. Nor did they know that Cultural Revolution guru Kang Sheng had been a key link between the Soviet secret police and Chinese students. The Red Guards were too young to understand that, at that time, to excel in these lessons (as Mao's elder son Anying/Serezha and Qu's daughter Tuya both did) was to fulfill a mission jointly conceived by elements in both the Soviet and Chinese Party elites.

Even after that underground school closed, the Soviet security apparatus was always on the lookout for promising young Chinese cadres. And so, when the first batch of graduates from the Russian international children's home arrived in Moscow Institutes in the 1940s, some were recruited for training in radio communications or other skills that would allow them, upon their return to China, to serve as conduits for information back to Moscow.[25] These were young people who had been raised to believe in "internationalism"—a one-to-one correspondence between the Chinese and Soviet revolutions—so many experienced no cognitive dissonance when asked to serve by a government that was, de facto, their own. It was dedication to the cause, not treason. In this case, it would seem, Red Guards did possess some information about these students, but had no way to properly contextualize it, even if they had wanted to.

Perhaps the most ironic espionage charges were those leveled against the group of Chinese students in Soviet institutes in the late 1940s who had founded an informal mutual support group in Moscow. As participants recall, the original impetus for the Chinese student association was desire to learn more about the rapidly evolving situation in China so as to better prepare for their futures there. As Chinese communists passed through Moscow, they would meet with the students, share news, and distribute much-needed financial assistance. The group was not exactly legal in the Soviet context but the authorities were aware of it. The Chinese student association created a microcosm of Chinese patriotism and dedication to the Chinese revolution via collective enthusiasm that sometimes shaded into peer pressure. And yet, for Red Guards who got wind of it, membership in a quasi-legal, semi-formal association in Moscow was a sure sign of treason, not a mark of patriotism.[26]

Later in the 1950s, the Soviet side would accuse some Chinese students in particularly sensitive specialties of being a bit too nosy, in other words, of attempting to learn on behalf of the Chinese revolution a bit more than the Soviets wanted to teach. It was dedication that went unnoticed during the Cultural Revolution, when not just Soviet-educated students were under suspicion, but so too were the very embassy staff who had managed them— all the way up to 1950s (Soviet-educated) ambassadors Zhang Wentian and Wang Jiaxiang, along with Foreign Minister Chen Yi, whose ministry was as wracked with conflict as the rest of the Chinese state.[27]

Experiences

Whatever accusations they initially faced, Sino-Soviet families found themselves in terrible circumstances once the real violence of the Cultural Revolution began, experiences that made solitary confinement in Qincheng look relatively bearable. Lena, the young Russian-born woman whose mother had tried so hard to turn her into a "real Chinese girl," was shocked when that very mother was accused of being a "capitalist-roader," the term used for people who had strayed off the true socialist path. "I could not conceive of a greater historical mockery," Lena recalls. "She was a one hundred percent fanatical Communist." She was so fanatical that in the 1930s in the Soviet Union she had given reports on her fellow Chinese students to the Chinese representatives of the secret police—a fact that had nothing to do with the accusations against her by Red Guards, who, ironically, knew nothing about it. Kang Sheng had at one point been a patron of Lena's mother, so, when the struggle sessions against her began, she wrote to Lena asking her to get a message to Kang via his niece, who was Lena's friend from childhood in Russia. But Kang refused to help. Lena's mother was locked up in a room close to her university library.[28] Later, Lena heard of her mother's fate from a half-sister who had been locked up with her:

> Night fell. They tortured "Enemy Number One." They inserted needles under nails, tore out her hair, would not let her get off her knees all night. The next morning . . . she was forced to stand in the back of a truck on display to the revolutionary masses and hauled to all of the schools in Changsha.[29]

One morning in May 1968, Lena's mother "was discovered hanging from a water pipe in the student lavatory" and was cremated before her family had seen her body. Lena herself only learned of her mother's death later. But, like many others, she had a terrible sense of foreboding, which led her to destroy her diaries and place her own daughter with a worker's family.[30]

In August, three months after the death of her mother, Lena saw the Red Guards come for her. Kang Sheng himself had decided that the Chinese children who had been raised in the Russian international children's home (with the exception of his niece) formed what was then called a "Petofi club," named after a group of Hungarian intellectuals whose criticisms of the communist regime there helped spark the 1956 uprising. It was an ironic name, since the Hungarian Petofi club opposed mandatory teaching of Russian in schools. Once they had been thus labeled, the Sino-Soviet "love children" did not stand a chance. Here again a social gathering—the last party held in 1963 at Eva and Emi's house—was used as an example of a supposedly criminal meeting, with a group photo that Kang's niece unwittingly provided him serving as evidence of who was included. Lena recalls her own imprisonment and torture in wrenching terms.

They drove my husband out into the courtyard, transferred my sleeping six-year-old son into the other room, and began mocking me in the fullest sense of the word. I had to stand at attention, answer all their questions, and call my mother a Soviet spy. The slightest disobedience evoked shouts, screams, insults, and curses. . . . I was locked up in a so-called political isolation cell. But this was only a minor misfortune. The main torment was that the "revolutionary pioneers" did not give me a moment's peace. . . . During the day, each of us waited our turn at the so-called "struggle meetings," where there were no rules, no limits, and total chaos. . . . They were bursting with hatred for the "devoted daughter of a Soviet spy," the label that the "revolutionary pioneers" affixed to me. . . . They started to beat me.[31]

In retrospect, Lena marveled that she did not lose her mind during this time, but she survived. Her husband managed to take her son to the worker's family as well, and he, unlike a number of other spouses, remained loyal to her through her ordeal. Given how horrific Lena's and her mother's experiences were, the decision of one of Lena's former Russian classmates to commit a joint suicide with her Russian-educated mother seems almost rational.[32] Other classmates lost their spouses, who either left them in an attempt to distance themselves from "Soviet spies" or were killed themselves.

While many people recall the struggle sessions as the worst part of the Cultural Revolution, at least one—Yura Huang Jian—felt differently, suggesting the variability of subjective experiences.

The difficult material circumstances, the beatings and various degrading "struggle with the enemy of the people" meetings—all of this I endured pretty steadfastly . . . but what was excruciatingly unbearable was the moral isolation, when they held me for a long time in solitary. They didn't let me talk to anyone or go anywhere. . . . Some of my friends couldn't handle it—they went insane or killed themselves. It's hard to believe, but it was even heartening when they called me for interrogations or when they made cruel accusations of my "crimes" at mass meetings. Standing for hours in a humiliating pose under the gaze of the "Red Guards," was, of course, both physically and morally difficult. But, however strange it may seem, several days after such humiliations I felt invigorated and ready for a new fight. The thing is, that even this—dear god let no one experience it—kind of socializing with people had a positive effect on my psyche. I felt myself to be a person and a fighter again.[33]

Yura remembered telling his captor, a former trainee of his, that in time it would become clear who the real enemy was. Like Lena, Yura was imprisoned—for fifteen months in his case—before being released and "sent down" to hard labor in the provinces. He and other Russian-raised Chinese explicitly connected hard labor during the Chinese Cultural Revolution to the tough conditions they had faced as children in the Soviet Union during World War II, feeling that because of those harsh times in the war they were better prepared for the Cultural Revolution brutality than other Chinese elites.

In fact, Red Guard attempts to wring confessions of treason out of the Russian-raised Chinese had the unintended consequence of focusing the victims' attention on the very past that was seen as so detrimental to China's future. Between interrogations they could not help but wrack their memories for details—perhaps, as Yura's comments suggest, even questioning their own loyalties and fighting to maintain equilibrium by recalling each and every scene or interaction they could remember from life in the Soviet Union. One memoirist sardonically thanked his time in captivity for spurring his reminiscences of childhood:

> In these 18 months, over and over again I had to recollect things from the past I had long since forgotten. To tell the truth, this stuff was of no use to anyone, like, certain anecdotes from my life. Of course, they weren't going to find what they wanted, because it just wasn't there. These 18 months spent thinking so hard led me to gradually restore some of the experiences and memories of my past.[34]

This man was the son of one of Emi's friends from France, Zhao Shiyan, who had been killed in 1927. He and his mother then came to Russia when he was just three. Sitting alone for a year and a half under intense pressure to produce something "useful" from his past, he instead discovered that his first memories of childhood were a trip to the Moscow zoo and the way his friend Vova nodded his head when he slept. But the Red Guards were intent on other things—particularly his participation in the Chinese student association while he was studying at Moscow Steel in the 1940s. What he remembered best, however, was how he and his fellow Chinese were so hungry that they broke university rules against students working part-time and unloaded vegetables on the docks of the Moscow River in exchange for potatoes. At some point, Red Guards suggested to him that he was not really Zhao Shiyan's son but rather a spy trained from birth by the Soviet Union and replaced for Zhao's real son. But the Russian memories his tormentors were stirring up strengthened his sense of self, and he dismissed this notion.

Defiant Romantics

People with direct ties to Soviet Russia were obviously targeted during the Cultural Revolution and were perhaps more likely than other intellectuals to face violent mass meetings or arrest and death. While some were killed, others survived a year or so in makeshift prisons, only to be sent to so-called May Seventh Cadre Schools for "reeducation" through labor in rural areas. Once there, they joined thousands of others in an experience that defined an entire generation of Chinese intellectuals. After the schools were disbanded, many young people found themselves doing manual labor in rural communes or border regions.

A key, well-known part of the Cultural Revolution was the restriction of access to books, magazines, or movies, especially foreign ones. Such restrictions hit literate people in the countryside the hardest. A privileged few in the cities still had access to pre-revolutionary books, since not all had been burned; home libraries of intellectual families still contained copies of Chinese classics and popular novels and translations of European literature. But after several years in the country without a book to read, some were willing to take a bit of a risk for the sake of literature.

By the 1970s, young Chinese in the countryside were unofficially writing and "publishing" fiction, via copies that circulated from hand to hand and were copied, recopied, and embellished. This "underground" or "samizdat" fiction was heavy on the romance that was so notably absent from officially sanctioned texts. One such "book" called "Open Love Letters" had in fact originated as real love letters among sent-down youths. Another story written by a sent-down student featured a protagonist who buys melon seeds and discovers they have been wrapped in a page of Pushkin; the author then sends his hero back, day after day, to buy more seeds until he has the entire book. In truth, Pushkin could have been substituted for Balzac or Dickens; by 1970, the prohibitions on foreign literature had worn down any preference for Russian novels that might have remained from the 1950s.[35]

Ironically, the large print runs of translated Soviet works of the 1950s meant that Russian socialist realist novels remained the most widely available—and semi-tolerated—pieces of foreign literature throughout the Cultural Revolution. One novel in particular—*How the Steel Was Tempered*—had at least a million copies in circulation and remained in print until 1966. In fact, in the aftermath of the Sino-Soviet split, the Chinese press ran articles accusing the Soviet Union of "abandoning" the novel's hero, Pavel Korchagin, just as it had abandoned socialist transformation, and inviting him to "come" to China. Parents who carefully monitored their children's access to books turned a blind eye when they found *How the Steel Was Tempered* under their pillows, which meant that by the end of the Cultural Revolution, this was the one foreign book that all literate young people had read.

And yet, reading—alone, with plenty of time to think—of the novel during the Cultural Revolution differed significantly from 1950s mass readings. At the height of Sino-Soviet "friendship," the Chinese Communist Party encouraged young people to emulate Pavel Korchagin, particularly in his rejection of his bourgeois girlfriend Tonya. But the Cultural Revolution's severe restriction of both the feminine and the private created a shortage of overtly feminine imagery in propaganda and fiction. The women gracing the covers of popular magazines were dressed androgynously and seemed happy to be part of a collective.[36] Tonya emerged as the new heroine of the novel in many young readers' minds. One literature specialist writes:

> For many young boys, Tonia thus represented their first contact with and love of the opposite sex. Liu Xiaofeng recalled in his memoir 20 years later that Tonia was his "first concrete image of a beauty"; he subsequently "conceptualized beauty in the form of Tonia." Literary critic Ding Fan admitted: "*How the Steel Was Tempered* was the first novel of my adolescent reading. Strangely, the love relationship between Pavel and Tonia, particularly descriptions of the adolescent fantasies of a romantic kind, impressed me deeply." Literary critic Li Jingze confesses that "Regardless whether Tonia is good or bad, there is something special about her. She is beautiful. Her sailor's blouse, short skirt,

her agile movement, and sunny laugh left an enduring impression on a Chinese boy in the early 1970s." It is impossible to tell whether Tonia awoke adolescent dreams of sexual love or whether the adolescent readers read their dreams into Tonia. In either case, unlike Korchagin, they did not grow disenchanted with Tonia; and unlike readers of the 1950s, they were not obliged to overcome or repress this sentiment.[37]

Whether or not the authorities were aware of the changing interpretations of the novel, it was, along with Gorky's *Mother*, the first foreign work to be released for official publication in 1972.

Liza's Release

Liza Kishkina sat in solitary confinement for eight years, to which she devotes less than thirty pages of a five-hundred-page memoir. After a period of intense, all-night interrogations in 1968, she was called from her cell once every few months, always to answer the same questions in a manner so routine that she ceased to fear them. Then the inquiries stopped entirely, for years. She remembers wondering if the authorities had forgotten about her. The only evidence to the contrary was her daily meal and walk, and according to the rules of Qincheng, just one prisoner walked in a given courtyard at a time. Many years later Liza discovered that Liu Shaoqi's wife Wang Guangmei was in the cell next to hers; Wang told her she heard and recognized Liza's Russian accent. Eva, who spent six years in Qincheng, remembers keeping elaborate daily routines of exercise and study inside her cell to stay sane, while Liza recited Russian poetry to herself and imagined that Li was somewhere in the same building. She closed her eyes and drew pictures of her future life, which always included grandchildren and a trip to Moscow.[38]

A soft washcloth pressed into her hand by a prison guard in 1972 was the first sign that life might improve. Soon thereafter a pile of books in Russian appeared in her cell—Marx, Engels, Lenin. Before that her only reading materials were a French translation of Mao's Little Red Book and People's Daily in Chinese. She regretted that she had not stuck with her Chinese studies. "I forced my way through the debris of the characters as through a dark forest, trying to guess at the meaning." Sometimes she knocked on her own door to ask a passing guard the pronunciation and meaning of a character, and the guards usually obliged her. In this way she finally learned to read Chinese; Eva described a similar process.

After the washcloth and the books came meals with meat and even milk products and dumplings. Liza's health had declined, and she was finally taken to a hospital and given medicine. When that didn't help, a female doctor who had recently been assigned to the prison began to visit her cell. One day, this doctor whispered in Liza's ear, "Why don't you ask to see your daughters? They're allowing visits now."[39]

In May 1975, Inna and Alla arrived for their first visit.

> The girls threw themselves toward me, and then I discovered that it had become difficult for me to speak Russian: the words weren't there on my tongue, I had to search my memory to find the word I needed. My daughters told me later that at that time I spoke like a foreigner who had at one point had a good grasp of the language, but now, it seemed, had forgotten it. Well—8 years in solitary! You even forget your native tongue.[40]

The girls evaded her references to Li and kept from her details of their own imprisonment. They had each spent over a year in prison and then several years at hard labor before returning to Beijing, where Alla was working in a factory. Inna, who was married and had given birth to Liza's long-imagined grandson, taught Russian at the Institute for Foreign Languages. This first visit lasted three hours, during which Liza ate the yogurt and marveled at the bread, candy, fruit, and cookies on which they had spent half a month's salary.

To her complete surprise, Liza was released from Qincheng not long after. Others who had been released a bit earlier, including Eva and Emi, had been allowed to go home to Beijing, but Liza and others who came out later were sent to provincial cities. A former colleague of hers arrived to accompany her to the town of Yongchen, where he stayed to be sure she was properly settled. Liza lived in a single-story house with two young women, a nurse and a librarian, who were to care for her. At night, the local police chief dropped by to play games and chat. He, like other local people, was genuinely curious about her, asked her many questions, and offered her advice on all sorts of practical matters, including how to dress for the cold. "Of course, I had no plans to dress like a Chinese village woman, but thanks to my time in Yongchen the distance between me and ordinary Chinese people shortened."[41]

In August of 1975, Inna arrived with her husband and son to visit. At long last Liza laid eyes on her grandson, Pavlik. Pavlik, to Liza's amazement, pointed at the steam coming from the pipes of the train engine and said in Russian, "Smoke, smoke." Despite all prohibitions Inna had spoken Russian to Pavlik since his birth. Inna took a look around at Liza's little house and said, "I don't recognize you, mother! Where are your housekeeping skills? You haven't even put up curtains." But in truth Liza didn't care. "It was like everything inside me had gone numb, as if the living cells of my soul had died off." Inna wanted to come and live with Liza, as other children did when their parents were released from prison into the provinces. But Liza was alive enough to refuse. She felt certain that her chances of returning to Beijing were greater if her daughters remained there.[42]

Inna saw the logic of her mother's decision, but, clever and determined, made one of her own. Overwhelmed with work and expecting a second child, Inna sent Pavlik to live with her mother—perhaps to counterbalance the shock Liza experienced when Inna finally told her, in early 1976, that Li had died the night before Liza's arrest. Upon hearing that she was to care for a toddler, Liza was terrified beyond belief: what if something happened to him? But as Inna had no doubt planned, it was Pavlik who brought her back to life. Suddenly she had something to think about and to do. She got a chicken, which laid eggs for Pavlik and provided much general entertainment. "Never in my life had I imagined I'd be socializing with a chicken!" she remembers. In the summer they walked to a milk farm and went to open air movies. "Pavlik became a bridge thrown across the abyss separating me from the world." It took three more years for the Chinese authorities to finally decide, in December 1978, to allow Liza back to Beijing.[43]

Revival

Liza and many other high-profile victims of the Chinese Cultural Revolution were eventually settled in modern apartment buildings scattered around the prestigious Muxidi district in Beijing. Liza and her daughters lived for many years in the same apartment building as Emi's son Vitya, just a short bike ride away from another complex that housed Tuya, Qu Qiubai's

Liza with her grandson Pavlik, 1978. Courtesy of Inna Li.

daughter, into old age. Though Qu had been gone for three decades when the Cultural Revolution began, he was still a victim of it. His grave at the main Babaoshan Cemetery for Communist Party dignitaries and martyrs was disinterred, and his daughter and wife were imprisoned. Yang Zhihua died in 1973, but Tuya survived. In the aftermath of the Cultural Revolution, she and the other elderly alumni of the Russian International Children's home began meeting up in Beijing to eat Russian food and sing Russian songs; eventually they began traveling en masse to the school's international reunions in Ivanovo. In 2015, Tuya, Liu Shaoqi's daughter Aiqin, and Mao's daughter Li Min were presented with awards by the Russian ambassador to China in connection with the seventieth anniversary of Russia's World War II victory.[44]

Liza enjoyed similar honors and awards. Like her Chinese counterparts in the aftermath of the Cultural Revolution, slowly but surely she began to build a new life for herself. She was given a fantastic apartment and 20,000 yuan in lost wages. At age sixty-four she started teaching at the Beijing

Foreign Languages Institute again, where she worked until 1996, "when an unexpected heart attack struck me down right at work and they carried me out on an ambulance stretcher."[45] Eventually, she and Li were both officially rehabilitated; she went on to serve in the ceremonial Chinese People's Political Consultative Congress. In 2013 at the age of ninety-nine, she was awarded the French Legion of Honor.

Liza's closest Chinese friends Ania and Lin Li had also been in prison all those years, as was Grania, but all three women emerged and gradually returned to their senses. Grania longed to return to Russia but was refused by the Soviet government and eventually emigrated with her son to Australia. Others emigrated as well. Lena, the daughter of Manchurian operatives who had been raised in the Interdom, became fascinated by Gorbachev's *glasnost* and active in China's dissident movement in the 1980s, emigrating to Monterey, California, in 1989. The great exile of the Sino-Soviet romance, Jiang Jingguo, lived out his days as president of Taiwan with Faina at his side, undertaking political liberalization on Taiwan in tandem with his Soviet counterparts. His children eventually moved to California. Even 1920s Trotskyist romantics Peng Shuzhi and Chen Bilan moved from Paris to Los Angeles in the 1970s.

Liza recalls how, in those early years, everyone who could leave China did. Or almost everyone; Eva Sandberg nursed Emi until his death in 1986 and remained in China until she died in 2001. "The late 1970s and early '80s were a time when nobody in China believed that 'this country' could have a future," Liza writes.

> Lots of people asked me "How come you don't leave?" But nowhere was pulling me. . . . Truly, after so many tragic peregrinations, without even noticing it myself I had somehow grown into Chinese life, and people, even the most orthodox elderly veterans, recognized me as their own. After all, I had lived through everything with them: "struggle sessions," and prison, and exile. And I was rewarded with human trust.[46]

It was almost as if the Chinese revolution had finally managed, in the course of a half century of passion and tragedy, to reconcile itself to the Russian woman who had always been one of the best parts of its own story. Liza Kishkina died in Beijing on May 12, 2015, at the age of 101.

20

Nostalgia
Wang's Search

IN THE WINTER of 2004, an old Chinese man sat on a Moscow-bound plane, passing time with the inflight sound system, looking for something he can't find. He heard Broadway show tunes, Italian operas, and Russian pop songs, but what he did not hear is music from the Soviet era, or even Russian folk songs.[1] It's an eight and a half hour flight, but he has been waiting a half-century to land in Moscow, so what difference does one more day of boredom make?

Actually, this is not his first trip to Moscow. In 1984, Wang Meng was invited to a film festival in Uzbekistan and passsed a single day in Moscow en route to Tashkent. Wang had spent a lifetime dreaming about Russia, weaving it into fiction inspired by his subjective experiences of the Chinese revolution. After being sent to the countryside during the anti-Rightist campaign of the late 1950s, Wang returned briefly to Beijing. When the Sino-Soviet split went public, he was devastated. "I can't help it, the Soviet Union was me at nineteen, it was my first love, it was the beginning of my literary career. . . . [W]hen I learned in the 1960s that the Soviet Union had become 'revisionist,' our enemy, what I felt was the pain of my own soul tearing apart. The pain was worse than if I had been executed myself. If a person is executed their ideals and dreams still exist, but if the Soviet Union goes revisionist then what?" For all this passionate talk, Wang took very practical action to ensure that he would not be executed. In 1963, sensing another storm, he applied for a transfer for himself and his family to Xinjiang, thinking he would rather spend a few years there than go through another wrenching Beijing political campaign with another possible separation from his wife and child.[2]

Wang and his family ultimately spent sixteen years in the Uighur town of Yining (also known as Kulja or Ili), less than fifty miles from the border of Soviet Kazakhstan. By the time Red Guards arrived there during the Cultural Revolution, their fervor was a bit muted, and Wang, who learned Uighur, had too many local friends willing to protect him for the campaign to do much damage. Wang continued writing fiction and submitting it for publication; in 1979 one of his stories was finally published in a mainstream literary journal. The Chinese Writer's Association called him back to Beijing, and his first 1950s novel, *Forever Young*, came out at long last. A movie based on this book earned him the 1984 invitation to the Tashkent film festival. On one hand, Wang felt at home and enjoyed himself in Tashkent, since Uzbekistan has a Uighur minority population and Uzbek, like Uighur, is a Turkic language.[3]

The problem with Tashkent, though, was that it was not Moscow. Like Qu Qiubai and other travelers in the 1920s who chafed at delays in the borderlands of the Far East, the Soviet Union that Wang Meng dreamed of was Russian, not Eurasian. That Wang could spend sixteen years growing to love the northwestern borderlands, yet still long for the big cities of European Russia shows just how enduring the distinction between the two really was, and just how important Russian culture, people, and history remained in the imaginations of even the most cosmopolitan second-generation Chinese communists. When Wang visited Moscow in 2004, he had traveled all over the world, not only as a famous Chinese writer but also, from 1986 to 1989, as China's minister of culture. In 2004 a volume of his fiction had just been translated into Russian, and he was awarded an honorary doctorate by the Russian Academy of Sciences, so his trip was sponsored by the Sino-Russian Friendship Association.[4] Yet his extended travelogue describes a personal quest that he undertook on behalf of like-minded intellectuals of his generation.

Even in 1984, Wang had traveled enough—the United States, Germany, Mexico—to draw some comparisons. Whereas he had been longing to see the Soviet Union since he was fifteen, the idea of a trip to America only occurred to him when he was forty-five. For a writer, he said in 1984, such a visit was easy. "As long as you have enough of a sense of humor, you'll have enough juice to digest your American experience. But not the Soviet Union."

No other country is like the Soviet Union; even though I haven't seen it with my own eyes, I already know it and understand it so well. I miss its cities, its countryside, its people, flags, slogans, fiction, poetry, drama, film, painting, song and dance so much. Arriving in Moscow, everything gives me déjà vu: the elderly people fishing on the Moscow river, the two blue eyed sentries standing motionless as statues in front of Lenin's tomb, the bells of the Kremlin clock tower announcing the hour ... such a sense of déjà vu is even chilling. Have I really arrived in the native land of Lenin and Stalin, Pushkin and Gorky, that Moscow that I've heard so many songs sung of, that I myself have sung so many songs about? ... No other foreign country caused me so much love, infatuation, and longing in my youth, and later ... so much confusion, pain, and even terror. Good or bad, our relationship to it is too deep, too close. My friends and I all felt a special kind of concern, we all wondered about it. ... Everything beautiful about it makes me sad but happy, everything not beautiful about it makes me happy but sad.[5]

Once Wang's 1984 single day in Moscow is over and he flies to Tashkent, his tone changes. He describes the normal hubbub of an international film festival, where he saw movies about places that he had probably thought about even less than the United States. His descriptions of the city and of subsequent visits to Samarkand and Tbilisi are precisely in the "tourist" mode he explicitly rejects for Moscow. In Georgia, the idea that he could be so close to Stalin's hometown yet have no visit to it on his itinerary clearly provoked frustration. Three weeks later, Wang was on the plane back to Beijing, where he quickly reworked his travel diary for publication.[6]

That Wang spent three years in the late 1980s as minister of culture without another visit to Moscow seems odd until one considers China's domestic situation. Wang was presiding over what has since been called "culture fever," optimistic years in the 1980s when writers, artists, filmmakers, and musicians unleashed a bewildering profusion of aesthetic visions the likes of which had not been seen in China since the May Fourth period. Wang himself had first risen to artistic prominence in the early 1950s and was associated with the youthful hopes of that time. Moreover, while other intellectuals his age had been suffering mercilessly in the 1960s and early 1970s, Wang had been busy learning Uighur and accumulating novel experiences in Xinjiang, which made his writing seem fresh and exciting in the early 1980s. At the end of the

1980s, he was busy defending avant-garde writers and talking his own daughter out of participating in the demonstrations at Tiananmen. No wonder he had no time for Moscow.

By the time Wang visited Russia again, the Soviet Union had collapsed—an event he regarded with all the dismay one might expect. Just as the Soviet Union he had loved had been Russian, so too the Russia he loved had been Soviet.

> When I think about the words "former Soviet Union" at first I feel strange, who doesn't know the Soviet Union is already "former"? Adding the word former is like taking your pants off to fart. But the experience of looking for music in the Russian plane reminded [me] of the sorrow of the "survivors" of the former Qing Dynasty. I jokingly call myself a survivor of the Soviet Union, so wasn't adding the word "former" the same for survivors of the "former Qing"? History causes so many "former" things of the past, the present, and even the future to go, never to return.[7]

The problem for Wang, like many communists in both countries, was that none of the futures he had dreamed of—for himself, for Soviet Russia, for China—had come to pass. Instead of a great transformation leading to a bright new future, both Russia and China had descended into violence and chaos, turned on each other, and then abandoned the core mission of their revolutions to the vagaries of "reform."

As the plane descended toward Sheremyetevo International Airport, he noticed, as many travelers do, just how thick the forest is right up to the edges of the airport, and he mentally corrected himself. In a short story he wrote, he had described these trees as beech trees, when in fact most are birch. Later, when he recounted this moment, he layered in an odd allusion.

> I've found that in Russian landscape paintings, trees, especially birch trees, often play the role of protagonists, such as Levitan's "Spring Floods." My pitiful art appreciation ability and background causes me to love Levitan better than the French or Dutch masters.
>
> But I'm also confused, because it's said that Levitan was Lithuanian, and Lithuania was among the most aggressive countries to detach from the Soviet Union and distance itself from Russia, and now it's joined NATO. So does Levitan still count as a Russian painter?[8]

Actually, Levitan, who was Jewish and born in 1860 in a shtetl in territory controlled by the Russian Empire, attended the Moscow Painting School, where he was taught by prominent Russian artists and became famous for his depictions of Russian landscapes. Soviet Russia repeatedly issued commemorative stamps of his paintings in the 1950s and 1960s, and Wang most likely first saw his artwork then. Levitan's "Russianness" as an artist is not really in dispute, which throws Wang's apparently obtuse rhetorical question into sharp relief.

Yet, the painting Wang mentioned looks nothing like the dense forests around Sheremyetevo. "Spring Floods" on first glance simply depicts a river that has flooded through a birch forest; the canvas is mostly water and sky. The trees are partially submerged but the river is calm and sun drenches the image. Only a home nearly floating in the distance alludes to the destructive power of the river just a day or two before. Otherwise it seems as though all is as it should be. "History," as Wang noted, "causes so many 'former' things of the past, the present, and even the future to go, never to return." However rueful he might have felt about being among the "former" things swept away, this particular reference gestures to an attempt to hold fast to the hopeful perspective of his youth, or at least a refusal to give in to despair.

At seventy, Wang went to Moscow not, as previous generations did, for a glimpse of China's future, but rather to find a piece of his personal past. And what he encountered was a Russian present from which glimmers of nostalgia could only be coaxed with finesse and patience. When he exited the plane he saw signs in English and international brands—the Nike checkmark, the Red, Black and Blue Squares of Johnny Walker, and even the presumably pink Victoria's Secret. He was reminded of the way in which writers from Hungary's PEN club insisted on speaking English at a meeting he attended there in 1988.

> I thought, could a commercial brand name be more enduring than, say, the magnificent, long U.N. speeches of the USSR's 1950s Deputy Foreign Minister Vyshinsky? Half a century ago, probably only a Chinese revolutionary youngster like me read so eagerly the speeches of a man who is said to have served so well during Stalin's Great Purge. Now, whether in Russia or China, how many people still think so often of that old guy?[9]

Who knows, but likely only Wang Meng could go from Johnny Walker to Vyshinsky with only a brief detour through Hungary. Vyshinsky was indeed notorious for his role in Stalin's show trials and went on to represent the Soviet Union at the Nuremburg trials. In this passage Wang contrasts the ubiquitous, light-hearted simplicities of the global capitalist present with the all but forgotten, heavy complexities of the global communist past. He seemingly declines to allow later knowledge of Vyshinsky's central role in Soviet repression of the 1930s to devalue his memories of reading the Soviet minister's speeches in the 1950s. It is a deliberate and knowing refusal to integrate present knowledge with past sentiment.

Wang took a basic tour of Moscow for several days. He went to the Kremlin and Red Square, to Lenin's tomb where he bowed solemnly in tribute. He took a walk down the all too commercial Arbat and ate dinner at a restaurant, whose Chicken Kiev reminded him of the grand opening of the Restaurant Moscow in Beijing. Twice he went to the Lenin Hills; repeatedly he admired Stalin-era architecture; daily he sat through traffic jams worse than what he remembered in Mexico City. He saw "Swan Lake" at the Bolshoi and was dismayed that the happy ending always danced during Soviet times had been replaced by a tragic one. He visited St. Petersburg, where he viewed a glorious Baltic sunset.[10] When it came time to make an author's appearance at a Moscow bookstore, he arrived to find an audience of several dozen curious readers. After a round of naive questions about contemporary China, someone from the audience asked him to sing some Soviet songs. While the audience could certainly sing Katyusha and Moscow Nights with him, when he went on to sing lesser-known wartime classics, voices from the audience died out and he sang alone. Afterward, an elderly woman approached and asked whether he knew a certain translator, whom Wang calls "Old G." Yes, he and Old G were in fact friends. The woman turned out to be a Latvian poetess, and she brought along a photo album to show him. In it are pictures of herself and Wang's friend in the 1950s when they had a love affair. Wang was amazed to see his friend looking so "handsome and cool," but the real surprise was that Old G had never told him about this Soviet girlfriend.[11]

However satisfying Wang's various Moscow experiences may have been, the high point of his trip—the moment he felt he had found what he was looking for—occurred in the restaurant of his hotel, the Soviet-era Cosmos, which featured evening concerts of Russian folk music.

What the airplane lacked I found on the ground. Two flawless young girls sang, accompanied by a man with a guitar. Sometimes the two of them picked up balalaikas or clappers. . . . The girls are still here, the songs are still here. They sang Katyusha, they sang The Hawthorn, they sang Cranberry Flowers and Moscow Nights . . . especially they sang Who Knows? with endless charm and unlimited innocence. They swayed as they sang, like flowers in the breeze. They had the femininity of springtime, the allure of dessert: their songs came straight out and straight in, no tricks, no artifice, no decoration, sighing to themselves, then bantering playfully, smart and casual at the same time. Each sentence was filled with rhyming ah, ya, nya, lia, da sounds, so much more open, warm, and touching than when they're sung in Chinese. Singing like this is irresistible, the sound enters your heart through your ears, it ravishes you, badly, it lingers. . . . It reminds me of my weekly visits to the Shichahai ice rink when I was nineteen.[12]

From the tenor of his descriptions it would almost seem as though the entire trip to Moscow had been worth it just to hear these two beautiful girls sing "Who Knows?," his favorite song of his favorite nights of his favorite year of his life. Bowing to Lenin was important, the Baltic sunset was unforgettable, but "Who Knows?" is why he came.

When the singing ended, though, Wang remembered that times have changed and that it's important to tip. "Art and tips aren't separate," he concludes. "Friendship, youth, love, and dreams aren't included in the tip. The creators and purveyors of art are people, and people care about profit. Russian singing girls don't refuse tips." Even here, in the very moment when he was most transported back to the ideals of his youth, he was also reminded of their failure.

Back in Beijing when Wang composes his travelogue, then, he begins:

It's not here.
It's still not here.
I never did find it.

Epilogue

At Yura's

ALL THE WAY from northwest to southeast Beijing on the metro, and a little walk past rows of small stores selling sporting goods.

Hot bright backstreet, followed by cool dark apartment. Yura and Valya have a beautiful Russian dinner prepared.

Yura is Chinese and at almost eighty has a big frame. Valya is all small with her clouds of half-Russian, half-Korean hair and ruffled apron. They speak Russian together and everything in the apartment including them is at ease. They talk about the cats and the plants, their way of introducing themselves.

Then Yura begins with his stories and Valya flits in and out with the familiarity of a wife who has heard them before, but the interest of a second wife who listens a bit differently. There is a twist, too: Yura has written a memoir, in Russian, and Valya has typed it up for translation and publication in Chinese. So what they say implicitly references what they have written. Stories unspool. Eat dinner, go back to the living room, curl up in the armchair, and now it's time to ask questions.

Whatever happened to Tamara? Yura chuckles and shakes his head. Valya thought and wondered about Tamara. She had seen a Russian TV show, "Looking for You," that accepted letters from viewers to long-lost loved ones, found the missing halves, and reunited the pairs on television. Valya took it upon herself to write a letter for Yura. They found Tamara.

Really? Were you on TV? Yes, in 1998! Do you want to see it?

The show begins with the obvious anticipation. Yura is ringing a doorbell, and then Tamara appears. She is old, with a thinning frizz of hair, lots of wrinkles, and a short, plump, bent figure. No trace of whatever pretty had been, never mind whatever sexy had been. Then the camera is on Yura. He breaks down and cries. There is just a moment of this before the video cuts to a different take. Music is playing and Yura and Tamara are dancing, in Tamara's living room, with the furniture cleared aside. He's too tall, she's too old, there is no spark, and it's awkward. Until it isn't. Suddenly, they forget this moment, for just a moment, and fall into their time and their music. It is a physical demonstration of an imaginary time in Sino-Soviet emotional history, that one instant when China and Russia simply danced.

ACKNOWLEDGMENTS

THIS BOOK WAS a quest, and in writing it I lost any innocence I might have had at the outset. But in exchange, I became acquainted with an array of such fascinating people that the story feels like a by-product of their varied effects on my imagination.

It began with a 2003 trip to Ivanovo, where I first met the Russian-born children of the Chinese revolutionaries who are the main subjects of this book, at a school reunion they had traveled from Beijing to attend. Shen Linru made a spot for me at his table, wrote his address in my notebook, and welcomed me to his apartment in Beijing a year later. Over time, he and his many friends not only shared their life stories on tape, but also showed me what it meant to *be* Sino-Soviet at dinners, birthday parties, and reunions. I am especially grateful to Roza Yubin, Dora Liuxia, Yura Huangjian, Inna Li, Elizaveta Kishkina, Victor Siao, Tolya Li, Yang Dong, Zhenya Chuven, Tuya Qu, Serezha Shpatov, Han Moning, Roza Tete, Galya Nini, Chen Zutao, Pasha Chen Yin, Liu Aiqin, Su Heqing, and Ira Zhao.

To make sense of the stories they told, I needed the help of a formidable group of teachers. At UC Berkeley, Ying Yang and I-Hao Li taught me Chinese with patience and wit, respectively. At Tsinghua, Liu Zhenxia tailored lessons using my primary sources and even her own wedding ceremony;

eventually, she traveled to Moscow with me, where she helped with archival materials handwritten in Chinese, refused to speak English, and became a true friend. Her sister, Liu Fujian, transcribed documents; Zhenxia also introduced me to Li Li, who transcribed interviews and hunted down memoirs. In Moscow, Victor Usov, Nastya Usova and Aleksandr Larin offered me the perspective of Russian Sinologists deeply concerned with the human dimension of Sino-Soviet history over blini and sometimes with music. In Ivanovo, Galina Ivanovna Shevchenko graciously welcomed me to the Interdom, while Sofia Ivanovna Kuznetsova flung open the doors of her archive and showed me, with her own broad-minded, deep-hearted generosity, the best of socialist internationalism. All along, Yu Miin-ling published a steady stream of pioneering articles about Sino-Soviet cultural relations to guide my way like crumbs on a forest path.

It was my dissertation committee who taught me to make meaning of my sources. Irina Paperno showed me how to read autobiographies with discipline and nuance, fed me dark chocolate and encouragement, and offered some of the best critique I have ever received. Wen-hsin Yeh welcomed me to the China field and opened door after door for me there with timely introductions to books and people. She also helped me bridge the divide from language student to historian in illuminating discussions of the documents I brought back from my travels. Yuri Slezkine is the best teacher I've ever had, whose sparing questions redefined the very acts of reading and writing that are so central to my life. He is my first and last reader, and his ear gave me my voice.

Truly magical were the friendships and intellectual encounters this project conjured. Claudia Verhoeven's conversation, writing, and style all inspired me, and her critique of my early chapters was formative. He Donghui's nuanced work on Chinese literature, sense of Sino-Soviet adventure, tireless practical help, and deep wisdom replenished my enthusiasm for the quest. Thomas Lahusen's approach to biography and history was an early touchstone for me; later, his engagement with this project at conferences and as a formal reader offered help and hope. Shen Zhihua's personal hospitality and raucous storytelling abilities made Beijing come alive with fun and mischief, even as his amazing archive, conference invitations, and generous vision of international scholarly cooperation made a serious contribution to my research. Katerina Clark's thoughtful reading of the manuscript, searching questions, and ongoing conversation about international socialist culture have helped shape this book.

The UC Berkeley kruzhok was a wonderful place to share ideas; Alexis Peri, Christine Evans, David Beecher, Miriam Neirick, Shawn Salmon, and Stephen Brain were all especially perceptive readers. In Moscow, Oscar Sanchez-Sibony and Jenny Kaminer made long cold weeks end with warmth and laughter; Debbie Yalen was a lovely roommate and friend; Charles Shaw was a great support on my most recent trip.

Friends from other times and places who are scholars and artists in their own right—Beth Johnston, Michelle Shih, Bill Bland, Thomas Dillingham, and William Wood—stepped in to read chapters, ask questions, and offer critique.

I am grateful for invitations to present pieces of my research from Tom Bernstein and Edward Tyerman at Columbia University, David Ransel at Indiana University, Alex Cook and Stefan-Ludwig Hoffman at UC Berkeley, Maike Lehmann at Humboldt University, Dan Edelstein at Stanford University, and Tara Zahra at the University of Chicago. Tom, David, and Alex all provided excellent feedback for articles published in conference volumes. While these articles are separate from this project, their insight has improved it all the same. William Kirby, Karin-Irene Eiermann, Glennys Young, Choi Chatterjee, and Lisa Kirschenbaum all gave interesting feedback as discussants and fellow conference panelists. Haiyan Lee generously read the manuscript and offered support; an early conversation with Lorenz Luthi gave me the confidence to pursue the romance metaphor that structures this book.

The Fulbright Program, Social Science Research Council, Phi Beta Kappa, as well as the UC Berkeley Center for Chinese Studies, Institute for International Studies, and History Department all provided funding for the research and writing of my dissertation. But the luckiest break was a postdoctoral fellowship at the Harvard Academy of International and Area Studies, a golden ticket to a book factory where Larry Winnie acted as Wonka, wandering into my office in the afternoons with a jar of literal chocolate for me and my officemate, Miriam Kingsberg. Miriam read my entire manuscript *three* times, each time offering spot-on critique along with her friendship, sly humor, and unerring restaurant selection.

The seven readers at the Harvard Academy author's conference—Timothy Colton, Susan Ferber, Sheila Fitzpatrick, Henrietta Harrison, Terry Martin, Sergey Radchenko, and Steve Smith—each gave insightful, constructive criticism that has guided me over the past five years as I transformed my dissertation into this book. Henrietta and Steve read the manuscript twice and gave margin comments both times, offering much-needed perspective at a key juncture. Timothy Colton, whose undergraduate lectures drew me to Soviet history years ago, offered renewed insight and empathy as an Academy mentor.

I am equally grateful for the comments and suggestions of three anonymous readers from Oxford University Press and for the help of its incredibly capable production team. Susan Ferber's early interest in publishing this project was inspiring and her unflagging support over the years has been a critical factor in driving it to completion. Her thoughtful suggestions, handwritten with great care on every page, transformed a meandering manuscript into a finished book.

My new colleagues at California State University, East Bay, have been incredibly encouraging as I have completed the final revisions to this manuscript in my first year of teaching there. Linda Ivey's emotional support was unwavering and her professional guidance, world-class. Dee Andrews has given excellent advice at every turn. As a research assistant, Sophia Flint's attention to detail has been a great help in the final stages; Yun-ling Wang helped with last-minute transcriptions. And I owe an enormous debt to Henry Reichman, who read my manuscript more times than I can count, wrote letters on my behalf, and just generally would not rest until he saw me safely into my new office at East Bay.

All along, Tatyana Mamut's deep generosity and care have sustained me in the best and worst of times. Edith Sheffer's fearless approach to research and everyday companionship made dissertation writing fun. Eleonor Gilburd's awesome knowledge has enriched this project, while her hidden reservoir of humor illuminated even the darkest stretches of the path, to its very end.

So long and difficult was this quest that the composition of my family changed in the course of it. Without Kris Twomey, I never would have had the courage to begin it. Without Amy McGuire, I might have gotten lost many times. Without Thadd Peterson, the end would have been lonelier. And Misha Twomey's fun-loving nonsense and radiant optimism remind me to live in the present and hope for the future, even as I write about the past.

This book is dedicated to my parents, Thomas Roger McGuire and Patricia Mae Ainsworth, who taught me how to tell stories and how to listen to them; how to travel and how to come home; and what romance is really all about.

ABBREVIATIONS

AVPRI   Arkhiv vneshnei politiki Rossiiskoi Imperii—Archive of
Foreign Policy of the Russian Empire

GARF   Gosudarstvennyi arkhiv Rossiiskoi Federatsii—State Archive
of the Russian Federation

HA   Hoover Archive

RGALI   Rossiisskii gosudarstvennyi arkhiv literatury i isskustva—
Russian State Archive of Literature and Art

RGANI   Rossiisskii gosudarstvennyi arkhiv noveishei istorii—Russian
State Archive of Contemporary History

RGASPI   Rossisskii gosudarstvennyi arkhiv sotsial'no-politicheskoi
istorii—Russian State Archive of Socio-Political history
(includes the materials of the Communist International and
the Soviet Komsomol)

WJBDAG   Wai jiao bu dang an guan—Foreign Ministry Archive of the
People's Republic of China

NOTES

Introduction
1. Whiting, *Soviet Policies in China*; North, *Moscow and Chinese*; Schwartz, *Rise of Mao*; Dirlik, *Origins of Chinese Communism*; van de Ven, *Friend to Comrade*.
2. Usov, "Finansovaia pomoshch"; "First Conversation," trans. Zubok for CWIHP. The Cold War International History Project at the Woodrow Wilson Center in Washington, DC, has played a critical role in promoting innovative new scholarship.
3. Elleman, *Diplomacy;* Pantsov, *Bolsheviks;* Wolff, "One Finger's"; Luthi, *Sino-Soviet Split;* Radchenko, *Two Suns;* Pantsov and Levine, *Mao;* Shen and Xia, *Mao and the Sino-Soviet;* Friedman, *Shadow Cold War;* Radchenko, *Unwanted Visionaries.*
4. Kotkin, *Magnetic Mountain;* Fitzpatrick, *Everyday Stalinism;* Weiner, *Making Sense;* Kirschenbaum, *Legacy;* Hellbeck, *Revolution;* Lahusen, *How Life;* Yurchak, *Everything Was Forever;* Evans, *Between Truth.*
5. Slezkine, *Arctic Mirrors;* Edgar, *Tribal Nation;* Martin, *Affirmative Action Empire;* Hirsch, *Empire of Nations;* Chakers, *Socialist Way of Life;* Scott, *Familiar Strangers.*
6. Young, *Communist Experience;* Zhuravlev, *"Malen'kie liudi";* Epstein, *Last Revolutionaries;* Shore, *Caviar and Ashes;* David-Fox, *Showcasing;* Chatterjee, *Americans Experience Russia;* David Fox, Holquist, and Martin, eds., *Fascination and Enmity;* Gilburd, "To See Paris and Die"; Gorsuch, *Soviet Tourism;* Clark, *Fourth Rome.*

7. Exceptions: Yu, "Sun Yat-sen University"; Yu, *Xingsu xinren*; Galitskii, *Tszian*; Pantsov and Spichak, "New Light"; Eiermann, "Autobiographies."

8. Levine, *Found*; Ye, *Seeking*; Reynolds and Reynolds, *East Meets East*; Rhoads, *Stepping*; Harrell, *Sowing*; Huang, *Chinese Students*.

9. Qu, "Chi du."

10. Pan, *When True Love Came*; Liu, *Revolution Plus Love*; Glosser, *Visions*; Lee, *Genealogy of Love*; Stites, *Revolutionary Dreams*; Naiman, *Sex in Public*; Fitzpatrick, *Cultural Front*; Bernstein, *Dictatorship of Sex*; Kaminer, *Bad Mother*.

11. Brinton, *Anatomy of Revolution*; Skocpol, *States and Social Revolutions*; Mayer, *Furies*; Smith, *Revolution*; Furet, *Marx*; Malia, *History's Locomotives;* Meisner, *Li Tachao.* Histories of the Comintern as an "exporter" of revolution summarized or referenced in McDermott, *Comintern.*

12. Wilbur and How, *Missionaries;* Shen, *Sulian zhuanjia*; Kaple, "Agents of Change." Pedagogical undertones in Sino-Soviet cultural relations: Bernstein and Li, eds., *China Learns;* Gamsa, *Russian Literature in China.*

13. Shlapentokh, *French Revolution in Russian Intellectual Life;* Shlapentokh, *Counter-revolution;* Gorsuch, " 'Cuba, My Love' "; Kirschenbaum, *International Communism.*

14. David-Fox, "Iron Curtain"; Katsakioris, "L'Union soviétique"; Matusevich, *No Easy Row*; Babiracki and Zimmer eds., *Cold War Crossings*; Sanchez Sibony, *Red Globalization;* Mehilli, "Socialist Encounters"; Ivaska, "Transnational Activist Politics"; Jersild, *Alliance;* Shen, *Sulian zhuanjia;* Cook, *Little Red Book;* Rozman, *Mirror.*

15. Geraci, *Window;* Ram, *Imperial Sublime*; Tolz, *Russia's Own Orient*; Fein, "Science and the Sacred"; Kirasirova, " 'Sons of Muslims' in Moscow."

16. Catherine quoted: Schimmelpenninck van der Oye, *Russian Orientalism*, 52.

17. The Russian Ecclesiastical Mission in Beijing produced occasional spurts of research and translation but was the exception. Widmer, *Russian Ecclesiastical*; Paine, *Imperial Rivals*; Lim, *China and Japan.*

18. Attention to China in 1920s: Tyerman, "Soviet Images"; 1960s: McGuire, "Fun House Mirror." Soviet cultural diplomacy focused on Europe: David-Fox, *Showcasing*, 56.

19. V. G. Gel'bras, *Kitaiskaia real'nost' Rossii*, 101–103, 118–120; Kalita and Panich, *Krosskul'turnoe issledovanie*, 81–94; Galenovich, *Rossiia v 'kitaiskom zerkale'*, 39.

20. Bassin, Glebov, and Laruelle, eds., *Between Europe and Asia*; Laruelle, *Russian Eurasianism.*

21. Marks, *Metaphors in International Relations.*

22. Hunt, *Family Romance;* Elshtain, *Family in Political Thought*; Chaihark and Bell, *Politics of Affective Relations.*

23. "Emotional regimes": Reddy, *Navigation of Feeling;* Plamper, *History of Emotions.* On socialist "brotherhood" and "friendship" specifically: Martin, *Affirmative Action Empire*; Applebaum, "Friendship of the Peoples."

24. Liu Wenfei quoted in He, "History of Russian Lit." Scholarship on Russian literature in China voluminous, e.g., Chen, *Er Shi*; Wang, *Youyuan*; Liu, *Hong Chang*; Zeng, *19 shi ji*; Cao, *E Su.*

25. Westad, *Brothers;* Dittmer, *Sino-Soviet Normalization*; see chapters on "Menage a Trois, 1945–1949," "Sino-Soviet Marriage, 1950–1960," "Romantic Triangle, 1969–1976."

26. In using a metaphor as structure, this book was directly inspired by Slezkine, *Jewish Century.*

Chapter 1

1. Xiao, *Zhengui*, 136; Siao, *Shi ji*, unnumbered photo section; Wang, *Xiao*, 170, 178–180; Emi's birth name was Xiao Zizhang. Gong, "Xiao," 186, 189.

2. Emi (Siao Emil') as first Chinese student from France: RGASPI f. 532, op. 1, d. 393, ll. 4, 14. The next Chinese students recorded as arriving from France are groups in April and November 1923.

3. Wang, *Xiao*, 2–4; Barr, "Four Schoolmasters," 68. The leader of the Taiping Rebellion, Hong Xiuquan, was a failed examination candidate. Elman, *Cultural History*, 366–370.

4. Wang, *Xiao*, 4, 15; Xiao, *Mao*, 18.

5. Liu, *Red Genesis*, 52.

6. Xiao, *Zhengui*, 117.

7. Xiao, *Zhengui*, 117–118; Xiao, *Mao*, 34.

8. Xiao, *Mao*, 34–35.

9. Liu, *Red Genesis*, 35, 57–58; Xiao, *Zhengui*, 119, 122, 123. Xiao, *Mao*, 32.

10. Xiao, *Mao*, 81. Yu's claim to be Mao's close friend is substantiated in their letters. Schram, *Mao's Road*, 70–82, 85–105 to Xiao Yu, 610 to Xiao Zizhang/Emi.

11. Significance of 1911: Esherick and Wei, *China*; Harrison, *Republican Citizen;* Fitzgerald, *Awakening China.*

12. Xiao, *Zhengui*, 120–121; Snow, *Red Star*, 141; Spence, *Mao*, 12; Esherick, *Reform*, 52–65.

13. Xiao, *Zhengui*, 122–123; Xiao, *Mao*, 58–60.

14. Xiao, *Zhengui*, 124–126. Boy Scouts in China imparting skills of group organization later useful in student protests: Wasserstrom, *Student Protests*, 82–83.

15. Schwarcz, *Chinese Enlightenment*, 4–5, 13, 46–54.

16. Zhu, *Xiwang (jixu)*, 5–7; Rhoads, *Stepping Forth*, 7–12; Harrell, *Sowing*, 11–39; Huang, *Chinese Students*, 1–16, 67; Wang, *Chinese Intellectuals*, 52–53.

17. Konishi, *Anarchist Modernity*; Huang, *Chinese Students*, 201–239.

18. Zhu, *Xiwang (jixu)*, 7–8; Wang, *Chinese Intellectuals*, 99–104, 111–116, 157–160; Chinese student experiences in the United States: Ye, *Seeking Modernity*.
19. AVPRI, f. 143, op. 491, d. 2752. This file contains individual petitions; refusal on grounds of national security, l. 68. Liu, "Shi yue," 195, 198.
20. Wang, *Xiao*, 85–86.
21. Wang, *Xiao*, 88–89, 98.
22. Zhou, *May Fourth*, 84–90.
23. Wang, *Xiao*, 99–100; Lanza, *Behind the Gate*, 169–173; Zhou, *May Fourth*, 105, 109–117.
24. Wang, *Xiao*, 102–107; Yeh, *Provincial Passages*.
25. Wang, *Xiao*, 107–108; Levine, *Found*, 51–52.
26. Wang, *Xiao*, 108–110.
27. Xiao, *Zhengui*, 28.
28. Zheng, *Oppositionist*, 4–5.
29. Wang, *Xiao*, 117–126.
30. Wang, *Xiao*, 130–131; Levine, *Found*, 80–81.
31. Wang, *Xiao*, 130–131.
32. Wang, *Xiao*, 131–132, 141–143; Xiao, *Zhengui*, 17–18.
33. Levine, *Found*, 36–37.
34. Zheng, *Oppositionist*, 17–18.
35. Levine, *Found*, 38–39.
36. Levine, *Found*, 115–134.
37. Wang, *Xiao*, 162–169; Barnouin and Yu, *Zhou*, 25–28; Levine, *Found*, 155.
38. Xiao, *Zhengui*, 131–134; Wang, *Xiao*, 170–171.
39. Xiao, *Zhengui*, 133. The student who had written to Emi from Moscow was Ren Bishi.
40. Xiao, *Zhengui*, 133–134.
41. Levine, *Found*, 169–172. Levine argues that the Comintern was not the mastermind of the European branch of the Chinese Communist Party. Subsequent correspondence from Paris to Moscow about sending students to Moscow to study supports this argument, reading as letters from one Chinese communist to another and make no reference to direct Comintern involvement. On the other hand, they were retained in the Comintern archive. RGASPI f. 532, op. 1, d. 14, ll. 3–16.
42. Wang, *Xiao*, 177–178.
43. Xiao, *Zhengui*, 9, 136.

Chapter 2
1. Mao, "Qiubai," 254.
2. Photos of Qu before, during, and after Moscow: *Qu Qiubai hua zhuan*, 43, 44, 49, and 55.
3. Xia, "Ch'u," 181–182; Li, "Ch'u," 1–8, 11.
4. Xia, "Ch'u," 183; Spence, *Gate*, 133.

5. Qu, *Duoyu*. 3.
6. AVPRI, f. 143, op. 491, d. 2042, l. 9–15; Tyerman, "Soviet Images," 56.
7. History of railroad: Wolff, *Harbin*. Russian language school: Fu, *Waiyu*, 22, 37 note 1; Qu, "E xiang," 268–269; Bugayevska, "Beijing Institute," 2–3.
8. Wolff, *Harbin*, 17, 32; Bugayevska, "Beijing Institute," 3–4.
9. Khokhlov, "Pokotilov," 40.
10. Chen, *Zhong E*, 40–43; Bugayevska, "Beijing Institute," 4–5, 9.
11. Pushkin, *Captain's Daughter*.
12. Shi, *Water Margin*; Chen, *Zhong E*. 58–60.
13. Price, *Russia and the Roots*, 193.
14. Hu, *Translation*, 106–120; Price, *Russia and the Roots*, 195–196.
15. Recent, succinct analysis of language and social revolution: Barlow, "History's Coffin."
16. Zhou, *May Fourth*, 61–65. Lin's translation has been discussed in classic scholarship such as Link, *Mandarin Ducks* and Lee, *Romantic Generation*.
17. Turgenev, trans. unknown, "Chun Chao."
18. Turgenev, *Torrents*.
19. *Qingnian zazhi*, no. 1.
20. Effects of translation on Chinese: Gunn, *Rewriting Chinese*; Liu, *Translingual Practice*.
21. Lee, *Lu Xun*, 49, 53–57,
22. Gamsa, *Reading*, 15–24; Gálik, *Genesis*, 30–31, 58, 74, 125, 134, 194, etc.; Dirlik, *Origins*, 26–27.
23. Konishi, *Anarchist Modernity*, 93–141, esp. 111–112; Zarrow, *Anarchism*, 25, 95–96; Bodde, *Tolstoy and China*, 56–57; 63–75, 81.
24. Chen, *Zhong E*, 265–339; Shneider, *Russkaia klassika*, 19–20.
25. Qu's nostalgia for gentry culture and his use of Russian literature to express it is also described in Widmer, "Qu," 103–125.
26. Bugayevska, "Beijing Institute," 6–7; Gálik, *Genesis*, 217–218.
27. Qu, *Duoyu*, 3.
28. Qu, "Xian tan," 197.
29. Qu, *Duoyu*, 4.
30. Li, "Ch'u," 25, 28–29; Shneider, *Tvorcheskii put'*, 21.
31. Qu, *Duoyu*, 5.
32. The other two were Yu Songhua and Li Zongwu, neither of whom achieved Qu's prominence. Li was a fellow student at the Russian language institute but lacked Qu's literary talent; Yu spoke no Russian. Li, "Ch'u," 43, 59.
33. Pickowicz, *Marxist Literary*, 25, note 55, p. 30; Shneider, *Tvorcheskii put'*, 20–21; Li, "Ch'u," 43–46; Xia, "Ch'u," 184–190.
34. Translation of eighteenth-century classic and Qu quote, Xia, "Ch'u," 190–191.
35. Old regimes: Paine, *Imperial Rivals*.
36. Qu Qiubai, *Zuopin*, 256.
37. Qu Qiubai, *Zuopin*, 256–257.

38. Qu Qiubai, *Zuopin*, 257.
39. Qu Qiubai, *Zuopin*, 257–258.
40. Qu Qiubai, *Zuopin*, 258–259.
41. On Harbin: Carter, *Harbin*; Wolff, *Harbin*; Lahusen, "Harbin."
42. Qu Qiubai, *Zuopin*, 259–261.
43. Qu Qiubai, *Zuopin*, 261, 265–266.
44. In addition to posting his reports back to *Chen Bao*, Qu also kept a "diary."
    Journey seems to be a collage of excerpts from that diary and selections from
    his *Chen Bao* reports. There is no known original of the diary, however.
    Journey was first published in Shanghai in 1922 as *Xin E guo you ji: cong
    Zhongguo dao Eguo de ji cheng* (Travel notes on new Russia: a travel diary
    from China to Russia).
45. Barlow, " 'History's Coffin,' " 263.
46. Qu Qiubai, *Zuopin*, 265.
47. Liu, *Translingual Practice*, 106–107.
48. Ding, *Qu Qiubai mulu*, 4–6.
49. Qu Qiubai, *Zuopin*, 271, 273.
50. Qu Qiubai, *Zuopin*, 275.
51. Qu Qiubai, *Zuopin*, 288–289.
52. Qu Qiubai, *Zuopin*, 273–274.
53. Larin, *Kitaitsy*, 13–23, 71–80; Qu Qiubai, *Zuopin*, 274; Liu, "Shi yue," 209–210.
54. Qu, *Zuopin*, 273, 289–290.
55. Qu, *Zuopin*, 274.
56. Qu, *Zuopin*, 275–277.
57. Qu, *Zuopin*, 279–280, 291, 293.
58. Li, "Ch'u," 59–60.
59. Interesting comparison to Africa: Baldwin, "Russian Routes." Li, "Ch'u,"
    61–62; Skachkov, *Bibliografiia Kitaia*, 489, 648. Kolokolov later published a
    well-regarded Russian-Chinese dictionary.
60. Qu, "Chi du," 307.
61. Qu, "Chi du," 311–312.
62. Qu, "Chi du," 310, 332–334.
63. Qu, "Chi du," 318–322. Sofia may have been enacting the kind of cultural
    diplomacy the Soviet regime expected of non-party intellectuals, or this may
    have been one of the many chance encounters between foreigners and Soviet
    citizens—both described by David-Fox, *Showcasing*, 49, 120.
64. Qu, *Zuopin*, 325–326.
65. Qu, *Zuopin*, 326–327.
66. Qu, *Zuopin*, 329–330.
67. Qu, *Zuopin*, 350, 339, 332–333.
68. Qu, *Zuopin*, 353.
69. Qu, *Zuopin*, 353–354.
70. Qu, *Zuopin*, 357–359.
71. Qu, *Zuopin*, 360–361.

Chapter 3

1. Zhang, *Rise*, vol. 1, 121.
2. Feigon, *Chen*, 37–43, 54–55, 71.
3. Chen, "On the Literary Revolution."
4. Jiang, *Xin E.*
5. Meisner, *Li Ta-chao*, 31–34, 60–70, 90–95; Dirlik, *Origins*, 24–32.
6. Elleman, *Diplomacy*, 24–27, 35–37; Smith, *Road*, 11–12; Zhang, *Rise*, vol. 1, 121–122. On widespread disappointment with Wilsonian ideals: Manela, *Wilsonian Moment.*
7. Go and Titarenko, eds., *Komintern*, vol. 1, 48; Lazić and Drachkovitch, *Dictionary*, 497–498; Dalin, *Memuary*, 42–43.
8. Zhonggong, ed., *Gongchanzhuyi*, vol. 1, 182.
9. Zhang, *Rise*, vol. 1, 121–124.
10. Smith, *Road*, 11–18; Sotnikova, "Komintern," 128. Voitinskii survived purges and war to become a respected Sinologist. Lenchner, "Khronika," 167–168.
11. Yu and Zhang, *Yang*, 1–7; Smith, *Road*, 16; Larin, *Kitaitsy*, 89–90; Benton, *Chinese Migrants.*
12. Bulgakov, "Chinese Tale," xiv–xv, 146–158. Other literary variations on the theme of the Chinese Red Army partisan are found in Platonov's *Cherengur*, Ostrovsky's *How the Steel Was Tempered*, and Ivanov's *Armored Train*, 14–69. Tyerman, "Soviet Images," 90–108.
13. Peng, *Memoires*, 183.
14. Usov, "Finansovaia pomoshch," 121. Even the Bolsheviks complained about the difficulty of finding cadres among Red Army Chinese. Larin, *Kitaitsy*, 112.
15. Xiao, "Fu Su," 2.
16. Xiao, "Fu Su," 5.
17. Peng, *Memoires*, 11–13.
18. Peng, *Memoires*, 135–139, 151–166.
19. Yeh, *Provincial Passages*, 208–212; Xiao, "Fu Su," 6–7; Fu, *Waiyu*, 46.
20. Bao, *Chi E*, 1–2.
21. Peng, *Memoires*, 229–231; Bao, *Chi E*, 3.
22. Xiao, "Fu Su," 7–11; Bao, *Chi E*, 5–8.
23. Peng, *Memoires*, 239–240.
24. Peng, *Memoires*, 240–245.
25. Gamsa, "Red Beards," explains that there was, actually, no Chinese bandit group called "Red Beards."
26. Peng, *Memoires*, 245–255.
27. Peng, *Memoires*, 262.

Chapter 4

1. Peng, *Memoires*, 263–264.
2. Peng, *Memoires*, 265–266, 275. Xiao, "Fu Su," 14–15.
3. Peng, *Memoires*, 277–279.

4. Li, *Liu*, 8; Zhu, *Xiwang*, 15; and *Xiwang (jixu)*, 421. The Liu talk was recalled by future PRC Foreign Ministry official Chen Xianyu.
5. Peng, *Memoires*, 268–270; David-Fox, *Showcasing*, 30–39.
6. Timofeeva, "Universitet, 1921–1925"; Timofeeva, "Universitet, 1926–1938." There is no English-language monograph on the school. See, however, McClellan, "Black Hajj," and Sokolov, *Komintern i V'etnam*. David-Fox, *Revolution of the Mind*, 87–88. Ch. 2, "Power and Everyday Life at Sverdlov University," provides an interesting comparison to Chinese experiences.
7. Broido (1885–1956) had been a Menshevik who joined the Bolsheviks in 1918. After spending several years during the Civil War in Turkestan he returned to Moscow in 1921 as deputy commissar of nationalities under Stalin and rector of Eastern University, where he remained until 1926. Lazić and Drakhovitch, *Dictionary*, 45. RGASPI f. 532, op. 1, d. 110, l. 16.
8. Timofeeva, "Universitet, 1921–1925," 47–48.
9. Numbers of foreign students: RGASPI f. 532, op. 1, d. 2, ll. 49–51; d. 12, ll. 53–54; d. 23, ll. 1–2; d. 25, ll. 37, 44; Timofeeva, "Universitet , 1921–1925," 51.
10. Keddie, *Iran*, 63–93; Manela, *Wilsonian Moment*; Scalapino and Lee, *Korea*, 3–32.
11. Peng, *Memoires*, 264–265; Zheng, *Oppositionist*, 53.
12. Zheng, *Oppositionist*, 29–30.
13. Zheng, *Oppositionist*, 51. Sample lists of names: RGASPI f. 532, op. 1, d. 8, ll. 9, 15.
14. Li, "Ch'u," 67.
15. Skachkov, *Bibliografiia Kitaia*, 488–492; Li, "Ch'u," 68; Peng, *Memoires*, 273.
16. Liu, *Zi shu*, 24–25.
17. Qu's system: Qu, *Wen ji*, vol. 3, 351–422.
18. Bao, *Chi E*, 22.
19. Peng, *Memoires*, 273.
20. Qu, *Duoyu*, 5.
21. Peng, *Memoires*, 288–289.
22. Cao, *Huiyi*, 41.
23. Xiao, "Fu Su," 11–12; Bao, *Chi E*, 55; Zheng, *Oppositionist*, 52; RGASPI f. 532, op. 1, d. 5, ll. 31–33.
24. Li, "Ch'u," 68.
25. Bao, *Chi E*, 55–56; Zheng, *Oppositionist*, 30–34, 52.
26. RGASPI f. 532, op. 1, d. 22, ll. 7–8; d. 293, l. 77; op. 7, d. 2, l. 217; Lazitch and Drachkovitch, *Dictionary*, 39–40.
27. RGASPI f. 532, op. 1, d. 22, ll. 11–17, 22; d. 23, ll. 11–24; Peng, *Memoires*, 272.
28. Xiao, "Fu Su," 12–13. Among the serious generals of the Chinese revolution who studied in Moscow besides Xiao Jingguang was Ye Ting, who was at Eastern University in 1924–1925. Xiao, *Zhengui*, 46. In the late 1920s the university designed a special military training course for Chinese. McGuire, "Sino-Soviet."

29. RGASPI, f. 532, op. 1, d. 17, l. 3.

30. RGASPI, f. 532, op. 1, d. 17, l. 3.

31. In the 1890s, Russian Social Democrats could not decide whether to tutor workers in ideological concepts or teach them activist techniques. Wildman, *Russian Social Democracy.*

32. RGASPI f. 532, op. 1, d. 23, 3–27; Zheng, *Oppositionist,* 54–55; Bao, *Chi E,* 23.

33. Bao, *Chi E,* 57–59.

34. Bao, *Chi E,* 47–53.

35. Peng, *Memoires,* 265, 327; Bao, *Chi E,* 28–29, 59–60; Murav'ev, *Tverskoi Bul'var,* 143.

36. Peng, *Memoires,* 294–302; Xiao, "Fu Su," 12.

37. Li, "Ch'u," 74, 76; Zhang, *Rise,* 201; Shneider, *Tvorcheskii put',* 33–35.

38. Bao, *Chi E,* 40. Bao Pu refers here to Zhang Guotao.

39. Scalapino and Lee, *Korea,* 41–42.

40. Bao, *Chi E,* 40; Zhang, *Rise,* 201.

41. Zhang, *Rise,* 201.

42. Zhang, *Rise,* 193.

43. Bao, *Chi E,* 37–38.

44. Bao, *Chi E*; Peng, *Memoires,* 302–303.

45. RGASPI f. 495, op. 30, d. 293, l. 12. In 1922, KUTV brought 1,000 students on a total of 51 excursions. RGASPI f. 532, op. 1, d. 5, ll. 35–40; Lianov, "Na prazdnike."

46. RGALI, f. 2653, op. 1, d. 68, ll. 1–4.

47. Xiao, *Zhengui,* 10.

48. Xiao, *Zhengui,* 10.

49. Gao, *Tianya,* 114; Murav'ev, *Tverskoi,* 130–137.

50. Babaev, *Khikmet,* 93; Fish, *Khikmet,* 34–54.

51. Xiao, *Zhengui,* 137–138; Xiao, *Wenji,* vol. 3, 16–18. Emi would rework the Internationale in 1939 with a short introduction explaining the history of its translation.

52. Xiao, "Fu Su," 16; Harrison, *Long March,* 37–38.

53. Xiao, *Zhengui,* 139; Gao, *Xiao San,* 115.

54. Another early example is a filmmaker, Shu Heqing, educated in the Soviet Union in the 1930s, whose footage of the Chinese revolution was used for a major Soviet documentary, which won him and his Soviet collaborators the Stalin prize. Du and Wang, *Zai Sulian,* 1–15; Shu Heqing, interview by author, Beijing, fall 2004.

55. Xiao, *Zhengui,* 141–142. Mayakovsky came to Eastern University in January 1925 to read his poem, "Lenin." RGALI, f. 963, op. 1, d. 1574, l. 1.

56. Xiao, *Zhengui,* 143–144.

57. Peng, *Memoires,* 281.

58. Peng's efforts to root out anarchists actually mirrored a similar effort in China 1920–1921. Dirlik, *Origins*, 211, 221–223; Feigon, *Chen*, 154–156; Van de Ven, *Friend*, 65; Bao, *Chi E*, 24–26.

59. Bao, *Chi E*, 43.

60. Xiao, *Zhengui*, 137; Zheng, *Oppositionist*, 55; Gao, *Tian ya*. 115.

61. RGASPI, f. 532, op. 1, d. 99, ll. 13, 21–25; d. 22, l. 23.

62. RGASPI, f. 532, op. 1, d. 23, ll. 1–3.

63. RGASPI, f. 532, op. 1, d. 4, l. 16.

64. RGASPI f. 532, op. 1, d. 7, ll. 32–33; d. 21, l. 2; d. 99, l. 14. The university also spent the most on the Chinese whose sheer numbers combined with cost of transportation made them by far the largest item in the recruiting budget. RGASPI f. 532, op. 1, d. 6., ll. 1–3.

65. Peng, *Memoires*, 367–370; Xiao, *Zhengui*, 140.

Chapter 5

1. Yang, "Yi Qiubai," 63; Kong, "Ji Qu," 145–146.

2. Li, "Ch'u," 110, 137; vitality and clothing: Ding, "Qu," 123–124; Zhou, "Qu," 269; Zhang, *Rise*, vol. 1, 297.

3. *Jiang nan*, photos pp. 2, 33, 37, 41, 44, 49, 55; Ding, "Qu," 115, and Yang, "Yi Qiubai," 63.

4. Li, "Ch'u," 108–109.

5. Qu, "'Shanghai daxue,'" 1–13; Yeh, *Alienated*, 152–156.

6. Yeh, *Alienated*; Wasserstrom, *Student Protests*, 45–46.

7. Yang, "Yi Qiubai," 63–64; Qu, "Duoyu," 14; Li, "Ch'u," 137–140.

8. Fu, *Waiyu*, 47; Qu, "Shanghai Daxue," 11.

9. Fu, *Waiyu*. 48–49.

10. Yeh, *Alienated*, 139–143, 147–150.

11. Smith, *Road*, 69.

12. Van de Ven, *Friend to Comrade*, 85–90.

13. Saich, *Maring*, 18–22.

14. Van de Ven, *Friend to Comrade*, 86–88.

15. Saich, *Maring*, 58, 78.

16. Drakhovitch, *Internationals*; Pantsov, *Bolsheviks*, 9–70 is an incomparable discussion of Trotskyist and Leninist views on China and foreign policy more broadly. Smith, *Road*, 213.

17. Zheng, *Oppositionist*, 73; Zhang, *Rise*, vol. 1, 224.

18. Saich, *Maring*, 475–479; Zhang, *Rise*, vol. 1, 300.

19. Zhang, *Rise*, vol. 1, 139.

20. Maring's other interpreter was Zhang Tailei, whose English was good. Zhang, *Rise*, 138; Saich, *Maring*, 555–587, 640, 858.

21. Saich, *Maring*, 560–570, 577–579; Li, "Ch'u," 125–126.

22. Kartunova, "Moscow's Policy," 69–70.

23. Holubnychy, *Borodin*, 1–4, 18–34, 40–50, 224, 246; Jacobs, *Borodin*, 1–3, 21–24, 41–51; Spence, *To Change China*, 184–185.
24. Holubnychy, *Borodin*, 220.
25. Holubnychy, *Borodin*, 220–245.
26. Yoshihiro, "Chinese National Revolution," 148; Li, "Ch'u," 144–146.
27. Yang, "Perspectives," 77–97; Yu, "Reassessment," 98–125.
28. Yang, "Perspectives," 77–79.
29. Yu, "Reassessment," 99, 102.
30. Peng, *Memoires*, 338–339.
31. Kartunova, "Military Aspect," 66–73.
32. Cherepanov, *Zapiski*, 47.
33. Rigby, *May 30th*.

Chapter 6

1. Zheng, *Oppositionist*, 146.
2. HA, Peng papers, Box 3, Ch. 3, 12–13.
3. HA, Peng papers, Box 3, Ch. 3, 14–15.
4. Gilmartin, *Engendering*; Gilmartin, "Inscribing Gender," 244–249.
5. Recent, high readable analysis of China's love revolution: Pan, *When True Love Came*.
6. Lang, *Chinese Family*, 202–203.
7. Zheng, *Oppositionist*, 95 and note p. 297; Link, *Mandarin Ducks*.
8. Liu, *Revolution Plus*, 17–20, 44–53; Xia, *Gate*, 62, 70, 77, 89; Zheng, *Oppositionist*, 50–51.
9. Zheng, *Oppositionist*, 94; Xia, *Gate*, 62, 73–76, 84; Li, "Ch'u," 112–116, 135.
10. Chen, *Zhong E*, 78–83.
11. Chen, *Zhong E*, 304–339.
12. Yoshihiro, *Formation*, 98; Tyerman, "Soviet Images," 38, 126–128, 149, 158, 186, 189–192.
13. Lee, *Revolution of the Heart*.
14. Ding, "Qu," 113–141 is the memoir; Qu signing as Weihu, p. 132. Fictionalized: Ding, "Wei Hu," 3–111. Partial English summary of "Wei Hu": see Liu, *Revolution Plus*, 126–134.
15. Ding, "Qu" 115–116, "Wei Hu," 4–6.
16. Ding, "Qu," 116.
17. Ding, "Wei Hu," 12.
18. Ding, "Qu," 116.
19. Ding, "Qu," 118–119.
20. Ding, "Qu," 119–120, 122.
21. Ding, "Qu," 121–125; Zhang, *Rise*, vol. 1, 298.
22. Pan, *When True Love Came*, 270–275.
23. HA, Peng papers, Box 3, Ch. 4, 5; Li, "Ch'u," 142. Ding, "Qu," 127–128.
24. Ding, "Qu," 123.

25. HA, Peng Papers, Box 3, Ch. 1, 1–7; Ch. 2, 3.
26. HA, Peng Papers, Box 3, Ch. 2, 1–3.
27. HA, Peng Papers, Box 3, Ch. 2, 3–16.
28. HA, Peng Papers, Box 3, Ch. 3, 15–18. Lively account of one such captivity: Xie, *Woman Soldier's*, 92–134.
29. HA, Peng Papers, Box 3, Ch. 3, 19–20, 24.
30. HA, Peng Papers, Box 3, Ch. 4, 14, Ch. 5, 2–3.
31. HA, Peng Papers, Box 3, Ch. 5, 20–21, 42.
32. HA, Peng Papers, Box 3, Ch. 5, 5, 10.
33. HA, Peng Papers, Box 3, Ch. 5, 10–18.
34. HA, Peng Papers, Box 3, Ch. 5, 21–22, Ch. 6, 1–2.
35. HA, Peng Papers, Box 3, Ch. 5.
36. Yang, "Yi Qiubai," 66–67.
37. Yang, "Yi Qiubai," 72; Zheng, *Oppositionist*, 140–141; Schoppa, *Blood Road*, 70.
38. Yang, "Yi Qiubai," 72–74.
39. Yang, "Yi Qiubai," 75; Zheng, *Oppositionist*, 89–90; Li, "Ch'u," 163.
40. HA, Peng Papers, Box 3, Ch. 6, 4–8.
41. HA, Peng Papers, Box 3, Ch. 6, 8–9.
42. HA, Peng Papers, Box 3, Ch. 6, 9–10.
43. HA, Peng Papers, Box 3, Ch. 7, 1.

Chapter 7

1. Chiang Kaishek is the popular Western spelling of Jiang Jieshi; I have chosen to call the father Chiang and the son Jiang.
2. Taylor, *Generalissimo's Son*, photo section after p. 188.
3. Jiang, *Biography*, 3–10; Ch'en, *Chiang*, 67.
4. Cline, *Chiang*, 153–154; Jiang, *Biography*, 13–14.
5. Peng, *Jiang*, 7–8.
6. Tuck, *Radek*, 50.
7. Yu, "Sun," 22.
8. Yu, "Sun," 17, 37, 41–42.
9. Sheng, *Sun*, 87–88; Wang, *Liu E*, 33–36; RGASPI f. 530, op. 4, d. 5, ll. 227–228; Liu, "Zi Fu," 304–307.
10. Sheng, *Sun*, 88.
11. Yu, "Sun," 148; Wang, *Liu E*, 38–39.
12. Kartunova, "Moscow's Policy," 67–68.
13. Pantsov, "Bolshevik Concepts," 30–43; Sheng, *Sun*, 33–34, 144–163.
14. English: Cline, *Jiang* Appendix, "My Days in Soviet Russia," 147–187. Chinese: Jiang, *Wo zai Sulian*.
15. Soviet autobiographers: Hellbeck, *Revolution;* foreign communists: Kirschenbaum, "Dolores."
16. Jiang, *Wo zai Sulian*, 2. All translations of Jiang's Chinese language text are my own.

17. Jiang, *Wo zai Sulian*, 2.
18. Differences in Russian and Chinese bathing rituals are a matter of frequent mention, e.g., Hu, "Liu E," 135–136; Wei, "Tan Wang," 159.
19. Jiang, *Wo zai Sulian*, 2–4.
20. Jiang, *Wo zai Sulian*, 4–8.
21. Tuck, *Radek*, 75–76, 80–81; Wang, *Liu E*, 35.
22. Sheng, *Sun*, 33–37; Ren, "Liu E," 76; Liu, "Zi Fu," 263.
23. Wang, *Liu E*, 37–38. The school acquired a dorm for married students in 1928. Sheng, "Sun," 89.
24. Gorsuch, *Youth*. Naiman, *Sex*.
25. Zheng, *Oppositionist*, 152–153.
26. RGASPI, f. 530, op. 4, d. 49, ll. 113, 116–116ob,
27. RGASPI, f. 530, op. 4, d. 49, ll. 101–101ob.
28. Hu, "Liu E," 133–136.
29. Galitskii, *Tszian*, 27, citing RGANI f. 550, op. 1, d. 2, l. 268; Yu, "Sun," 174–175.
30. Cline, *Jiang*, 157–158.
31. Galitskii, *Tszian*, 27.
32. RGASPI f. 530, op. 4, d. 49, l. 115–115ob.
33. RGASPI f. 530, op. 4, d. 49, l. 93.
34. RGASPI f. 530, op. 4, d. 49, ll. 113ob, 114, 116ob.
35. Yu, "E guo," 113–115; Galitskii, *Tszian*, 28.
36. Sheng, *Sun*, 111–116; RGASPI f. 530, op. 4, d. 5, *passim*. The Chinese wrote Rafailovshchina, inserting an "ov" into the more typical Russian formulations, Rafailshchina or Raphaelshchina.
37. RGASPI f. 532, op. 1, d. 99, ll. 5–9. The idea of merging the two groups of Chinese was much debated. RGASPI f. 532, op. 1, d. 393, ll. 14–20; d. 398, ll. 26–32; RGASPI f. 532, op. 1, d. 35, ll. 100–102; RGASPI f. 532, op. 1, d. 36, ll. 91, 94, 95; RGASPI f. 532, op. 1, d. 50, *passim*.
38. Ren, "Liu E," 73–79. Lenin's tomb was an obligatory field trip for most Chinese students. Wang, *Liu E*, 28–32.
39. Wilbur and How, *Missionaries*, 527–528.
40. RGASPI, f. 530, op. 4, d. 5, ll. 35–48; f. 532, op. 2, d. 97, ll. 15–19. Sun, "Guanyu Zhongguo," 180–183.
41. Wang, *Liu E*, 36.
42. HA, Peng Papers, Box 3, Ch. 7, 13–14.
43. Zheng, *Oppositionist*, 142–146.
44. Numerous cases of "flag-switching" described: Zheng, *Oppositionist*, 138–153; Sheng, "Sun," 113.
45. RGASPI, f. 530, op. 4, d. 49, l. 105, 113.
46. Ren, "Liu E," 76.
47. Ren, "Liu E," 76; Yu, "Sun," 103–104; RGASPI f. 530, op. 4, d. 5, 49–57, ll. 227–228. The idea of a secret, puritanical, anti-Russian, Chinese organization in Moscow haunted Soviet authorities for years—as is

evidenced by a reinvestigation of it in 1940. RGASPI f. 532, op. 4, d. 1, ll. 1–3.

48. Sheng, *Sun*, 112–116. Sheng's wife was a student in the school; presumably this account of Krupskaia's meeting with the girl students comes from her. Yu, "Sun," 133, 152–158, citing RGASPI f. 530, op. 4, d. 49, l. 105.

49. RGASPI f. 530, op. 2, d. 49, 3–4a, 80–96.

50. RGASPI f. 532, op. 1, d. 401, ll. 122–123ob.

51. Gudkov as Shen Zemin, see Go (Krymov), *Zapiski*, 179. Shen's wife, Zhang Qinqiu, was with him in Moscow. Shen came to Chinese University in November 1926. RGASPI f. 532, op. 1, d. 27, ll. 12–13; RGASPI f. 530, op. 4, d. 5, ll. 26–34.

52. Sheng, "Sun," 79–80. Sheng estimated that even after two years in Moscow less than 10 percent of Chinese students achieved Russian proficiency. High-ranking Chinese with wives/girlfriends in Moscow: Cai Hesen and Xiang Jingyu; Zhang Guotao and Yang Zilie; Wang Ming and Meng Qingshu; Zhu De and his wife, and more. Ren Bishi brought his first, arranged-marriage wife. She had bound feet and did not study. Shao Lizi came to Moscow as a widower and married a younger woman, Fu Xuewen. Others came with wives and had affairs with Russians. Sheng, "Sun," 44, 147; Praeger Young, *Choosing Revolution*, 62, 78–79; Wei, "Tan Wang," 159; Ren, "Liu E," 78.

Chapter 8

1. Sheng, *Sun*, 118–120.

2. Zhelokhovtsev, "Mayakovsky's Poetry in China," 165; L. E. Cherkasskii, *Maiakovskii v Kitae*, 62–74; Tyerman, "Soviet Images," 9–10, 60–61, 108–114, 326–354. This play was re-performed in the early 1950s and was subject to much criticism from the Chinese themselves, including Emi.

3. Trampedach, "Chiang Kaishek, 1926/27," 131.

4. Classic Trotskyist interpretation: Isaacs, *Tragedy*; Trotsky, *Trotsky on China*, esp. 149–198; Stalin: Pantsov, *Bolsheviks*, 152–153; Borodin: Jacobs, *Borodin*, 286.

5. Liu, *Revolution Plus*, Ch. 1; Smith, *Road*, 126; Wang, *Memoirs*, 29–32; Pan, *When True Love Came*, 254–275, suggests that after 1927, revolution replaced love as a focus for young Chinese radicals and that Russia became associated with loveless sex.

6. Communists after 1927: Stranahan, *Underground*; Wakeman, *Policing Shanghai*, particularly Ch. 9, "Reds." Tyerman, "Soviet Images," 355–413 is an extended discussion of the "bio-interview."

7. Wang, *Memoirs*, 42.

8. Sheng, *Sun*, 48; Wang, *Memoirs*, 44. Similar reaction to Spanish exiles after Republican defeat: Young, "To Russia with Spain."

9. RGASPI, f. 532, op. 1, d. 35, ll. 117–118.

10. Elleman, *Moscow and Nanchang*, 122–138.

11. Li, "Ch'u," 270–273. On Guangdong: Tsin, *Canton*.

12. Deutscher, *Prophet Unarmed*, 286–288.

13. Pantsov, *Bolsheviks*, 123.

14. Pantsov, *Bolsheviks*, 183–184. No arrests: Wang, *Memoirs*, 62–67.

15. Pantsov, *Bolsheviks*, 189–208. Zheng, *Oppositionist*, xv–xvi. Chen describes their fate vividly in her memoir. HA, Peng Papers, Box 3.

16. Zhang, *Rise*, vol. 2, 68; Wang, *Memoirs*, 116–117.

17. Du and Wang, *Hongse houdai*, 15–16: the memoir of Qu Duyi, who was six at the time.

18. Smith, "Moscow," 222–227; Eiermann, "Chinese Comintern Delegates"; Eiermann, "Chinesische Komintern-Delegierte." Tensions among translators: RGAPSI f. 530, op. 4, d. 5, *passim*.

19. Harrison, *Long March*, 156. These numbers of delegates come from 1950s Communist Party histories; no list is included in relatively recently published document collections such as Go and Titarenko, *VKPb, Komintern i Kitai* or Saich, *Maring*.

20. Sheng, *Sun*, 184–187.

21. Sheng, *Sun*, 185.

22. Steve Smith, "Moscow," 238. Based on a careful examination of the evidence, Smith concludes: "The brute fact was that a national revolution based on workers and peasants, capable of proceeding in a socialist direction, could not have succeeded in 1927 because objective conditions were overwhelmingly unfavorable."

23. Zhang, *Rise*, vol. 2, 75–76.

24. Zhang, *Rise*, vol. 2, 78; Sheng, *Sun*, 187–197.

25. The other Politburo members were Xiang Zhongfa, Li Lisan, Zhou Enlai, Cai Hesen, Zhang Guotao, and Xiang Ying. Harrison, *Long March*, 165–157. Of the twenty-odd Central Committee members elected, 11 had already or subsequently would study in the Soviet Union. Bartke, *Biographical Dictionary*, 364–365; Zhang, *Rise*, vol. 2, 83–84.

26. Zhang, *Rise*, vol. 2, 114–115.

27. Zhang, *Rise*, vol. 2, 114–115.

28. Zhang, *Rise*, vol. 2, 116.

29. Brown, "Russification of Wang," 5–6, quoting Feng Yuxiang. On rector in 1925: see Ch. 4 of this book.

30. Brown, "Russification of Wang," 14–32. Wang Ming left no detailed firsthand account of his early years in Moscow; even a recently published memoir contains little about his Soviet 1920s and 1930s. Wang, *Huiyilu*; Zhang, *Rise*, vol. 2, 77.

31. Sheng, *Sun*, 205–228.

32. Smith, *Revolution*, 58–66.

33. Heated debates about zemliachestvo in 1928: RGASPI, f. 530, op. 4, d. 5, *passim*; Mif as instigator, l. 213; Chinese restaurants, l. 26; see also Yu, "Sun," 203–205.

34. Wang, *Er shi jiu*; Sheng, *Sun*, 205–261.
35. Zhang, *Rise*, vol. 2, 87–91.
36. Zhang, *Rise*, vol. 2, 94–96.
37. Zhang, *Rise*, vol. 2, 95; Sheng, *Sun*, 218–219.
38. Zhang, *Rise*, vol. 2, 95.
39. Sheng, *Sun*, 178.
40. Ma, *Lu Su*, 124–125.
41. Pantsov, *Bolsheviks*, 204–206.
42. Pantsov, *Bolsheviks*, 207–208; Pantsov and Spichak, "New Light," 32–45. Daria Spichak is the leading expert on Chinese students at the International Lenin School (MLSh). According to the admittedly incomplete information contained in the Sakharov Center database, in June of 1929, one Li Haozhou, of primary education only and unknown occupation, was sentenced to death for espionage; he was shot on September 16, 1930. Only later in the 1930s were larger numbers of Chinese sentenced to death.
43. Sheng, *Sun*, 223–224; Sin-Lin, *Shattered Families*, n. 52, p. 441, notes that Qu's brother had been exiled; Wang, *Memoirs*, 82; Zhang, *Rise*, vol. 2, 102–105.
44. Spence, *Search*, 387–399. Zhang tells the story of his own Long March in vol. 2 of his memoirs, pp. 181–473.
45. Usov, *Sovetskaia Razvedka*, 222–239; Whymant, *Sorge*, 30–40.
46. Wakeman, *Policing Shanghai*, 135–142.
47. Notable examples include Yang Shangkun, who was president of China 1988–1993 and who played a key role in the outcome of the Tiananmen Square demonstrations, as well as Wang Jiaxiang and Zhang Wentian, who were both early PRC ambassadors to the Soviet Union and major figures in PRC diplomacy. Bartke, Biographical Dictionary, 268–269, 216–217, 303.
48. Fu, "Zhui nian Qu," 261; Widmer, "Qu," 118–122; Pickowicz, *Marxist Literary*, Chs. 6–11, engage carefully with Qu's literary polemics.
49. Barlow, "'History's Coffin,'" 282–284.
50. Pickowicz, *Marxist Literary*, 192, 209; Xu, *Qu Qiubai yu Lu Xun*. Mao Dun describes how Qu helped shape his writing in Mao Dun, "Hui yi Qiubai," 254–259.
51. Yang, *From Revolution*, 73–82. Yang argues that the Russia connection was not decisive in faction formation.
52. Chang and Halliday, *Mao*, 113–119, 122.
53. Xia, "Ch'u"—the translations here are from him. Newer work that reinterprets "Superfluous Words" as a prism for Qu's biography: Roux and Wang, *Des mots de trop*.
54. Qu, "Duoyu," 35–36. My translation.
55. Xia, "Ch'u," 212. I use Xia's translation here.
56. North, *Moscow and Chinese*, 165.
57. Xia, "Ch'u," 205–211.

Chapter 9

1. RGASPI f. 530, op. 4, d. 49, l. 80–81.
2. Yu, "E guo," 120.
3. RGASPI f. 530, op. 4, d. 49, l. 89–91; Yu, "E guo," 111.
4. Sheng, *Sun*, 89, 113.
5. Sheng, *Sun*, 122.
6. Galitskii, *Tszian*, 55–63; Yu, "E guo," 123–124.
7. Sheng, *Sun*, 141–143. Shao Lizi's son sent him a similar letter: "You are a counter-revolutionary you are no longer my father and henceforth shall be my enemy." Smith, *Road*, 123.
8. Jiang, *Wo zai Sulian*, 21–29. In his English memoirs he calls this person "General Malshev"; it is possible this was Malyshev, who was a Tolmachev graduate and also ran summer camps to teach military skills to students from Chinese University.
9. Galitskii, *Tszian*, 22, 80–81.
10. Jiang, *Wo zai Sulian*, 38–44.
11. These letters are wonderful glimpses of Chinese life in unmediated contact with the Soviet Union. Hundreds of pages of handwritten Chinese originals are in RGASPI f. 514, op. 1, d. 601, 602, 603, 604 and 973, 974.
12. Galitskii, *Tszian*, 80–87.
13. Jiang, *Wo zai Sulian*, 46–48; Cline, *Chiang*, 170–174.
14. Cline, *Chiang*, 170–174; Galitskii, *Tszian*, 93–94, citing RTsKhIDNI (RGASPI), f. 495, op. 225, d. 932, ll. 30, 117.
15. Hellbeck, *Revolution*. Kotkin, *Magnetic Mountain*. Lahusen, *How Life*.
16. Jiang, *Wo zai Sulian*, 49–52.
17. Cline, *Chiang*, 174–177; Galitskii, *Tszian*, 228.
18. Galitskii, *Tszian*, 119.
19. Cline, *Chiang*, 182.
20. Galitskii, *Tszian*, 139, 142.
21. Jiang, *Wo zai Sulian*, 66.
22. Cline, *Chiang*, 186–187.

Chapter 10

1. Kishkina, *Iz Rossii*, 86
2. Kishkina, *Iz Rossii*, 85.
3. Kishkina, *Iz Rossii*, 11, 13–14, 20–21, 31.
4. Kishkina, *Iz Rossii*, 21–22.
5. Kishkina, *Iz Rossii*, 13, 18, 25.
6. Kishkina, *Iz Rossii*, 34, 36–38, 43, 47–48.
7. Kishkina, *Iz Rossii*, 11, 49–53, 59.
8. Kishkina, *Iz Rossii*, 62–63, 66–68.
9. Kishkina, *Iz Rossii*, 73–75, 89.
10. Kishkina, *Iz Rossii*, 80, 89–90.

11. Kishkina, *Iz Rossii*, 86.
12. Kishkina, *Iz Rossii*, 77–79.
13. Kishkina, *Iz Rossii*, 88–93. Multigenerational Sinologists in Vladivostok: Kriukov, *29 Ulitsa Mol'era*.
14. Kishkina, *Iz Rossii*, 97.
15. Kishkina, *Iz Rossii*, 95. Interviews and conversations by author with Liza, family and friends, Beijing, Fall 2004.
16. Kishkina, *Iz Rossii*, 97–98.
17. Kishkina, *Iz Rossii*, 98–99.
18. Photo: Spence, *Search*, photo after p. 327.
19. Kishkina, *Iz Rossii*, 99.
20. Kishkina, *Iz Rossii*, 101–102.
21. Kishkina, *Iz Rossii*, 101–103.
22. Kishkina, *Iz Rossii*, 103–104.
23. Kishkina, *Iz Rossii*, 106–112.
24. Kishkina, *Iz Rossii*, 113.
25. Kishkina, *Iz Rossii*, 113–114.
26. Kishkina, *Iz Rossii*, 117–118, 120.
27. Kishkina, *Iz Rossii*, 117, 120.
28. "Save the Homeland" was *Jiu guo shi bao*, published in New York, 1938.
29. Wang, *Kua guo zhi lian*, 91.
30. Him, *Chinese American,* 65, 84 and 85.
31. Wang, *Kua guo zhi lian*, 53–76.
32. Lescot, *Before Mao*, 165–167. First published in French in 1999 as *L'Empire Rouge: Moscow-Pekin, 1919–1989,* the book came out in English in 2004 under two separate titles, *The Red Empires: A Tale of Love Divided* and *Before Mao.*
33. RGASPI, f. 514, op. 1, d. 973, ll. 6–7.
34. RGASPI, f. 514, op. 1, d. 973, ll. 42–43.
35. RGASPI, f. 514, op. l. 41.
36. RGASPI, f. 514, op. ll. 41–43.
37. RGASPI, f. 514, op. l. 40.
38. Kishkina, *Iz Rossii*, 140.
39. Kishkina, *Iz Rossii*, 147.
40. Kishkina, *Iz Rossii*, 149, 152.
41. Kishkina, *Iz Rossii*, 186–216.
42. Kishkina, *Iz Rossii*, 225–228.

Chapter 11

1. Khikmet, *Izbrannoe*, 275–288, Russian translation. English: Hikmet, *Poems*, 6–7. Hikmet blurred Chinese demonstrations in Paris during the May 30 Movement in 1925 and events in China in 1927. As Hikmet well knew, Emi left France in 1921.

2. Meisner, *Mao*, 40–41; Terrill, *Mao*, 100; Chang and Halliday, *Mao*, 34–35; Wang, *Xiao*, 200–226; Smith, *Road*, 172–173.

3. Wang, *Xiao*, 230; Siao, *Shi ji*, 22. Photo: Gao, *Xiao*, 303.

4. Siao, *Shi ji*, 21; Wang, *Xiao*, 231; Kishkina, *Iz Rossii*, 290: "Lively, energetic, he attracted female attention."

5. RGASPI, f. 495, op. 225, d. 96, l. 30. This is the *lichnoe delo* for Emi Siao which appeared to be organized in chronological order, backward. All subsequent references to page numbers in this file are counting from the back.

6. Wang, *Xiao*, 229–231.

7. RGASPI, f. 495, op. 225, d. 96, l. 30; Wang, *Xiao*, 234–236; Siao, *Shi ji*, 21.

8. RGASPI, f. 495, op. 255, d. 96, ll. 22–29; Wang, *Xiao*, 237.

9. RGASPI, f. 495, op. 255, d. 96, l. 30.

10. Wang, *Xiao*, 239–240; RGASPI, f. 495, op. 255, d. 96, ll. 30, 33–34.

11. Xiao, *Shi wenji*, 195–197; Wang, *Xiao*, 244–247.

12. Reznik, "Romm's Unpublished," 2–10. Drucker, "Formalism's Other," 750. Tsareva, "Romm."

13. Xiao, *Shi wenji*, vol. 2, 197. Gao Tao, *Xiao*, 235–238; RGALI, f. 1495, op. 1, d. 101, l. 2.

14. RGALI, f. 1495, op. 1, d. 101, l. 2.

15. RGALI, f. 1495, op. 1, d. 131, l. 3–8. Xiao, *Shi wenji*, vol. 2, 197.

16. Xiao, *Izbrannoe*, 11–14; Xiao, *Shi wenji*, 18–21.

17. Siao, *Shi ji*, 13.

18. Wang, *Xiao*, 248, Gao Tao, *Xiao*, 1, 8–10, 240.

19. Martin, *Affirmative Action Empire*, 185–200.

20. De Francis, *Nationalism and Language*, 92–97. Chinese language reform is, of course, a major issue of scholarly research in its own right: Zhou, *Language Policy*; Emi: RGASPI f. 514, op. 1, d. 666, l. 13–320b.

21. RGASPI, f. 495, op. 225, d. 96, l. 40–43.

22. Among the writers Emi wrote to invite was Cao Jinghua, with whom he had attended Eastern University in the early 1920s and who was at the time teaching and translating in Leningrad, but Cao could not attend. He was, according to Emi, in the process of disguising his entire family as ordinary "overseas Chinese" to return to China and could not publicly represent "left-wing" writers. Xiao, *Shi wenji*, vol. 2, 198.

23. "Stenograficheskii otchet," 365–366.

24. Wang, *Xiao*, 272–278.

25. Hu, "In a German Women's Prison," 74–75; Kisch, *Egon*.

26. RGALI, f. 631, op. 1, d. 836, l. 1–23. Quote: p. 6.

27. Siao, *Shi ji*, 5.

28. Siao, *Shi ji*, 7–8. It seems likely that this collective farm was one of the model sites described by David-Fox, *Showcasing*, 106–122.

29. Siao, *Shi ji*, 22–23.

30. Siao, *Shi ji*, 14.
31. Siao, *Shi ji*, 17–18.
32. Xiao, *Izbrannoe*, 105–109.
33. RGALI, f. 1495, op. 1, d. 101, l. 4.
34. RGALI, f. 631, op. 15, d. 199, l. 47–56. Quote: 48–49.
35. RGALI, f. 631, op. 15, d. 199, l. 55–56.
36. Fitzpatrick, *Cultural Front*, 196–205; Clark, *Fourth Rome*, 211–212.
37. Clark, *Fourth Rome*, 242–251.
38. Siao, *Shi ji*, 21, 26–28.
39. Siao, *Shi ji*, photo section, 14, 31.
40. Pirozhkova, *Vospominaniia*, 289.
41. Siao, *Shi ji*, 48.
42. Siao, *Shi ji*, 24.
43. Siao, *Shi ji*, 41; Gao, *Xiao*, 300–305.
44. Siao, *Shi ji*, 46–54.
45. Xiao, *Shi wenji*, vol. 2, 200–201.
46. RGASPI f. 514, op. 1, d. 1040, ll. 4–7.
47. RGASPI f. 514, op. 1, d. 1040, ll. 72–74.
48. Chang and Halliday, *Mao*, 208, 217.
49. RGASPI, f. 495, op. 225, d. 96, l. 57.
50. RGASPI, f. 495, op. 225, d. 96, l. 50–51.
51. RGASPI, f. 495, op. 225, d. 96, ll. 57–58, 40–43; English language version of Mao biography: Siao, *Mao*.
52. Siao, *Shi ji*, 56.
53. Siao, *Shi ji*, 54–58. Advocating for release: Interview by author, Xiao Weijia, Beijing, August 2005; Proceeds and activities: RGASPI, f. 495, op. 225, d. 96, l. 59, 62; RGALI f. 1495, op. 1, d. 131, l. 13.
54. Wang, *Xiao*, 348–350.

Chapter 12

1. Since it is awkward in English to call her "He," she is referred to here as Zizhen.
2. Chang and Halliday, *Mao*, 22–25, 81–87.
3. Wang, *He Zizhen*; Chang and Halliday, *Mao*, 58–59.
4. Cheng, *He*, 20, 50; Ip, "Fashioning Appearances," 344.
5. Wang, *He Zizhen*, 17; Cheng, *He*, 74–82.
6. Averill, *Jinggangshan*, 77–78, 180, 188. Averill cites the local historian Liu Xiaonong, who wrote "Mao Zedong dierci hunyin neiqing" as well as a historical novel called *Jinggang yanyi*. Chang and Halliday, *Mao*, 58.
7. The first child was a daughter who was lost and apparently died; the second was a son who was left behind with her sister, who was married to Mao's little brother Zetan. A third child had died a few months after birth. Chang and Halliday, *Mao*, 59 and 111, 124–125.

8. Gilmartin, *Engendering*, 215–216; Praeger Young, *Choosing Revolution*; Shu, *Long March*, 132–155.
9. Chang and Halliday, *Mao*, 148–151.
10. Li, *Moi otets*, 1.
11. Li, *Moi otets*, 3–7.
12. Niu, *Ya'nan to the World*.
13. Price, *Agnes Smedley*, 303–309.
14. Wang, *Xiao*, 290, 295–299, 306–311.
15. RGALI f. 631, op. 15, d. 510, l. 9–9a.
16. Siao, *Shi ji*, 66–67.
17. Xiao, "Wang Shi," 528.
18. Wang, *Xiao*, 313.
19. Wang, *Xiao*, 278, 313–317. Emi also spoke at the Yan'an forum but apparently did not deliver his talk very well.
20. Siao, *Shi ji*, 67–93.
21. Emi's relationship with the Chinese woman: Jiang, "Ganlou yu Xiao," 42–45.
22. Price, *Agnes Smedley*, 315–320; Chang and Halliday, *Mao*, 195; Snow, "Mao's Love Affair," cited in Price, 310
23. RGASPI, f. 495, op. 225, d. 420, ll. 5–6 on her arrival with a group of sick party members and a brief note admitting her to the Kremlin's Polyklinik no. 1 on January 20, 1938. In the Russian archives she appears under the pseudonym "Ven Iun."
24. RGASPI, f. 495, op. 225, d. 420, l. 4. Zizhen's *roddom* was called Sechenov.
25. Li, *Moi Otets*, 12–14.
26. Lee, *Manchuria;* Levine, *Anvil of Victory*.
27. RGASPI f. 532, op. 1, d. 402, ll. 52–56. Sukharchuk, "Uchennyi- Internatsionalist."
28. Byron and Pack, *Kang Sheng*, 112–114, 117–118, 122–123; Yu, "Sun," 291–297; Mayer, *The Furies*.
29. Byron and Pack, 112–114, 122–123; RGASPI f. 532, op. 2, d. 107, *passim*.
30. RGASPI f. 532, op. 2, d. 107, ll. 7–16. If the Chinese students were not taken to see the performance, it might also have been because it was considered too elite—Mei inspired long theoretical responses from cultural giants including Eisenstein, and Brecht, as well as Sergei Tretiakov; Clark, *Fourth Rome*, 192–209.
31. Kraevskii's lectures: RGASPI f. 532, op. 1, d. 171, ll. 1–73. Quote: ll. 15–19.
32. RGASPI f. 532, op. 1, d. 402, 139–143a. Battle of Madrid November 1936 especially influential among international socialists, including Mao: Tanner, *Battle for Manchuria*, 8–9. One Chinese woman at the school named her baby daughter Dora after Dolores Ibarruri. Similar enthusiasm on the part of Soviet citizens: Kirschenbaum, "Dolores Ibarruri"; Soviet citizens naming children Dolores, Young, "To Russia with Spain," 404.

33. RGASPI f. 532, op. 1, d. 402, ll. 35–36, 39–40.
34. RGASPI f. 495, op. 18, d. 1073, ll. 191–192. My thanks to Shen Zhihua for providing me with a copy of this document. RGASPI f. 532, op. 1, d. 402, ll. 119–123.
35. RGASPI f. 532, op. 1, d. 404, ll. 69–70. Weapons, location: 66–68.
36. RGASPI f. 532, op. 1, d. 405, l. 23.
37. RGASPI f. 532, op. 1, d. 40, ll. 23–230b.
38. RGASPI f. 532, op. 1, d. 405, ll. 23–24. Reports on individual students note their relationships with women (including Eastern University employee Mariia Kirsanova) or nights away from school. One Van Khuan (born 1908, a partisan in 1933–34) was said to have met a girl named Lena Gavrilova, who got pregnant by him. RGASPI f. 532, op. 1, d. 405, 50–60.
39. RGASPI f. 532, op. 1, d. 405, 26–260b.
40. RGASPI f. 532, op. 1, d. 404, ll. 58–60. Kang Sheng's action, p. 60.
41. RGASPI f. 532, op. 1, d. 403, ll. 59–67 is the entire report; Q & A: 62–63.
42. RGASPI f. 532, op. 1, d. 404, ll. 58.
43. Fitzpatrick describes the ongoing controversies in Soviet society more generally over abandoned wives in the 1930s in *Everyday Stalinism*, 143–147.
44. RGASPI, f. 514, op. 1, d. 973, ll. 48–51.
45. "Yi Su Keqin," 30–51. The story was corroborated in interviews by the author with her daughters' friends in Beijing in 2004. Similar observations regarding Spanish exiles during these years, including difficulties in defining "appropriate" romance and "good" women: Kirschenbaum, "Dolores Ibarruri," 574–575, 581–583, 586–587.
46. For a popular, contemporary version of this story [in Chinese] see http://sq.k12.com.cn/discuz/thread-343378-1-1.html.
47. Sin Lin, *Shattered Families*, 345; Postoiannaia, *Butovskii Poligon.* Sakharov Center database includes over sixty Chinese sentenced to death, including numerous people who are listed as working in laundries, and about a half dozen students from the Eastern University, Colonial Research Institute, or the Moscow Lenin School.
48. The Mao brothers remembered that she studied at Eastern University even before she gave birth.
49. Lin, "Wangshi," 95; Shi, *Zai Lishi*, 132.
50. Lin, "Wangshi"; RGASPI f. 495, op. 30, d. 1206, ll. 1–25, 1–5 for Zhou's letter.
51. Failure to improve health: RGASPI f. 495, op. 30, d. 1206, ll. 1–5; Closure of school and dispersal of students: GARF f. 8265, op. 4, d. 70, ll. 1–61; d. 76, l. 16.

Chapter 13

1. Jian, "Bol' i schast'e," 4.
2. Ball, *Abandoned Children.* 176–178, 183–184.

3. Tuya/Qu Duyi, interview by author, Beijing, August 2004; Qu, "Nan yi minmie de jiyi," 15–16.
4. Tuya/Qu Duyi, interview by author. Vaskino as a summer house for Eastern University: RGAPSI, f. 532, op. 1, d. 26. Vaskino as a home for eighty foreign children: GARF f. 8265, op. 1, d. 672, ll. 1, 11.
5. Xiao, *Shi xuan*, 34–36.
6. Interview by author, Zhao Shige, Beijing, September 2004.
7. Kishkina, *Iz Rossii*, 111–112.
8. Vova Neverov/Shen Linru, interview by author, Beijing, Fall 2004.
9. Kishkina, *Iz Rossii*, 93; RGASPI f. 495, op. 225, d. 1144, l. 3.
10. I have completed the research for a history of this home, tentatively titled *Communist Neverland: History of a Russian International Children's Home. 1933–2013.*
11. Some of these children are listed clearly in the school's record books, others (Dennis, Pak, Bierut) I have interviewed, others are simply well-known in the oral history of the school or are listed in memoirs, e.g., Sin-Lin, *Shattered Families.* 86–87.
12. These statistics come from my own database, compiled from the Interdom's record books of students and their arrivals and departures, "Osnovnaia Kniga," and "Kniga Ucheta."
13. "Broshiura Fritsa Beisa o detskom dome MOPRa v g. Ivanovo, Stat'ia p polozhenii detei politzakliuchennykh 1922–1936" in RGASPI f. 539, o. 5, d. 35, ll. 82–115; *Internatsional'nyi Maiak*, e.g., no. 17–18, June 1932, p. 13, and no. 31, November 1932, pp. 10–11; Postcards: Sofia Ivanovna Kuznetsova, interview by author, Ivanovo, Fall 2005.
14. GARF, f. 8265, op. 1, d. 55.
15. Zhao Shige, interviews by author, fall 2004. Photo albums and loose photos in Interdom archive depict the bears and toys.
16. Group memoir of Chinese Interdom students is a rich source on life in the home: Du and Wang, *Hongse houdai*.
17. Jian, "Bol' i schast'e," 6.
18. Jian, "Bol' i schast'e," 7.
19. Jian, "Bol' i schast'e," 9.
20. Tuya, interview by author. Yang: RGASPI, f. 495, op. 205, d. 554, l. 40b.
21. RGASPI, f. 17, op. 130, d. 10, ll. 10, 49; d. 16, ll. 38–42.
22. RGASPI f. 532, op. 1, d. 403, l. 3.
23. RGASPI, f. 495, op. 225, d. 2799, l. 7. MOPR may have funded a children's home in Shanghai in 1930: RGASPI, f. 539, op. 3, d. 21.
24. Du and Wang, "Bu kui Mao," 63–66; Chang and Halliday, *Mao*, 177–178, 190–191.
25. RGASPI, f. 532, op. 1, d. 403, ll. 63–64.
26. RGASPI, f. 532, op. l, l. 64.
27. RGASPI, f. 532, op. 1, d. 403.

28. RGASPI, f. 532, op. 1, ll. 63–65; interview by author, Tuya; in Interdom records Karl was listed in the "Uchetnaia kniga," entry number 499, "Strakhov Karl (Tsiu-Tsiu Karl). Strakhov had been Qu's Russian pseudonym, though Qu had kept his Chinese name in Russian, Tsiu Tsiubo. Tuya was not the only young woman from the youth sector to have a child there; Su Zhaozheng's daughter "Liva" gave birth at age nineteen. RGASPI f. 495, op. 225, d. 2800, l. 6.

29. GARF f. 8265, op. 1, d. 100, ll. 102–132.

30. Zhao Shige, interview by author; GARF f. 8265, op. 4, d. 70, l. 49 refers to "Dom otdykha TsK MOPR SSSR v Monino Byv. Vtoroi IDD" and is dated November 26, 1939, indicating that by then Monino was no longer functioning as a children's home. At the same time, this document is one of several sending Chinese adults and children to Monino.

31. Qualls, "Niños to Soviets?"

32. Shi, *Zai lishi*, 99. Lists: GARF f. 8265, op. 4, d. 70, ll. 5, 9, 15, 16, 18.

33. GARF f. 8265, op. 4, d. 60, ll. 121, 136.

34. GARF f. 8265, op. 4, d. 70, ll. 47 and 48 are lists of children who arrived in Moscow on November 16 and November 23.

35. Liu, "Zai shenghuo," 132–138.

36. Du and Wang, "Xin Zhongguo," 343–345; Chen Xiaoda, "Bu gai," *Hongse houdai*, 449–453.

37. Jian, "Bol' i schast'e," 11.

38. Content of "Monument": Turner, *Translations*, 24.

39. Liu, "Zai shenghuo," 139–140.

40. Din-Savva, *Iz Moskvy*, 24–25; Li, *Moi Otets*, 17–18.

41. *Hong Yingtao* (Red Cherry) was made in 1995 about the Interdom during the war. It is available with English subtitles in some US libraries.

42. Du and Wang, "Shuai men," 205–211.

43. GARF, f. 8265, op. 4, d. 139, ll. 1–24.

44. RGASPI, f. 495, op. 73, d. 180, ll. 18, 20–24. GARF f. 8265, op. 1, d. 221, 172–173, 197–199; op. 4, d. 104, ll. 11–24. Many stories of wartime experiences in Du and Wang, *Hongse houdai*, e.g., 99–102.

45. Fritz Shtraube, interviews by author, Berlin, August 2005 and July 2008. Similar relief among some Spanish child refugees: Qualls, "From Niños to Soviets?", 290–291.

46. Shtraube, interviews by author; letter from Fernanda Lacerda to me, July 29, 2008.

47. Shtraube, interviews by author; RGASPI, f. 495, op. 73, d. 180, ll. 19–20.

48. Usov, "Kitaiskie vospitanniki," 109. Usov takes the letters from a collection of Mao's writings. On the Interdom's attempts to procure Chinese language materials, see GARF f. 8265, op. 1, d. 277, l. 17; interview by author, Monia Kibalchik, Beijing, October 2004.

49. RGASPI f. 495, op. 73, d. 180, ll. 14–15; f. 495, op. 225, d. 2799, l. 23.

50. The original letters are in the local Ivanovo archive, Ivanovo Gosudarvennyi Arkhiv, f. r-25, op.1, d. 9.

51. Letter from Serezha to Fritz, 1943, in Fritz's personal archive. Serezha thanks Fritz "with all his heart for the open, honest, comradely criticism" Fritz has given him.

52. Zhao Shige, "Shuo shuo wo de xiao huo ban he wo ziji," 308–309.

53. Yura, interview by author.

54. Yura, interview by author.

55. Yura, interview by author.

56. Zhao Shige, interview by author.

57. Du and Wang, *Hongse houdai*, 55–56, 101–103.

58. Usov, "O Zhizni," 106–107.

59. Du and Wang, *Hongse houdai*, 102, 346–352.

Chapter 14

1. Liu, "Zai shenghuo," 142. Aiqin remembered that when her father saw her dresses he "shook his head with dissatisfaction."

2. Chen, *Mao's China and the Cold War*, 44–46; Chen, "The Sino-Soviet Alliance," 11–17; Radchenko and Wolff, "To the Summit," 110–111.

3. Study or work: Liu Shaoqi, Zhu De, Ren Bishi, Chen Yun, Kang Sheng, Dong Biwu, Lin Boqu, Zhang Wentian, and Deng Xiaoping. Children or adopted children: Liu, Zhu, Lin, Zhang, plus Mao Zedong, Zhou Enlai, and Gao Gang. No affiliation: Peng Zhen, Peng Dehuai. Information compiled from Bartke, *Biographical Dictionary*, and Du and Wang, *Hongse houdai*.

4. Liu, "Zai shenghuo," 142–143.

5. Liu, "Zai shenghuo," 142–143.

6. Interview by author, Liu Aiqin, Beijing, fall 2004; Liu, "Zai shenghuo," 141–142.

7. Siao, *Shi ji*, photo section.

8. Siao, *Shi ji*, 102–103.

9. Siao, *Shi ji*, 102–103; Siao, *China*, 206–207.

10. Siao, *Shiji*, 101–103; Siao, *China*, 204.

11. Siao, *Shiji*, 107–108.

12. Siao, *Shiji*, 108–111.

13. Hess, "Big Brother," 161; Yu, "Learning," 105–106.

14. Hess, "Big Brother," 178.

15. Hess, "Big Brother," 112; Pringsheim, "Sino-Soviet Friendship" 151–164. On construction of Soviet-style buildings to house Friendship Societies in numerous cities, as well as later construction of Beijing's Soviet Exhibition Center, see Li, "Building Friendship."

16. Siao, *Shiji*, 112; Xiao, "Sulian de wenhua."

17. Siao, *Shiji*, 114.

18. Pringsheim, "Friendship Association," 33.

19. Pringsheim, "Friendship Association," 37.
20. "Su wenhua daibiao"; Pringsheim, "Friendship Association," 41.
21. "Zong Su," Yu, "Learning," 102; Siao, *Shiji*, 122–124.
22. Wolff and Radchenko, "To the Summit," 111.
23. Comprehensive description of Mao-Stalin talks in English: Heinzig, *Soviet Union*, 263–384.
24. "Record of Conversation." Tone: Westad, "Unwrapping."
25. Shen, "1950 nian."
26. Radchenko and Wolff, "To the Summit," 105.
27. Radchenko and Wolff, "To the Summit," 106–109, 111; Chang and Halliday, *Mao*, 338–339, 350–351.
28. Chang and Halliday, *Mao*, 350.
29. Chang and Halliday, *Mao*, 351–353.
30. Zubok, "'To Hell with Yalta!'" 25; Chang and Halliday, *Mao*, 351–353.
31. Zubok, "'To Hell with Yalta!'" 24–27; Westad, "Fighting for Friendship," 224–226.
32. Wolff and Radchenko, "To the Summit," 111; Chang and Halliday, *Mao*, 352–355.
33. Honeymoon: Shen and Xia, "Hidden Currents during the Honeymoon." Earlier useage: Luthi, *Sino-Soviet Split*, 38, quotes John Gittings's use of the term "honeymoon," in his *Survey of the Sino-Soviet Dispute*, 19. Marriage: Dittmer, *Sino-Soviet Normalization*, 167.
34. Experts: Jersild, *Sino-Soviet Alliance*; Shen, *Sulian zhuanjia*; Kaple, "Soviet Advisors."
35. Jersild, *Sino-Soviet Alliance*, 31, 39–42, 45–46.
36. Li, *Mao and the Economic*; Kaple, "Agents of Change."
37. http://www.china-underground.com/magazine/cool-sino-soviet-propaganda-images. Accessed July 5, 2015. Other images show two men, one Chinese and one Russian, holding in hands in various poses, sometimes standing very close with arms around shoulders, with hands intertwined, or embracing.

Chapter 15

1. Wang, *Ban sheng,* 60.
2. Wang, *Ban sheng,* 60; Gladkov, *Cement.*
3. Tanner, *Battle for Manchuria*, 44–47.
4. Yick, *Urban Revolution,* 6, 66–68.
5. Wang, *Ban sheng*, 40–41.
6. Wang, *Ban sheng*, 58.
7. Wang, *Ban sheng*, 39–40.
8. Wang, *Ban sheng*, 42, 54. Role of charismatic students in general: Yick, *Making Urban Revolution*, 40–45.
9. Wang, *Ban sheng*, 54, 58, 60; Curiously, both "I am the son of the working people" and "Rainbow" had been translated into Chinese by Qu Qiubai's

old friend, Cao Jinghua. Chen, *Zhong E*, 327, 340–341; Robert Busch, "Gladkov's Cement."

10. Wang, *Ban sheng*, 61.
11. Arrests of student communists in Beijing in the fall of 1947: Yick, 112–113.
12. Wang, *Ban sheng*, 63.
13. Wang, *Ban sheng*, 65.
14. Wang, *Ban sheng*, 75–81, 86–91.
15. Wang, *Ban sheng*, 107.
16. Volland, "Translating," 66. Volland argues that translations from foreign literature were somewhat protected from the new regime's determination to achieve linguistic conformity in literature. Volland, "Linguistic Enclave"; Chen, *Zhong E,* 159.
17. He, "Coming of Age," 406; Yu, "Pavel Korchagin."
18. Tyerman, "Soviet Images," 93–94; Clark, *Soviet Novel*.
19. He, "Coming of Age," 403–404, quoting Wang Meng, *Season of Love*, 9.
20. He, "Coming of Age," 403, quoting Chinese writer Liu Xinwu.
21. Chen, "Film and Gender," 423, 425, 428–430.
22. Chen, "Film and Gender," 430–431, 438–439.
23. Wang, *Ban sheng*, 90.
24. Wang, *Ban sheng*. Zoya was a household name in China because a Soviet children's book about her had been released in translation in 1952 with a print run of 1.3 million copies, additional versions for young children, and a side-by-side Chinese/Russian version for language students. Volland, "Translating," 63.
25. Wang, *Ban sheng*, 90.
26. Wang, *Ban sheng*, 108. Pushkin translation from Russian original, mine.
27. Wang, *Ban sheng*, 108, 117. Tolstoy, *Anna Karenina*, 26–29.
28. Wang, *Ban sheng*, 110–112.
29. Melvin and Cai, *Rhapsody in Red*, 165; Jones, *Yellow Music*; Yu, "Cong gao."
30. Yu "Cong gao"; Wang, *Ban sheng*, 89.
31. Wang, *Ban sheng*, 120–126.
32. Wagner, *Chinese Prose*, 194–195. Later a Chinese theater group attempted a stage version of the story. Jersild, *Sino-Soviet Alliance*, 152.
33. Wang, *The Butterfly*, 189–190.
34. Wang, *The Butterfly*, 210, 213–214.
35. Wang, *The Butterfly*, 216, 236–238. Wagner, *Chinese Prose*.
36. Wagner, *Chinese Prose*, 203.
37. Zha, "Servant."
38. Wang, *Ban sheng*, 126.

Chapter 16

1. Cheng, *Zhang*, 589.
2. Zhu, *Xiwang (jixu)*, 417, 421, 426.
3. Cheng, *Zhang*, 105.

4. Wang and Dong, *Tebie jingli*, 123–124.
5. Li, *Zhonghua,* vol. 1, 220. This is a two-volume collection of official documents regarding Chinese students abroad after 1949. Zhu, *Xiwang (jixu)*, 441; RGANI, f. 535, op. 1, d. 58, l. 9; RGASPI, f. m1, op. 46, d. 248, l. 11.
6. Zhu, *Xiwang (jixu),* 441. In seeking Soviet technical, not political expertise, the Chinese were typical of postwar foreign students from developing countries. Engerman, "Second World's," 205–207.
7. Li, *Zhonghua,* contains numerous documents on student selection, e.g. pp. 98, 11–112, 118–119.
8. Redlining: Li, *Zhonghua*, 148; Liu: Liu Shaoqi to Li Fuchun, September 18, 1952. I received a copy of this document from the Ministry of Education archives from a team of researchers led by Zhou Wen at Huadong Shifan Daxue's Russian Research Center. Li's daughter: interview by author, Vova Neverov, Beijing, July 2004.
9. Zhu, *Xiwang*, 15; Du and Wang, *Hongse houdai*, 115–118.
10. Zhu, *Xiwang.* 15.
11. Interview by author, Tan Aoshuang, Moscow, November 2003.
12. Du and Wang, *Hongse houdai*, 647; Li, *Zhonghua*, 237, 244.
13. Liu, *Zi shu*, 262–263.
14. Liu, *Zi shu*, 259–260.
15. RGASPI, f. m1, op. 46, d. 125, ll. 12–15, 24–26; d. 135, ll. 10–15; d. 208, ll. 43–56; d. 184, ll. 47–50, 61–77; d. 176, ll. 109–113. On another, later group of critical foreign students, see Maxim Matusevich, "Visions of Grandeur," 361–366.
16. RGASPI, f. m1, op. 46, d. 184, l. 24–25; d. 293, l. 25; d. 247, l. 54–55.
17. RGASPI, f. m1, op. 46, d. 152, ll. 10–12, 64–69, 72–76; d. 164, ll. 7–12, 37–39; d. 135, ll. 3–6; d. 208, ll. 10–36. Hessler, "Death of an African"; Katsakioris, "Soviet-South Encounter," 153–160.
18. Zhu, *Xiwang*, 88–91, 103–106; RGASPI, f. m1, op. 46, d. 135, l. 39. Julie Hessler has described similar instances of student resentment over being exploited for political purposes on the part of Africans, "Death of an African Student," 46–47.
19. Zhu, *Xiwang*, 125–128.
20. Pohl, "Virgin Lands."
21. Zhu, *Xiwang*, 135–136. Soviet student dissatisfaction: Tromly, *Making the Soviet Intelligentsia*, 176–183.
22. Zhu, *Xiwang,* 134–137.
23. Paperno, *Chernyshevsky*, 23–29, for plot summary; more broadly, Paperno describes how early Russian radicals, like later Chinese ones, scripted their behavior using fictional texts, e.g., 29–36.
24. Zhu, *Xiwang*, 234–239.
25. Zhu, *Xiwang*, 222–225, 146–147.
26. Zhu, *Xiwang*, 168–171.

27. Even in Sino-Soviet friendship propaganda of the late 1940s the mother theme was prominent. Hess, "Big Brother Is Watching," 179–180.
28. Katsakioris, "Soviet-South Encounter," 153, 157; Quist-Adade, "The African Russians," 153–173; Zheng Yifan interviews by author, Beijing, September 2004; Zheng himself married a fellow Chinese student and has the wedding certificate to prove it; Wang interview by author (name has been changed at request of interviewee), September 12, 2004, Beijing; interview by author, Ren Xiang, Beijing, October 2004.
29. Interview by author, Ren Xiang.
30. RGANI f. 5, op. 30, d. 369, l. 106. Eastern European students who married Soviet citizens and applied to return together to their home countries had a surprisingly high success rate. Tromly, "Brother or Other," 94.
31. The prohibition extended to foreigners in China as well. Forbidden affairs: Jersild *Sino-Soviet Alliance*, 97–102.

Chapter 17

1. Kishkina, *Iz Rossii*, 254–255; Soviet permission: GARF f. 8265, op. 4, d. 156, l. 172.
2. Kishkina, *Iz Rossii*, 249–250.
3. Kishkina, *Iz Rossii*, 256.
4. Manchester, "Repatriation," 354–360, 374–377; Kishkina, *Iz Rossii*, 251–253
5. Kishkina, *Iz Rossii*, 265, 277.
6. Kishkina, *Iz Rossii*, 255–262, 329.
7. Kishkina, *Iz Rossii*, 274–276.
8. Kishkina, *Iz Rossii*, 277–280.
9. Kishkina, *Iz Rossii*, 281, 285–286.
10. "Cable, Kovalev to Stalin, 17 May 1949," APRF f. 45, op. 1, d. 331, ll. 50–55, trans. Sergey Radchenko, republished in *Cold War International History Project Bulletin* 16 (Fall 2007/Winter 2008), 161–164.
11. Kishkina, *Iz Rossii*, 288, 295–296, 312.
12. Kishkina, *Iz Rossii*, 292–293, 332–333.
13. Kishkina, *Iz Rossii*, 314–315.
14. Kishkina, *Iz Rossii*, 313, 317, 324, 330–331, 333.
15. Kishkina, *Iz Rossii*, 317–318, 334.
16. Kishkina, *Iz Rossii*, 315, 318–322.
17. Kishkina, *Iz Rossii*, 336.
18. Kishkina, *Iz Rossii*, 326–328, 334–335
19. Kishkina, *Iz Rossii*, 321.
20. Kishkina, *Iz Rossii*, 338. Babaevskii, *Cavalier;* Weiner, *Making Sense of War*, 50–52. Babaevskii was criticized by Soviet "Village Prose" writers of the 1950s who rejected idealized versions of collective farms. Kozlov, *Readers.* 49.
21. Kishkina, *Iz Rossii*, 300, 309–311.
22. Kishkina, *Iz Rossii*, 92, 197, 285, 338.

23. Kishkina, *Iz Rossii*, 339–340.
24. Kishkina, *Iz Rossii*.
25. Li [Liza Kishkina], *Wo de Zhongguo*, 230.
26. Jersild, *Sino-Soviet Alliance*, 15.
27. Pringsheim, "Friendship Association," 57; Fu, *Zhongguo waiyu*, 71.
28. Kishkina, *Iz Rossii*, 383.
29. Kishkina, *Iz Rossii*, 386; Kaple, "Soviet Advisors," 129.
30. Expert attitudes and behavior: Jersild, *Sino-Soviet Alliance*, 23, 44.
31. Kishkina, *Iz Rossii*, 398.
32. Siao, *Heping*; Siao, *China* 224, 229, 236; Siao, *China: Photographien*. 17; Siao, *Zhongguo*, 132–133; Siao, *Shi ji*, 123–131.
33. Siao, *Shi ji*, 131–138.
34. Siao, *Shi ji*, 138–144.
35. Siao, *Shi ji*, 149–150. Siao and Alley, *Peking Opera*. Alley, like many "friends of China," was a somewhat controversial person. Brady, *Friend of China*.
36. Siao, *Shi ji*, 151–153.
37. Siao, *China*. 265–266.
38. Siao, *China: Photographien*. 130.
39. Siao, *China*, 267; Siao and Uhse, *Peking*.
40. Siao, *Shi ji*, 155–158.
41. Siao, *Shi ji*, 158–159.
42. Turkevich, "Second Congress," 31–34.
43. RGALI, f. 631, op. 15, d. 199, ll. 55–56.
44. Sincerity: Kozlov, *Readers*, Ch. 2; Jones, "Breaking the Silence"; Siao, *Shi ji*, 158–159.
45. Garrard, *Inside*, 70. Beginning in 1953 Ambassador Zhang Wentian did write good reports of changing Soviet attitudes toward Stalin, but the Chinese leadership in Beijing paid little attention until Khrushchev's Secret Speech. Luthi, *Sino-Soviet Split*, 46–50.
46. Siao, *Shi ji*, 160–161.

Chapter 18

1. Kishkina, *Iz Rossii*, 387.
2. Dates: Interdom, *Prikazy*, 1949-1953, pp. 96–97; WJBDAG, 109-0050-02 (1), p. 10.
3. WJBDAG 109-0050-02 (1), 4–12.
4. Din-Savva, *Iz Moskvy*, 39–40.
5. Din-Savva, *Iz Moskvy*, 43. Sea cucumber: Interview by author, Dora Liuxia, Summer 2004,
6. Xue, *Bai fa*, 96–97; Din Savve, *Iz Moskvy*, 44–46.
7. Mao Anqing's personal file at RGASPI states that he arrived for his first stay in January of 1952. He came and went throughout the 1950s, finally departing Russia for good in 1959. RGASPI f. 495, op. 225, d. 2799, ll. 30–37.
8. Zhenya Chuwen, interview by author, Beijing, Fall 2004.

9. Dora Liu Xia, interview by author, Beijing, Summer 2004.

10. In November 2003 "Amazonka"—Tan Aoshuang—was still alive and well in Moscow, where she told her side of the story.

11. Dora, interview by author.

12. Lena has published two overlapping but not identical memoirs, one in Russian and one in English, already cited here: Sin-Lin, *Shattered Families,* and Din-Savva, *Iz Moskvy.* Sin Lin, *Shattered Families,* 45–55, 57–58, 79.

13. Sin Lin, *Shattered Families,* 14–15.

14. Sin Lin, *Shattered Families,* 18.

15. Sin Lin, *Shattered Families,* 20–23.

16. Sin Lin, *Shattered Families,* 23–24, 28, 32.

17. Stories of culture clash in industrial settings: Zhao Shige, interview by author, Beijing, Fall 2004, and Han Moning, Beijing, interview, Fall 2004. Zhao worked as a railroad expert and Han was a hydraulic engineer.

18. Yura Huang Jian, interview by author, September 2004.

19. Jian, "Bol' i schast'e," 20, 58, 87.

20. Jian, "Bol' i schast'e," 23, 63–64.

21. Jian, "Bol' i schast'e," 32–33, 86–87.

22. Jian, "Bol' i schast'e," 32–33.

23. Jian, "Bol' i schast'e," 71.

24. Jian, "Bol' i schast'e," 27–28, 57, 90, 105.

25. Jian, "Bol' i schast'e," 92, 111, 109–114.

26. Jian, "Bol' i schast'e," 108, 120–121.

27. Jian, "Bol' i schast'e," 55–57.

28. This record was not internationally recognized as China had boycotted the Olympics. In summer 2008, when China finally hosted the Olympics, Zhen was chosen as one of eight highly symbolic flag-bearers. Si, "Zheng's Great Leap."

29. Siao, *Shi ji,* 166–167.

30. Siao, *Shi ji,* 163–164.

31. Siao, *China,* 288–289; Siao, *Shi ji,* 165.

32. Siao, *Shi ji,* 176–181.

33. Dikotter, *Mao's Great Famine;* discussion of "revolutionary" and "bureaucratic" Stalinism in the Chinese context: Luthi, *Sino-Soviet Split,* 21–23, 41–45, 82–90. Luthi repeatedly shows Mao directly referencing Stalin's policies, suggesting that for all Mao's insistence on the independence of his revolution, Soviet Russia was his main external reference point.

34. Luthi, *Sino-Soviet Split,* 115–115, 125–150; Radchenko, *Two Suns,* 12–14, 25–30.

35. Kishkina, *Iz Rossii,* 400–401. Luthi's review of the evidence shows that there was no separate communication; Luthi, *Sino-Soviet Split,* 124–125.

36. Kishkina, *Iz Rossii,* 402.

37. Kishkina, *Iz Rossii,* 402.

38. Kishkina, *Iz Rossii,* 402.

39. Kishkina, *Iz Rossii*, 398, 405.

40. Kishkina, *Iz Rossii*, 399, 401.

41. Kishkina, *Iz Rossii*, 400–401.

42. MacFarquhar, *Origins of the Cultural Revolution*, vol. 3, 131–134, Ch. 7.

43. Kishkina, *Iz Rossii*, 403–404. In fact, there was a movement afoot, led by the Soviet-educated former ambassador Wang Jiaxiang, to rethink China's relationship with the Soviet Union, but it failed. Luthi, *Sino-Soviet Split*, 212–218.

44. Kishkina, *Iz Rossii*, 405.

45. Siao, *Shi ji*, 183–189.

46. Siao, *China*, 353–354, Siao, *Shi ji*, 190–191.

47. Siao, *China* 372–373, Siao *Shi ji*, 205.

48. Siao, *Shi ji*, 198–201, 205.

49. Siao, *Shi ji*, 206.

50. Siao, *Shi ji*, 206–207.

51. Siao, *Shi ji*, 210–211.

52. Siao, *Shi ji*, 211, 214, 218, 222.

Chapter 19

1. Kishkina, *Iz Rossii*, 408.

2. Radchenko, *Two Suns*, 120–137, 148–164.

3. Din-Savva, *Iz Moskvy*, 220; Sin Lin, *Shattered Families*, 157.

4. Din-Savva, *Iz Moskvy*, 220–226; Sin Lin, *Shattered Families*, 157–162.

5. Din-Savva, *Iz Moskvy*, 229.

6. Kishkina, *Iz Rossii*, 376, 409–410.

7. Kishkina, *Iz Rossii*, 409.

8. Kishkina, *Iz Rossii*, 410–411, 415; Sin Lin, *Shattered Families*, 164.

9. Siao, *Shi ji*, 228–229.

10. Kishkina, *Iz Rossii*, 410–411; Sin Lin, *Shattered Families*, 163–164.

11. Kishkina, *Iz Rossii*, 413–416.

12. Kishkina, *Iz Rossii*, 417–420.

13. Kishkina, *Iz Rossii*, 423–424.

14. Kishkina, *Iz Rossii*, 424–425.

15. Kishkina, *Iz Rossii*, 425–426.

16. Kishkina, *Iz Rossii*, 426.

17. Kishkina, *Iz Rossii*, 427.

18. Kishkina, *Iz Rossii*, 428.

19. Kishkina, *Iz Rossii*, 428–430.

20. Kishkina, *Iz Rossii*, 431–437.

21. Macfarquhar and Schoenhals, *Mao's Last Revolution*, 145–146.

22. Du and Wang, *Hongse houdai*. 130.

23. "Statement from A. G. Krymov," trans. Jersild.

24. Kishkina, *Iz Rossii*, 438–444.

25. Du and Wang, *Hongse houdai*, 102, 184–187.

26. Interview by author, Chen Zutao, Beijing, Fall 2004; interview by author, Zhao Shige, Beijing, October 2004.

27. Ma, *Cultural Revolution*.

28. Sin Lin, *Shattered Families*, 171–174.

29. Sin Lin, *Shattered Families*, 173–174.

30. Sin Lin, *Shattered Families*, 175–176.

31. Sin Lin, *Shattered Families*, 176–178.

32. Du and Wang, *Hongse houdai*, 229–230.

33. Jian, "Bol' i schast'e," 40–41.

34. Du and Wang, *Hongse houdai*, 299.

35. Clark, *Cultural Revolution*, 226–231; Qin, "The Sublime and the Profane," 240–265.

36. Andrews and Shen, "Chinese Women," 139–142.

37. He, "Coming of Age," 408.

38. Kishkina, *Iz Rossii*, 445, 456; Siao, *Shi ji*, 268.

39. Kishkina, *Iz Rossii*, 452–455.

40. Kishkina, *Iz Rossii*, 456.

41. Kishkina, *Iz Rossii*, 470.

42. Kishkina, *Iz Rossii*, 466–468.

43. Kishkina, *Iz Rossii*, 469–473.

44. http://www.womenofchina.cn/womenofchina/html1/news/china/1504/1764-1.htm. Accessed July 27, 2015.

45. Kishkina, *Iz Rossii*, 347–348.

46. Kishkina, *Iz Rossii*, 477–478.

Chapter 20

1. Wang, *Sulian ji*, 15. For an interesting review of *Sulian ji*, see Nicolai Volland, "Mourning the Soviet Union," *China Beat*, August 7, 2011. All quotes here are my translation. For biographical sketch: Zha, "Servant of the State." For more detail: Wang, *Ban sheng*.

2. Wang, *Sulian ji*, 21.

3. Wang, *Sulian ji*, 99–100.

4. Wang, *Sulian ji*, 35–36.

5. Wang, *Sulian ji*, 54–55.

6. Wang, *Sulian ji*, 95–121.

7. Wang, *Sulian ji*, 15.

8. Wang, *Sulian ji*, 18.

9. Wang, *Sulian ji*, 18.

10. Wang, *Sulian ji*, 21–35.

11. Wang, *Sulian ji*, 21–22.

12. Wang, *Sulian ji*, 19–21.

BIBLIOGRAPHY OF WORKS CITED

Andrews, Julia F. and Kuiyi Shen. "Chinese Women and Lifestyle Magazines in the Late 1990s." In *Popular China: Unofficial Culture in a Globalizing Society,* ed. Perry Link, Richard Madsen, and Paul Pickowicz. Lanham, MD: Rowman & Littlefield, 2002.

Applebaum, Rachel. "Friendship of the Peoples: Soviet-Czechoslovak Cultural and Social Contacts from the Battle for Prague to the Prague Spring, 1945–1969." Ph.D. diss., University of Chicago, 2012.

Arendt, Hannah. *On Revolution.* New York: Penguin Books, 1990.

Averill, Stephen. *Revolution in the Highlands: China's Jinggangshan Base Area.* Lanham, MD: Rowman & Littlefield, 2006.

Babaev, A.A. *Nazym Khikmet: Zhizn' i tvorchestvo.* Moscow: Nauka, 1975.

Babaevskii, Semen. *Cavalier of the Gold Star.* Trans. Ruth Kisch. London: Lawrence & Wishart, 1956.

Babiracki, Patryk and Kenyon Zimmer, eds. *Cold War Crossings: International Travel and Exchange across the Soviet Bloc, 1940s–1960s.* With an introduction by Vladislav Zubok. College Station: Texas A & M University Press, 2014.

Baldwin, Kate. "The Russian Routes of Claude McKay's Internationalism." In *Africa in Russia, Russia in Africa*, ed. Maxim Matusevich. Trenton, NJ: Africa World Press, 2007.

Ball, Alan. *And Now My Soul Is Hardened: Abandoned Children in Soviet Russia, 1918–1930.* Berkeley: University of California Press, 1994.

Bao, Pu. *Chi E you ji.* Shanghai: Bei xin shu ju, 1927.

Barlow, Tani. "'History's Coffin Can Never Be Closed': Qu Qiubai Translates Social Science." *boundary 2* 43, no. 3 (2016): 253–286.

Barnouin, Barbara and Changgen Yu. *Zhou Enlai: A Political Life*. Hong
    Kong: Chinese University Press, 2006.
Barr, Allan. "Four Schoolmasters: Educational Issues in Li Hai-Kuan's Lamp at the
    Crossroads." In *Education and Society in Late Imperial China, 1600–1900*. Ed.
    Benjamin Elman and Alexander Woodside. Berkeley: University of California
    Press, 1994.
Bartke, Wolfgang. *Biographical Dictionary and Analysis of China's Party Leadership,
    1922–1988*. München: K. G. Saur, 1990.
Bassin, Mark, Sergey Glebov, and Marlene Laruelle, eds. *Between Europe
    and Asia: The Origins, Theories, and Legacies of Russian Eurasianism*.
    Pittsburgh: University of Pittsburgh Press, 2015.
Benton, Gregor. *Chinese Migrants and Internationalism: Forgotten Histories, 1917–
    1945*. London: Routledge, 2007.
Bernstein, Frances Lee. *The Dictatorship of Sex: Lifestyle Advice for the Soviet Masses*.
    DeKalb: Northern Illinois University Press, 2007.
Bernstein, Thomas and Hua-yu Li, eds. *China Learns from the Soviet Union, 1949–
    Present*. Lanham, MD: Lexington Books, 2010.
Bodde, Derek. *Tolstoy and China*. Princeton, NJ: Princeton University Press, 1950.
Brady, Anne-Marie. *Friend of China: The Myth of Rewi Alley*.
    London: RoutledgeCurzon, 1996.
Brinton, Crane. *The Anatomy of Revolution*. New York: Vintage Books, 1938.
Brown, Zora Anderson. "The Russification of Wang Ming: A Study of the
    Comintern Career of Chen Shao-yu, 1925–1937." Ph.D. diss., Mississippi State
    University, 1977.
Bugayevska, Kateryna. "The Beijing Institute of Russian Language and Translation
    of Russian Literature in 20th Century China." Paper presented at Columbia
    University conference: *Russia in East Asia: Imagination, Exchange, Travel,
    Translation*. New York, February 28, 2014.
Bulgakov, Mikhail. "A Chinese Tale." In *Diaboliad and Other Stories*. Ed. Ellendea
    Proffer and Carl R. Proffer, Trans. Carl R. Proffer. Bloomington, IN: Indiana
    University Press, 1972.
Busch, Robert. "Gladkov's Cement: The Making of a Soviet Classic." *Slavic and
    East European Journal* 22, no. 3 (1978): 348–361.
Byron, John and Robert Pack. *The Claws of the Dragon: Kang Sheng, the Evil
    Genius behind Mao and His Legacy of Terror in People's China*. New York: Simon
    & Schuster, 1992.
Cao, Jinghua. *E Su wenxue shi*. Changsha: Hunan jiaoyu chubanshe, 1992.
Cao, Jinghua. *Xiao mi de huiyi*. Hefei: Anhui de jiaoyu chubanshe, 1997.
Carter, James H. *Creating a Chinese Harbin: Nationalism in an International City,
    1916–1932*. Ithaca, NY: Cornell University Press, 2002.
Chaihark, Hahm and Daniel Bell. *The Politics of Affective Relations: East Asia and
    Beyond*. Lanham, MD: Lexington Books, 2004.
Chakers, Melissa. *The Socialist Way of Life in Siberia: Transformation in Buryatia*.
    Budapest: Central European University Press, 2014.

Chatterjee, Choi. *Americans Experience Russia: Encountering the Enigma, 1917–Present*. New York: Routledge, 2013.

Chen, Duxiu. "On the Literary Revolution," *Xin qingnian*, January 1, 1917. Quoted in Zhou, *May Fourth*.

Chen, Jian. *Mao's China and the Cold War*. Chapel Hill: University of North Carolina Press, 2001.

Chen, Jian. "The Sino-Soviet Alliance and China's Entry into the Korean War." Working Paper #1, *Cold War International History Project*, Woodrow Wilson International Center for Scholars, Washington, DC, June 1992.

Chen, Jianhua. *Er shi shiji Zhong E wenxue guanxi*. Beijing: Gao deng jiaoyu chubanshe, 2002.

Chen, Jieru. *Chiang Kai-shek's Secret Past: The Memoir of His Second Wife, Ch'en Chieh-ju*. Ed. Lloyd E. Eastman. Boulder, CO: Westview Press, 1993.

Chen, Tina Mai. "Film and Gender in Sino-Soviet Cultural Exchange, 1949–1969." In China Learns, ed. Bernstein and Li.

Cheng, Tingyi. *He Min san jiemei: san jiemei de san zhong butong mingyun*. Beijing: Dongfang chubanshe, 2003.

Cheng, Zhongyuan. *Zhang Wentian zhuan*. Beijing: Dang dai Zhongguo chubanshe: Xinhua shudian jingxiao, 1993.

Cherepanov, A. I. *Zapiski voennogo sovetnika v Kitae*. Moscow: Nauka, 1976.

Cherkasskii, L. E. *Maiakovskii v Kitae*. Moscow: Nauka, 1976.

Clark, Katerina. *Moscow, the Fourth Rome: Stalinism, Cosmopolitanism, and the Evolution of Soviet Culture, 1931–1941*. Cambridge, MA: Harvard University Press, 2011.

Clark, Katerina. *The Soviet Novel: History as Ritual*. Chicago: University of Chicago Press, 1981.

Clark, Paul. *The Chinese Cultural Revolution: A History*. Cambridge: Cambridge University Press, 2008.

Cline, Ray. *Chiang Ching-kuo Remembered: The Man and His Political Legacy*. Washington, DC: United States Global Strategy Council, 1989.

"Conversation between I. V. Stalin and Mao Zedong, Moscow," December 16, 1949, History and Public Policy Program Digital Archive, Archive of the President, Russian Federation (APRF), f. 45, op. 1, d. 329, ll. 9–17. Trans. Danny Rozas. http://digitalarchive.wilsoncenter.org/document/111240.

Cook, Alexander C., ed. *Mao's Little Red Book: A Global History*. Cambridge: Cambridge University Press, 2014.

Dalin, S. A. *Kitaiskie memuary*. Moscow: Nauka, 1982.

David-Fox, Michael. "The Iron Curtain as Semipermeable Membrane: Origins and Demise of the Soviet Superiority Complex." In *Cold War Crossings*, ed. Babiracki and Zimmer.

David-Fox, Michael. *Revolution of the Mind: Higher Learning among the Bolsheviks, 1918–1929*. Ithaca, NY: Cornell University Press, 1997.

David-Fox, Michael. *Showcasing the Great Experiment: Cultural Diplomacy and Western Visitors to the Soviet Union, 1921–1941*. New York: Oxford University Press, 2012.

David-Fox, Michael, Peter Holquist, and Alexander Martin, eds. *Fascination and Enmity: Russia and Germany as Entangled Histories, 1914–1945*. Pittsburgh: University of Pittsburgh Press, 2012.

De Francis, John. *Nationalism and Language Reform in China*. Princeton, NJ: Princeton University Press, 1950.

Deutscher, Isaac. *The Prophet Unarmed: Trotsky 1921–1929*. London: Verso, 2003.

Dikotter, Frank. *Mao's Great Famine: The History of China's Most Devastating Catastrophe, 1958–1962*. New York: Walker, 2010.

Din-Savva, Lena. *Iz Moskvy da v Pekin: vospominaniia*. Tenafly: Hermitage, 2000.

Ding, Jingtang and Yanmo Ding, eds. *Qu Qiubai yinxiang*. Shanghai: Xue lin chubanshe, 1997.

Ding, Jingtang and Cao Wen, eds. *Qu Qiubai zhu yi xi nian mulu*. Shanghai: Shanghai renmin chubanshe, 1959.

Ding, Ling. "Wei Hu." In *Ding Ling quanj ji*. Vol. 1. Ed. Zhang Jiong. Shijiazhuang: Hebei Renmin chubanshe, 2001.

Ding, Ling. "Wo suo renshi de Qu Qiubai tongzhi." In *Qu Qiubai yinxiang*, ed. Ding and Ding.

Dirlik, Arif. *The Origins of Chinese Communism*. New York: Oxford University Press, 1989.

Dittmer, Lowell. *Sino-Soviet Normalization and Its International Implications, 1945–1990*. Seattle: University of Washington Press, 1992.

Drucker, Johanna. "Formalism's Other History." *Art Bulletin* 78, no. 4 (1996): 750–751.

Du, Weihua and Yiqiu Wang, "Bu kui Mao," in Du and Wang eds. *Zai Sulian zhangda*.

Du, Weihua and Yiqiu Wang, "Shuai men," in Du and Wang eds. *Zai Sulian zhangda*.

Du, Weihua and Yiqiu Wang, "Xin Zhongguo," in Du and Wang eds. *Zai Sulian zhangda*.

Du, Weihua and Yiqiu Wang, eds. *Zai Sulian zhangda de hongse houdai*. Beijing: Shijie zhishi chubanshe, 2000.

Edgar, Adrienne. *Tribal Nation: The Making of Soviet Turkmenistan, 1924–1938*. Princeton. NJ: Princeton University Press, 1999.

Eiermann, Karin Irene. "Chinese Comintern Delegates in Moscow in the 1920s and 1930s—Lost in Translation and Begging for Money." Paper presented at the American Association for the Advancement of Slavic Studies Annual Convention, 2007.

Eiermann, Karin-Irene. "'When I Entered Middle School, I Was a Great Pessimist': The Autobiographies of Chinese Communist Women in Moscow in the 1920s." *Twentieth-Century China* 33, no. 2 (2007): 4–28.

Elleman, Bruce. *Diplomacy and Deception: The Secret History of Sino-Soviet Diplomatic Relations, 1917–1927*. Armonk, NY: M. E. Sharpe, 1997.

Elleman, Bruce. *Moscow and the Emergence of Communist Power in China, 1925–30: The Nanchang Uprising and the Birth of the Red Army.* London: Routledge, 2009.

Elman, Benjamin. *A Cultural History of Civil Examinations in Late Imperial China.* Berkeley: University of California Press, 2000.

Elshtain, Jean. *The Family in Political Thought.* Amherst: University of Massachusetts Press, 1982.

Engerman, David. "The Second World's Third World." *Kritika* 12, no. 1 (2011): 183–211.

Epstein, Catherine. *The Last Revolutionaries: German Communists and Their Century.* Cambridge, MA: Harvard University Press, 2003.

Esherick, Joseph. *Reform and Revolution in China: The 1911 Revolution in Hunan and Hubei.* Berkeley: University of California Press, 1976.

Esherick, Joseph and C. X. George Wei. *China: How the Empire Fell.* London: Routledge, 2014.

Evans, Christine Elaine. *Between Truth and Time: A History of Soviet Central Television.* New Haven, CT: Yale University Press, 2016.

Feigon, Lee. *Chen Duxiu, Founder of the Chinese Communist Party.* Princeton, NJ: Princeton University Press, 1983.

Fein, Julia. "Science and the Sacred in Buddhist Buryatia: The Politics of Chita's Museum-Temple, 1899–1914." *Ab Imperio*, no. 2 (2011): 417–425.

Fitzpatrick, Sheila. *The Cultural Front: Power and Culture in Revolutionary Russia.* Ithaca, NY: Cornell University Press, 1992.

Fitzpatrick, Sheila. *Everyday Stalinism: Ordinary Life in Extraordinary Times: Soviet Russia in the 1930s.* New York: Oxford University Press, 1999.

"First Conversation between N.S. Khrushchev and Mao Zedong, Hall of Huaizhentan [Beijing]" July 31, 1958, History and Public Policy Program Digital Archive, Archive of the President of the Russian Federation (APRF), f. 52, op. 1, d. 498, ll. 44–477, copy in Dmitry Volkogonov Collection, Manuscript Division, Library of Congress, Washington, DC. Translated for CWIHP by Vladislav M. Zubok. http://digitalarchive.wilsoncenter.org/document/112080.

Fish, Radii. *Nazym Khikmet: ocherk zhizni i tvorchestva.* Moscow: Sovetskii pisatel', 1960.

Fitzgerald, John. *Awakening China: Politics, Culture, and Class in the Nationalist Revolution.* Stanford, CA: Stanford University Press, 1996.

Friedman, Jeremy. *Shadow Cold War: The Sino-Soviet Competition for the Third World.* Chapel Hill, NC: University of North Carolina Press, 2015.

Fu, Ke. *Zhongguo waiyu jiaoyu shi.* Shanghai: Shanghai waiyu jiaoyu chubanshe, 1986.

Fu, Yan. "Zhui nian Qu Qiubai tongzhi." In *Qu Qiubai yinxiang*, ed. Ding and Ding.

Furet, Francois. *Marx and the French Revolution.* Chicago: University of Chicago Press, 1988.

Galenovich, Iu. M. *Rossiia v "kitaiskom zerkale," traktovka v KNR v nachale XXI veka istorii Rossii i russko-kitaiskikh otnoshenii.* Moscow: Vostochnaia kniga, 2011.

Gálik, Marian. *The Genesis of Modern Chinese Literary Criticism.* London: Curzon Press, 1980.

Galitskii, Vladimir. *Tszian Tszingo: Tragediia i triumf syna Chan Kaishi.* Moscow: GAU-Universitet, 2002.

Gamsa, Mark. "How a Republic of Chinese Red Beards Was Invented in Paris." *Modern Asian Studies* 36, no. 4 (2002): 993–1010.

Gamsa, Mark. *The Reading of Russian Literature in China: A Moral Example and Manual of Practice.* New York: Palgrave Macmillan, 2010.

Gao, Tao. *Tian ya ping zong: ji Xiao San.* Beijing: Zhongguo qingnian chubanshe, 1991.

Gao, Tao. *Xiao San yi shi yi pin.* Beijing: Wenhua yishu chubanshe, 2010.

Garrard, John and Carol Garrard. *Inside the Soviet Writers' Union.* New York: Free Press, 1990.

Gel'bras, V. G. *Kitaiskaia real'nost' Rossii.* Moscow: Muravei, 2001.

Geraci, Robert. *Window on the East: National and Imperial Identities in Late Tsarist Russia.* Ithaca, NY: Cornell University Press, 2001.

Gilburd, Eleonory. "To See Paris and Die: Western Culture in the Soviet Union, 1950s and 1960s." Ph.D. diss., University of California, Berkeley, 2010.

Gilmartin, Christina Kelley. *Engendering the Chinese Revolution: Radical Women, Communist Politics, and Mass Movements in the 1920s.* Berkeley: University of California Press, 1995.

Gilmartin, Christina Kelley. "Inscribing Gender Codes: Male-Feminists in the Early Chinese Communist Party." In *Chinese Revolution,* ed. Leutner.

Gladkov, F.V. *Cement.* Trans. A. S. Arthur and C. Ashleigh. New York: International Publishers, 1929.

Glosser, Susan. *Chinese Visions of Family and State, 1915–1953.* Berkeley: University of California Press, 2003.

Go, Khen"iui and M. L. Titarenko, eds. *VKPb, Komintern i natsional'no-revoliutsionnoe dvizhenie v Kitae: dokumenty.* Vol. 1. Moscow: AO "Buklet," RTsKhIDNI, 1994.

Gong, Mu. "Xiao San ping zhuan." *Xin wenxue shiliao* (January 1999): 186–197.

Gorsuch, Anne. *All This Is Your World: Soviet Tourism at Home and Abroad after Stalin.* Oxford: Oxford University Press, 2013.

Gorsuch, Anne. " 'Cuba, My Love': The Romance of Revolutionary Cuba in the Soviet Sixties. *American Historical Review* 120, no. 2 (2015): 497–526.

Gorsuch, Anne. *Youth in Revolutionary Russia: Enthusiasts, Bohemians, Delinquents.* Bloomington, IN: Indiana University Press, 2000.

Gunn, Edward. *Rewriting Chinese: Style and Innovation in Twentieth-Century Chinese Prose.* Stanford, CA: Stanford University Press, 1991.

Harrell, Paula. *Sowing the Seeds of Change: Japanese Teachers, Chinese Students, 1895–1905.* Stanford, CA: Stanford University Press, 1992.

Harrison, Henrietta. *The Making of the Republican Citizen: Political Ceremonies and Symbols in China, 1911–1929*. Oxford: Oxford University Press, 2000.

Harrison, James Pinckney. *The Long March to Power: A History of the Chinese Communist Party, 1921–1972*. New York: Praeger, 1972.

He, Donghui. "Coming of Age in the Brave New World." In *China Learns*, ed. Bernstein and Li.

Heinzig, Dieter. *The Soviet Union and Communist China, 1945–1950*. Armonk, NY: M. E. Sharpe, 2004.

Hellbeck, Jochen. *Revolution on My Mind*. Cambridge, MA: Harvard University Press, 2006.

Hess, Christian A. "Big Brother Is Watching: Local Sino-Soviet Relations and the Building of Dalian, 1945–1955." In *Dilemmas of Victory: The Early Years of the People's Republic of China*, ed. Jeremy Brown and Paul Pickowicz. Cambridge, MA: Harvard University Press, 2010.

Hessler, Julie. "Death of an African Student in Moscow: Race, Politics, and the Cold War." *Cahiers du Monde Russe* 41, no. 1–2 (2006): 33–64.

Hikmet, Naʿzim. *Poems of Nazim Hikmet*. Trans. Randy Blasing and Mutlu Konuk Blasing. New York: Persea Books, 1994.

Him, Mark Lai. *Chinese American Transnational Politics*. Ed. Madeline Y. Hsu. Urbana: University of Illinois Press, 1985.

Hirsch, Francine. *Empire of Nations: Ethnographic Knowledge and the Making of the Soviet Union*. Ithaca, NY: Cornell University Press, 2005.

Holubnychy, Lydia. *Michael Borodin and the Chinese Revolution*. Ann Arbor: Published for East Asian Institute, Columbia University by University Microfilms International, 1979.

Huang, Fuqing. *Chinese Students in Japan in the Late Ch'ing Period*. Trans. Katherine P. K. Whitaker. Tokyo: Centre for East Asian Cultural Studies, 1982.

Hu, Lanqi. "In a German Women's Prison." In *Writing Women in Modern China: The Revolutionary Years, 1936–1976*, ed. Amy B. Dooling. New York: Columbia University Press, 2005.

Hu, Mulan. "Liu E huiyi." In *Liu shi nian lai*, ed. Zhonghua.

Hu, Ying. *Tales of Translation: Composing the New Woman in China, 1899–1918*. Stanford, CA: Stanford University Press, 2000.

Hunt, Lynn. *The Family Romance of the French Revolution*. Berkeley: University of California Press, 1992.

Ip, Hung-Yok. "Fashioning Appearances: Feminine Beauty in Chinese Communist Revolutionary Culture." *Modern China* 29, no. 3 (2003): 329–361.

Isaacs, Harold. *The Tragedy of the Chinese Revolution*. Stanford, CA: Stanford University Press, 1951.

Ivaska, Andrew. "Transnational Activist Politics in in Dar Es Salaam's Long 1960s: Tales from a Movement Hub." Paper presented at University of California, Berkeley conference: *Socialist Internationalism*, April 2014.

Jacobs, Dan N. *Borodin: Stalin's Man in China*. Cambridge, MA: Harvard University Press, 1981.

Jersild, Austin. *The Sino-Soviet Alliance: An International History*. Chapel Hill: University of North Carolina Press, 2014.

Jian, Yura Huang. "Bol' i schast'e starogo trenera," unpublished Russian memoir. A version was translated and published in Chinese: *Tiao zhan gao du: Yi ge jiaolian de huiyi*. Beijing: Tongxin chubanshe, 2000.

Jiang, Jingguo. *Jiang Jingguo xiansheng quanji*. Taibei: Xing zheng yuan xin wen ju, 1992.

Jiang, Jingguo. *Wo zai Sulian de shenghuo*. Shanghai: Qianfeng chubanshe, 1947.

Jiang, Jungen. "Ganlou yu Xiao San de aiqing beige." *Ming ren zhuanji* 44, no. 1 (2001): 42–45.

Jiang, Kanghu. *Xin E you ji*. Shanghai: Shang wu yin shu guan, 1923.

Jiang, Nan. *The Biography of Jiang Jingguo*. Hong Kong: Morning Star, 2000.

Jones, Andrew. *Yellow Music: Media Culture and Colonial Modernity in the Chinese Jazz Age*. Durham, NC: Duke University Press, 2001.

Jones, Polly. "Breaking the Silence: Iurii Bondarev's Quietness between the 'Sincerity' and 'Civic Emotion' of the Thaw." In *Interpreting Emotions in Russia and Eastern Europe*, ed. Mark Steinberg and Valeria Sobol. Dekalb: Northern Illinois University Press, 2011.

Jung, Chang and Jon Halliday. *Mao: The Unknown Story*. New York: Alfred A. Knopf, 2005.

Kalita, V. V. and I. E. Panich. *Krosskult'turnoe issledovanie dinamiki etnicheskikh stereotipov russkikh i kitaitsev*. Vladivostok: Dal'nauka, 2012.

Kaminer, Jenny. *Women with a Thirst for Destruction: The Bad Mother in Russian Culture*. Chicago: Northwestern University Press, 2014.

Kaple, Deborah. "Agents of Change: Soviet Advisers and High Stalinist Management in China, 1949–1960." *Journal of Cold War Studies* 18, no. 1 (2016): 5–30.

Kaple, Deborah. "Soviet Advisors in China in the 1950s." In *Brothers in Arms,* ed. Westad.

Kartunova, Anastasia. "Moscow's Policy towards the National-Revolutionary Movement in China: The Military Aspect, 1923–1927." In *Chinese Revolution*, ed. Leutner.

Khikmet, Nazym. *Izbrannoe. Stikhotvoreniia, poemy, avtobiografiia*. Moscow: Khudozhestvennaia Literatura, 1974.

Kisch, Egon. *Egon Kisch berichtet: China geheim*. Berlin: E. Reiss, 1933.

Kong, Lingjing. "Ji Qu Qiubai." In *Qu Qiubai yinxiang*, ed. Ding and Ding.

Katsakioris, Constantin. "L'Union soviétique et les intellectuels africains: Internationalisme, panafricanisme et négritude pendant les années de la décolonisation, 1954–1964," *Cahiers du Monde Russe* 47, no. 1 (2006): 15–32.

Keddie, Nikki. *Roots of Revolution: An Interpretive History of Modern Iran*. New Haven, CT: Yale University Press, 1981.

Khokhlov, A. N. " 'Dmitrii' Dmitrievich Pokotilov." *Voprosy Istorii,* no. 5 (2011): 36–54.

Kirasirova, Masha. " 'Sons of Muslims' in Moscow: Soviet Central Asian Mediators to the Foreign East, 1955–1962." *Ab Imperio* no. 4 (2011): 106–132.

Kirschenbaum, Lisa. "Exile, Gender and Communist Self-Fashioning: Dolores Ibarruri (La Pasionara) in the Soviet Union." *Slavic Review* 71, no. 3 (2012): 566–589.

Kirschenbaum, Lisa. *International Communism and the Spanish Civil War: Solidarity and Suspicion.* Cambridge: Cambridge University Press, 2015.

Kirschenbaum, Lisa. *The Legacy of the Siege of Leningrad, 1941–1995: Myths, Memories, and Monuments.* New York: Cambridge University Press, 2006.

Kishkina, Elizaveta. *Iz Rossii v Kitai: Put' dlinoiu v sto let.* Moscow: Izdatel'skii proekt, 2014.

Konishi, Sho. *Anarchist Modernity: Cooperatism and Japanese-Russian Intellectual Relations in Modern Japan.* Cambridge, MA: Harvard University Asia Center, 2013.

Kotkin, Steven. *Magnetic Mountain: Stalinism as a Civilization.* Berkeley: University of California Press, 1997.

Kozlov, Denis. *Readers of Novyi Mir: Coming to Terms with the Stalinist Past.* Cambridge, MA: Harvard University Press, 2013.

Kriukov, M. *29 Ulitsa Mol'era: sekretnaia missiia polkovnika Popova.* Moscow: Pamiatniki istoricheskoi mysli, 2000.

Krymov, A. G. *Istoriko-memuarnye zapiski kitaiskogo revoliutsionera.* Moscow: Nauka, 1990.

Lahusen, Thomas, ed. "Harbin and Manchuria: Place, Space and Identity." Special issue of the *South Atlantic Quarterly* 99, no. 1 (2000).

Lahusen, Thomas. *How Life Writes the Book: Real Socialism and Socialist Realism in Stalin's Russia.* Ithaca, NY: Cornell University Press, 1997.

Lang, Olga. *Chinese Family and Society.* New Haven, CT: Yale University Press, 1946.

Lanza, Fabio. *Behind the Gate: Inventing Students in Beijing.* New York: Columbia University Press, 2010.

Larin, A. G. *Kitaitsy v Rossii vchera i segodnia, istoricheskii ocherk.* Moscow: Muravei, 2003.

Laruelle, Marlene. *Russian Eurasianism: An Ideology of Empire.* Trans. Mischa Gabowitsch. Washington, DC: Woodrow Wilson Center Press, 2008.

Lazić, Branko and Mildorad M. Drachkovitch. *Biographical Dictionary of the Comintern.* Stanford, CA: Hoover Institution Press, 1973.

Lee, Chong-Sik. *Revolutionary Struggle in Manchuria: Chinese Communism and Soviet Interest, 1922–1945.* Berkeley: University of California Press, 1983.

Lee, Haiyan. *Revolution of the Heart: A Genealogy of Love in China, 1900–1950.* Stanford, CA: Stanford University Press, 2007.

Lee, Leo Ou-fan. *The Romantic Generation of Modern Chinese Writers.* Cambridge, MA: Harvard University Press, 1973.

Lee, Leo Ou-fan. *Voices from the Iron House: A Study of Lu Xun.* Bloomington, IN: Indiana University Press, 1987.

Lenchner, S. "Khronika. Istoricheskaia nauka v SSSR. Rabota Sektora Noveiisheii Istorii Instituta Istorii Akademii Nauk SSSR v 1946 i 1947 godakh." *Voprosy istorii,* no. 5 (1947).

Lescot, Patrick. *Before Mao: The Untold Story of Li Lisan and the Creation of Communist China.* Trans. Steven Rendall. New York: HarperCollins, 2004.

Leutner, Mechthild et al., eds. *The Chinese Revolution in the 1920s: Between Triumph and Disaster.* London: RoutledgeCurzon, 2002.

Levine, Marilyn. *The Found Generation: Chinese Communists in Europe during the Twenties.* Seattle: University of Washington Press, 1993.

Levine, Steven. *Anvil of Victory: The Communist Revolution in Manchuria, 1945–1948.* New York: Columbia University Press, 1987.

Li, Hua-yu. *Mao and the Economic Stalinization of China, 1948–1953.* Lanham, MD: Rowman & Littlefield, 2006.

Li, Min'. *Moi otets Mao Tzedun.* Trans. Dora Liu Sia, Inna Li, Liu Chzhen. Ed E. P. Kishkina. Beijing: Izdatel'stvo literatury na inostrannykh iazykakh, 2004.

Li, Mingjiang. *Soft Power: China's Emerging Strategy in International Politics.* Lanham, MD: Lexington Books, 2009.

Li, Sha [Liza Kishkina]. *Wo de Zhongguo yuanfen: Li Lisan furen Li Sha huiyilu.* Beijing: Waiyu jiaoxue yuyanjiu chubanshe, 2009.

Li, Tao, ed. *Zhonghua liuxue jiaoyu shilu 1949 yihou.* Vol. 1. Beijing: Gaodeng jiaoyu chubanshe, 2000.

Li, Tien-min. *Liu Shao-ch'i: Mao's First Heir Apparent.* Taipei: Institute of International Relations Republic of China, 1975.

Li, Yan. "Building Friendship: Soviet Influence, Socialist Modernity, and Chinese Cityscape in the 1950s." *Quarterly Journal of Chinese Studies* 2, no. 3 (2014): 48–66.

Li, Yu-ning. "A Biography of Ch'ü Ch'iu-pai: From Youth to Party Leadership (1899–1928)." Ph.D. diss., Columbia University, 1967.

Lianov, L. "Na prazdinke narodov vostoka, 1'i vypusk studentov KUTV." *Zhizn' Natsional'nostei: Ezhenedel'nyi organ Narkomnatsa,* April 1, 1922.

Lim, Susanna. *China and Japan in the Russian Imagination, 1685–1922.* London: Routledge, Taylor and Francis Group, 2013.

Lin, Li. "Wangshi suo ji: Wo yu Sun Weishi de di yi ci woshou." *Zhonghua er nu,* no. 209 (2004).

Link, Perry. *Mandarin Ducks and Butterflies: Popular Fiction in Early Twentieth Century Chinese Cities.* Berkeley: University of California Press, 1981.

Liu, Aiqin. "Zai shenghuo de dili zhong chengda." in Du and Wang eds. *Zai Sulian zhangda.*

Liu, Jianmei. *Revolution Plus Love: Literary History, Women's Bodies, and Thematic Repetition in Twentieth-Century Chinese Fiction.* Honolulu: University of Hawaii Press, 2003.

Liu, Liyan. *Red Genesis: The Hunan Normal School and the Creation of Chinese Communism, 1903–1921.* Albany: State University of New York Press, 2012.

Liu, Lydia. *Translingual Practice: Literature, National Culture, and Translated Modernity: China, 1900–1937.* Stanford, CA: Stanford University Press, 1995.

Liu, Longyao. "Zi fu jian shu." In *Liu shi nian lai,* ed. Zhonghua.

Liu, Shaoqi. *Liu Shaoqi zi shu*. Beijing: Jie fang jun wenyi chubanshe, 2007.

Liu, Wenfei. *Hong chang man bu*. Kunming Shi: Yunnan renmin chubanshe, 2000.

Liu, Zerong. "Shi yue geming qianhou wo zai Sulian de yi duan jingli." *Wen shi ziliao xuanji*, no. 60: 195–231.

Lu, Yi. "Chinese Communist Party History: The Traitor Huang Ping," *Bai nian chao*, (2010), no 4.

Luthi, Lorenz. *The Sino-Soviet Split: Cold War in the Communist World*. Princeton, NJ: Princeton University Press, 2008.

Ma, Jisen. *Cultural Revolution in the Foreign Ministry of China*. Hong Kong: Chinese University Press, 2004.

Ma, Yuansheng. *Lu Su Jishi*. Beijing: Qun zhong chubanshe, 1987.

MacFarquhar, Roderick. *The Coming of the Cataclysm, 1961–1966*. Vol. 3, *The Origins of the Cultural Revolution*. Oxford: Published for the Royal Institute of International Affairs Studies of the East Asian Institute by Oxford University Press and Columbia University Press, 1997.

MacFarquhar, Roderick and Michael Schoenhals. *Mao's Last Revolution*. Cambridge, MA: Belknap Press of Harvard University Press, 2006.

Malia, Martin. *History's Locomotives: Revolutions and the Making of the Modern World*. Ed. Terence Emmons. New Haven, CT: Yale University Press, 2006.

Manchester, Laurie. "Repatriation to a Totalitarian Homeland: The Ambiguous Alterity of Russian Repatriates from China to the USSR." *Diaspora: A Journal of Transnational Studies* 16, no. 3 (2007): 353–388.

Manela, Erez. *The Wilsonian Moment: Self-determination and the International Origins of Anticolonial Nationalism*. Oxford: Oxford University Press, 2007.

Mao, Dun. "Hui yi Qiubai lieshi." In *Qu Qiubai yinxiang*, ed. Ding and Ding.

Marks, Michael. *Metaphors in International Relations Theory*. New York: Palgrave Macmillan, 2011.

Martin, Terry. *The Affirmative Action Empire: Nations and Nationalism in the Soviet Union, 1923–1939*. Ithaca, NY: Cornell University Press, 2001.

Matusevich, Maxim. *Africa in Russia, Russian in Africa: Three Centuries of Encounters*. Ed. Maxim Matusevich. Trenton, NJ: Africa World Press, 2007.

Matusevich, Maxim. *No Easy Row for a Russian Hoe: Ideology and Pragmatism in Nigerian-Soviet Relations, 1960–1991*. Trenton, NJ: Africa World Press, 2003.

Matusevich, Maxim. "Visions of Grandeur Interrupted: The Soviet Union through Nigerian Eyes." In *Africa in Russia*, ed. Matusevich.

Mayer, Arno. *The Furies: Violence and Terror in the French and Russian Revolutions*. Princeton, NJ: Princeton University Press, 2000.

McClellan, Woodford. "Black Hajj to 'Red Mecca': Africans and Afro-Americans at KUTV, 1925–1938." In *Africa in Russia*, ed. Matusevich.

McDermott, Kevin. *The Comintern: A History of International Communism from Lenin to Stalin*. New York: St. Martin's Press, 1997.

McGuire, Elizabeth. "China, the Fun House Mirror: Soviet Reactions to the Chinese Cultural Revolution, 1966–1969." Berkeley Program in Soviet and Post-Soviet Studies Working Paper, Spring 2001.

McGuire, Elizabeth. "Sino-Soviet, Every Day: Chinese Revolutionaries in Moscow Military Schools, 1927–1930." In *Everyday Life in Russia Past and Present*, ed. Choi Chatterjee et al. Bloomington, IN: Indiana-Michigan Series in Russian and East European Studies, 2015.

Mehilli, Elidor. "Socialist Encounters: Albania and the Transnational Eastern Bloc in the 1950s." In *Cold War Crossings*, ed. Babiracki and Zimmer.

Meisner, Maurice. *Li Tachao and the Origins of Chinese Marxism*. Cambridge, MA: Harvard University Press, 1967.

Meisner, Maurice. *Mao Zedong: A Political and Intellectual Portrait*. Cambridge: Polity Press, 2007.

Melvin, Sheila and Jindong Cai. *Rhapsody in Red: How Western Classical Music Became Chinese*. New York: Algora, 2004.

Murav'ev, Vladimir. *Tverskoi bul'var*. Moscow: Klassika plius, 1996.

Naiman, Eric. *Sex in Public: The Incarnation of Early Soviet Ideology*. Princeton, NJ: Princeton University Press, 1997.

Niu, Jun. *From Yan'an to the World: The Origin and Development of Chinese Foreign Policy*. Trans. Steven Levine. Norwalk: EastBridge, 2005.

North, Robert. *Moscow and Chinese Communists*. Stanford, CA: Stanford University Press, 1954.

Nye, Joseph. *Soft Power: The Means to Success in World Politics*. New York: Public Affairs, 2004.

Paine, S. C. M. *Imperial Rivals: China, Russia and Their Disputed Frontier*. Armonk, NY: M. E. Sharpe, 1996.

Pan, Lynn. *When True Love Came to China*. Hong Kong: Hong Kong University Press, 2015.

Pantsov, Alexander. *The Bolsheviks and the Chinese Revolution, 1919–1927*. Richmond, UK: Curzon Press, 2000.

Pantsov, Alexander. "Bolshevik Concepts." In *The Chinese Revolution*, ed. Leutner.

Pantsov, Alexander and Daria Spichak. "New Light from the Russian Archives: Chinese Stalinists and the International Lenin School in Moscow, 1926–1938." *Twentieth-Century China* 33, no. 2 (2008): 29–50.

Pantsov, Alexander and Steven Levine. *Mao: The Real Story*. New York: Simon & Schuster, 2007.

Paperno, Irina. *Chernyshevsky and the Age of Realism: A Study in the Semiotics of Behavior*. Stanford, CA: Stanford University Press, 1988.

Peng, Shuzhi, Claude Cadart, and Yingxiang Zheng. *L'envol du communisme en Chine: mémoires de Peng Shuzhi*. Paris: Gallimard, 1983.

Peng, Zheyu and Yan Nong. *Jiang Jingguo zai Mosike*. Jiulong: Zhongyuan chubanshe, 1986.

Pickowicz, Paul. *Marxist Literary Thought in China: the Influence of Ch'ü Ch'iu-pai*. Berkeley: University of California Press, 1981.

Pirozhkova, A. N. *Ia pytaius' vosstanovit' cherty: vospominaniia o Babele—i ne tol'ko o nem*. Moscow: Izdatel'stvo AST, 2013.

Plamper, Jan. *The History of Emotions: An Introduction*. Trans. Keith Tribe. Oxford: Oxford University Press, 2015.

Pohl, Michaela. "The Virgin Lands between Memory and Forgetting: People and Transformation in the Soviet Union, 1954–1960." Ph.D. diss., Indiana University, 1999.

Postoiannaia mezhvedomstvennaia komissiia pravitel'stva Moskvy po vosstanovleniiu prav reabilitirovannykh zhertv politicheskikh repressii, ed. *Butovskii Poligon, 1937–1938*. Moscow, 2000.

Praeger Young, Helen. *Choosing Revolution: Chinese Women Soldiers on the Long March*. Urbana: University of Illinois Press, 2001.

Price, Don C. *Russia and the Roots of Chinese Revolution, 1896–1911*. Cambridge, MA: Harvard University Press, 1974.

Price, Ruth. *The Lives of Agnes Smedley*. New York: Oxford University Press, 2005.

Pringsheim, Klaus H. "The Sino-Soviet Friendship Association, 1949–1951." Master's thesis, Columbia University, 1959.

Pushkin, Alexander. *The Captain's Daughter and Other Great Stories*. Mattituck, NY: Amereon House, 1990.

Qin, Liyan. "The Sublime and the Profane: A Comparative Analysis of Two Fictional Narratives about Sent-down Youth." In *The Chinese Cultural Revolution as History,* ed. Joseph Esherick, Paul Pickowicz, and Andrew Walder. Stanford, CA: Stanford University Press, 2006.

Qu, Duyi. "Nan yi minmie de jiyi," in Du and Wang, eds. *Zai Sulian.*

Qu, Qiubai. "Chi du xin shi." In *Qu Qiubai zuopin jingbian*, ed. Ni Fan, Wei Yu, and Hanbo Lu. Lijiang: Lijiang chubanshe, 2004.

Qu, Qiubai. *Duoyu de hua*. Beijing: Renmin wenxue chubanshe, 1973.

Qu, Qiubai. "E xiang ji cheng: xin E guo you ji." In *Qu Qiubai zuopin jingbian*, ed. Ni Fan, Wei Yu, and Hanbo Lu. Lijiang: Lijiang chubanshe, 2004.

Qu, Qiubai. *Qu Qiubai wen ji*. Vol. 3. Beijing: Renmin wenxue chubanshe, 1985.

Qu, Qiubai. "Xian tan." *Xin Zhongguo*, September 15, 1919.

Qu, Qiubai, "Xiandai Zhongguo suo dang you de 'Shanghai daxue.' " In *Shanghai Daxue Shiliao*, ed. Huang Meizhen, Shi Yuanhua, and Zhang Yun. Shanghai: Fudan daxue chubanshe, 1984.

Qu, Qiubai. *Xin E guo you ji: cong Zhongguo dao Eguo de ji cheng*. Shanghai: Shang wu yin shuguan, 1922.

Qu Qiubai ji nian guan, ed. *Jiang nan di yi yan: Qu Qiubai hua zhuan*. Shanghai: Shanghai shudian, 2002.

Qualls, Karl. "From Ninos to Soviets? Raising Spanish Refugee Children in House No. 1, 1937–1951." *Canadian-American Slavic Studies* 48, no. 3 (2014): 288–307.

Quist-Adade, Charles. "The African Russians: Children of the Cold War." In *Africa in Russia*, ed. Matusevich.

Radchenko, Sergey. *Two Suns in the Heavens: The Sino-Soviet Struggle for Supremacy, 1962–1967*. Washington, DC: Woodrow Wilson Center, 2009.

Radchenko, Sergey. *Unwanted Visionaries: The Soviet Failure in Asia at the End of the Cold War*. New York: Oxford University Press, 2014.

Radchenko, Sergey and Wolff, David. "To the Summit via Proxy Summits: New Evidence from Soviet and Chinese Archives on Mao's Long March to Moscow,

1949." *Cold War International History Project Bulletin* 16 (Fall 2007/Winter 2008): 105–182.

Ram, Harsha. *The Imperial Sublime: A Russian Poetics of Empire.* Madison: University of Wisconsin Press, 2003.

Reddy, William. *The Navigation of Feeling: A Framework for the History of Emotions.* Cambridge: Cambridge University Press, 2001.

Ren, Zhuoxuan. "Liu E ji gui guo hou de huiyi." In *Liu shi nian lai,* ed. Zhonghua.

Reynolds, Douglas R. and Carol T. Reynolds. *East Meets East: Chinese Discover the Modern World in Japan, 1854–1898, a Window on the Intellectual and Social Transformation of Modern China.* Ann Arbor, MI: Association for Asian Studies, 2014.

Reznik, Vladislava. "A Long Rendezvous: Aleksandr Romm's Unpublished Works on Ferdinand de Saussure." *Slavonic and East European Review* 86, no. 1 (2008): 1–25.

Rhoads, Edward. *Stepping Forth into the World: The Chinese Educational Mission to the United States, 1872–1881.* Hong Kong: Hong Kong University Press, 2011.

Rigby, Richard W. *The May 30th Movement.* Canberra: Australian National Research University Press, 1980.

Rozman, Gilbert. *A Mirror for Socialism: Soviet Criticisms of China.* Princeton, NJ: Princeton University Press, 1985.

Roux, Alain and Xiaoling Wang. *Qu Qiubai (1899–1935), "Des mots de trop" (duoyu de hua). L'autobiographie d'un intellectuel engagé chinois.* Paris-Louvain: Bibliothèque de l'INALCO n°8, Centre d'Études chinoises, 2005.

Saich, Tony. *The Origins of the First United Front: The Role of Sneevliet alias Maring.* Leiden: E. J. Brill, 1991.

Sanchez Sibony, Oscar. *Red Globalization: The Political Economy of the Soviet Cold War from Stalin to Khrushchev.* Cambridge: Cambridge University Press, 2014.

Scalapino, Robert and Chong-sik Lee. *Communism in Korea.* Berkeley: University of California Press, 1972.

Schimmelpenninck van der Oye, David. *Russian Orientalism: Asia in the Russian Mind from Peter the Great to the Emigration.* New Haven, CT: Yale University Press, 2010.

Schoppa, Keith R. *Blood Road: The Mystery of Shen Dingyi in Revolutionary China.* Berkeley: University of California Press, 1995.

Schram, Stuart, ed. *Mao's Road to Power: Revolutionary Writings, 1912–1949.* Armonk, NY: M. E. Sharpe, 1992.

Schwarcz, Vera. *The Chinese Enlightenment: Intellectuals and the Legacy of the May Fourth Movement of 1919.* Berkeley: University of California Press, 1986.

Schwartz, Benjamin. *Chinese Communism and the Rise of Mao.* Cambridge, MA: Harvard University Press, 1979.

Scott, Erik. *Familiar Strangers: The Georgian Diaspora and the Evolution of Soviet Empire.* New York, NY: Oxford University Press, 2016.

Shen, Zhihua. "1950 nian Zhong Su tiaoyu tanpan zhong de liyi chongtu ji qi jiejue." *Lishi yanjiu,* no. 2 (2001). [English translation: *Zhongguo shehui kexue,* no. 3 (2002).

Shen, Zhihua. *Sulian zhuanjia zai Zhongguo*. Beijing: Zhongguo guoji guangbo chubanshe, 2003.

Shen, Zhihua and Yafeng Xia. "Hidden Currents during the Honeymoon: Mao, Khrushchev, and the 1957 Moscow Conference." *Journal of Cold War Studies* 11, no. 4 (2009): 74–117.

Shen, Zhihua and Yafeng Xia. *Mao and the Sino-Soviet Partnership, 1945– 1959: A New History*. Lanham, MD: Lexington Books, 2015.

Sheng, Yueh. *Sun Yat-sen University in Moscow and the Chinese Revolution: A Personal Account*. Lawrence: University of Kansas Center for East Asian Studies, 1971.

Shi, Naian. *The Water Margin: Outlaws of the Marsh*. Trans. J. H. Jackson. North Clarendon, VT: Tuttle, 2010.

Shi, Zhe. *Zai lishi juren de shenbian*. Beijing: Zhongyang wenxian chubanshe, 1991.

Shlapentokh, Dmitry. *The Counter-revolution in Revolution: Images of Thermidor and Napoleon at the Time of Russian Revolution and Civil War*. New York: St. Martin's Press, 1999.

Shlapentokh, Dmitry. *The French Revolution in Russian Intellectual Life: 1895–1905*. New Brunswick, NJ: Transaction, 1997.

Shneider, M. E. *Russkaia klassika v Kitae: perevody, otsenki, tvorcheskoe osvoenie*. Moscow: Nauka, 1977.

Shneider, M.E. *Tvorcheskii put' Tsiui Tsiu-bo, 1899–1935*. Moscow: Nauka, 1964.

Shore, Marci. *Caviar and Ashes: A Warsaw Generation's Life and Death in Marxism, 1918–1968*. New Haven, CT: Yale University Press, 2006.

Shu, Shuyan. *The Long March*. London: HarperPress, 2006.

Si, Tingting. "Zheng's Great Leap," *China Daily*, December 28, 2007. http://www. chinadaily.com.cn/olympics/2007-12/28/content_6355805.htm. Accessed August 22, 2016.

Siao, Emi. *Mao Tse-tung: His Childhood and Youth*. Bombay: People's Publishing House, 1953.

Siao, Eva. *China: Photographien 1949–1967*. Heidelberg: Edition Braus, 1996.

Siao, Eva. *Shi ji zhi lian: wo yu Xiao San*. Trans. Zhu Yandong. Beijing: Zhongguo shehui chubanshe, 1999.

Siao, Eva. *Zhongguo: wo de meng, wo de ai: Ye Hua yan li de Zhongguo*. Shijiazhuang: Hebei mei shu chubanshe, 1999.

Siao, Eva and Rewi Alley. *Peking Opera*. Beijing: New World Press, 1957.

Siao, Eva and Bodo Uhse. *Peking; Eindrücke und Begegnungen*. Dresden: Sachsenverlag, 1956.

Sin-Lin. *Shattered Families, Broken Dreams: Little Known Episodes from the History of the Persecution of Chinese Revolutionaries in Stalin's Gulag: Rescued Memoirs and Archival Revelations*. Trans. Steven Levine. Portland, ME: MerwinAsia, 2012.

Skachkov, Petr. *Bibliografiia Kitaia*. Moscow: Izdatel'stvo Vostochnoi Literatury, 1960.

Skocpol, Theda. *States and Social Revolutions: A Comparative Analysis of France, Russia, and China*. Cambridge: Cambridge University Press, 1979.

Slezkine, Yuri. *Arctic Mirrors: Russia and the Small Peoples of the North*. Ithaca, NY: Cornell University Press, 1994.

Slezkine, Yuri. *Jewish Century*. Princeton, NJ: Princeton University Press, 2004.

Smith, Steve. "Moscow and the Armed Uprisings in Shanghai, 1927." In *Chinese Revolution*, ed. Leutner.

Smith, Steve. *Revolution and the People in Russia and China*. Cambridge: Cambridge University Press, 2008.

Smith, Steve. *A Road Is Made: Communism in Shanghai, 1920–1927*. Honolulu: University of Hawaii Press, 2000.

Snow, Edgar. *Red Star over China*. New York: Grove Press, 1968.

Sokolov, A. A. *Komintern i v'etnam: podgotovka v'etnamskikh politicheskikh kadrov v kommunisticheskhikh vuzakh SSSR 20-30-e gody*. Moscow: IV RAN, 1998.

Sotnikova, I. "Komintern i nachalo kommunisticheskoi raboty v Kitae." *Problemy Dal'nego Vostoka*, no. 6, (2011): 126–134.

Spence, Jonathan. *To Change China: Western Advisors in China*. New York: Penguin Books, 2002.

Spence, Jonathan. *The Gate of Heavenly Peace: The Chinese and Their Revolution, 1895–1930*. New York: Viking Press, 1981.

Spence, Jonathan. *Mao Zedong*. New York: Penguin Group, 1999.

Spence, Jonathan. *The Search for Modern China*. New York: W.W. Norton, 1999.

"Statement from A.G. Krymov (Guo Zhaotang), a Prisoner in Noril'sk and Former Member of the Chinese Communist Party and the Executive Committee of the Comintern," January 24, 1954, History and Public Policy Program Digital Archive, RGANI f. 5, op. 28, 1954, r. 5112, d. 185, l. 27–31. Obtained and translated for CWIHP by Austin Jersild. http://digitalarchive.wilsoncenter.org/document/116806.

"Stenograficheskii otchet: Pervyi vsesoiuznyi s"ezd Sovetskikh pisatelei." Moscow: Izd. Sovetskii pisatel', 1934.

Stites, Richard. *Revolutionary Dreams: Utopian Vision and Experimental Life in the Russian Revolution*. New York: Oxford University Press, 1989.

Stranahan, Patricia. *Underground: The Shanghai Communist Party and the Politics of Survival, 1927–1937*. Lanham, MD: Rowman & Littlefield, 1998.

Sukharchuk, Grigorii Dmitrievich. "Uchennyi-Internatsionalist: A.G. Krymov-Go Shaotan." *Problemy Dal'nego Vostoka*. no. 5 (1989): 125–133.

"Su wenhua daibiao tuan di chen: dongbei Zhong Su youxie juban huanying wanhui (Xinhua she Shenyang 30 ri dian)," *Renmin Ribao*, October 31, 1949.

"Sulian de wenhua jiaoyu: 1949 nian 9 yue 12 ri wan 8 shi zai Zhong Su youxie zhuban de jiangyan hui shang, Xiao San jiang," *Renmin Ribao*, October 3, 1949.

Sun, Naixiu. *Tugeniefu yu Zhongguo*. Shanghai: Xuelin chubanshe, 1988.

Sun, Yefang. "Guanyu Zhongguo lu Mo zhibu." Zhong gong dang shi ziliao, no. 1 (1982): 180–183.

Tanner, Harold M. *The Battle for Manchuria and the Fate of China: Siping, 1946*. Bloomington, IN: Indiana University Press, 2013.

Taylor, Jay. *The Generalissimo's Son: Chiang Ching-kuo and the Revolutions in China and Taiwan*. Cambridge, MA: Harvard University Press, 2000.

Terrill, Ross. *Madame Mao: The White-Boned Demon*. Sydney: Hale & Iremonger, 1995.

Terrill, Ross. *Mao: A Biography*. Stanford, CA: Stanford University Press, 1999.

Timofeeva, N. N. "Kommunisticheskii Universitet Trudiashchikhsia Vostoka (KUTV) 1921–1925." *Narody Azii i Afriki*, no. 2 (1976): 47–57.

Timofeeva, N. N. "Kommunisticheskii Universitet Trudiashchikhsia Vostoka (KUTV) 1926–1938." *Narody Azii i Afriki*, no. 5 (1979): 30–42.

Tolstoy, Leo. *Anna Karenina*. New York: W.W. Norton, 1970.

Tolz, Vera. *Russia's Own Orient: The Politics of Identity and Oriental Studies in the Late Imperial and Early Soviet Periods*. New York: Oxford University Press, 2011.

Trampedach, Tim. "Chiang Kaishek between Revolution and Militarism, 1926/27." In *Chinese Revolution*, ed. Leutner.

Tromly, Benjamin. "Brother or Other? East European Students in Soviet Higher Education Establishments, 1948–1956." *European History Quarterly* 44, no. 1 (2014): 80–102.

Trotsky, Leon. *Leon Trotsky on China*. Ed. Les Evans and Russell Blocks, Intro. Peng Shu-tse. New York: Monad Press, 1976.

Tsareva, Ekaterina. "Aleksandr Il'ich Romm (1898-1943)." Internet Journal Leksikon, December 1, 2012. http://www.lexicon555.com/voina2/romm.html. Accessed November 5, 2014.

Tsin, Michael. *Nation, Governance and Modernity in China: Canton, 1900–1927*. Stanford, CA: Stanford University Press, 1999.

Tuck, Jim. *Engine of Mischief: An Analytical Biography of Karl Radek*. New York: Greenwood Press, 1988.

Turgenev, Ivan. "Chun Chao." Trans. unknown. *Qingnian zazhi* 1, no. 1. Shanghai: Qiuyi Shushe, 1915.

Turgenev, Ivan. *The Torrents of Spring*. Trans. Ivy and Tatiana Litvinov. New York: Grove Press, 1996.

Turkevich, Lyudmilla. "The Second Congress of Soviet Writers." *Books Abroad* 30, no. 1 (1956): 31–34.

Pushkin, Aleksander. "My Monument." In *Translations from Poushkin in Memory of the Hundredth Anniversary of the Poet's Birthday*. Trans. Charles Turner. St. Petersburg: K. L. Ricker, 1899.

Tyerman, Edward. "The Search for an Internationalist Aesthetics: Soviet Images of China, 1920–1935." Ph.D. diss., Columbia University, 2014.

Usov, V. "Finansovaia pomoshch Kominterna KPK v 20-30 gode XX V." *Problemy Dal'nego Vostoka*, no. 1 (2007): 112–138.

Usov, V. "Kitaiskie vospitanniki interdomov Rossii." *Problemy Dal'nego Vostoka*, no. 4 (1997): 102–117.

Usov, V. "O zhizni detei Predsedatelia KNR Liu Shaotsi v SSSR i ob ikh dal'neishei sud'be." *Problemy Dal'nego Vostoka*, no. 4 (1998): 105–111.

Usov, V. *Sovietskaia razvedka v Kitae: 30-e gody XX veka*. Moscow: Tovarishchestvo nauchnykh izdanii KMK, 2007.

Van de Ven, Hans. *From Friend to Comrade: The Founding of the Chinese Communist Party, 1920–1927*. Berkeley: University of California Press, 1991.

Volland, Nicolai. "A Linguistic Enclave: Translation and Language Policies in the Early People's Republic of China." *Modern China* 35, no. 5 (2009): 467–494.

Volland, Nicolai. "Translating the Socialist State: Cultural Exchange, National Identity, and the Socialist World in the Early PRC." *Twentieth-Century China* 33, no. 2 (April 2007): 51–72.

Wagner, Rudolf. *Inside a Service Trade: Studies in Contemporary Chinese Prose*. Cambridge, MA: Council on East Asian Studies, Harvard University, 1992.

Wakeman, Frederic. *Policing Shanghai, 1927–1937*. Berkeley: University of California Press, 1995.

Wang, Fan and Ping Dong. *Tebie jingli: shi wei lishi jian zheng ren de lishi shi lu*. Beijing: Zhong gong dang shi chubanshe, 2008.

Wang, Fanxi. *Memoirs of a Chinese Revolutionary*. Trans. Gregor Benton. New York: Columbia University Press, 1991.

Wang, Jian, ed. *Soft Power in China: Public Diplomacy through Communication*. New York: Palgrave Macmillan, 2011.

Wang, Jiaxiang. *Kua guo zhi lian: liang ge Zhongguo nanren yu liang ge Sulian nü ren*. Beijing: Zhongguo qingnian chubanshe: Xinhua shudian jingxiao, 1996.

Wang, Jiezhi and Jianhua Chen. *Youyuan de huixiang: Eluosi zuojia yu Zhongguo wenhua*. Yinchuan: Ningxia renmin chubanshe, 2002.

Wang, Jueyuan. *Liu E huiyilu*. Taibei: Sanmin shuju, 1969.

Wang, Meng. *Ban sheng duo shi*. Vol. 1, *Wang Meng zi zhuan*. Guangzhou: Huacheng chubanshe, 2006.

Wang, Meng. *The Butterfly and Other Stories*. Beijing: Chinese Literature, 1983.

Wang, Meng. *Sulian ji*. Beijing: Zuojia chubanshe, 2006.

Wang, Ming. *Wang Ming huiyilu*. Hong Kong: Ha ya chubanshe, 2009.

Wang, Xingjuan. *He Zizhen de Lu*. Beijing: Zuojia chubanshe, 1985.

Wang, Yi Chu. *Chinese Intellectuals and the West, 1872–1949*. Chapel Hill: University of North Carolina Press, 1966.

Wang, Yunsheng. *Er shi jiu ge ren de li shi*. Beijing: Kunlun chubanshe, 1999.

Wang, Zhengming. *Xiao San zhuan*. Chengdu: Sichuan wenyi chubanshe, 1992.

Wasserstrom, Jeffrey. *Student Protests in Twentieth-Century China: The View from Shanghai*. Stanford, CA: Stanford University Press, 1991.

Wei, Chao. "Tan Wang Shi." In *Liu shi nian lai*, ed. Zhonghua.

Weiner, Amir. *Making Sense of War: The Second World War and the Fate of the Bolshevik Revolution*. Princeton, NJ: Princeton University Press, 2001.

Westad, Odd Arne, ed. *Brothers in Arms: The Rise and Fall of the Sino-Soviet Alliance, 1945–1963*. Washington, DC and Stanford, CA: Woodrow Wilson Center Press and Stanford University Press, 1998.

Westad, Odd Arne. "Fighting for Friendship: Mao, Stalin, and the Sino-Soviet Treaty of 1950." *Cold War International History Bulletin*, no. 8/9 (1996): 224–236.

Westad, Odd Arne. "Unwrapping the Stalin-Mao Talks: Setting the Record Straight." *Cold War International History Project Bulletin*, no. 6/7 (1995–1996): 23–24.

Whiting, Allen S. *Soviet Policies in China, 1917–1924*. New York: Columbia University Press, 1954.

Whymant, Robert. *Richard Sorge and the Tokyo Espionage Ring*. London: I. B. Tauris, 1996.

Widmer, Ellen. "Qu Qiubai and Russian Literature." In *Modern Chinese Literature in the May Fourth Era*, ed. Merle Goldman. Cambridge, MA: Harvard University Press, 1977.

Widmer, Eric. *The Russian Ecclesiastical Mission in Peking during the Eighteenth Century*. Cambridge, MA: East Asian Research Center, Harvard University, 1976.

Wilbur, C. Martin and Julie Lien-ying How. *Missionaries of Revolution: Soviet Advisors and Nationalist China, 1920–1927*. Cambridge, MA: Harvard University Press, 1989.

Wildman, Allan. *Making of a Worker's Revolution: Russian Social Democracy 1891–1903*. Chicago: University of Chicago Press, 1967.

Wolff, David. "'One Finger's Worth of Historical Events': New Russian and Chinese Evidence on the Sino-Soviet Alliance and Split, 1948–1959." *Cold War International History Project* Working Paper no. 30 (August 2000).

Wolff, David. *To the Harbin Station: The Liberal Alternative in Russian Manchuria, 1898–1914*. Stanford, CA: Stanford University Press, 1999.

Woodside, Alexander. "The Divorce between the Political Center and Educational Creativity in Late Imperial China." In *Education and Society in Late Imperial China, 1600–1900,* ed. Benjamin Elman and Alexander Woodside. Berkeley: University of California Press, 1994.

Wu, He. "History of Russian Lit in China Short but Profound." *Chinese Social Sciences Today*, January 8, 2016. http://www.csstoday.com/Item/2996.aspx. Accessed August 27, 2016.

Xia, Ji'an. "Ch'u Ch'iu-pai's Autobiographical Writings; the Making and Destruction of a 'Tender-Hearted' Communist." *China Quarterly*, no. 25 (1966): 176–212.

Xia, Ji'an. *The Gate of Darkness: Studies on the Leftist Literary Movement in China*. Seattle: University of Washington Press, 1968.

Xiao, Jingguang. "Fu Su xuexi qianhou." *Geming shi ziliao*, no. 3 (1981): 1–21.

Xiao, San, ed. *Heping zhi lu*. Beijing: Renmin wenxue chubanshe, 1952.

Xiao, San. *Izbrannoe*. Ed. I. Frenkel. Moscow: Izdatel'stvo Inostrannoi Literatury, 1954.

Xiao, San. *Xiao San shi wenji*. Vol. 3. Beijing: Beijing tushuguan chubanshe, 1996.

Xiao, San. *Xian San shi xuan*. Beijing: Renmin wenxue chubanshe, 1985.

Xiao, San. *Zhengui de jinian*. Tianjin: Tianjin renmin chubanshe, 1983.

Xiao, Yu. *Mao Tse-tung and I Were Beggars*. Syracuse, NY: Syracuse University Press, 1959.

Xie, Bingying. *A Woman Soldier's Own Story: The Autobiography of Xie Bingying*. Trans. Lily Chia Brissman and Barry Brissman. New York: Columbia University Press, 2001.

Xu, Jingsheng. *Qu Qiubai yu Lu Xun*. Beijing: Huawen chubanshe, 1999.

Xue, Wen. *Bai fa huishou*. Beijing: Beijing tushuguan chubanshe, 2000.

Yang, Benjamin. *From Revolution to Politics: Chinese Communists on the Long March*. Boulder, CO: Westview Press, 1990.

Yang, Tianshi. "Perspectives on Chiang Kaishek's Early Thought from His Unpublished Diary." In *Chinese Revolution,* ed. Leutner.

Yang, Zhihua. "Yi Qiubai." In *Qu Qiubai Yinxiang*, ed. Ding and Ding.

Ye, Weili. *Seeking Modernity in China's Name: Chinese Students in the United States, 1900–1927*. Stanford, CA: Stanford University Press, 2001.

Yeh, Wen-hsin. *The Alienated Academy: Culture and Politics in Republican China, 1919–1937*. Cambridge, MA: Council on East Asian Studies, Harvard University, 1990.

Yeh, Wen-hsin. *Provincial Passages: Culture, Space, and the Origins of Chinese Communism*. Berkeley: University of California Press, 1996.

"Yi Su Keqin tongzhi," *Yunnan xiandai shi yanjiu ziliao* (date unknown): 30–51.

Yick, Joseph K. S. *Making Urban Revolution in China: The CCP-GMD Struggle for Beijing-Tianjin, 1945–1949*. Armonk, NY: M. E. Sharpe, 1995.

Yoshihiro, Ishikawa. "The Chinese National Revolution and the Eighth ECCI Plenum: Exploring the Role of 'Chugunov,'" In *The Chinese Revolution*, ed. Leutner.

Yoshihiro, Ishikawa. *The Formation of the Chinese Communist Party*. Trans. Joshua A. Fogel. New York: Columbia University Press, 2013.

You zhe. *Xin E huixianglu: yi qian jiu bai nian yi nian Youzhe guan cha*. Peking: Publisher unknown, 1925.

Young, Glennys. *The Communist Experience in the 20th Century: A Global History through Sources*. Oxford: Oxford University Press, 2013.

Young, Glennys. "To Russia with Spain: Spanish Exiles in the USSR and the Longue Duree of Soviet History." *Kritika* 15, no. 2 (Spring 2014): 395–419.

Yu, Miin-ling. "Cong gao ge dao di chang: Sulian qunyuan gequ zai Zhongguo." *Zhongyang yanjiu yuan jindai shi yanjiu suo jikan*, no. 53 (2006): 149–191.

Yu, Miin-ling. "E guo dangan zhong de liu Su xuesheng Jiang Jingguo." *Zhongyang yanjiu yuan jindai shi yanjiu suo jikan*, no. 29 (1998): 103–130.

Yu, Miin-Ling. "Learning from the Soviet Union: CPC Publicity and Its Effects—A Study Centered on the Sino-Soviet Friendship Association." *Social Sciences in China* 26, no. 2 (2005): 100–111.

Yu, Miin-ling. "A Reassessment of Chiang Kaishek and the Policy of Alliance with the Soviet Union." In *Chinese Revolution*, ed. Leutner.

Yu, Miin-ling. "A Soviet Hero, Pavel Korchagin, Comes to China." *Russian History-Histoire Russe* 29, no. 2-4 (2002): 329–355

Yu, Miin-ling. "Sun Yat-sen University in Moscow, 1925–1930." Ph.D. diss., New York University, 1995.

Yu, Miin-ling. Xingsu xinren : Zhonggong xuanchuan yu Sulian jingyan. Taipei: Institute of Modern History, Academia Sinica, 2015.

Yu, Shicheng. *Yang Mingzhai*. Ed. Shengshan Zhang. Beijing: Zhonggong dangshi ziliao chubanshe, Xinhua shudian jingxiao, 1988.

Yurchak, Alexei. *Everything Was Forever until It Was No More: The Last Soviet Generation*. Princeton, NJ: Princeton University Press, 2006.

Zarrow, Peter. *Anarchism and Chinese Political Culture*. New York: Columbia University Press, 1990.

Zeng, Siyi. *19 shiji E guo weimeizhuyi wenxue yanjiu: lilun yu chuangzuo*. Beijing: Beijing daxue chubanshe, 2015.

Zha, Jianying. "Servant of the State: Is China's Most Eminent Writer a Reformer or an Apologist?" *New Yorker*, November 8, 2010.

Zhang, Guotao. *The Rise of the Chinese Communist Party: The Autobiography of Chang Kuo-t'ao*. 2 vols. Lawrence: University Press of Kansas, 1971–72.

Zhao, Shige, "Shuo shuo wo de xiao huo ban he wo ziji," in Du and Wang eds. *Zai Sulian zhangda*.

Zheng, Chaolin. *An Oppositionist for Life: Memoirs of the Chinese Revolutionary Zheng Chaolin*. Trans. Gregor Benton. Atlantic Highlands, NJ: Humanities Press, 1997.

Zhelokhovtsev, Alexei. "Mayakovsky's Poetry in China." *Soviet Literature*, no. 6 (1983).

Zhonggong zhongyang dangshi ziliao zhengji weiyuanhui, ed. *Gongchanzhuyi xiaozu*. Beijing: Zhong gong dang shi ziliao chubanshe chuban faxing, 1987.

Zhonghua min guo liu E tong xue hui, ed. *Liu shi nian lai Zhongguo liu E xue sheng zhi feng shuang zhuo li*. Taibei: Zhonghua wenhua ji jin hui: Zhonghua tu shu chubanshe, 1988.

"Zhong Su youxie zonghui: ganshi hui mingdan queding, Qian Junrui danren zong ganshi," *Renmin Ribao*, 11 November 1949.

Zhou, Cezong. *The May Fourth Movement: Intellectual Revolution in Modern China*. Cambridge, MA: Harvard University Press, 1960

Zhou, Jianren. "Wo suo zhidao de Qu Qiubai tongzhi." In *Qu Qiubai Yinxiang*, ed. Ding and Ding.

Zhou, Minglang, ed. *Language Policy in the Peoples Republic of China: Theory and Practice since 1949*. Boston: Kluwar Academic Publishers, 2004.

Zhu, Xun, ed. *Xiwang jituo zai nimen de shen shang: yi liu Su suiyue*. Beijing: Zhongguo jiliang chubanshe, 1997.

Zhu, Xun, ed. *Xiwang jituo zai nimen de shen shang (jixu): nan wang de zhongrong suiyue*. Beijing: Zhongguo jiliang chubanshe, 1997.

Zhuravlev, Sergei. *"Malen'kie liudi" i "Bol'shaia Istoriia."* Moscow: Rosspen, 2000.

Zubok, Vladislav. " 'To Hell with Yalta!'—Stalin Opts for a New Status Quo." *Cold War International History Project Bulletin*, no. 6/7 (1995–1996): 24–27.

INDEX